INTERNATIONAL RELATIONS
THEORY TODAY

INTERNATIONAL RELATIONS THEORY TODAY

Edited by
Ken Booth *and* Steve Smith

Polity Press

First published in 1995 by Polity Press
in association with Blackwell Publishers.

Editorial office:
Polity Press
65 Bridge Street
Cambridge CB2 1UR, UK

Marketing and production:
Blackwell Publishers
108 Cowley Road
Oxford OX4 1JF, UK

ISBN 0 7456 1165 6
ISBN 0 7456 1166 4 (pbk)

A CIP catalogue record for this book is available from the British Library.

Typeset in 11 on 12 pt Garamond Stempel
by CentraCet Ltd, Cambridge
Printed in Great Britain by Hartnolls Ltd, Bodmin, Cornwall

This book is printed on acid-free paper.

Contents

The Contributors

Ken Booth is Professor of International Politics at the University of Wales, Aberystwyth. He has been a Scholar-in-Residence at the US Naval War College, Senior Research Fellow at the Center for Foreign Policy Studies, Dalhousie University (Canada) and Visiting MacArthur Professor in the Faculty of Social and Political Sciences, Cambridge University. Among his books are *Strategy and Ethnocentrism* (1979), *Law, Force and Diplomacy at Sea* (1985) and, as editor, *New Thinking about Strategy and International Security* (1991).

Chris Brown is Professor of Politics at the University of Southampton. His recent publications include *International Relations Theory: New Normative Approaches* (1992) and, as editor, *Political Restructuring in Europe: Ethical Perspectives* (1994). He has written numerous articles on international relations theory.

Barry Buzan is Professor of International Studies at the University of Warwick, and a Project Director at the Center for Peace and Conflict Research in the University of Copenhagen. His books include *People, States and Fear: The National Security Problem in International Relations* (1983, revised 1991) and *An Introduction to Strategic Studies: Military Technology and International Relations* (1987). Jointly written works include *The Logic of Anarchy: Neorealism to Structural Realism* (1993) and *Identity, Migration, and the New Security Agenda in Europe* (1993).

Jean Bethke Elshtain is Laura Spelman Rockefeller Professor of Social and Political Ethics at the University of Chicago. Among her many books are *Public Man, Private Woman* (1981), *Women* *and War* (1987), as editor, *Just War Theory* (1992), and *Democracy on Trial* (1994).

Cynthia Enloe is Professor of Government at Clark University and the author of a number of works on the military and gender. Her most recent books are *Bananas, Beaches and Bases: Making Feminist Sense of International Politics* (1989) and *The Morning After: Sexual Politics at the End of the Cold War* (1993).

Fred Halliday is Professor of International Politics at the London School of Economics. He has written widely on international relations, the Cold War and the politics of the Middle East. His most recent books are *Revolution and Foreign Policy: The Case of South Yemen, 1967–1987* (1990) and *Rethinking International Relations* (1994).

Andrew Hurrell is University Lecturer in International Relations and Fellow of Nuffield College, Oxford. His interests cover international relations theory, the environment and Latin America. His publications include, as co-editor, *The International Politics of the Environment* (1992) and *Regionalism and International Order* (forthcoming).

Robert H. Jackson is a Professor at the University of British Columbia in Vancouver and a Visiting Senior Research Fellow at Jesus College, Oxford (1993–4). He is currently working on a study of international society after the Cold War. His latest book is *Quasi-States* (1990), and he has recently co-edited *States in a Changing World* (1993).

Andrew Linklater is Professor of International Relations at Keele University. He has also taught at Monash University, Australia. Among his publications are *Men and Citizens in the Theory of International Relations* (1982, 2nd edn 1990), *Beyond Realism and Marxism: Critical Theory and International Relations* 1990), and, as co-editor, *New Dimensions in World Politics* (1975).

Richard Little is Professor of Politics at Bristol University. He has also taught at the Open University and Lancaster University. He has published mainly in the areas of intervention and international relations theory. His most recent books are, as joint author, *The Logic of Anarchy: Neorealism to Structuralism* (1993) and, as co-editor, *Perspectives on World Politics: A Reader* (2nd edn 1991).

Steve Smith is Professor of International Politics at the University of Wales, Aberystwyth. He has previously taught at the State University of New York and at the University of East Anglia. His most recent books are, as joint author, *Explaining and Understanding International Relations* (1990) and, as co-editor, *European Foreign Policy* (1994). He is editor of the Cambridge University Press/British International Studies Association series *Studies in International Relations*.

Susan Strange is currently Visiting Professor at the University of Warwick. As well as being a journalist for the *Observer* she has held professorships at the London School of Economics and the European Institute in Florence. Her most recent publications are *States and Markets* (1988) and, as joint author, *Rival States, Rival Firms: Competition for World Market Share* (1991).

J. Ann Tickner is Associate Professor of Political Science at the College of the Holy Cross, Worcester, Massachusetts, where she teaches international relations. She has been a Visiting Research Scholar at the Wellesley College Center for Research on Women. Her publications include *Self-Reliance Versus Power Politics: American and Indian Experiences in Building Nation States* (1987) and *Gender in International Relations: Feminist Perspectives on Achieving Global Security* (1992).

John A. Vasquez is Professor of Political Science at Vanderbilt University. His publications include *The War Puzzle* (1993), *The Power of Power Politics* (1983) and, as joint author, *In Search of Theory* (1981). He has edited *Classics of International Relations* (1990).

R. B. J. (Rob) Walker is Professor of Political Science at the University of Victoria, British Columbia, Canada, and editor of the journal *Alternatives*. He has held visiting positions at Princeton University, the Australian National University and the University of British Columbia. He is the author of *One World, Many Worlds* (1988), *Inside/Outside: International Relations as Political Theory* (1993) and is editor of *Culture, Ideology and World Order* (1984).

Marysia Zalewski is Lecturer in International Politics at the University of Wales, Aberystwyth. She has published mainly in the areas of gender and international relations, and is currently writing *Gender and International Politics*. She is convenor of the British International Studies Association working group on gender and international relations.

Preface

This is a confusing yet exciting and important time for those who study international relations. We hope that this collection of essays about the major theoretical questions today will convey both the intellectual ferment of the subject and its interrelationships with the compelling issues of contemporary world politics.

We began work on this book by identifying the most interesting questions at the frontiers of international relations theory. The questions range over such areas as how we think about theory, the interplay between theoretical development and the changing context of world politics, and the condition of the discipline of international relations. Having identified the questions we then looked for people we knew would write a thought-provoking essay on the state of thinking about their particular topic, and at the same time push the argument forward in their own individual way. The previous work of the contributors can be identified with one (or more) of the distinctive approaches, methodologies or subfields of international relations. The authors include those who would describe themselves, *inter alia*, as neo-realists, critical theorists, postmodernists or specialists on gender, international political economy and international society – as well as several authors who are difficult to label. We believe that we have brought together an important set of questions with an excellent group of contributors.

Theorizing about politics has traditionally taken place at one of three sites: the domestic arena, international relations and global politics. Over the centuries, speculation about politics in the domestic setting has obviously been the most abundant and influential, despite Kant's injunction 200 years ago that the international should have primacy, since the good life at home cannot be achieved until the world has freed itself from international conflict. Although academic traditions and momentum generally continue to maintain the boundaries between the three traditions of speculation, it is our contention that it is increasingly untenable to consider the three sites as spatially separate; instead, we should understand theorizing about politics as analogous to a palimpsest. On a particular issue one or other of the three sites will be the main focus of interest but the other narratives will nearly always intrude with more or less clarity. The different texts of political theory exist on the same page, not in different books. Each narrative – 'domestic', 'international' and 'world' – develops within a context in part shaped by the others. Domestic political theory cannot proceed far without reference to the context of inter-state relations and trends in world politics. The study of politics at the site of inter-state relations – traditional 'international politics' – must increasingly (even at significant cost to its disciplinary focus) recognize that it too cannot be a discipline unto itself. The more it recognizes this, and takes advantage of its global perspective, the more it has the opportunity, as is said later, to become the subject of all subjects in the social sciences.

The book is aimed at all levels of students of international relations, from undergraduates to professors; we believe that the quality of essays is such that everybody will be able to get something out of them, but that senior undergraduates and postgraduates in particular will gain a good deal. The individual authors were asked to write in an accessible but advanced way about the condition of theoretical speculation on their particular topic. We hope that after finishing the book the reader will have learned something about the empirical state of the world, but even more importantly will be more aware of the problems involved in theorizing about international relations in world politics.

We have incurred a number of debts in preparing this book. The most important is to Anthony Giddens, for suggesting to us a work on international relations theory today in the first place. To Donna Griffin and Elaine Lowe thanks are due for efficient and cheerful typing; and to our contributors, whose enthusiasm and responsiveness have made editing this book an easy and rewarding task.

Ken Booth and Steve Smith

1

The Self-Images of a Discipline: A Genealogy of International Relations Theory

Steve Smith

The purpose of this introductory chapter is to provide a context within which the individual chapters may be read. My principal concern is to offer an account of the main divisions in international relations theory, and to illuminate the interesting, and often contradictory, categorizations of international theory that have become commonplace. In this sense, this chapter aims to provide an overview of how international theory is described and categorized. But it also aims to do something rather more unsettling, namely to show how the history of international theory, and specifically the ways in which international thought has been categorized, has created privileged, that is to say primary and dominant, understandings and interpretations. My focus, then, is on how the discipline of international relations has portrayed its theories and the distinctions between them: what are the self-images of the discipline, and what do these self-images tell us?

THEORIES AND PRACTICES

I want to provide a context for reading the essays that follow in the light of the work of two writers. The first influence on this chapter is Zygmunt Bauman's book *Modernity and the Holocaust* (1989). In this important work Bauman argues that sociology has been strangely silent about the Holocaust, seeing it as an exception that cannot be explained or as the last outpost of pre-modern barbarism. In contrast, Bauman argues that the Holocaust was one manifestation of modern political life and of the dominance of 'reason' and 'rationality'. As he puts it, the Holocaust 'was a legitimate resident in the house of modernity; indeed, one who would not be at home in any other house' (p. 17). Its stress on rational solutions, its use of technology and its reliance on advanced bureaucratic machinery made the Holocaust very much a product of Western 'reason'. In this sense Bauman echoes the arguments of Max Horkheimer and Theodor Adorno in their 1944 book *Dialectic of Enlightenment* (1979), where they argue that it is mistaken to see the Enlightenment as necessarily progressive; rather, there is a negative side to the Enlightenment, as clearly indicated by the Nazi period in German history. These views are controversial. Many claim that an explanation of the Holocaust needs to be couched more in terms of German history and culture rather than the Enlightenment *per se*, whilst others see the Enlightenment providing the means for essentially pre-Enlightenment thinking. I do not want to discuss the specific claims of Bauman's view of the Holocaust since I do not want any such discussion to detract from the general issue he raises about the nature of the power/knowledge relationship; specifically, the point I want to stress is that a discipline's silences are often its most significant feature. Silences are the loudest voices.

The significance of Bauman's comments on sociology's silence about the Holocaust for a discussion of international theory may at first sight seem unclear; but I want to argue that what Bauman, Adorno and Horkheimer have to say about the Enlightenment and about reason resonates with theorizing within the discipline of international relations. The connection is that the ways in which international theory has been categorized, and the debates within it presented, fail to acknowledge the link between social practice and the constitution of social knowledge. International theory tends to speak of international practice as if the 'reason' of theoretical understanding can be opposed to, or separated from, the 'unreason' or 'irrationality' of the anarchy of international society: the discipline comments on, or observes, or evaluates, or explains an empirical domain; it does not constitute it. Yet, just as sociology remains silent about the Holocaust, so international theory remains silent about massive areas of the social reality of the international, treating it as a realm of pre-modern barbarism or as a temporal and spatial domain isolated from cultural identity and interpretation. It is *a* domain, defined by its own practices and, in an important sense, trans-historical, totalizing and given. It is a distinct and separate realm of enquiry in which regularities in behaviour are seen as proof of the very separateness that needs to be questioned. What, in short, are the silences of international theory, and what is the relationship between the study of international relations and *a particular view* of what constitutes international practice?

What international theory rarely accepts, although there have been important, and always marginalized, exceptions throughout its history (for example, the work within peace studies or much of the inter-war work on improving inter-state relations), is that our rationalization of the international is itself constitutive of that practice. The selfsame 'reason' which rules our thinking also helps constitute international practice. In short, international theory is implicated in international practice because of the way that theory, in the main, divorces ethics from politics, and instead promotes understanding via a 'reason' separated from ethical or moral concerns. There are exceptions to this general trend, most notably the work of many writing before the establishment of a separate discipline of international relations, and many traditional realists such as Niebuhr, Wolfers and Carr. But in the received wisdom of the discipline, these normative and ethical elements tend to be played down or seen as implying a specific realist interpretation. My claim is that the dominant strain in international theory has been one which sees ethics as applicable to the kind of community that international society cannot be. Thus, in the name of enlightenment and knowledge, international theory has tended to be a discourse accepting of, and complicit in, the creation and re-creation of international practices that threaten, discipline and do violence to others. Nuclear strategy, and especially its treatment of arms races as natural phenomena, is merely the most explicit example of this tendency; the other areas of international thought confirm it. It is 'reason' which is implicated in the re-creation and reaffirmation of international practices of domination and subordination, and through which the identity of others is legitimized.

The second, and more fundamental, influence on the aims of this chapter is Michel Foucault. I will use his writings on the archaeology and the genealogy of knowledge to illuminate what stories international theory has told about itself. I am more interested in Foucault's later writings on genealogy than his earlier work on the archaeology of knowledge, and the difference between the two is a good way of illustrating what I want to do in this chapter.

This difference represents the main distinction between the earlier and the later works of Foucault. In works such as *Madness and Civilization* (1967, first published in 1961), *The Birth of the Clinic* (1975, first published in 1963), *The Order of Things* (1970, first published in 1966), and *The Archaeology of Knowledge* (1972, first published in 1971), Foucault undertakes an archaeological examination of the rules that regulate discourses. His method is one of scholarly detachment from the subject matter, with the aim of showing how discursive practices operated in history. This is not merely a version of the history of ideas, since Foucault does not see any smooth evolution of ideas, but rather gaps, discontinuities and violent changes. As Smart (1985, p. 54) has put it: 'Through such an analysis the meanings, beliefs, and truths of a past are revealed to be merely so many interpretations rather than progressive approximations to the reality of things in themselves.'

In contrast, the later works of Foucault, especially his work on punishment (*Discipline and Punish* 1977, first published in 1975) and on sexuality – *The History of Sexuality*, Volumes 1, 2 and 3 (1979, 1987 (first published 1984) and 1988 (first published 1984)) – reveal more of a concern with genealogy, that is to say with the linkage between social practice and discourses. In these later works Foucault looks at discourses as embodying social power, and specifically seeks to critique what the human sciences take as given. Of course, there are very clear continuities between the two approaches (thus I reject any notion of a break between the earlier and later Foucault), but there is a clear shift of emphasis, and it is genealogy that seems to offer most for the study of international theory.

Foucault outlines his genealogical method most clearly in a 1971 paper (1986, first published in English in 1977). The title of this paper, 'Nietzsche, Genealogy, History', makes very clear the intellectual debt that Foucault owes to Nietzsche's work on genealogy. Genealogy is to be distinguished from tracing the origins of the identity of the essence of human behaviour. Rather, a genealogist 'finds that there is "something altogether different" behind things: not a timeless and essential secret, but the secret that they have no essence or that their essence was fabricated in a piecemeal fashion from alien forms. Examining the history of reason, he learns that it was born in an altogether "reasonable" fashion – from chance' (1986, p. 78). The key process at work is that of domination. In this sense history is a series of dominations, and discourses a central mechanism of these dominations. There being no universal truths or essences, the clash between discourses is a place of confrontation,

> a 'non-place', a pure distance, which indicates that the adversaries do not belong to a common space . . . In a sense, only a single drama is ever staged in this 'non-place', the endlessly repeated play of dominations . . . Humanity does not gradually progress from combat to combat until it arrives at universal reciprocity, where the rule of law finally replaces warfare; humanity installs each of its violences in a system of rules and thus proceeds from domination to domination . . . The successes of history belong to those who are capable of seizing these rules. (1986, pp. 85–6)

James Der Derian's excellent study of diplomacy shows very clearly what a genealogical account looks like. As he comments

> it means to act on a suspicion, supported by historical research, that the given origins of diplomacy have been defined more by diplomacy's present status and needs than by its past principles and practices . . . It most assuredly will not reproduce the certitude of traditional diplomatic historians who study diplomacy as an unfolding story of the past neatly creating the present . . .; but to project the present on to the past, discover laws of development, or assert some continuous movement towards a single *telos* is to abuse history. (1987, p. 3)

Centrally, his account shows how diplomatic practice was sustained and constituted by the discursive practice of diplomacy, a fact reflected in much of the writing about international relations undertaken before the formation of a separate discipline.

What does adopting a genealogical approach to international theory involve? Richard Ashley has noted five overlapping aspects of a genealogical attitude. First, it involves a shift away from uncovering structures of history and towards a focus on 'the movement and clashes of historical practices that would impose or resist structure . . . With this shift . . . social inquiry is increasingly disposed to find its focus in the posing of "how" questions, not "what" questions' (1987, p. 409). Second, all history is seen as the clash of multiple wills, even history which produces order. In this light, discursive practices 'are to be understood as containing their own exemplary and replicable strategies and technologies for the disciplining of plural historical practices in the production of historical modes of domination' (p. 409). Third, a genealogical attitude is particularly concerned with how discursive practices emerge and are disciplined. Boundaries are seen as especially problematic, as are claims of unity, identity and autonomy within a field of practice. In short, academic disciplines are to be seen as the results of multiple practices and as historically constituted, and not at all as autonomous and natural or given. They are fields of battle between rival interpretations: 'the "autonomy" and "identity" of a field [are] a consequence of the play of power among plural elements. One is disposed to look for the strategies . . . by which multiple themes . . . are excluded, silenced, dispersed . . . thereby to privilege some elements over others, impose boundaries, and discipline practice in a manner producing just this normalized division of practical space' (p. 410). Fourth, there are no transcendental subjects with existences formed prior to practice. Instead, subjects 'emerge in consequence of the power political struggle among concepts, themes, and modes of practice. As such, the subject is itself a site of power political contest' (p. 410). Finally, academic approaches which claim to provide access to the universal truths, hidden essences, underlying structures or moral imperatives are seen as 'political practice intimately engaged in the interpretation, production, and normalization of modes of imposed order, modes of domination. They are seen as means by which practice is disciplined and domination advances in history' (pp. 410–11).

A genealogical approach is, therefore, one which analyses both descent and emergence. As Smart (1985, pp. 56–60) points out, the analysis of descent questions notions of unity and identity, and attacks the assumption of an unbroken continuity of history. The study of emergence looks at how historical forms are merely transitory manifestations of subjugation and domination. What it means for international theory is that it calls into question the self-images of the discipline, whereby international theory is portrayed as a developing discursive field with clear boundaries and transcendental concerns. Rather than being a 'natural' and 'autonomous' discipline with a series of unfolding debates which get ever closer to explaining reality, from a genealogical perspective international theory appears as a historical manifestation of a series of conflicting interpretations, whose unity and identity are the product of a victory in this conflict. Crucially, a genealogical analysis focuses our attention on to the picture of the discipline that the discipline tells itself. What is the self-image of international theory that dominates debates, and which graduate students are given as *the* history of international thought? What assumptions are hidden in the way that the history of the discipline is presented? What voices are silenced and which marginalized in the canon of international theory? Above all, what power-political practices infuse the self-images of international theory?

TEN SELF-IMAGES OF INTERNATIONAL THEORY

I will now turn to look at the ways in which international theorists have tended to talk about the field. I am concerned to look at how international theorists have described the debates within the field, and particularly to focus on the depiction of the key disputes and positions within it. Of the ten that follow some are clearly more widely accepted categorizations of the discipline than others, but each has been used as a typology of the discipline, or as a way of pronouncing on what are the 'key' debates and positions within the discipline. In each case I am more interested in what is silenced or pronounced inappropriate than with reiterating the claims of the specific categorization.

International Theory versus Political Theory

This way of thinking about international theory has been particularly important among those who fit within what is usually, if inaccurately, termed the 'English' school (for a definitive statement of this see Bull, 1977). The argument was best expressed in an influential 1966 paper by Martin Wight, in which he defined international theory as being 'a tradition of speculation about the society of states, or the family of nations, or the international community' (1966, p. 18), in contrast to political theory, which was concerned with 'speculation about the state' (p. 18). His argument was not that there could be no international theory; rather, that there was no body of international theory to rival the achievements of political theory. Not only was there no body of international theory before the twentieth century to match the work of the great political theorists but also what international theory had existed had been marked by 'intellectual and moral poverty' (p. 20). He put this down to the dominance of the state as the focal point for political theory, which made it difficult to think beyond the state to notions of a world community or of individuals having rights outside the framework of the state. Moreover, international theory did not fit well in an era dominated by a belief in progress. Above all, Wight argued that to talk of international theory required using the language of domestic political theory, and that this was inappropriate to a realm where survival was the main concern. Instead, Wight argued, there is no international theory apart from the philosophy of history; it is historians who could best explain 'the nature of foreign policy and the working of the states-system' (p. 32).

The problem with this view is that it sets up a false dichotomy between political and international theory, one which can only load the dice against international theory. As Roy Jones has pointed out, Wight's view that there can be no international theory should really be rephrased to read: 'in the English school there can be no theory of international relations because the English school has cut itself off from the classical theme of political thought' (1981, p. 2). For Chris Brown the problem lies in the definition of political theory that Wight uses. It is a narrow definition, focusing on the state; such a definition axiomatically limits international theory to a minor role since it cannot deal with the kinds of questions raised by political theory. Yet, there are other definitions of political theory which do not focus on the state, and which indicate that there are significant overlaps between political and international theory, so that each is involved in very much the same type of enterprise. As Brown puts it: 'the theory of international relations is not a long-lost, newly invigorated twin of political theory but an integral part of the later discourse. Wight's mistake was not to misunderstand international theory but to mischaracterise *political* theory . . . Wight's definition of political theory is highly contentious' (1992, pp. 6–7). Brown then points out that a definition of political theory for Plato would have involved notions of justice, and such a definition would be one that united political and international theory; each deals with differing aspects of questions of justice. Wight's starting point, which results in his verdict on why there can be no international theory, is therefore nothing like as 'natural' or 'neutral' as Wight suggested. This view depends on a highly specific reading of political theory, and can therefore not simply be taken for granted. Rather, it is his definition, rooted in a historically specific view of what politics was about, that leads to his conclusion. Contrary to his view, political and international theory share the same concerns and imperatives and are part of the same theoretical enterprise, albeit dealing with different constructions of the political world. Indeed, one might make the more radical point, radical at least for the self-image of international politics, that international theory is but one aspect of a much wider range of social, political, ethical and economic theory and that they are aspects of international theory. The conventionally accepted divisions between, say, sociology and politics, must, in this light, be seen as social constructions, and not as natural. As R. B. J. Walker (1993) has persuasively shown, the discourses of political theory and international theory have been presented as distinct, yet presume each other.

Communitarian versus Cosmopolitan Thought

This categorization refers to a debate which has been particularly influential in the development of what is termed normative theory. This is rather a misleading term since it implies that there is any such thing as non-normative theory. The basic distinction is simple: communitarian theories argue that political communities are the bearers of rights and duties in international society; cosmopolitan theories argue that moral arguments should be based not on communities but on either humanity as a whole or on individuals (see the debate between Brown and Hoffman in Brown, 1987, 1988; Hoffman, 1988a). The debate between these positions has opened up considerable space both for developing normative international theory and for linking international theory with similar debates in other disciplines, particularly moral philosophy, and social and political theory. This has been most evident in the works of Brown (1992), Beitz (1979), Nardin (1983) and Frost (1986), which explicitly use the cosmopolitan/communitarian debate to link international theory with the wider philosophical and social science literatures, notably the works of Walzer (1980), Barry (1989), and Rawls (1971).

The main problem with this categorization is that the vast majority of international theory has proceeded as if it did not exist. The central thrust of the discipline since its emergence as a separate subject in the aftermath of the First World War has been to create an *autonomous* theory of international politics. This requires treating the international as distinct from the other reference points of social and political theory, let alone the obtuse debates within contemporary moral philosophy. The dominance of realism furthered this tendency with its stress on practical and scientific knowledge and the consequent belittling of normative theory. For realists, the international political sphere is one of necessity, regularity and danger, wholly unsuitable for the moral philosopher. Moralizing belongs in the pulpit, not in the classroom or in the corridors of power. Taking normative concerns seriously would at best mislead students as to the *real* nature of international relations and, at worst, court national disaster. The problems with this viewpoint are threefold: first, it is based on an implicit assumption that non-normative theory is possible; second, it assumes that the 'political' and the 'international' are in some way natural categories, not at all the product of the ways in which we think about the social world; finally, it assumes that realism does not already adopt, albeit implicitly, moral principles. On this last point it is fair to point out that some classical realists, such as Kennan, Morgenthau and Niebuhr, did sometimes speak of the international sphere as one suitable for moral reasoning, but they also spoke of the preponderance of power-political considerations and warned against the dangers of a moral foreign policy. Moreover, although this strain of practical realism has been influential it has been dominated by a more technical realism in which there is absolutely no room for normative reasoning. Writers like Morgenthau adopt each position in different places in their writings, but in my view it is technical realism that lies at the centre of their analysis. It is only recently that this dominant view has come under sustained attack, most powerfully from Chris Brown (1992).

Nonetheless, the cosmopolitan/communitarian debate does have the difficulty that it places at the centre of our analysis moral and ethical concerns. This is problematic because of the discipline's focus on scientific approaches, which eschew concern with ought-type questions. It is also problematic because of the focus on policy relevance. How can international theory fare when the policy analysts want answers to today's problems, answers that are costed and evaluated for political risk? The worry is that the cosmopolitan/communitarian debate results in a marginalization of international theory. More important still is the worry that the debate is really rather too narrow, because it is based on debates within philosophy and political theory that are themselves coming under attack for what they leave out of the equation. In this sense the cosmopolitan/communitarian debate merely defers to work in other disciplines regardless of the constructed nature of the categories and concepts within these privileged narratives; that is to say that international questions are defined and answered in terms derived from political theory. Thus, although not predetermined, the debates within normative international theory all too often sound like the concerns of white, Western, wealthy males. Once other definitions of rights or of referent points enter the frame, the categories can no longer carry the analytical weight assigned to them. It is for this reason that agreement between communitarians and cosmopolitans is very difficult, maybe impossible, since there exists no independent ground for resolving differences. Finally, it is obvious that within each of the broad camps there are enormous differences of emphasis, and a corresponding set of very serious weaknesses. But centrally, the debate is one framed within terms that are themselves socially constructed, and therefore open to question. Yet it is this very fact which points to one significant strength of the work in this area: in my judgement anything which links international theory to developments in philosophy and the other social sciences is to be welcomed. The problem is that this categorization of international theory refers to a very small part of what passes for international theory and therefore runs the risk of further marginalizing normative theory.

The Three Rs

Martin Wight's threefold categorization has been particularly influential in the development of the 'English' school of international theory. Originally given as a series of lectures at the London School of Economics in the 1950s, and published only long after his death (Wight, 1991), Wight's division of international theory into three traditions has been the dominant categorization of traditions among those who work at the intersection between international and political theory, and, like Wight, attempt to create the kind of international theory that, as noted earlier, was hitherto absent. Wight's legacy is astonishing for one who, as Hedley Bull (1976, p. 101) notes, published so little in his lifetime, though he wrote prodigiously (one 68-page pamphlet and half a dozen chapters and articles). Yet his legacy has clearly been particularly profound for those who attended his lectures and later worked with him in the British Committee on the Theory of International Politics.

For Wight, international theorists can be divided into three traditions, known either as realists, rationalists and revolutionists or as Machiavellians, Grotians and Kantians. In each case, the first group saw international politics as anarchical, a potential war of all against all; the second saw it as a mixed domain of conflict and co-operation, in which a society of states existed, in which rules of behaviour also existed and were observed; the third group saw international politics as really about humanity, the *civitas maxima*, on account of whom the international society of states had to be transcended.

There are three main problems with this categorization. The first is that there are other ways of dividing international political theory; Michael Donelan (1990) lists five traditions (natural law, realism, fideism, rationalism, historicism), whilst Nardin and Mapel (1992) offer twelve ways of thinking about international ethics. This is not simply a matter of semantics but, rather, a question of what distinct positions exist.

The second problem is that many scholars, and certainly most major political thinkers, do not fit at all easily within one tradition. Thus, a false sense of unity is created, and nuances and subtleties lost. Of course, this is a problem with any categorization, but it is particularly marked in Wight's case, a problem made more pressing by the extensive re-evaluation of political thinkers that has occurred since Wight gave his lectures. For Hedley Bull (1976, p. 111), Wight's categories do not bear the weight he assigned to them. In his defence, Timothy Dunne (1993, pp. 312–13) has noted that Wight was well aware of the difficulty in putting thinkers into categories; for Wight, 'the greatest political writers in international theory almost all straddle the frontiers dividing two of the traditions' (1991, p. 259). Yet, for Bull it is doubtful whether much of the thinking about international politics relates to the debate within and between the three traditions: 'There is a point at which the debate Wight is describing ceases to be one that has actually taken place, and becomes one that he has invented; at this point his work is not an exercise in the history of ideas, so much as the exposition of an imaginary philosophical conversation' (1976, p. 111). The problem is not that imaginary philosophical conversations are unhelpful, indeed Michael Donelan has used these to very good effect in his recent study (1990); rather, the problem is that Wight needs to impute to thinkers views they did not express in order to deal with many of the central issues in international theory.

The final problem is whether debate between the three traditions can be resolved or whether such a categorization is, in the final analysis, relativistic. Dunne argues that the three traditions are meant to be seen as historically rather than ethically relativistic, in the sense that each tended to dominate at various times in historical practice; but the problem remains that, as with communitarianism and cosmopolitanism, there is no basis for deciding between the traditions that is external to each but not external to all. By this I mean that each tradition had its own, and distinct, evaluative criteria, with no criteria being agreed on by the three traditions; there was no foundation for evaluating truth claims outside each tradition. Wight himself was firmly in the Grotian or rationalist tradition, although Alan James (1982, p. 118) has placed him unambiguously in the Machiavellian or realist tradition. However, Wight was also clear that understanding international relations required dealing with all three traditions, with the main concern being not to prove one right but, rather, to see the debate between the three as of central importance. Truth was not an attribute of any one tradition but of the dialogue between them. This raises the obvious questions of 'Which dialogue?' and 'Is any dialogue as good as any other dialogue?' The problem with this, of course, is that the grounds for making choices between the arguments of each tradition on any given issue must, in the absence of an external foundation, depend on the values and beliefs of the person involved. In Wight's case, for example, this has led to a debate over whether or not his Christian beliefs led to a bias against the Kantian or revolutionary tradition. What the three traditions leave us with, then, is a set of theories from which the analyst can 'pick and mix'. This problem is compounded if the traditions are not accurate reflections of what cited thinkers thought; the danger is then one of tautology. The main issue, however, is not really whether thinker X fits accurately into tradition Y, but how do we choose between the various traditions that are used in international theory.

The Three Waves or The 'Great Debates'

A much wider characterization of the development of international theory than the previous ones has been that based on a chronological view of development (usually tied to some notion of progress).

Such a perspective has tended to divide up the history of the discipline into phases when a specific theoretical position dominated over rival views, with the periods of transition between hegemonic voices being marked by 'great debates'.

Starting from the assumption that international relations as a separate discipline began with the foundation by David Davies of the Woodrow Wilson Chair at Aberystwyth in 1919, such accounts usually speak of three main phases in the development of international theory. As John Vasquez puts it: 'The twentieth-century history of international relations inquiry can be roughly divided into three stages: the idealist phase; the realist tradition; and the "behavioral" revolt' (1983, p. 13). Hedley Bull, in a widely cited overview of the growth of international theory, adopts the same characterization, with rough dates to delineate the periods of dominance: 'it is helpful to recognise three successive waves of theoretical activity: the "idealist" or progressive doctrines that predominated in the 1920s and early 1930s, the "realist" or conservative theories that developed in reaction to them in the late 1930s and 1940s, and the "social scientific" theories of the late 1950s and 1960s, whose origin lay in dissatisfaction with the methodologies on which both the earlier kinds of theory were based' (1972, p. 33).

If idealism, realism and behaviouralism dominated the discipline successively, then much attention becomes focused on the periods of transition; accordingly the literature is full of references to two 'great debates'. The first of these was between idealism and realism in the late 1930s and early 1940s; the second was between realism and behaviouralism in the late 1950s and 1960s. More recently, some scholars have spoken of a third 'great debate'; however, there are differences over who are the protagonists of this third debate. Maghroori and Ramberg (1982) accept the chronological interpretation of the development of the subject just summarized, but see a third debate developing between state-centric realists and transnationalists, whereby the latter (usually including idealists and behaviouralists) see other actors centrally involved in international politics. Yosef Lapid (1989), on the other hand, characterizes the third debate as one between positivism (which characterized all previously dominant theories) and post-positivism, a collection of views that challenge the central assumptions of positivism.

For Arend Lijphart (1974a and 1974b), the first three waves of theory and the two 'great debates' between then can best be understood as social science examples of Thomas Kuhn's concept of a paradigm. Lijphart argues that the second 'great debate' was much more important than the first debate, because it involved a more fundamental dispute than that between realism and idealism. As he notes, both realism and idealism were part of the traditional paradigm opposed in the second debate by the scientific paradigm (1974a, p. 20). Accordingly, the chronological periods when first idealism, then realism, and then behaviouralism dominated were periods of Kuhnian normal science, with the 'great debates' representing times of paradigm crisis (1974b, pp. 54–9).

There are a number of problems with this characterization of the development of international theory. The first difficulty comprises a number of points and relates to the use of Kuhn's work on paradigms, which, as we will see in the next section, has become a common way of talking about international theory. My comments here about the problems of using the concept of paradigm in international theory will, obviously, apply to the other usages as well. But the Lijphart view is a particularly appropriate place to start because it involves explicitly both Kuhn's comments on 'normal science' and his work on paradigm crisis and change (Kuhn, 1970a). The central difficulty is that Kuhn's version of scientific progress is itself hotly contested within the philosophy of science, yet its usage in international theory tends to deal with it as if it was unproblematic. To cite just one obvious problem: Kuhn is very imprecise over what he means by a paradigm. As Margaret Masterman (1970, pp. 61–5) notes, Kuhn uses the term in twenty-one different ways. But to this must be added the major debates over the picture Kuhn paints of scientific activity (for a good starting point see the essays in Lakatos and Musgrave, 1970). The second problem with using Kuhn's work is that he was clear that his argument applied only to the 'mature' sciences, and not to either the 'proto-sciences' or to the arts and social sciences. Third, there is an absolutely key problem with Kuhn's argument that has far more bearing on any social science application than it does for any science application. This is the question of whether Kuhn is a relativist; in turn this boils down to what Kuhn means when he talks of 'reality'. This is not the place to discuss this in any depth, except to note that Kuhn walks a very fine line between implying that he is a relativist (1970b, pp. 259–66), and arguing that he is not since there is a reality against which paradigms can be tested (1970a, pp. 205–7).

Consider these two statements as an example of the deep waters involved: 'Most of the puzzles of normal science are directly presented by nature . . . For me, scientific development is, like biological evolution, unidirectional and irreversible' (Kuhn, 1970b, pp. 263–4); 'There is, I think, no theory-independent way to reconstruct phrases like "really there", the notion of a match between the ontology of a theory and its "real" counterpart in nature now seems to me illusive in principle . . . I can see in [the] succession [of theories] no coherent direction of ontological development' (Kuhn, 1970a, p. 206). Whatever the problems of dealing with this issue in the natural sciences, it will clearly cause more fundamental problems in international theory, where the notion of 'reality' can be seen in qualitatively distinct terms. If reality is a problem for scientists consider what introducing the notion of a socially constructed reality does to the discussion. Think, for example, of the meaning of terms such as society, or the family, or masculinity. In short, if Kuhn sees relativism avoided by recourse to a notion of a reality, even if our theories of it see it in different ways, then dealing with a reality in which our theories are themselves constitutive of that reality is much more problematic; hence Kuhn's view that his arguments applied only to the natural, or, as he termed them, mature sciences.

In addition to the problems involved in using Kuhn's work, there are other difficulties in presenting the discipline in the Bull/Vasquez/Lijphart way. The first is that it makes the process far more clinically exact than it actually was. The chronology is appealing but is also misleading. International theory did not move so effortlessly through the three phases, much like a car accelerating through the gears. Such a version of events silences all the debates and conflict between rival interpretations and in effect awards a winner's medal to the dominant voice. The chronological version of events is therefore too simplistic and offers far too neat and tidy a version of theoretical development; it is as if all realists suddenly realized the folly of their ways, renounced their sins and converted to the new theory immediately.

A second problem is that the paradigms were nothing like as united as this version of events implies. The idealist or realist camps contained a wide variety of theoretical positions and certainly cannot be forced into a box of shared views and assumptions. In stressing common themes, diversity and complexity are downplayed. What results is a simplified, even simplistic, version of theoretical development with neat changeover points and common manifestos. This does considerable violence to actual theoretical development, and imposes on events a logic that is that of the observer, not of the participants. A related difficulty is that the chronology implies theoretical progress, with deposed theories fading away in much the same way as Einstein succeeds Newton. This is simply wrong as a statement about international theory. What is termed idealist thinking is still powerful in contemporary theoretical debates, and realism still probably dominates the teaching of the discipline. The strands of thought outlined in this version of events should instead be seen as rival conceptions of international reality, with no one version superseding the others for all time.

Moreover, there is the question of what this characterization of international theory omits. The idealist/realist/behaviouralist progression is in fact a narrow, and particularly political, reading of international theory. Where, for example, is class, or ethnicity, or gender in this self-image? Where are the concerns of developing countries to be found in this canon? It is, in fact, a Western/white/male/conservative view of international theory.

Finally, the 'great debates' are much overstated in this version of events. Neither 'debate' was really a debate; rather, each was really only a series of statements of faith, with political or sociological factors determining which voice was heard. I do not read the 'triumph' of realism over idealism as a debate; nor do I think much light was shed by the traditionalist/behaviouralist debate. Indeed, the latter 'debate' shows just how limited is this conception of international theory. As John Vasquez (1983) has shown, the debate between traditionalists and behaviouralists was not a debate about theory but one limited to methodological questions. The main protagonists, Bull and Kaplan for example, saw much the same world and explained it in similar ways, albeit using different methods. They shared a view of what the world of international relations was like (its ontology), and saw similar processes at work in inter-state relations. Bull, however, chose to study this via what were termed traditional methods whilst Kaplan came to very much the same conclusions by using 'scientific' language. Ontologically, though, their underlying theories of international relations were essentially identical. In this sense Lijphart was quite wrong to claim that the second 'great debate' was more fundamental than the first; I would say the opposite, because the first was about far more basic questions dealing with the nature of social reality.

The Inter-Paradigm Debate

This categorization of international theory has been influential since the mid-1980s, being the organizing schema for major texts and readers (Little and Smith, 1991; Olson and Groom, 1991; McGrew and Lewis, 1992; Viotti and Kauppi, 1993) and the starting point for many studies of contemporary international theory (see, for example, Holsti, 1985; Hoffman, 1987; Whitworth, 1989). It was first adopted by Michael Banks (see 1984, 1985) in 1984 and refers to the situation in international theory in the aftermath of the behavioural 'revolution'. In this sense it describes the state of international theory from the early 1980s onwards, and has become the accepted wisdom of most international theorists. The central argument is straightforward. Whereas international theory had traditionally been marked by successive dominant paradigms (idealism/realism/behaviouralism), the situation by the start of the 1980s was that no one approach dominated the literature. Instead there were three alternative accounts, each of which offered a relatively coherent and logical account of international politics (albeit not the same international politics). The three main paradigms were realism/neo-realism, liberalism/globalism/pluralism and neo-Marxism/structuralism. The labels are clearly problematic, since neo-realism is often also called structural realism, and both the world society (Burton, 1972) and the globalization (Scholte, 1993) approaches sit uneasily between pluralism and neo-Marxism; indeed, Holsti (1985, pp. 11–12) sees the two alternatives to realism as being world society and neo-Marxist accounts.

Nonetheless, the view of international theory as comprising three main competing paradigms is a tenable one, and one excellent for introducing students to the variety of theories available in the discipline. Accordingly, each paradigm can be summarized in terms of its answers to questions such as: 'Who are the main actors?', 'What are the main issues in international politics?', 'What are the main processes at work in international society?' and 'What are the main outcomes?' Clearly, each paradigm gives different answers to these questions, so that the student gets three different interpretations of international politics. At this point, two crucial questions arise: first, 'Are the paradigms compatible?' and, second, 'Which one is correct?' The temptation is to say that each offers a view of a different aspect of international politics, with realism dealing with war and peace, liberalism with the management of international regimes in which states and non-states are active, and neo-Marxism dealing with global poverty and development issues. The question of which one is correct is therefore avoided, since each is 'correct' with regard to the aspect of international politics that it deals with. For Michael Banks and others who use the concept of an inter-paradigm debate, its main advantage is that it offers three interpretations of international relations and invites debate between them.

There are a number of points to make about this, the dominant self-image of contemporary international theory. The first, and rather predictable, point is that the divisions between the three paradigms are questionable. The three views are nothing like as distinct as the categorization implies. Similarly, within the divisions there is much more diversity than is implied by the labelling of each paradigm. But this will be the case with any such attempt to distil the logical kernels of overlapping arguments, and must therefore be seen as mainly a matter of accurate representation of the main claims of the various positions.

A second problem is that the division of international theory into these three paradigms reflects a specific view of what international theory consists of. In short, a large proportion of international political and economic activity is left out of the inter-paradigm debate. For Holsti, a paradigm of international theory must deal with three issues: the causes of war ('the raison d'être of the field'); the essential actors; and images of the world system/society of states (1985, pp. 7–8). To put it simply, this leaves much out of international theory, and puts any inter-paradigm debate onto advantageous terrain for realism, since that is the theory that has traditionally focused on war. Thus, dividing the discipline into these three paradigms really does restrict what counts as international theory, and silences many other interpretations. Crucially, it makes it difficult for any paradigm that challenges the three criteria that Holsti outlines, most importantly that concerning war as the *raison d'être* of the discipline.

A third problem is that the notion of an inter-paradigm *debate* is really misleading, since it implies that the three paradigms can confront one another over how to explain international relations. The problem is that there has been very little at all in the way of a debate between the rival positions. Rather, each has had its supporters, and these have referenced one another, been on one another's conference panels, and built incrementally on one another's work. Very rare is any attempt to debate between the paradigms (for one very clear attempt to do so see Tooze, 1992). Paradigms are more akin to research frameworks within which identifiable groups work.

This leads to a fourth problem, which is that if there is little in the way of debate then the characterization of this 'debate' as the defining feature of international theory is very limited and conservative. In effect each paradigm deals with its own research agenda and leaves the others alone. This is an effective way of marginalizing dissident voices. Even pluralist and structuralist challenges to realism can be ghettoed and thereby ignored by realist scholars, although the neo-realist/neo-liberal institutionalist debate is an example of a genuine debate between rival accounts. Yet, there, as we will see below, the debate is on very precise and narrow terms, and sees neo-realism defining the terms of debate. The overall picture, then, is one where little in the way of alternative versions of reality are allowed space to debate. This is particularly so if the dice are loaded by stating that any paradigm must deal with an agenda laid down by the realist paradigm.

A fifth problem is that the idea of an inter-paradigm debate hides the extent to which most international theory is realist. The worry is that in the name of theoretical plurality, all that is happening is a form of Marcusian repressive tolerance; by this I mean that the discipline appears liberal, tolerant and open, but all that happens is that radical voices are merely co-opted onto the realist agenda, and are thereby effectively marginalized since they cannot explain that agenda (nor would they wish to) as well as can realism. Certainly, the 1984 paper by Alker and Biersteker indicated that the vast bulk of international politics writing fell within the realist paradigm, whatever the methodological slant of the work involved; nearly 70 per cent of work cited in their survey of reading lists in the main US departments of international relations were realist or neo-realist, with only some 6 per cent fitting within the neo-marxist tradition (1984, pp. 129–30).

Finally, note that the idea of an inter-paradigm debate involves hidden complications over the question of whether the paradigms are three different aspects of the same world or whether they are three views of different worlds. The notion of an inter-paradigm debate implies that these are three accounts of the same world, which the student can then compare to see which offers the 'best' account. Yet if these are the terms of the debate this is a debate that realism seems certain to win. The worrying thought is that the three paradigms each see a different world, and that they are therefore in an important sense incommensurable. If so, the alternatives to realism can be seen as dealing with peripheral issues. The temptation for students is to adopt a 'pick and mix' attitude, using each paradigm to explain the areas in which it is strongest, without realizing that the three cannot simply be added together to form an overall account of international politics since they are based on incompatible assumptions. In short, very complex issues are involved here, despite the beguiling attraction of this presentation of international theory.

State-Centrism versus Transnationalism

We have already mentioned this categorization in connection with the chronological account offered by Bull, Vasquez, Maghroori and Ramberg, and Lijphart. According to Maghroori and Ramberg, the debate between state-centric and transnationalist accounts comprised the third 'great debate' in the history of international theory. At its simplest, the dispute is between state-centrists (who also happened in the main to be realists in the first debate, and traditionalists in the second), and globalists, or transnationalists (who tended to be idealists and behaviouralists in the previous two debates), over the role of the state in international politics. The resulting pictures of the world offered by the rival approaches are thereby very different. The point for Maghroori and Ramberg is that neither of the earlier 'great debates' involved any discussion of who acted in international politics; it was always assumed to be the state (1982), as Vasquez shows very clearly in his study of behaviouralism (1983). In this light the third debate is the most fundamental debate in the history of international theory.

This is a view of international theory that is rooted in a specific time period and geographical and political location. It is a child of the 1970s, and an approach reflecting the policy concerns of the US in the era of detente. It is important to note that it was in many ways the forerunner of the pluralist paradigm of the 1980s and of the neo-liberal institutionalist paradigm of the 1990s, but it was nonetheless a narrow debate in international theory. This is indicated by the way in which the debate developed in the 1980s and 1990s, with attention turning to look more at the regimes and institutional settings of actors, rather than dealing solely with the question of whether or not they were states.

The central weakness of this categorization is that it led to a focus on quantitative measures of actor activity. It thereby tended to downplay the role of the state, seeing it as one actor among many. At its best (see Mansbach and Vasquez, 1981) it provided a sophisticated framework for moving beyond power politics to a focus on issue politics. But in the main the work undertaken confused activity with impact, analysing the activities of each actor quantitatively, for example so as to show that states were not as dominant in international interactions as previously thought, regardless of what each action consisted of (see Mansbach, Ferguson and Lampert, 1976, for one such study). When the international climate shifted back to a form of cold war in the early 1980s, transnationalism seemed to have little to say about the main issues confronting international theorists. Similarly, the 1980s witnessed a major increase in the role of the state in international economic activity, which obviously undermined the transnationalist account.

A related problem is that the transnationalist literature adopted a specific perspective on political economy. As Robert Gilpin (1987, pp. 25–64) has shown there are at least three main ways of accounting for international political economic behaviour. Of these the transnationalists worked within a liberal perspective. The problem, of course, is that the other two accounts (nationalist, which equates to political realism, and Marxist, which, unsurprisingly, links to structuralism) offer powerful critiques of the liberal view of political economy. In this sense, it is caught between two powerful frameworks, each of which stresses the importance of a structure (of national power in the case of nationalism, and of class power in the Marxist case); yet, transnationalists tended to have no clear idea of the role of international structures, a position only fully resolved with the development of neo-liberalism in the 1990s.

Neo-realism and Neo-liberalism

As has been noted above, this characterization of international theory is the latest round of an ongoing debate. It had its origins in the debate between state-centrism and transnationalism, but has much more to do with the debates between pluralist and neo-realist paradigms of the 1980s (for the classic statements of neo-realism, see Waltz, 1979; Gilpin, 1981; Keohane, 1986; and for its most sophisticated treatment see Buzan, Jones and Little,

1993. For pluralism see Keohane and Nye, 1977; Krasner, 1983; Keohane, 1984). In many ways this debate is currently the most significant within the mainstream of US international theory, and is certainly the dominant debate in one of the leading US journals, *International Organization*. According to David Baldwin (1993) in his introduction to a collection of the main articles dealing with the debate, there are six points of dispute between the two schools of thought (pp. 4–8).

The first concerns the nature and consequences of anarchy, with neo-realists seeing concerns over physical security as producing far more of the motivations of state action than do neo-liberals. Second, neo-realists think that international co-operation is much harder to achieve than do neo-liberals. Third, neo-realists stress the centrality of relative gains for decision-makers in dealing with international co-operation, whereas neo-liberals stress the importance of absolute gains. Fourth, neo-realists tend to deal with national security issues, whilst neo-liberals tend to look at political economy, with the result that each sees rather different prospects for co-operation. Fifth, neo-realists concentrate on capabilities rather than intentions, whilst neo-liberals look more at intentions and perceptions. Finally, whereas neo-liberals see institutions as able to mitigate international anarchy, neo-realists doubt this.

There is no doubt that this is an important debate, one made even more relevant by the end of the Cold War and a subsequent concern with the ability of institutions to mitigate anarchy. Indeed, for many the future of European co-operation is a test of the two approaches (see Baldwin, 1993, p. 5; Keohane, Nye and Hoffmann, 1993). However, there are some serious limitations of this current view of the state of international theory.

The main limitation is that this is an extraordinarily narrow view of what are the topics to debate in international theory. If it is true that this debate is at the forefront of contemporary international theory, that is a stunning indictment of the myopic and ethnocentric nature of international theory. Of course it matters whether states pursue relative or absolute gains, and the role of international institutions is vitally important both practically and theoretically; but to claim that in a world of extreme danger and violence these are *the* crucial questions for international theory seems perverse. Of course, it is important to enquire whether or not states can develop policies of common security in a world full of dangerous weapons, but this is both a limited definition of types of violence in the world, and, more importantly, is a narrow definition of the central issues and concerns of international theory. The debate is a Western, even north Atlantic, one. It hardly begins to deal with the concerns of the vast majority of humanity, and very effectively silences those who do not fit into this US view of what international politics is all about.

Linked to this is the thought that the two accounts are very similar; think of how close they are in their positions on Baldwin's six points noted above. In an important sense they are part of a specific view of international politics rather than two alternatives that together define the space within which debate about international theory can take place. If this is where the action is, it takes place within a very narrow space.

The Post-Positivist Debate

In the last few years a number of powerful attacks on realism have been mounted by scholars from a diffuse grouping of positions. For Yosef Lapid (1989), these together constitute the post-positivist challenge to the realist dominance of international theory. There are four main groupings involved in this challenge. The first comes from critical theory, and is focused on the work of Robert Cox (1981, 1987), Mark Hoffman (1987) and Andrew Linklater (1982, 1990, 1992). For critical theorists, knowledge of the world is always to be understood within a context of interests, following on from the pioneering work of the Frankfurt School, most notably Jurgen Habermas. Knowledge is not neutral, as positivists suggest. For critical theorists, problem-solving positivism needs to be replaced by a critical theory, aware of the political interests it represents, and with an overt commitment to emancipation.

A second strand of thought has developed from a concern with the overlap between sociology and international relations, under the general heading of historical sociology. This is a broad grouping, ranging from the meticulous historical research of Michael Mann (1986, 1993) and Charles Tilly (1975, 1990) to the very specific studies of social revolutions by Theda Skocpol (1979). The point here is that historical sociologists show that the state, made by war in many cases, is the product of the interaction between internal forces and an external setting. This undermines realist, and especially neo-realist, claims of the power of the external setting in determining state behaviour, and of the functional equivalence of states, whatever their internal make-up and regardless of their location in time and space. Having said which, this grouping is the least post-positivist of the four, since it uses very much the same methods and relies on similar assumptions as are found, for example, in the inter-paradigm debate. Its findings, however, represent a significant undermining of neo-realism.

The third grouping comprises feminist writers. This is such a wide category that it is difficult to pin down many common themes and assumptions; but one main concern for feminist scholars is the construction of gender. Work done by feminist international relations writers ranges from those concerned to look at issues concerning women, through those interested in structures of male dominance, to writers examining the nature of identity and gender. Cynthia Enloe (1989, 1993), for example, looks at where women actually *are* in international relations, as well as exploring how socially constructed notions of masculinity and femininity help to oil and turn the wheels of international politics. Jean Elshtain (1987) discusses the assumptions about females and males in thinking and writing about war, whilst Spike Peterson and Anne Sisson Runyan (1993) look at the manifestations of global gender inequality. Arguably more radically still, Christine Sylvester (1994) offers a postmodern feminist repainting of international politics in a postmodern era. Centrally, each of these writers challenges the assumed genderless nature of international theory, and shows how assumptions about gendered roles, and even gendered knowledge, run through international theory. International theory is not so much gender neutral as gender blind.

Finally, there are those writers concerned to develop postmodern readings of international relations. Taking their cues from writers such as Foucault, Derrida, Nietzsche, Heidegger and Virilio, postmodern international theorists attack the very notions of reality, or truth, or structure or identity that are central to international theory as well as all other human sciences. Whilst I am well aware that all literatures are full of nuances and sophistications, and am convinced, for example, that realism has been subject to gross oversimplification (stressing the technical rather than the practical aspects of realist writings), the problem is far more acute in the case of postmodernism. This is an impossible literature to summarize without crass oversimplification, but representative examples of the work in this area would be R.B.J. Walker's re-reading of political and international theory (1993),

James Der Derian's study of 'anti-diplomacy' (1992) and David Campbell's interpretation of US foreign policy (1992).

What these four sets of writings have in common is a commitment to an international theory far removed from the assumptions of positivism and realism. They are in that sense post-positivist, although they are massively different in terms of what they want to put in its place. The most helpful distinction is between foundationalist and anti-foundationalist approaches, which, as we shall see later, is becoming a crucial division in contemporary international theory. Put simply, critical theory, historical sociology and much feminist work are firmly located within foundationalism, and are explicitly part of what can be called an Enlightenment tradition. Some feminist work and all postmodern writings would not see themselves as anti-foundationalist so much as unsure of the security of a claim of foundationalism.

There are problems with this categorization, as the last point suggests. The main worry is that these are so different accounts that they cannot be grouped together. In this sense they are not united by what they agree on but by what they oppose. Each approach has its own problems, and there is not space to enter into the massive literatures involved (a fact that has not stopped many in the discipline from commenting on the inadequacies of these new voices in international theory). These are complex literatures, especially in the cases of feminist theory and postmodernism, and any critique of them has to be far more aware of their claims and nuances than is usually the case. The one point I would stress is that they do not add up to *a* post-positivist international theory; they are often mutually incompatible, and cannot be seen as easily combinable. What they have in common is a rejection of the simplistic philosophy of science that underlines most positivistic scholarship in international theory. Thus, to ask any of these approaches to comment on a realist agenda is massively to load the dice against the post-positivist argument. Asking a postmodernist to list his or her policies for the Bosnian crisis is to allocate disciplinary power in a most effective way.

Constitutive versus Explanatory Theory

In my view this is the main meta-theoretical issue facing international theory today. The emerging fundamental division in the discipline is between those theories that seek to offer explanatory accounts of international relations, and those that see theory as constitutive of that reality. At base this boils down to a difference over what the social world is like; is it to be seen as scientists think of the 'natural' world, that is to say as something outside of our theories, or is the social world what we make it? Radically different types of theory are needed to deal with each of these cases, and these theories are not combinable so as to form one overarching theory of the social world. There have been many attempts to overcome the tension between the two types of account, most notably the scientific realism of Bhaskar and the structuration theory of Giddens, but in my view these attempts cannot succeed. I should be clear that my reading of this division in social theory is one hotly contested by those who hope to make either constitutive theory yield ultimately to explanatory theory (Bhaskar) or vice versa (Giddens); that is to say that Giddens sees constitutive theory as in the end able to encompass the structural and external factors dealt with by explanatory theory, whilst Bhaskar sees explanatory theory as able to deal with meanings and understandings. My view would also be rejected by those who do not accept the division in the first place, arguing, for example, that it sets up a false dichotomy, one which reflects a specific view of epistemology and ultimately of the ontology of the social world. In this latter group would be most postmodernist writers who are wary of the utility of claims of foundationalism. Nonetheless, in my judgement this really is a fundamental divide within social theory, one which gives space to attempts to ground theory via hermeneutics as well as by appeal to functional or structural notions. (For my developing position on this see Hollis and Smith, 1986, 1990, 1991, 1992, 1994; and Smith, 1994.)

But in international theory the dispute between explanatory and constitutive theory seems to be central, even if, as we will see below, the constitutive theorists subsequently fall out over what kind of constitutive theory is appropriate. Most of the work of postmodernists and critical theorists, and that of some feminists, fits into this broad category of constitutive theory, with the work of Alexander Wendt (1987, 1991, 1992a, 1992b; Wendt and Duvall, 1989), John Ruggie (1983, 1993), Nicholas Onuf (1989) and Walter Carlsnaes (1992, 1994) being the clearest examples of attempts to create this kind of international theory. Opposed to this stands virtually all the work contained in the three dominant paradigms of the 1980s, realism, pluralism and neo-Marxism. Indeed, Robert Keohane made the point in his 1988 presidential address to the

International Studies Association that the task of international institutional theorists was to examine the merits of explanatory and constitutive theories, or, as he named them, rationalistic and reflective accounts (Keohane, 1988; see also Goldstein and Keohane, 1993).

The contrast is very clear in Jim George's (1993) review of Waltz's neo-realism, in which he argues that Waltz's positivism results in an account which is 'banal', 'ahistorical' and 'depoliticised' (p. 210). As George puts it: 'My own position on [Waltz's] *Theory of International Politics* and (to a lesser degree) *Man, the State and War* is that they stand as major indictments of an IR community which, closed to critical reflective capacity for so long, has accorded such high status to works of so little substance' (p. 207).

However, one effect of thinking about international theory in terms of a divide between constitutive and explanatory theory is that it makes it possible to be more sophisticated in thinking about realism. This is because there are very significant overlaps between contemporary constitutive theory and the work of the 'English' school of international theory (especially the work of Bull) and of some realist (but not neo-realist) thinkers (especially Niebuhr and Carr). The central debate within each of these categories is basically the same. For the 'English' school that issue is whether the meanings and interpretations of international society are constitutive of that society or are mere ciphers for structural forces. Within realism, the central division is between practical and technical realism, with the dispute turning on precisely this same question. In each case these are versions of the exact issue that lies at the heart of the dispute between explanatory and constitutive theory.

Foundationalist and Anti-Foundationalist International Theory

If the previous division is the most important categorization at the grand theoretical level of international theory, then in my view the most exciting debate within constitutive theory is between two very different epistemologies. Mark Hoffman and Nick Rengger have proposed that there are really two distinct types of post-positivist international theory. This view emerged out of an initial disagreement between them (Rengger, 1988; Hoffman, 1988b) over the nature of critical international theory, but led to a joint paper which makes a useful distinction between the two types of theory (Rengger and Hoffman, 1992, pp. 132–4). There they distinguish between critical interpretative theory and radical interpretativism. The former is the work on critical theory discussed above, which Rengger and Hoffman see as implying a 'minimal foundationalism'. By this they mean that there are grounds for judging between rival truth claims. These grounds are derived from Habermas's concept of communicative competence and, crucially, his notion of an ideal speech situation. These provide a basis by which it is possible to evaluate the 'knowledge-constitutive interests' involved in differing theories. Critical interpretative theorists argue that the main criterion for assessing truth claims is whether or not these theories are emancipatory, as distinct from mere problem-solving theories. The former attempt to better the human condition, whereas the latter are seen as taking the world as it is and concentrating on working within that setting, not changing it. Problem-solving theories are seen as positivist, whereas critical interpretative theory is seen as emancipatory. Radical interpretativism, on the other hand, shares with critical interpretative theory this rejection of positivism, but does not share its minimal foundationalism. Instead, it posits a power–knowledge relationship that calls into question even the emancipatory claims of critical interpretative theory. In Lyotard's famous phrase, radical interpretative theory involves 'incredulity toward metanarratives' (1986, p. xxiv). By this he means that there are no foundations outside any individual theory which can serve as a neutral arbiter between competing accounts. For radical interpretative theorists, critical interpretative theory is 'just' another attempt to provide such a metanarrative. After all, they point out, whose emancipation is involved here? For critical theorists, emancipation means something very different from what many radical feminists mean by it. In short, whereas critical theorists want to establish a minimal foundationalism, radical interpretativists argue that this is just as illusory as are positivist claims about truth as correspondence (i.e. that theories can be assessed by whether they fit 'reality').

This is not the place to judge these two approaches, since there exist no common standards by which such a judgement might be made. My point is not to offer my view about which of these positions is better, let alone 'right'; rather, to indicate that this categorization seems to me to be exactly where the frontiers of constitutive international theory are today. As such this is a far deeper debate than that offered by the inter-paradigm debate or by the dispute between neo-realists and neo-liberal institutionalists. Is is a particularly interesting and important debate because it propels international theory towards the central debates within the other social sciences. In this sense, it undermines the very misleading characterization of international theory as autonomous and distinct which has dominated virtually all the self-images discussed above. By so doing, it requires international theory to be less parochial and exclusive. I have put this debate at the end of my list because I feel it to be the most important one for the future of international theory. For too long, under the shadow of positivism, international relations has been dominated by explanatory theory which rested on an outdated and fundamentally contested view of both the content of international theory and the nature of social scientific enquiry. Focusing on foundationalism/anti-foundationalism returns international theory to a more humble, and more central, place within the human sciences.

CONCLUSION

These categorizations represent ten self-images of international relations theory. My introductory comments about Bauman and Foucault will make it clear where my sympathies lie, although I should point out that I have travelled a long, and positivist, road to get here. What interests me about international relations theory today is that these ten readings of that theory offer different accounts of what international theory is about, and what should rightly be its concern. As my comments above indicate, I am most interested with the final two self-images, since they seem to me to focus on the concerns raised by my discussion of Bauman and Foucault at the start of this chapter. But, of course, these categorizations are themselves partial and obviously reflect a political and theoretical agenda. The central claim of this chapter, though, is that *all* self-images reflect normative concerns. There is no more normative theorist than one who proudly boasts that he or she will simply deal with 'the facts'. The problem with this is which 'facts'. Crucially, focusing on questions about the contrast between explanatory and constitutive theories and the competing claims of foundationalist and anti-foundationalist accounts makes us think about international theory as intimately connected with the other human sciences. It is vitally important that international theorists question the assumption that international theory is a separate field of enquiry. Instead it should be seen as one arena in which both the clash between explanatory and constitutive theories and that between foundationalism and anti-foundationalism take place.

Having said which, I must stress that the contributors to this book occupy a variety of positions in these self-images, and there is no orthodoxy shared by them all. What, however, is shared is not only an engagement with the self-images and categorizations within which they work, but also a concern with international relations theory as more than a free-standing discipline. Each contributor deals with issues that are on the frontier of the discipline, and which the reader needs to contextualize within the self-images noted above. My aim has been to give the reader a set of lenses through which to think about the contributions that follow, and thereby to read into the contributions to see not only what voices are present, and which are privileged, but also which voices are absent. I leave open to the reader whether or not he or she sees one lens are providing *the* answer, whether more than one lens is needed to comprehend international relations, or whether the problem is that the different lenses are incompatible. The underlying question for the reader is whether the self-images and debates dealt with above are different accounts of the same world, or whether they are accounts of different worlds. That question again returns international theory to the most fundamental debates within the social sciences.

Finally, if the central message of Foucault's genealogical method is to enquire into the way in which certain categorizations of thought dominate over others, then the reader needs to think about what the self-images of international theorists tell us about the discourse of international theory. Which accounts have dominated and *why*? Which voices are dominant? Which 'reality' is dominant? If Bauman makes us think about that over which we remain silent, perhaps it is appropriate to end by asking the reader to reflect on how Bauman's central claim about sociology and the Holocaust translates into the relationship between international theory and international practice: 'the Holocaust has more to say about the state of sociology than sociology in its present shape is able to add to our knowledge of the Holocaust' (1989, p. 3). What do the self-images of international theory tell us? What are the silences, identities and discontinuities submerged within the dominant discourses of international theory? Does the practice of international politics tell us more about international theory than the dominant debates within international theory can tell us about international politics? Together the work of Bauman and Foucault should alert us to the link between theory and practice. What do the self-images tell us about the social practice of international theory? Whose interests get represented in international theory? Whose interests and identities are ignored and silenced and seen as irrelevant? Above all, *why* is international theory?

Note

I would like to thank Ken Booth, Tim Dunne, Richard Wyn Jones, Nick Wheeler and Marysia Zalewski for their particularly helpful and incisive comments on an earlier draft of this chapter.

References

Alker, H. and Biersteker, T. 1984: The dialectics of world order: notes for a future archeologist of international savoir faire. *International Studies Quarterly*, 28(2), 121–42.

Ashley, R. 1987: The geopolitics of geopolitical space: toward a critical social theory of international politics. *Alternatives*, 12(4), 403–34.

Baldwin, D. (ed.) 1993: *Neorealism and Neoliberalism: The Contemporary Debate*. New York: Columbia University Press.

Banks, M. 1984: The evolution of international relations theory. In M. Banks (ed.), *Conflict in World Society: A New Perspective on International Relations*, Brighton: Wheatsheaf Books, 3–21.

Banks, M. 1985: The inter-paradigm debate. In M. Light and A. J. R. Groom (eds), *International Relations: A Handbook of Current Theory*, London: Frances Pinter, 7–26.

Barry, B. 1989: *Theories of Justice*. Hemel Hempstead: Harvester Wheatsheaf.

Bauman, Z. 1989: *Modernity and the Holocaust*. Cambridge: Polity Press.

Beitz, C. 1979: *Political Theory and International Relations*. Princeton, N.J.: Princeton University Press.

Brown, C. 1987: Not my department? Normative theory and international relations. *Paradigms*, 1(2), 104–3.

Brown, C. 1988: Cosmopolitan confusions: a reply to Hoffman. *Paradigms*, 2(2), 102–11.

Brown, C. 1992: *International Relations Theory: New Normative Approaches*. Hemel Hempstead: Harvester Wheatsheaf.

Bull, H. 1972: The theory of international politics, 1919–1969. In B. Porter (ed.), *The Aberystwyth Papers: International Politics 1919–69*, Oxford: Oxford University Press, 30–55.
Bull, H. 1976: Martin Wight and the theory of international relations. *British Journal of International Studies*, 2(2), 101–6.
Bull, H. 1977: *The Anarchical Society: A Study of Order in World Politics*. London: Macmillan.
Burton, J. 1972: *World Society*, Cambridge: Cambridge University Press.
Buzan, B., Jones, C. and Little, R. 1993: *The Logic of Anarchy: Neorealism to Structural Realism*. New York: Columbia University Press.
Campbell, D. 1992: *Writing Security: United States Foreign Policy and the Politics of Identity*. Manchester: Manchester University Press.
Carlsnaes, W. 1992: The agency-structure problem in foreign policy analysis. *International Studies Quarterly*, 36(3), 245–70.
Carlsnaes, W. 1994: In lieu of a conclusion: compatibility and the agency-structure issue in foreign policy analysis. In W. Carlsnaes and S. Smith (eds), *European Foreign Policy*, London: Sage, 274–87.
Cox, R. 1981: Social forces, states and world orders: beyond international relations theory. *Millennium: Journal of International Studies*, 10(2), 126–55.
Cox, R. 1987: *Production, Power and World Order: Social Forces in the Making of History*. New York: Columbia University Press.
Der Derian, J. 1987: *On Diplomacy: A Genealogy of Western Estrangement*. Oxford: Basil Blackwell.
Der Derian, J. 1992: *Anti-Diplomacy: Spies, Terror, Speed, and War*. Oxford: Basil Blackwell.
Donelan, M. 1990: *Elements of International Political Theory*. Oxford: Clarendon Press.
Dunne, T. 1993: Mythology or methodology? Traditions in international relations. *Review of International Studies*, 19(3), 305–18.
Elshtain, J. 1987: *Women and War*. Brighton: Harvester Press.
Enloe, C. 1989: *Bananas, Beaches and Bases: Making Feminist Sense of International Politics*. London: Pandora Books.
Enloe, C. 1993: *The Morning After: Sexual Politics at the End of the Cold War*. Berkeley: University of California Press.
Foucault, M. 1967: *Madness and Civilization: A History of Insanity in the Age of Reason* (first published 1961). London: Tavistock Publications.
Foucault, M. 1970: *The Order of Things: An Archaeology of the Human Sciences* (first published 1966). New York: Random House.
Foucault, M. 1972: *The Archaeology of Knowledge* (first published 1971). New York: Pantheon Books.
Foucault, M. 1975: *The Birth of the Clinic: An Archaeology of Medical Perception* (first published 1963). New York: Vintage Books.
Foucault, M. 1977: *Discipline and Punish: The Birth of the Prison* (first published 1975). Harmondsworth: Allen Lane.

Foucault, M. 1979: *The History of Sexuality Vol. 1: An Introduction*. Harmondsworth: Allen Lane.

Foucault, M. 1986: Nietzsche, genealogy, history. In P. Rabinow (ed.), *The Foucault Reader*, Harmondsworth: Peregrine Books, 76–100.

Foucault, M. 1987: *The Use of Pleasure: The History of Sexuality* Vol. 2 (first published 1984). Harmondsworth: Peregrine Books.

Foucault, M. 1988: *The Care of the Self: The History of Sexuality* Vol. 3 (first published 1984). Harmondsworth: Allen Lane.

Frost, M. 1986: *Towards A Normative Theory of International Relations*. Cambridge: Cambridge University Press.

George, J. 1993: Of incarceration and closure: neo-realism and the new/old world orders. *Millennium: Journal of International Studies*, 22(2), 197–234.

Gilpin, R. 1981: *War and Change in World Politics*. Cambridge: Cambridge University Press.

Gilpin, R. 1987: *The Political Economy of International Relations*. Princeton, N. J.: Princeton University Press.

Goldstein, J. and Keohane, R. (eds) 1993: *Ideas and Foreign Policy: Beliefs, Institutions & Political Change*. Ithaca, N.Y.: Cornell University Press.

Hoffman, M. 1987: Critical theory and the inter-paradigm debate. *Millennium: Journal of International Studies*, 16(2), 231–49.

Hoffman, M. 1988a: States, cosmopolitanism and normative international theory. *Paradigms*, 2(1), 60–75.

Hoffman, M. 1988b: Conversations on critical international relations theory. *Millennium: Journal of International Studies*, 17(1), 91–5.

Hollis, M. and Smith, S. 1986: Roles and reasons in foreign policy decision-making. *British Journal of Political Science*, 16(3), 269–86.

Hollis, M. and Smith S. 1990: *Explaining and Understanding International Relations*. Oxford: Clarendon Press.

Hollis, M. and Smith, S. 1991: Beware of gurus: structure and action in international relations. *Review of International Studies*, 17(4), 393–410.

Hollis, M. and Smith, S. 1992: Structure and action: further comment. *Review of International Studies*, 18(2), 187–8.

Hollis, M. and Smith, S. 1994: Two stories about structure and agency. *Review of International Studies*, 20(3) forthcoming.

Holsti, K. 1985: *The Dividing Discipline: Hegemony and Diversity in International Theory*. London: Allen & Unwin.

Horkheimer, M. and Adorno, T. 1979: *Dialectic of Enlightenment* (first published 1944). London: Verso.

James, A. 1982: Michael Nicholson on Martin Wight: a mind passing in the night. *Review of International Studies*, 8(2), 117–23.

Jones, R. 1981: The English school of international relations: a case for closure. *Review of International Studies*, 7(1), 1–13.

Keohane, R. 1984: *After Hegemony: Cooperation and Discord in the World Political Economy*. Princeton, N. J.: Princeton University Press.

Keohane, R. (ed.) 1986: *Neo-Realism and Its Critics*. New York: Columbia University Press.
Keohane, R. 1988: International institutions: two approaches. *International Studies Quarterly*, 32(4), 379–91.
Keohane, R. and Nye, J. 1977: *Power and Interdependence: World Politics in Transition*. Boston: Little, Brown & Co.
Keohane, R., Nye J. and Hoffmann, S. (eds) 1993: *After the Cold War: International Institutions and State Strategies in Europe 1989–1991*. Cambridge, Mass.: Harvard University Press.
Krasner, S. (ed.) 1983: *International Regimes*. Ithaca N.Y.: Cornell University Press.
Kuhn, T. 1970a: *The Structure of Scientific Revolutions*. Chicago: University of Chicago Press.
Kuhn, T. 1970b: Reflections on my critics. In I. Lakatos and Musgrave (1970), 231–78.
Lakatos, I. and Musgrave, M. (eds) 1970: *Criticism and the Growth of Knowledge*. Cambridge: Cambridge University Press.
Lapid, Y. 1989: The third debate: on the prospects of international theory in a post-positivist era. *International Studies Quarterly*, 33(3), 235–54.
Lijphart, A. 1974a: International relations theory: great debates and lesser debates. *International Social Science Journal*, 26(1), 11–21.
Lijphart, A. 1974b: The structure of the theoretical revolution in international relations. *International Studies Quarterly*, 18(1), 41–74.
Linklater, A. 1982: *Men and Citizens in the Theory of International Relations*. Houndmills, Basingstoke: Macmillan Press.
Linklater, A. 1990: *Beyond Realism and Marxism: Critical Theory and International Relations*. Houndmills, Basingstoke: Macmillan Press.
Linklater, A. 1992: The question of the next stage in international relations theory: a critical-theoretical point of view. *Millennium: Journal of International Studies*, 21(1), 77–98.
Little, R. and Smith M. (eds) 1991: *Perspectives on World Politics*, 2nd ed. London: Routledge.
Lyotard, J.-F. 1986: *The Postmodern Condition: A Report on Knowledge*. Manchester: Manchester University Press.
Maghroori, R. and Ramberg, B. (eds) 1982: *Globalism versus Realism: International Relations' Third Debate*. Boulder, Colorado: Westview Press.
Mann, M. 1986: *The Sources of Social Power*, Vol. 1: *A History of Power from the Beginning to A.D. 1760*. Cambridge: Cambridge University Press
Mann, M. 1993: *The Sources of Social Power*, Vol. 2: *The Rise of Classes and Nation-States, 1760–1914*. Cambridge: Cambridge University Press..
Mansbach, R., Ferguson, Y. and Lampert, D. 1976: *The Web of World Politics: Non-State Actors in the Global System*. Englewood Cliffs N.J.: Prentice-Hall.

Mansbach, R. and Vasquez, J. 1981: *In Search of Theory: A New Paradigm for Global Politics*. New York: Columbia University Press.
Masterman, M. 1970: The nature of a paradigm. In Lakatos and Musgrave (1970), 59–89.
McGrew, A. and Lewis, P. (eds) 1992: *Global Politics: Globalization & the Nation-State*. Cambridge: Polity Press.
Nardin, T. 1983: *Law, Morality and the Relations of States*. Princeton N.J.: Princeton University Press.
Nardin, T. and Mapel, D. (eds) 1992: *Traditions of International Ethics*. Cambridge: Cambridge University Press.
Olson, W. and Groom, A. 1991: *International Relations Then and Now: Origins and Trends in Interpretation*. London: Harper Collins Academic.
Onuf, N. 1989: *World of Our Making: Rules and Rule in Social Theory and International Relations*. Columbia, S.C.: University of South Carolina Press.
Peterson, V. S. and Sisson Runyan, A. 1993: *Global Gender Issues*. Boulder, Colorado: Westview Press.
Rawls, J. 1971: *A Theory of Justice*. Oxford: Oxford University Press.
Rengger, N. 1988: Going critical? A Response to Hoffman. *Millennium: Journal of International Studies*, 17(1), 81–9.
Rengger, N. and Hoffman, M. 1992: Modernity, post-modernism and international relations. In J. Doherty, E. Graham and M. Malek (eds), *Post-Modernism in the Social Sciences*. Houndmills, Basingstoke: Macmillan Press, 127–46.
Ruggie, J. 1983: Continuity and transformation in the world polity: toward a neorealist synthesis. *World Politics*, 35(2), 261–85.
Ruggie, J. 1993: Territoriality and beyond: problematizing modernity in international relations. *International Organization*, 47(1), 139–74.
Scholte, J. 1993: *International Relations of Social Change*. Buckingham: Open University Press.
Skocpol, T. 1979: *States and Social Revolutions: A Comparative Analysis of France, Russia, and China*. Cambridge: Cambridge University Press.
Smart, B. 1985: *Michel Foucault*. London: Routledge.
Smith, S. 1994: Foreign policy theory and the new Europe. In W. Carlsnaes and S. Smith (eds), *European Foreign Policy*, London: Sage, 1–20.
Sylvester, C. 1994: *Feminist Theory and International Relations in a Post-Modern Era*. Cambridge: Cambridge University Press.
Tilly, C. (ed.) 1975: *The Formation of National States in Western Europe*. Princeton, N.J.: Princeton University Press.
Tilly, C. 1990: *Coercion, Capital, and European States, A.D. 990–1990*. Oxford: Basil Blackwell.
Tooze, R. 1992: Conceptualising the global economy. In McGrew and Lewis (1992), 233–49.
Vasquez, J. 1983: *The Power of Power Politics: A Critique*. London: Frances Pinter.

Viotti, P. and Kauppi, M. 1993: *International Relations Theory: Realism, Pluralism, Globalism*, 2nd ed. New York: Macmillan.
Walker, R. B. J. 1993: *Inside/Outside: International Relations as Political Theory*. Cambridge: Cambridge University Press.
Waltz, K. N. 1979: *Theory of International Politics*. Reading, Mass.: Addison-Wesley.
Walzer, M. 1980: *Just and Unjust Wars: A Moral Argument with Historical Illustrations*. Harmondsworth: Penguin.
Wendt, A. 1987: The agent-structure problem in international relations theory. *International Organization*, 41(3), 335–70.
Wendt, A. 1991: Bridging the theory/meta-theory gap in international relations. *Review of International Studies*, 17(4), 383–92.
Wendt, A. 1992a: Levels of analysis vs. agents and structures: part III. *Review of International Studies*, 18(2), 181–5.
Wendt, A. 1992b: Anarchy is what states make of it: the social construction of power politics. *International Organization*, 46(2), 391–425.
Wendt, A. and Duvall, R. 1989: Institutions and international order. In E.-O. Czempiel and J. Rosenau (eds), *Global Changes and Theoretical Challenges: Approaches to World Politics for the 1990s*, Lexington, Mass.: Lexington Books, 51–73.
Wight, M. 1966: Why is there no international theory? In H. Butterfield and M. Wight (eds), *Diplomatic Investigations: Essays in the Theory of International Politics*, London: Allen & Unwin, 17–34.
Wight, M. 1991: *International Theory: The Three Traditions*. Leicester: Leicester University Press.
Whitworth, S. 1989: Gender in the inter-paradigm debate. *Millennium: Journal of International Studies*, 18(2), 265–72.

2

The End of the Cold War and International Relations: Some Analytic and Theoretical Conclusions

Fred Halliday

INTRODUCTION: THE CHALLENGES OF THE REAL

The end of the Cold War presents international relations as an academic discipline with a special, triple, challenge: the first two components of this challenge may be self-evident, the third rather less so. On the one hand, it poses a range of empirical and analytical questions, pertaining to what has happened, why it happened and what the longer-run implications for the course of international relations may be. On the other, it poses a theoretical challenge, namely that of assessing how far the course of events over the past few years, and the broader revision of how we see historical trends in the twentieth century that it occasions, lead us to identify weaknesses, what in Kuhn's language would be anomalies, in existing theories of international relations and suggest where further theoretical work may be in order. International relations, to its credit and profit, has not in recent years been dominated by one single paradigm, but has enjoyed a healthy pluralism, even if at times this has led to indulgence of modish apparitions (such as postmodernism) at the expense of substantial theoretical engagement and debate: the end of the Cold War may nonetheless pose a challenge across the range of established theories.

Any confrontation with these two questions rests, however,

upon an assumed answer to the third, one that underlies much work on international relations but which is of such a sensitivity that it is all too rarely addressed in its own right, and that is the relationship between international relations as a theoretical and analytic academic discipline and events in the outside, so-called 'real', world. If all branches of the social sciences have evolved in response to events and challenges in the 'real', and if all make it part of their professional identity and *amour propre* to suggest some orthodox, non-ideological, relationship to that 'real', few if any are as sensitive as international relations about their ties to external events. One has only to identify those practices that are most abhorred in international relations – the temptations of international history, the virus of 'presentism', the corruption of 'current affairs' – to see how deep-seated this concern about external contamination is. Its most firm and peremptory variant is to be found in the kind of assertion common in realism that there is really nothing new in the international, and that all we need to know can be found in the doleful utterances of the classics – Thucydides, Hobbes, Machiavelli – or in the parsimonious and atemporal maxims of Waltz's neo-realism.

It is one of the beguiling paradoxes of international relations that while it served to legitimize an international practice that dominated the postwar world, that of cold war and the attendant mobilizations of states and other resources, the Cold War itself was subjected to almost no theoretical analysis at all, on the grounds that there was nothing particularly new in it. The virtual aphasia which confronts international relations in the face of what has been, and remains, the most formative international process of the past five hundred years, capitalism, is even more striking (on which see the brilliant analysis in Rosenberg, 1994). Buried in the terms 'international society' and, more recently, 'interdependence', this silence is the most striking of all within the discipline. International relations is not alone in its theoretical blindnesses: the inability of economics to create a theory that deals with interest groups and irrational behaviour, of politics to specify the socio-economic, as distinct from the purely constitutional and procedural, preconditions for democracy or of sociology to say anything until the 1970s about nationalism, are parallel cases. It is not casual therefore that the most apparently rigorous, and therefore theoretically comfortable, response to the events of the past few years is to say that they have made, and should make, no difference at all to the theory or teaching of international relations.

This inbuilt silence is of course not only inherently implausible, but is undesirable, in that it avoids discussion of the proper response of a social science to the external world. The dangers of 'presentism' and of current affairs are real enough, and especially so in international relations. The history of the subject is replete with examples of work that is warped and conditioned by transient changes, or by the identification of processes as recent when they have in fact a much longer, and often classically discussed, provenance – interdependence being an obvious example. The Anglo-Saxon instantaneous too easily becomes the global trend. But a major upheaval in world history, which the events of the past few years certainly are, merits more than canonical repetition. The First World War produced international relations as an academic discipline and generated a field of theoretical work, the much-maligned 'utopianism', which dominated the inter-war years. The Second World War, and the Cold War that followed, marked the domination of realism, still, despite many a competitor, the dominant paradigm in the field. The works of Carr, Niebuhr and Morgenthau did not emerge simply from reflections in a library. It would hardly be surprising if the collapse of the Soviet Bloc in 1989, arguably the third great cataclysm of the twentieth century, and one that drew a line under the previous two, should not also pose theoretical questions for international relations. The issue is not whether it does or not, but, rather, what the issues of substance posed by the past really are, and which processes currently under way in the world outside merit our prospective analytic and theoretical attention. We may well get it wrong – as the 'utopians' and 'realists' in their time certainly did: but this is no reason to avoid the challenge which the end of the Cold War poses.

THE COLLAPSE OF THE SOVIET BLOC

The historical outlines and originality of what happened in the late 1980s can be summarized in brief. In a bloc of states, dominated by the USSR, which had since the 1940s been engaged in great power competition with the West, and which had, in the form of the USSR itself, been challenging the Western world since 1917, the political system collapsed (Blackburn, 1991). The originality of this system's collapse needs mention: it occurred without inter-state war, in a very short space of time, without the presence of evident forms of political vanguards or opposition organization and without significant bloodshed. Moreover, in contrast to other revolutions since 1789 which had to some degree claimed to defy the international norm or advocate something 'new', those propounding change in this context wanted not, as had hitherto almost always been the case, the creation of something 'new', an alternative to the prevailing world order, but, rather, conformity to that order, a recruitment and incorporation, as rapid and painless as possible, into what was deemed to be the prevailing norm, be it 'civilization', 'democracy', the 'West' or 'modernity': hence Habermas's (1991) term *die nachholende Revolution*, the 'catching-up revolution'.

At this interim point, certain qualifications of a major kind are necessary: most of those ruled by communist parties in 1988 (1.7 billion) still are (1.4 billion); there is no certainty about what kinds of government will emerge in the former Soviet Union, or in many of its former allies; the future pattern of Russian foreign policy is obscure. But nonetheless a cataclysm of great proportions has occurred, and one that brings to an end not only the Cold War and the challenge of the Bolshevik revolution but also a longer period of international history in which a movement of contestation of the hegemonic capitalist form was identifiable. At the risk of what one could term 'megalo-presentism', it could be suggested that 1989 brought to the end a period of history that began in 1789 with the French Revolution. In this sense the argument of Fukuyama (1992), that what is new about the contemporary situation is that there is only one set of answers now acceptable on a world scale, is to a considerable degree valid. It is in this above all that the historic importance of 1989 consists (Halliday, 1991, 1992a).

In this perspective the 'end of the Cold War' is a composite phenomenon involving four broad historical trends, each of which will take time to work itself out and each of which may have identifiable theoretical implications.

Altered Relations Between Great Powers

The end of the Cold War marks the end of the inter-state conflict that has dominated the world since 1945 and of the Soviet–US nuclear confrontation. Two obvious prospective issues are whether this marks an end of great power military rivalry as a whole, at least for a generation or so, and whether a new pattern of inter-state blocs and of hegemony will emerge to replace the old. The argument on the former would seem to have considerable historical force – that for a century since the Sino–Japanese war of 1894 great powers have been engaged in major military confrontation, or in the threat thereof, and that this era is now over. The prospect of this now seems definitely to have receded and while there are those who foresee new great power conflicts in the future, the pattern of the past century would appear to have been broken. As for hegemony, we now see a situation of great fluidity in which no bloc of states seems likely to emerge to match the US, but where the US itself appears reluctant to play the unipolar 'Roman' role which the collapse of the USSR has allotted to it. The argument that war between states is almost precluded when they are liberal democratic states has much to recommend it and, if true, would focus our attention on the consequences were some of the great powers, Russia or Japan, in the longer run to diverge from this democratic model (see Doyle, 1983a, 1983b, 1986, for the classic formulation of this view, but see also the qualifications below). The implications of this for the international system will be examined later, in the penultimate section of this chapter.

The End of Communism

The second dimension of the end of the Cold War is the end of communism as a political force. As already indicated this is, as yet, a phenomenon confined to Europe: but the trend within China would seem to indicate a move towards capitalism, if not liberalism, and the remaining communist states (Cuba, Vietnam, North Korea) are unable to provide an international alternative. Two large questions arise here: first, what the future of an alternative to capitalism now is, and if there is one at all; second, what the historical import of the whole communist experience was. In regard to the first it seems that no programme of political challenge to liberal capitalism from the left now has any serious credit or support: the communist revolutionary challenge is exhausted. What remains are variants of social-democratic adaptation within advanced capitalism, but ones that are more and more restricted in part by international conditions, in part by changing social and political configurations within individual countries themselves. It is conventional to state that the collapse of social democracy is in part a result of the failure of communism: the reverse may, however, be the case – the dynamic of social democracy and its equivalents was broken in most advanced countries (Britain, the US, Australia, Germany) in the 1970s, and the very lack of a credible middle, or third, road meant that the choices facing communist reformers in the late 1980s were all the starker.

The question of what was communism, too near to allow of an easy perspective, has occasioned several candidate explanations: a dictatorial tendency whereby revolutionary elites seized control of societies, a flawed movement for the self-emancipation of the working class, an expression of messianism, a product of oriental despotism, a failed developmentalist project. One author has recently suggested that it may end up being comparable to the Jesuit experiment in Paraguay, a rational attempt at insulating a section of the world from international pressures and sustaining an alternative development path, and one that was much idealized by intellectuals at the time, but one which was in the end to collapse almost without trace (Anderson, 1992). Some explanation involving different elements of the candidates listed above may be appropriate: what is perhaps most striking is that this attempt to escape the conventional path of capitalist development was for a time remarkably successful, not least in the ideological and military challenge it posed to the West, but was in the end forced to capitulate, and to do so almost without a semblance of resistance. Although now seen as inevitable, this was not how the communist experiment appeared for many decades: among both those who supported it and those who feared it, there was a belief in the efficacy of socialist state intervention that subsequent events have belied. If nothing else, the communist collapse deserves careful study from the perspective of those who believe in or state-dictated social and economic development, or in 'totalitarianism'.

Changing the Inter-State Map

The third element in the end of the Cold War is the break-up of the USSR, and of its attendant alliance system. Here it is not at all clear if the process is complete, not only with regard to Eastern Europe but also to Russia itself: the Russian Federation is subject to substantial centrifugal forces and may yet break up into three parts under international and internal pressure. Even if the process of fragmentation is already complete, it has unleashed powerful changes in the international arena. On the one hand, it has created a situation in which, with the break-up of the pre-existing order, new regional alliances and new potential hegemons have emerged: in Europe – Germany; in the Caucasus, Black Sea and Central Asia – Turkey. In the Far East the realignments are less major, because Soviet power was weaker, but it has encouraged and coincided with an increase in both Chinese and Japanese power; and the impact on Indo-China, with the removal of the Soviet role in Cambodia and Vietnam, and in the North-East Asian region, is nonetheless substantial and continuous. Some of these regional changes take us back to a situation before 1914 – the pattern of alliances in the Balkans and in the Baltic are cases in point. Others are new, the Turkish–Iranian contest in Central Asia being only a remote descendant of earlier ones.

The other strategic consequence of the collapse of communism is that it has broken a 'regime' that prevailed since the end of the Second World War, in terms of which the existing map of the world, whatever its iniquities and arbitrariness, was maintained. For all the talk of secession and unification that marked the post-1945 epoch, it is striking how, until 1989, the map more or less held. States became independent, some lost bits of territory, but the actual division into 170-odd states was more or less frozen. Unification or fusion occurred only by force and at moments of uncertainty arising from decolonization (Palestine, Western Sahara, Timor and, it can be argued, Tibet). Secession succeeded only in the case of Bangladesh in 1971, but that was of an entity that was already geographically separated from the rest of Pakistan.

Since 1989 both fusion and fission have come again on to the order of the day: the fusion of the Yemens and the Germanys will be followed, albeit with some delay, by that of the Koreas and probably, in some form or other, of the (three) Chinas. On the other hand, fission has been the fate of the multi-ethnic states of the former communist system (USSR, Yugoslavia, Ethiopia, Czechoslovakia), with the result that in the space of two years over twenty new sovereign states have come into existence. No one can yet tell what the longer-term demonstration effects of this process are going to be, but there can be little doubt that the breaking of the post-1945 regime will encourage many others to think that they too can achieve separate statehood. This will affect some areas more than others: but parts of Europe and Africa, as well as India, are likely to be subject to increased strains, now that it has been shown that secession is allowed.

The Spread of 'Democracy'

The collapse of communism and the apparent spread of liberal democratic political forms to a range of countries, post-communist and Third World, has led some to suggest that a new era of global democracy is at hand. This is in essence the argument of Fukuyama, although he is careful to state that he distinguishes between the claim that there is no other viable model on offer from the claim that its consolidation in all countries is imminent or even plausible (Halliday, 1992b). In certain respects this claim is a valid one, in that the end of communism has, in spite of the survival of the Asian communist bloc, underlined the extent to which the old, alternative revolutionary, path of political development is not viable or attractive.

Yet some major qualifications need to be made here. First, the attainment of a democratic system is not a rapid or once-and-for-all process, but takes a long period of transition: Britain and the US became fully democratic, in the sense of one person, one vote, only in the 1960s, after hundreds of years of development. Many other states are in the process of attaining this through various forms of 'semi-democratic' evolution – Mexico and Egypt being cases in point (Therborn, 1977). Second, no one can be sure if a democratic system is established for at least a generation: the fate of the Weimar Republic and of a range of Third World democracies (Lebanon, Liberia, Ceylon) that appeared reasonably secure in the 1960s should make that clear. The political strains within most countries newly arrived at pluralism indicate that matters may take a very different turn in the years ahead. Third, while the left authoritarian model has been discredited, capitalist states are far from unanimous that democracy on some kind of American-European model is most desirable. In the Far East in particular there is a range of states where alternative forms of capitalism, not of the most brutal but authoritarian nonetheless, can be identified and which may provide a more attractive model for former communist states, China and even Russia among them. Finally, the long-run stability of liberal capitalist states themselves may be insecure, as a combination of socio-economic strains and falling political participation threaten established, and in themselves far from ideal, norms. There are also a number of trends within advanced industrial society which make for more, rather than less, democracy: these include the new potentialities for electronic and media manipulation and surveillance, rising levels of electoral abstention and social alienation, and the collapse of the working class movements which for the first three-quarters of the twentieth century ensured a degree of political and social compromise in these societies.

The implications of this precariousness of democracy for international relations are twofold. First, if there is some reasonably binding relationship between liberal democracy and peace, the travails of democratization will have a major impact on the future course of inter-state relations. The precondition for world peace is the consolidation of democracy on a world scale: this process, not the salience of international law, was, of course, the central argument in Woodrow Wilson's supposedly 'utopian' view of international politics. Second, the process of democratization itself, and the degree to which all states in the world are pressured into conforming to it, focuses attention on how international norms and mechanisms such as foreign aid and trading conditionality can now operate to enforce a single mode of domestic political and economic practice. In other words, it raises the question, which is also raised by the fall of communism itself, of how far, beyond acceptance of certain international norms, states are also compelled by the system to conform internally, or to pay a higher price for not doing so. That has always been one of the underlying dimensions of international relations, but one which recent events enable us to look at in a fresh light. (Halliday, 1992c, 1992d).

EXPLAINING THE END OF THE COLD WAR

The argument so far has looked at implications for the international system of the end of the Cold War, and the consequences of the four different processes that are subsumed under that heading. The implications of 1989 for international relations involve, however, an additional exploration, namely of why it was that the Cold War ended, and indeed of what the Cold War itself was. The latter in turn presupposes some view of what the two component forces in this conflict ('capitalism' and 'communism') were, and of the manner in which each sought to compete with and, to a certain extent, prevail over the other. If we are still here in uncharted territory, the least that can be said is that some interesting questions for international relations are posed by this nexus of issues.

There is no shortage of explanations as to why the Cold War ended: the arms race, the democratic upsurge of peoples, the economic exhaustion of communism and particularly of the USSR are all widespread explanations. Yet it may be worth probing deeper, since the phenomenon itself is, as already indicated, very striking – a rapid, almost effortless, surrender by an elite that had hitherto shown remarkable tenacity and ingenuity in rivalling the West. The arms race itself cannot be a sufficient explanation, since while many resources went on arms, the inefficiency of the rest of the economy would still not be explained by it. Resistance from below there was, but remarkably little, with the intermittent exception of Poland. Certainly the system was performing less well than the West, but in its own terms, and in terms of a generational comparison, it had still achieved a great deal, doubling living standards in the USSR in a generation.

What above all led to the end of the Cold War was not, in Lenin's terms, that the ruled would not go on being ruled in the old way but, rather, that the rulers could not go on ruling in the old way: this is what needs explanation. If the central factor that needs explaining is why the USSR leadership lost its nerve, and engaged in a reform process, *perestroika*, that was itself doomed to failure, then three interlocking issues seem to have played the crucial role: the inability to compete with the US in the military dimensions of the third industrial revolution, the growing gridlock of the command economy and its inability to innovate and sustain earlier levels of growth, and the growing realization among the elite itself that the West was drawing ahead not only in political and military spheres but also in economic performance and in particular in the provision of consumer goods (Halliday, 1992a).

The first of these issues is self-evident, and is a more precise formulation of the impact of the arms race than a generic assertion of overspending and competitive inequality. The second is something that became clearer and clearer in the 1970s and 1960s, and compounded the sense, highlighted by the Prague invasion of 1968, that the system could not evolve in a political direction either. The third is what is most important, and from the point of view of international relations, most interesting, for it focuses our attention on a particular form of international competition and interaction distinct from the interaction of states and also of non-state transnational actors such as business enterprises or banks. These two were certainly very important in forming part of the challenge of the West to communism, but on their own they were not decisive. What is most significant, and what needs explanation in historical and theoretical terms, is the mechanism by which the example, the very demonstrated success, should have undermined the ability of the Soviet elite to continue as before. As I have put it elsewhere, it was the tee-shirt, not the gunboat, that broke down the communist system's resistance to global capitalism (Halliday, 1992a).

The question that is linked to this is, of course, the issue of what the Cold War itself was about. This has been discussed elsewhere and can only be summarized here (Halliday, 1991, 1992c). Suffice it to say that there were four broad schools of thought about what the Cold War constituted: a realist explanation, that it was no different from other forms of great power conflict; a critical, 'internalist', school, according to which it was not a contest at all but, rather, a mechanism by which the dominant groups in each bloc could better control their subject populations and clients; a 'misperception' school, which saw the Cold War was a mistake, an exaggeration of ideological differences and international conflict as a result of historical and individual misperceptions; and an 'inter-systemic' approach, that saw the Cold War as one between two rival social systems, each of which sought, albeit with much exaggeration and, as a result of nuclear weapons, some prudence, to prevail over the other.

This last point of view, that the Cold War was to some extent 'about' ideology, was under-represented in most academic literature, partly because it sounded like a Cold War stereotype, in taking the claims of the protagonists seriously, and partly because it involved an assertion of the importance of internal political and social organization for international relations. The 'inter-systemic' theory claimed that what was at stake in the Cold War, and more generally in international relations, was not just 'international society' as normally defined, the acceptance of common norms of inter-state behaviour, but the conformity of societies and states to certain, broadly defined, homogeneous norms. Yet the Cold War ended above all because the pressures on the Soviet system to conform were, after seventy years, too great.

Inter-systemic conflict theory argued that the Cold War, while certainly invested with elements of great power conflict, was more than that and about more than that. It also denied that the conflict was only the result of misperception. It recognized the importance of endogenous factors, but suggested that each side was fighting over something albeit within limits, and that the Cold War could end only when one side had prevailed over the other. This is exactly what happened. What broke the will of the Soviet leadership was not an absolute failure, or mass revolt from below, but a comparative historical judgement, that their societies were not like those of the West, and showed no sign of so becoming, either through a dramatic burst of growth and innovation in the East, or through a collapse of the capitalist system in the West. Once this had become evident, Gorbachev and his associates organized what was, in effect, an unconditional surrender: it was this that brought the Cold War to the end.

THEORETICAL ISSUES

At least four broad, interrelated theoretical issues, ones that go to the heart of international relations, would seem to arise from the above analysis. They are as follows: first, homogeneity and 'international society' – how far the international system does operate on the basis not only of shared inter-state norms, but also of common internal norms; second, the mechanisms of inter-society relationships under capitalism, and of how the dynamic of globalization under capitalism operates, with both incorporation and blockages to development; third, the mechanisms of power in the contemporary world, of the relationship of military to economic and ideological power; fourth, the workings of the balance of power in an era without major great power conflict. These are large themes: summary observations, picking up on and developing remarks earlier in the text, follow.

Homogeneity: the Stronger Variant of 'International Society'

The issue of homogeneity, i.e. the need for societies to share common internal norms, has been inadequately studied in international relations, most obviously because it seemed to fall into the trap of 'reductionism' castigated by Waltz. Where it has arisen, in the work of writers on interdependence, it has usually been seen as a recent phenomenon. Yet there are grounds for arguing that it underlies the whole history of the international system, and explains why deviations from internal norms are so threatening to international relations. The conundrum of much conflict in the international system is that while revolutions make some challenge to international order these challenges are rather limited: the inter-state rationale for counter-revolution would appear to be rather weak. Yet if homogeneity is made the issue the reason for such conflicts becomes clearer. No one saw this more clearly than Burke (1852) who, in his 'Letters on a Regicide Peace', sketched out the bases of what could be a powerful theory of homogeneity: that social and political peace within one state requires that others conform to broadly the same norms; that states are inevitably affected by changes in their neighbours, even if the latter do not challenge them internationally; and that status quo powers have an obligation to suppress deviations in the international norm to prevent instability from spreading. Burke suggests indeed that there is an 'international society' in the much stronger sense of a society of entities with shared values and it is the protection of this that should dominate inter-state relations (see Halliday, 1992c, 1992d, for more extended discussion of this issue). The work of historical sociologists (Mann, 1986, 1988, following Hintze and Skocpol, and Tilly, 1975: as discussed in Halliday, 1989) suggests a parallel line of enquiry, since it shows how what appear to be discrete, insulated, processes of national evolution and state formation are in fact compelled to conform to prevailing international trends and to imitate each other in order the better to compete. International rivalry therefore acts as a homogenizing force, so that the growth of governmental structures, or of political forms, has, over a period of decades, a convergent character.

There are two obvious objections to this claim for homogeneity. The first is that for long periods of modern history no such pattern has been observed: in the past century, and within the more developed but still semi-peripheral countries, we have seen major deviations to the right (in mid-twentieth-century Germany, Japan, Italy, Spain and Portugal and, in milder form, Ireland; in the 1970s the 'bureaucratic-authoritarian' regimes of Chile, Argentina, Brazil and Uruguay) and to the left (Russia and other communist states). There have also been attempts at more qualified autarchic development under capitalism (Peronist Argentina and Whitlam's Australia being, at certain points, cases of this). Yet in the end both forms have been contained, some by world war, some by transnational erosion and incorporation. What the Second World War did to Germany, Italy and Japan, the European Community and its evident economic success did to Spain, Portugal, Ireland and, in the end, the USSR. In the case of the Latin American countries, the exhaustion of the authoritarian project within, and changing international norms without, combined to produce a continent-wide redemocratization in the late 1980s. The urge towards semi-peripheral escape and deviation is very strong: yet the mechanisms of reincorporation are over a longer period even stronger. If you cannot beat them, you have to try to join them.

The second objection to the homegeneity thesis is that for all the spread of capitalism over the past five hundred years, and especially in the past century, the degree of inequality of wealth and variation in political form between more and less developed countries has increased, and may be continuing to do so. To address this involves some observations on the dynamics of the capitalist system itself.

The Dynamics of Capitalism

It has already been observed that international relations has a curious shyness about the concept of capitalism, an idea by no means specific to Marxists, and one accepted in other social sciences such as sociology. The failure to treat this in its own terms affects not just the general understanding of the international system over the past five hundred years, but also more recent forms of international conflict, be these rivalries surrounding empire, which had an at least indirect relationship to capitalism, or the analysis of the Cold War, since one part of the conflict remains beyond analytic bounds (Hobsbawm, 1987, gives a measured assessment of the relationship of post-1870s imperialism to capitalism). Either it is assumed that capitalism is not globalizing, something the evidence of the past two centuries would hardly support, or it is implied that while it wishes to be dominant, it also needs an 'enemy': communism was such an enemy and now that it has lost it is busy reinventing another one, such as Islam. Yet it is precisely the globalizing dynamic of capitalism which explains the growth of the whole international system, since Columbus set sail in 1492, and which explains how and why the West prevailed over the communist world in the Cold War: as a thwarted development project communism was a product of the tensions of capitalist society, socially, ideologically and internationally, but it was in the end destroyed by it.

To assert this global dynamic is not, however, to provide a complete answer since at least three large issues remain. First, if this is so, why has the spread of capitalism been, and continued to be, so uneven? Second, why, if a global economy is in the making, do separate states needed to be created, with even more appearing now, and appear to remain for the foreseeable future the main locus of political power? Third, it has to be asked what the particular mechanisms of its expansion are. The issue of the uneven spread of industrialization and its political concomitant, democracy, allows of no easy resolution. Many have, for a century or more, believed that with leads and lags this process of universalization of the Western model will prevail. Most early nineteenth-century liberals and radicals, including Marx, held to this, and in its most recent form it is reflected in Fukuyama's work: in the peremptory phrase he takes from Kojeve, all that is now involved is 'the realignment of the provinces'. Yet for all the globalization of capitalism, and the secular desirability of democracy on political and ethical grounds, this is far from being what has occurred. Indeed, the record of the last century, and of the post-1945 period, is of slowly rising living standards in most of the world, but of a growing gap between rich and poor.

Later Marxist writers summarized this process in the theories of dependency, which, while often overstated and too static, contained an enduring strength in that they recognized the persistence and increase in global inequality. This has received recent elaboration in the reformulation by Giovanni Arrighi (1991) of the concept of 'oligarchic wealth': according to this, the wealth of the rich presupposed the subordination and relative deprivation of the majority. The realization of the ecological limits of global economic activity have only added to this. The weaknesses of this theory persist, however: first, what the necessity of this oligarchic wealth consists of remains obscure – what it is within capitalism that requires such global disparities of wealth, any more than it requires, as distinct from benefiting from them for a time, inequalities of race and gender; second, the evidence, if by that is meant the record of the past and particularly the recent past extrapolated into the future, can be read in support of either conclusion. Those who, in the 1960s, said that it was impossible for capitalism to attain a number of goals in the Third World that had been attained in the developed world have been proved partly wrong: the standard list of what capitalism could 'not' do usually comprised industrialization, land reform, independence and political democracy. Yet the very widening of North–South gaps, and of South–South performance, suggests that no simple extrapolation is possible either. (For the classic rebuttal of dependency theory within a Marxist framework, see Warren, 1980.)

The issue of separate states has long puzzled analysts of international relations as those of a system: they have tended, for a variety of reasons, to stress the degree to which the international prevails over the national. This bias is all the stronger since the conventional explanations for the existence of separate states are manifestly spurious: that they reflect some given distribution of the world into nations, or that they reflect some earlier proto-democratic constitution of communities (the 'social contract'). Historical sociology, in the work of Tilly in particular, has reminded us just how brutal, and arbitrary, the constitution of states has been. The tendency to overstate internationalization has been especially strong over the past two decades, both in the writings of the interdependence school and in sociological theories of globalization of culture and society.

While forms of internationalization have certainly altered, and will continue to do so, not least in the face of ecological change, the pertinence of states remains and has in many ways become more evident: it is states that underlie the consensus of the European Community, or the disputes over global warming, or the conflicts over international trade. The fashionable Anglo-Saxon myth (always historically inaccurate) that the 'market' accounts for economic growth has been contradicted by the experience, and now by the proclaimed ideology, of East Asian states (for an early refutation of market hagiography see Polanyi, 1944; for later correctives see Sen, 1984; Wade, 1991). The controversy aroused throughout the developed world by such issues as welfare, educational attainment and migration indicates just how strong the state is and will continue to be. The spread of nationalism, in developed and newer states, shows that the issue of control of the state's resources, and the issues of identity surrounding it, are as powerful as ever. Hobsbawn (1990) has shown that the nation-state, i.e. the identification of a political unit with ethnicity, is less and less the viable unit for the functioning of the modern system: but this is distinct from saying that the state itself, with all its changing functions, no longer retains a central role.

To say this is not to concede the traditional realist view that international relations can be regarded as primarily relations between states. Equally, it is not to accept the liberal interdependence view that while inter-state relations were predominant until the postwar epoch, things have recently changed (curiously a fable that Fukuyama also holds). An alternative argument can be made that inter-state relations were never primary in the sense in which this is conventionally assumed. The emergence of the modern state system was parallel with, and in many respects presupposed, the existence of transnational economic processes and transnational cultural, including religious, and political communities: indeed, far from the states existing first and then gradually reaching out to one another, as realist narrative would suggest, a common market and a common culture were preconditions for the emergence of the state system as we know it. What we see today is a development of that transnationalism in both the economic and cultural spheres, with many unexpected, and contradictory, effects: the erosion of communist autarchy in Europe and increasingly in Asia, the spread of some forms of global mediatic culture, the creation of new multi-ethnic and multicultural urban communities (Los Angeles, New York, Paris, London, Berlin, Sydney to name but some). The global dynamic is, but always was, a combination of all three levels of international interaction: political, economic and cultural. The mistake is to think either that the recent prominence of this negates the importance of the state, or that it is something fundamentally novel. What we are seeing is the dynamic of the international system as it has been operating for half a millennium.

Power in the Contemporary World

The analysis of the international system rests upon, and has recently occasioned, a discussion of the nature of power, and specifically of military power. Three questions in particular have been posed in the literature: the relationship between the traditional core of power (military) and other forms – political, economic, cultural and ideological; the patterns of 'rise and decline' of powers and the varying interpretations of this; and the relationship between the power of individual units – states/societies – and other transnational or international entities, be these alliances and inter-state bodies (notably the European Community) or 'de-stated' structures in the sense that Susan Strange (1988) uses this latter term. The crisis and collapse of the USSR should raise a fourth, already adumbrated, namely the extent to which *international* power relies upon and ultimately has to prevail in the context of the projection of a globally hegemonic pattern of *internal* socio-economic organization.

Here there is space only to comment in summary form on each of these. The issue of what constitutes power is posed sharply by the end of the Cold War, because it has produced a world in which, in relations between more developed countries, military power appears to be less pertinent. How low the salience of military power will be in intra-OECD (Organization for Economic Co-operation and Development) relations remains to be seen: but it clearly is, and appears set to remain, far less relevant than in any other period of modern history. (Nye, 1990, is one suggestive if already outdated discussion of this). It will retain an irreducible relevance, in part for domestic economic and technological reasons, in part as a symbol of powerful status, but more importantly because the security situation outside the OECD shows no sign whatsoever of losing its military character. Military power was never the sole form of international power – as witness the strength of Holland in the seventeenth century – but it will remain relevant. What is changing, but in a way not liable to precise calibration, is its relationship to other forms of power.

On the one hand, coercive potential on the international scale will retain a core function, broadly similar to that of coercion in the domestic sphere: as Gramsci has argued with regard to internal politics (Anderson, 1976), coercion will be the gold around which the fiduciary issue of non-military power will be constructed. There has been much speculation about forms of 'hegemony' in international relations, borrowing loosely from Gramsci (for one set of essays on economic policy see Gill, 1993), but as yet there has been no systematic application of his theory of ideological and cultural power to international relations, and its relationship to military and economic power. On the other hand, those states (Japan, Germany) that, under the peculiar and transient conditions of the post-1945 world, attained international prominence without any remotely commensurate military skill will begin to acquire greater military potential, albeit in a changed international environment. There is an argument for saying that it may be more appropriate for them to do so in a clear, responsible and multilateral context; the alternative is to abjure even a low potential for military action abroad, and to engage in an abnegation that is bound, sooner or later, to lurch into belated and unilateral self-assertion.

The most interesting question raised by Japan's power is not whether it can be maintained without military correlates: it cannot, and never was, since the US substituted for Japan in the past four decades and this will gradually change. More difficult is whether a major economic power can maintain and expand its position without a correlative cultural power. All previous empires, from the Romans and the Arabs to the Americans and the Russians, have accompanied their imperial endeavours with cultural expansion, most notably at the linguistic levels. Today US hegemony is inextricably linked with forms of cultural and information hegemony. Yet Japan is reticent, in some respects recalcitrant, about spreading its language and is stereotypically reserved about whether it has a potentially hegemonic culture at all. It may be that, like so many other empires, its cultural hegemony will be established through the appropriation for its own use of the cultural achievements of others: the Arabs took much from the Byzantines, the British did not invent Christianity, the Americans did not entirely invent their language. It may be that just as territory is no longer intrinsic to hegemony, so culture may not be either: but the asymmetry in international cultural power between the US and Japan is as striking as the economic asymmetry of the US and the USSR in the cold war. Many Japanese claim they have no cultural capital to deploy: but shrine gateways, flower arrangement and karaoke are an imperfect rendering of Japan's cultural potential and a small reserve upon which to base a hegemonic project.

This issue of power has obvious implications for the future and, not least, the question of the balance of power. The end of the Cold War has brought to an end a century or so in which relations between the great powers had been dominated by military conflict, or the threat of it. Beginning in the Far East in the two decades before 1914 (Sino–Japanese, Russo–Japanese wars), and later encompassing Europe as well, this century of conflict was at first dominated by rivalry of imperial powers that were broadly similar in their internal constitution and aspirations, then marked by competition between democratic and dictatorial capitalist states, and subsequently by the ideologically formed Cold War in which great power competition was overlaid by heterogeneity at the socio-economic level. For the first time since 1894, there is no major threat of great power war.

It would be plausible to argue that this will not last, and that the international system will revert, following its anarchical nature, to great power rivalry, armed or muted, in the decades to come.

Proponents of balance of power theory have long held that with the decline of the USSR some new international coalition can emerge to counterbalance what would otherwise be US unipolarity. Some such as Rosecrance (1992) see a return to such rivalry unless a central coalition is soon established on a reasonably formal basis. Rosecrance's thesis is backed by an argument to the effect that the traditional balance of power did not maintain peace even for the period when its defenders claimed it did, and by a claim that nuclear deterrence, which he distinguishes from the balance of power, was far more precarious than appeared at the time. Others believed that the economic rivalry currently evident between the US, Japan and the EC will lead to three major trading blocs and concomitant politico-military formations emerging: this is the stuff of much speculation in the US. Others seek to re-establish regional balances of power, to offset potential hegemons – Japan in the Far East, Germany in Europe. All of these rest on some extrapolation of past patterns to the future.

It is possible, however, to project a more peaceful future for the international system based on the view that we are faced with a major disjuncture in its history. Economic power is now the main form of international power and need not necessarily lead to increasing competition: a combination of shared prosperity and good diplomacy could ensure a different result. The supposed candidate for world hegemony, the US, is markedly uninterested in assuming, benefiting from or paying for, this role: not only Bush, but also his opponents and critics, such as Chomsky, misread the significance of the Gulf War, which did not establish a new order of US domination, but acted as little more than a consolation for US decline and was, in this sense, a diversion from the main trend in international relations. If the balance of power is restored, it will not be through the emergence of a new hegemon to rival the US, but through a reduction in US international aspirations and needs to nearer the level of other great powers.

CONCLUSION

If it is impossible to know how relations between the great powers will evolve in the coming decades, it does appear that pre-existing theories, based on the necessity of great power rivalry or the prominence of military power, are now in question, as the world emerges from the great inter-hegemonic war of the past century.

A new theorization of international relations may, therefore, be needed, to deal with what may be a long period of intra-hegemonic peace. Much will, however, depend on how the central underpinnings of this new period (international economic prosperity, the consolidation of liberal democracy in major states, a reduction in North–South tensions) are consolidated.

A crisis in any one of these could seriously threaten the bases of the new international system, and there is reason enough to be anxious on all three. The two decades of postwar boom have given way to two further decades of recession and powerful recovery, with major negative consequences within the developed countries themselves. No one can be sure if the conditions for social peace within states, or inter-state co-operation abroad, can be maintained. Liberal democracy is at present apparently secure in some two dozen states in the world, but precariously and tentatively implanted elsewhere: there is no inevitability about its spread or, if it is established, about its duration: Russia may be a re-run, speeded up, of the Weimar Republic. Moreover, even within apparently established states there are trends which could, if continued, lead to very different forms of state, authoritarian if not classically fascist: the question of where Japan is going, and how far it provides the bases for a distinctive political model that will prevail in the Far East, is of concern to more than its neighbours.

The issue of North–South relations, encompassing as it does a range of economic, political and strategic conflicts, seems set to provide the basis for many conflicts in the decades ahead: oil and migration alone are sufficient to ensure this. In a range of Third World countries the stresses of development have engendered new political and social explosions – Islamist movements, state fragmentations, South Asian chauvinisms, to name but some. As long as capitalist development fails to provide the mass of the world's population with the economic and political achievements of the more developed states, or to offer a reasonable prospect of such a provision, political and social tensions in the Third World will continue. An increasing tendency to fence off the Third World, rather than incorporate it under traditional forms of domination, may characterize the policy of OECD states, leading to an expeditionary rather than an annexationist model of hegemonic control. But as more and more analysis demonstrates, no such insulation is possible and the whole international system is facing long-term challenges to meet which will involve concerted action by states. The sober predictions of crisis on a range of issues –

demographic, ecological and technological – allow no optimism (Kennedy, 1993).

The most fundamental issue of all, the unfinished business inherited from the Cold War, from the century of inter-hegemonic wars, and indeed from the half-millennium of the system's evolution, is that of the formation of an international society, not in the sense of a club of states with common rules, but of a community of political units united by economic and other transnational ties, and characterized by a broad sharing of political and social values. The Cold War was one episode in the evolution of that system, a phase of the conflict in which one group of states, guided by an ideology that challenged the prevailing models of political and economic development, sought to pioneer an alternative path, and in so doing came into international conflict with the dominant powers of the West. That challenge is now over, and no other plausible answer of global relevance is now apparent. The question is whether the potential for an international society in the stronger sense of the term can now be created by overcoming not only the anarchy of states but also the anarchies of the market and of the ethnic identification (on variant conceptions of 'anarchy' in the international sphere, see Rosenberg, 1994), as well as the new globalized pressures of ecology and population. This is the unfinished business of the Cold War, and indeed of international relations as a whole, a challenge to fulfil an old agenda, amid an international context beset by new dangers and tensions.

Note

This chapter is based on a paper originally presented to a conference at the Australian National University, Canberra, in July 1992. An earlier version of this essay was first published in Richard Leaver and James L. Richardson (eds), *Charting the Post-Cold War Order: Diagnoses and Prognoses*, Allen & Unwin, Australia; Westview Press, Boulder Co, 1993. My thanks are due to Richard Leaver, Andy Mack, James Richardson and the other participants in that conference for their helpful suggestions.

References

Anderson, P. 1976: The antinomies of Antonio Gramsci. *New Left Review*, 100 (Nov.–Dec.), 5–79.

Anderson, P. 1992: *A Zone of Engagement*. London: Verso.
Arrighi, G. 1991: World income inequalities and the future of socialism. *New Left Review*, 189 (Sept.–Oct.), 39–65.
Blackburn, R. (ed.) 1991: *After the Fall, The Fall of Communism and the Future of Socialism*. London: Verso.
Burke, E. 1852: Letters on a regicide peace. In *The Works and Correspondence of Edmund Burke*, vol. 5. London: Francis and John Rivington.
Doyle, M. 1983a: Kant, liberal legacies and foreign affairs. *Philosophy and Public Affairs*, 12(3), 205–35.
Doyle, M. 1983b: Kant, liberal legacies and foreign affairs, part 2. *Philosophy and Public Affairs*, 12(4), 323–53.
Doyle, M. 1986: Liberalism and world politics. *American Political Science Review*, 80(4), 1151–69.
Fukuyama, F. 1992: *The End of History and the Last Man*. London: Hamish Hamilton.
Gill, S. (ed.) 1993: *Gramsci, Historical Materialism and International Relations*. Cambridge: Cambridge University Press.
Habermas, J. 1991: What does socialism mean today? The revolutions of recuperation and the need for new thinking. In Blackburn (1991), 25–46.
Halliday, F. 1989: State and society in international relations. In H. Dyer and L. Mangassarian (eds), *International Relations, the State of the Art*. Houndmills, Basingstoke: Macmillan (and in Halliday (1994), 74–93).
Halliday, F. 1991: The ends of Cold War (and in Blackburn (1991), 78–99).
Halliday, F. 1992a: A singular collapse: the Soviet Union, market pressure and inter-state competition. *Contention*, 2(1), 121–41 (and in Halliday (1994), 191–215).
Halliday, F. 1992b: An encounter with Fukuyama. *New Left Review*, 193 (May–June).
Halliday, F. 1992c: the Cold War as inter-systemic conflicts – initial theses. In M. Bowker and R. Brown (eds), *From Cold War to Collapse: Theory and World Politics in the 1980s*. Cambridge: Cambridge University Press, 21–34 (and in Halliday, (1994), 19–215).
Halliday, F. 1992d: International society as homegeneity: Burke, Marx, Fukuyama. *Millennium Journal of International Studies*, 21(3), 435–61 (and in Halliday (1994), 94–123).
Halliday, F. 1994: *Rethinking International Relations*. Houndmills, Basingstoke: Macmillan.
Hobsbawm, E. 1987: *The Age of Empire: 1875–1914*. London: Weidenfeld and Nicolson.
Hobsbawn, E. 1990: *Nationalism and Self-Preservation*. Cambridge: Cambridge University Press.
Kennedy, P. 1993: *Preparing for the Twenty-First Century*. London: Harper Collins.
Mann, M. 1986: *The Sources of Social Power*, vol. 1: *A History of Power from the Beginning to A.D. 1760*. Cambridge: Cambridge University Press.

Mann, M. 1988: *States, War and Capitalism*. Oxford: Basil Blackwell.
Nye, J. 1990: *Bound to Lead*. New York: Basic Books.
Polanyi, K. 1944: *The Great Transformation: The Political and Economic Origins of Our Time*. Boston: Beacon Press.
Rosecrance, R. 1992: A new concert of powers. *Foreign Affairs*, 71(2), 64–82.
Rosenberg, J. 1994: *The Empire of Civil Society: a Critique of the Realist Theory of International Relations*. London: Verso.
Sen, G. 1984: *The Military Origins of Industrialisation and International Trade Rivalry*. London: Frances Pinter.
Strange, S. 1988: *States and Markets: an Introduction to International Political Economy*. London: Frances Pinter.
Therborn, G. 1977: The rule of capital and the rise of democracy. *New Left Review*, 103 (May–June), 3–41.
Tilly, C. 1975: *The Formation of National States in Europe*. Princeton: Princeton University Press.
Wade, R. 1991: *Governing the Market*. Princeton: Princeton University Press.
Warren, B. 1980: *Imperialism, Pioneer of Capitalism*. London: Verso.

3

International Relations and the Triumph of Capitalism

Richard Little

It has frequently been argued in the aftermath of the Soviet Union's demise not only that the West won the Cold War but also that the claims made in favour of capitalism have finally been vindicated. Across the political spectrum, according to Kumar (1992), it has been widely accepted that there is no future for any alternative form of utopian thinking. The triumph of capitalism is seen to be complete. No doubt there are reasons to be sceptical of this assessment. But it is a proposition which on the face of it has important implications for the study of international relations and which deserves to be examined seriously by theorists in the discipline. Although most mainstream theorists of international relations have eschewed the task, further afield there have been attempts to come to grips with the possibility that capitalism has become the universally accepted mode of political and economic organization.

This chapter examines the work of two theorists, Fukuyama and Wallerstein, who start from this premise. It outlines their competing theoretical orientations and assesses how these orientations impinge on the study of international relations. These two theorists operate on diametrically opposed positions of the political spectrum and subscribe to very different conceptions of capitalism. But both are very serious about exploring the implications which flow from the putative global triumph of capitalism. Francis Fukuyama in *The End of History and the Last Man* (1992) applauds the globalization of capitalism and sees the development as the end point of a rational working out of historical forces. By contrast, Wallerstein is acutely conscious of the oppression which exists in the prevailing system and seeks to identify anti-systemic forces which will help to move the world on to another phase beyond capitalism. While Fukuyama's views have been developed in a single text, Wallerstein's ideas have generated a wide-ranging school of thought, identified as world systems analysis, and the views of this school have been expressed in a large body of publications.

Although working from radically different perspectives, these two theorists both challenge mainstream thought in the study of international relations. The central aim of this chapter is to outline the positions adopted by the two theorists and to evaluate how seriously the challenge should be taken by theorists working within the mainstream. Before setting out the views of the two theorists, however, it is necessary to assess the role of capitalism in the mainstream study of international relations.

CAPITALISM AND THE END OF THE COLD WAR IN INTERNATIONAL RELATIONS THEORY

For forty years after the end of the Second World War, international politics was conventionally considered to be dominated by an ideological struggle between capitalism and communism. These concepts played a central role in the political discourse of the Cold War. Western leaders continuously vilified communism while the leaders of the Eastern regimes habitually attacked capitalism. In the course of this process, the concepts were often reduced to rhetorical slogans. Yet behind the slogans the differences were real and substantial. The study of international relations in the West, however, paid little attention to the competing ideologies which operated on either side of the iron curtain. Although the ideological divide was readily acknowledged, it was almost universally accepted that the Cold War could best be understood as a power struggle and discussed in terms of the balance of military power between the two competing blocs. Comparisons were frequently made with earlier struggles between, for example, Athens and Sparta or Rome and Carthage. But in contrast to these earlier military contests, which resulted in the ultimate victory of one of the powers, it was asserted with increasing confidence as the Cold War persisted that the military balance between the Soviet Union and the United States was so stable that the resulting bipolar structures would stay in place if not indefinitely then for a very considerable period of time in the future (DePorte, 1986; Gaddis, 1987).

The speed with which the bipolar structures were dismantled when the Cold War came to an end and the Soviet Union was dissolved took most if not all mainstream international relations theorists in the West completely by surprise. Yet their failure to anticipate this transformation is explicable once it is acknowledged that the structures maintaining bipolarity collapsed not as the result of a military victory but as a consequence of the massive ideological shift which took place in Eastern Europe and the Soviet Union. Support for communism simply evaporated and at the same time the basic tenets of capitalism were enthusiastically taken on board. Even the Kremlin watchers, who were constantly monitoring the shifts and turns in the ideological rhetoric employed by Soviet leaders, were taken by surprise because they too had assumed that the military strength of the Soviet Union rendered these leaders unassailable.

Despite the speed and scale of the changes which accompanied the collapse of Soviet power, mainstream theorists have had little difficulty accommodating their thinking to the new circumstances, although there is still substantial disagreement about the ultimate shape of the structures which will emerge in the wake of bipolarity. Erstwhile analysts who had argued with such confidence during the Cold War about the durability of the bipolar division between the Soviet Union and the US have now entered into an intense debate about whether bipolarity will be replaced by a new multipolar world centred on Europe, the US and Japan, or whether the US is in a position to fill the vacuum left by the Soviet Union and establish a unipolar world with the US exercising hegemonic power. The debate has proved to be so absorbing that the failure to anticipate the collapse of the Cold War structures has scarcely been acknowledged.

Critics of mainstream international relations, however, have not let this lacuna pass unnoticed and they have argued that it is a consequence of the stranglehold of realism on the discipline (Kratochwil, 1993). Attention has focused, in particular, on the writings of Waltz (1979), who is widely acknowledged to have provided the most authoritative contemporary realist or neo-realist account of the international system. In fact, the criticism is in part misplaced, because Waltz is quite explicit about the inability of his theory to account for change. Systemic analysis, he insists, can explain only the continued existence of the international system.

To accommodate structural change, a reductionist mode of explanation must be sought within the internal dynamics of the state.

So realism does make provision, therefore, for the analysis and explanation of change, but it remains true, nevertheless, that analysts working in Waltz's neo-realist mould during the Cold War have tended to operate almost exclusively in systemic terms. Ideology and many other 'reductionist' variables, in Waltz's terminology, were thereby pushed to one side and there was, as a consequence, a probably unnoticed predisposition either to deny or at any rate to ignore the potential for change. It is perhaps worth noting in parenthesis that Soviet specialists in international relations were, by contrast, attuned to looking for evidence of structural change in the international system. For most of the Cold War they denigrated the idea of the balance of military power as a crude mechanistic tool which failed to capture the essence of what was actually happening in the international system. Soviet specialists preferred to use what they called the correlation of forces, which focused attention on socio-economic factors, in the analysis of international politics. But, perhaps significantly, as the communist regimes found it increasingly difficult to compete in the socio-economic arenas during the 1980s and the legitimacy of these regimes became ever more precarious, there were increasing references to the military balance and an acknowledgement that this balance of power was the primary source of stability in the international system.

Realism has certainly played an important role in the Western study of international relations since the end of the Second World War, but the claim that realism has dominated the discipline, promoting a static image of the international system and diverting attention from the significance of capitalism, is open to serious question. Throughout most of the Cold War, continuous interest in the processes of transnationalism, integration and interdependence within the international system has been sustained by a group of theorists often identified as pluralists. Although generally not explicit, these theorists have been endeavouring, in practice, to accommodate what they see as the impact of capitalism on international relations. Whereas realists have stressed factors which help to sustain the independence and autonomy of the state, the pluralists have been more conscious of factors associated with the evolution of capitalism which are serving to undermine the independence of the state. There is an obvious tension between these two schools of thought which has only partly been alleviated by the existence of a largely unacknowledged division of labour in the mainstream study of international relations, with the realists monitoring East–West Relations and the pluralists focusing on international developments in capitalism within the Western world.

Although the ending of the Cold War and the demise of the Soviet Union are often treated in the West as emblematic events which foreshadow the inevitable demise of communism and the triumph of capitalism, there are few signs that the entrenched division of labour between realists and pluralists is about to dissolve. The division persists because both realists and pluralists tend to agree that ideological division is still an important feature of the international system, despite the elimination of bipolarity. They see no evidence that a world eschewing ideological division is likely to emerge in the near future.

On either side of the mainstream, however, it is possible to identify two competing schools of thought, operating from very different theoretical and ideological premises, which have contemplated the consequences of a world held together by a common ideological base. Both schools are openly and self-consciously polemical and it is this orientation which distinguishes their approaches so sharply from theorists working within the mainstream. The distinction has been captured by Cox (1981), who separates critical theorists from problem-solving theorists. Critical theorists work on the basis of a theory of history which gives them a handle on historical processes, enabling them to assess the existing structure of reality in terms of the historical evolution of the international system. These theorists are not only interested in analysing the world, they wish to restructure the established order, and their intention is to adopt a position which makes it possible for them to transcend the existing order and look for ways of transforming it.

Mainstream theorists in international relations, and, from Cox's perspective, particularly neo-realists, fit squarely into the second category of problem-solving theorists. Neo-realists are seen to accept the world as they find it, and their preoccupation is with getting the world to run more smoothly within the existing structural constraints. They are seen to adopt an ahistorical perspective premised on the assumption that there is a universal and unchanging order which embraces autonomous states within an anarchic international system. While pluralists, on the other hand, are interested in the process of change in the contemporary international system, they also lack any overarching theory of history which allows them to make trans-historical judgements. On the contrary: pluralists tend to be deeply suspicious of such theories.

Fukuyama and Wallerstein, by contrast, can both be characterized as critical theorists because their analysis is premised on a theory of history which they self-consciously use to make trans-historical assessments. Once their theoretical positions have been articulated, in the next two sections, the significance of their approaches for mainstream, problem-solving theorists in international relations can then be assessed.

FUKUYAMA AND THE TRIUMPH OF CAPITALISM

Although Fukuyama's thesis does not initially derive from a study of international relations, an investigation of *The End of History and the Last Man* quickly reveals that it relies very heavily on a perspective which has important implications for the theory of international relations. His thesis, which explains why capitalism and liberal democracy are inseparable features in the modern world and why these features will eventually become global in scope, is firmly established on the basis of assumptions about international relations and the international system.

Before exploring the international implications of Fukuyama's work, however, it is necessary to examine briefly the perspective from which he is operating. It is important to recognize in the first place that when Fukuyama refers to the 'end of history' he is not identifying history simply in terms of past events. He is endeavouring to resurrect Hegel's idea of a philosophy of history which assumes that we can discern a shape and direction in the flow of events which make up human history. In the nineteenth century there was a widespread tendency to work on the basis of an optimistic and progressive philosophy of history. The world in which Victorians were living was seen to be steadily improving. Fukuyama notes, however, that in the twentieth century the experience of world war and genocide has led to the acceptance of a much bleaker philosophy of history. History is seen to be leading not to a steady improvement in our lives, but to an inexorable deterioration. This picture painted by the pessimists, however superficially persuasive, according to Fukuyama, draws attention away from the real or more profound course of history, correctly discerned by Hegel, and which has been revealed once more by the peaceful or 'velvet' revolutions which started in Eastern Europe in 1989. What these revolutions demonstrated for Fukuyama is the persuasive power of liberal ideas. Fukuyama is not so naive or so ignorant as to believe that the world is now being run on liberal principles. 'What is emerging victorious', he argues, 'is not so much liberal practice as the liberal idea' (1992, p. 45). This distinction, of course, makes it extremely difficult to test the validity of Fukuyama's proposition. How do we know that the liberal idea is 'emerging victorious'? The proposition is more polemical than empirical and is no doubt designed, in part, to establish a self-fulfilling prophecy.

Nevertheless, for Fukuyama, the philosophy of history describes the struggle over ideas about a desirable political, economic and social order. And as far as Fukuyama is concerned, that struggle is coming to an end. Although he accepts that no liberal democracy existed before the formation of the US in 1776, he insists that the liberal conception of political, economic and social order is slowly but surely consolidating. With the 'velvet' revolutions, the number of liberal democracies, according to Fukuyama's reckoning, increased to sixty-one. Critics have been quick to point out that these assessments are extremely questionable. The emergence of fully enfranchised states is much more recent than Fukuyama seems to recognize. As Jones (1993, p. 202) points out, slavery, after all, was still an important institution in the US in 1776. And many Americans were systematically disenfranchised until the 1960s (Therborn, 1977). Moreover, the number of stable liberal democracies is far lower than Fukuyama estimates.

Acknowledging Fukuyama's exaggerated assessment of liberalism's success, he is still at liberty to speculate that 'if we are now at a point where we cannot imagine a world substantially different from our own, in which there is no apparent or obvious way in which the future will represent a fundamental improvement over our current order, then we must also take into consideration the possibility that History itself might be at an end' (1992, p. 51). As it happens, Fukuyama accepts that it is not possible to envisage any 'fundamental improvement' in a liberal world order. He justifies his faith in liberal democracy on two levels both of which are premised on the idea that there is a universal direction to history. On the first level, universality and directionality are tied to the development of science, which is seen to be incontrovertably directional and cumulative. The role science plays in giving direction to history is seen to operate in two very different spheres. First, there is a direct link identified between science and military technology. Fukuyama insists that in the final analysis attributes such as bravery and leadership will always succumb to superior military technology. The perennial and ubiquitous possibility of war is then seen to represent 'a great force for rationalization of societies, and for the creation of uniform social structures across cultures' (p. 73). Military technology, therefore, gives a universal direction to history with scientifically advanced and thus militarily superior states leading the way. Ironically, Fukuyama fails to recognize that this argument also underpins the realist position advocated by Waltz (1979).

A second sphere where the role of science gives direction to history is through its link to economic development. Science permits the conquest of nature and by this process human material needs can be increasingly satisfied. Because Fukuyama does not believe that it is possible to reverse the rising tide of economic expectations which accompanies the process of economic development, this process is also seen to give a universal direction to history. The latest stage in this process is the universal acceptance of the superiority of capitalism – the application of liberal principles to the economy – over all competing forms of economic management.

Neither military technology nor economic development, however, demonstrates a necessary connection between liberal capitalism and the end of history. But Fukuyama believes economic development does eventually establish such a link and he endeavours to show how the enormously complex economic systems associated with the post-industrial societies which have emerged in the West can operate only in the decentralized and market-orientated systems which are propagated by liberal democracies. While he readily accepts that the centralized and bureaucratized systems found in the Soviet Union and Eastern Europe were able to bring about an industrial revolution with a reasonable degree of success, he insists that they were incapable of managing the changes which were necessary if the communist states were to compete effectively with the post-industrial West. To do that, the communist states would have to be transformed into liberal democracies.

From Fukuyama's perspective, however, history is not driven simply by scientific advancement. Drawing again on Hegel, the universal direction to history can be accounted for at another and more profound level, and at this level too it becomes apparent why liberal democracies represent the end point of history. Throughout history, he argues, individuals have engaged in a struggle for what he refers to as *thymos* or recognition. This Hegelian idea may seem strange to a contemporary audience, argues Fukuyama, but this is only because of the 'successful "economization" of our thinking that has occurred in the last four hundred years' (1992, p. 145). By this he means that human beings now assume that life can be defined in cost–benefit terms. But human beings, Hegel insisted, become fully human only through a process of mutual recognition. In the past, individuals have achieved recognition most easily by subordinating others. But by definition such a process negates the universal satisfaction of the need for recognition. The reason the worldwide acceptance of liberalism does, ultimately, represent the 'end of history' is because within a society run on liberal principles 'there is a reciprocal and equal agreement amongst citizens to mutually recognize each other' (p. 200).

It is against this background that Fukuyama develops his discussion of international relations. He starts from the premise that the nation-state is likely to remain the central point of identification for most people for some considerable time. He justifies this claim by pointing to the substantial economic and cultural differences which continue to divide inhabitants of one state from another. These differences, he insists, are unlikely to disappear in the near future. Liberal capitalism continues to take many forms as a comparison of the US and Japan quickly makes apparent. Fukuyama observes a worldwide resistance to the forces of homogenization and indeed sees a reassertion of the desire for separate cultural identities across the globe. Universal demands for a distinct identity by all nations 'ultimately reinforce existing barriers between people and nations' (p. 244). As a consequence, he sees no evidence of a movement towards a universal and homogeneous form of state.

Nevertheless, he goes on, if there is a direction to history which is moving us towards the point where people in states around the world are governed by identical principles derived from liberalism, then as we move along this historical trajectory there must be important implications for the conduct of international relations. Specialists in international relations, argues Fukuyama, have failed to identify the evidence supporting the idea of a historical trajectory because of the dominating influence of realism. Whereas

Fukuyama is endeavouring to reveal that we are approaching the end of history, realists, by contrast, are accused of adopting a completely ahistorical perspective. These theorists 'talk as if history did not exist' (p. 246). International relations are seen to be conducted in a rigid and unchanging anarchic international system. The underlying assumption which informs all realist thinking is that 'insecurity is a universal and permanent feature of the international order' (p. 247). Under conditions of anarchy, the relations between states are inherently competitive because what realists see as the only prudent option for a state is to rely on its own power to ensure survival. Even defensive actions will be interpreted as potentially threatening and lead, as a consequence, to reactions which will perpetuate a system characterized by fear and mistrust.

Fukuyama recognizes, therefore, that realists are locked into a conception of the international system which does not allow for any improvement. There is no provision for change or evolution. States are seen to perpetuate an endless cycle of conflict. War and imperialism, constrained only by a shifting balance of power, are identified as the realists' defining characteristics of international relations. But Fukuyama also believes that realists are not only observers of international relations. He insists that they have had a decisive influence on the formulation of US foreign policy since the Second World War. Realism has provided 'the dominant framework for understanding international relations, and shapes the thinking of virtually every foreign policy professional today in the United States and much of the rest of the world' (p. 246). Fukuyama does not deny that realism represents an important and even a useful perspective on international relations and he accepts that it was fortunate that US decision-makers adopted a realist perspective after 1945 when the world was divided along lines of mutually hostile ideologies. The mistake of these decision-makers was to believe that 'realist principles represented timeless truths' (p. 251).

The inadequacies of realism become all too apparent for Fukuyama when attention is drawn to the strange proposals put forward by realists in the post-Cold War era. He points, for example, to the suggestion from Gaddis in 1990 that an attempt should be made to ensure that the Warsaw Pact survived in order to preserve the stability enjoyed in Europe in the period after 1945. Fukuyama considers the proposal preposterous and that it demonstrates the weakness of realist tenets. The fatal flaw in the realist mode of analysis is seen to stem from its reductionist mode of understanding. Realists are seen to argue that because the unchanging structure of the international system constrains the behaviour of the states which constitute the system, so states are compelled to reproduce conflictual patterns of behaviour. The reference to reductionism here must not be confused, however, with Waltz's use of the same term. For Waltz, reductionism refers to analysis which looks at the internal characteristics of states to account for their behaviour. By contrast, Fukuyama relates reductionism to the tendency to focus exclusively on one variable – the structure of the international system – when attempting to account for the international behaviour of states. Fukuyama argues that this reductionist line of argument ignores the importance of agency which becomes apparent when the level of analysis is changed. The realist mistake of restricting their explanatory frame of reference to the structure of the system thereby blinds them to the importance of the internal characteristics of the units. It is crystal clear to Fukuyama that any attempt to explain the behaviour of states must take account of these characteristics. What the realists are seen to ignore is the capacity of these units to evolve and, as a consequence, to change their behaviour in the international system.

At the heart of Fukuyama's thesis about international relations is the assertion that liberal states are 'fundamentally unwarlike'. This characteristic becomes very evident when observing the 'extraordinarily peaceful relations they maintain among one another' (p. 262). It follows, then, that as the number of liberal states in the international system increases, so too does the arena of pacific relations. As ever more states recognize the virtues of liberalism, so the globe will come to approximate a 'pacific union'. Fukuyama makes no pretence to originality in developing this line of argument. He readily acknowledges Kant's *Perpetual Peace* as providing the key source. But whereas Kant was working from first principles at the end of the eighteenth century, at the dawn of liberal democratic states, Fukuyama believes that the course of history serves to verify Kant's original insights. It follows, therefore, that just as the adoption of liberal principles has helped to promote human progress at the domestic level, so these changes have fed through to effect an improvement at the international level. From this perspective, then, it is fallacious to think, as the realists do, that the international system is a rigid immutable structure, constraining states to reproduce competitive and power-orientated policies. Liberal democracies can and will overcome the structural constraints imposed by the anarchic structure of the international system and begin to operate on the basis of peaceful principles. This line of argument, of course, presupposes the existence of a rising number of liberal states in the international system. But as pointed out earlier, this assumption has been questioned. Moreover, as Suganami (1990) has pointed out, even if it is true that war has not taken place between liberal states in the past, before we can be sure that war will not occur between liberal states in the future we need a theory which explains why war is ruled out between liberal states. Suganami argues that such a theory has not yet been spelled out.

Fukuyama, therefore, is relying on a somewhat optimistic picture of the future of international relations. But it is worth noting that there is a curious and ironic twist in Fukuyama's tail which emerges when he comes to contemplate the future consequences of the final triumph of capitalism after the world is 'filled up' with liberal democracies (1992, p. 330). Here he bravely confronts what he sees as the internal and external problems and contradictions thrown up by his preferred solution. He sees at one extreme that in a post-historical era, human beings, the 'last men', might degenerate, and become no better than 'domesticated dogs', totally satisfied with their lot. Paradoxically, he observes, human beings seem to 'require injustice, for the struggle against injustice is what calls forth what is highest in man' (p. 311). At the other extreme, Fukuyama fears that humans might return to being 'first men' and engage in 'bloody and pointless prestige battles' (p. 328). He looks sympathetically at Hegel's notion that wars will persist after the 'end of history' because human beings would not be satisfied by 'peace and prosperity'. Fukuyama argues that experience suggests that human beings in such a world may become bored and will struggle against such a world because they cannot envisage a world which precludes struggle. As a consequence, 'if the greater part of the world in which they live is characterised by peaceful and prosperous liberal democracy, then they will struggle *against* that peace and prosperity, and against democracy' (p. 330). Fukuyama here seems to be acknowledging that there may be a fatal flaw in human beings which encourages them to negate the rational forces which underlie history and makes it impossible for them to live in peace and harmony. Traditional realists must surely smile wryly at such an assessment, which is so close to the starting point of their own analysis.

The inability to eliminate what, from the perspective of the rational process of history, looks like human irrationality obviously disturbs Fukuyama. It is curious, therefore, as Halliday (1992) notes, that there is no mention of Freud in his discourse. Freud spent much of his life endeavouring to formulate a theory which would account for the apparently irrational and neurotic behaviour of human beings. Having opened this Pandora's box, however, Fukuyama quickly closes it again and ends by making reference to a favourite myth frequently drawn upon in the US. To recapitulate his theme, Fukuyama depicts the historical progress of states as wagons in a wagon train heading for a desirable destination in the West. The wagons become separated and some even get lost but most are seen, eventually, to reach the destination at the 'end of history' in safety. But in a final sentence, Fukuyama is unable to resist lifting the lid one last time and wondering if the destination will, in fact, prove satisfactory, or whether, having looked around, the wagons will set off on 'a new and more distant journey' (1992, p. 339).

WALLERSTEIN AND THE TRIUMPH OF CAPITALISM

Although Fukuyama opens up the possibility that the triumph of capitalism may prove, in practice, to be just another staging post along the endless track of history, his thesis is designed to demonstrate, of course, that liberal democracy and capitalism do, in fact, represent the 'end of history' because they provide the optimum conditions within which human beings can operate. There is no need, therefore, for the wagons to move on. Wallerstein wishes to argue, by contrast, that there is another and better destination than the one signalled by the triumph of capitalism. It is inevitable, therefore, that Wallerstein and Fukuyama should find themselves directly at odds with each other.

The confrontation between Fukuyama and Wallerstein reflects their very different conceptions of history. Fukuyama has been accused by some philosophers of history of 'American exceptionalism' – a tendency to see the US playing a unique role in history. Wallerstein, on the other hand, has been described as providing the 'most influential attempt' to overcome 'American exceptionalism' (Tyrrell, 1991, p. 1042). The justification for linking Fukuyama with 'American exceptionalism' arises because he is said to propagate the image of the US starting life at the 'end of history' and acting as a beacon to guide other states to this ultimate destination. Wallerstein's assessment could not be more different and, unsurprisingly, he is found by Fukuyama to have produced 'a highly tendentious reading of history' (Fukuyama, 1992, p. 358) as a result.

This is not a criticism which is likely to cause Wallerstein undue concern. From his perspective, Fukuyama's thesis, despite the unusual nature of its Hegelian trappings, rests on a central and fundamental flaw which it shares with the whole of American social science. The flaw is laid bare in the metaphor of the wagon train, which reveals Fukuyama's belief that states can be treated as separate and independent agents which can move in any direction depending upon the wishes of the inhabitants or at least their leaders. Acting upon the basis of this flawed assumption, according to Wallerstein, modernization theorists in the US were confident that just as the European economies 'took off' after the Second World War, so too would the economies of the European colonies once they had shaken off the shackles imposed on them by the metropolitan powers. In practice, the former colonies failed to catch up economically with the Western world because, argues Wallerstein, they were not independent agents but dependent cogs in a larger world system; they represented part of the dependent periphery to the Western core of the system.

Fukuyama is familiar with this line of argument and he insists that it is easily refuted by pointing to the success of the little Asian dragon countries, such as Taiwan, Singapore, and more recently, South Korea and Thailand. These countries, according to Fukuyama, have not been locked into a pattern of behaviour by the structure of the system which has forced them to maintain their dependent status at the periphery of a world system. On the contrary, they have transformed the nature of their economies in a way which has allowed them to compete effectively with the advanced Western countries. But Wallerstein denies that these countries have now moved to the core of the system, insisting that the states at the centre of the system, although constantly jockeying for position, have remained unchanged, apart from the addition of Japan, for over a hundred years. The critical statistic which needs to be observed reveals that although economies have grown at the periphery as well as at the centre, the gap between the rich countries and the poor countries continues to widen over time. This is not accidental, or purely the product of inefficient economic policies implemented by countries at the periphery; it is the consequence of the way the capitalist world system operates.

Given this starting point, it is inevitable that Wallerstein will have a very different assessment of the triumph of capitalism from the one offered by Fukuyama. But it can also be argued that his assessment is potentially more interesting for the analysis of international relations because it is developed outside the familiar framework associated with the debate between idealists and realists. Wallerstein is one of the few theorists to have developed a distinctively different framework for studying international relations. The framework gives rise to an internationalized conception of capitalism and it is this factor which leads to the distinctive assessment of the triumph of capitalism.

From Wallerstein's perspective, it needs to be established in the first instance that the triumph of capitalism is not a recent development as Fukuyama might suggest. Because Fukuyama believes that capitalism can be delimited within the boundaries of a state, its ultimate triumph can emerge only when all states adopt a capitalist mode of production. But Wallerstein works from a very different perspective and views capitalism 'as an entire system' (Shannon, 1989, p. 23) and a world system at that. Wallerstein does not thereby imply that capitalism has been global in extent from its inception. But he does argue that capitalism characterized the first and only world system that managed, during the nineteenth century, to extend across the globe. For Wallerstein, then, the triumph of capitalism can be traced from that point. Given this position, Wallerstein is inevitably led along a line of analysis which challenges much conventional thinking. When the Bolsheviks took control in Russia in 1917 and the communists in China in 1949, for example, these states are seen to have remained part of the ongoing capitalist system. From Wallerstein's perspective, they were not withdrawn from that system but remained an integral part of it. By the same token, he does not accept that with the demise of communism in Eastern Europe and the Soviet Union this area suddenly joined the capitalist system because, as far as he is concerned, it had never left the system. Wallerstein is not, of course, suggesting that the events surrounding the rise and demise of communism in the Soviet Union are insignificant. He readily acknowledges their importance. But his theoretical framework leads him to place a very different interpretation on these events from the ones emerging from either the realist or indeed Fukuyama's perspective. For Wallerstein, the collapse of the Soviet Union represents not the triumph of capitalism but part of a serious challenge to its survival.

To understand Wallerstein's interpretation of recent events, however, it is necessary to look more closely at his theoretical framework. It is important to recognize in the first place that Wallerstein's approach leads him to work on a very broad historical canvas. Unlike Fukuyama, however, Wallerstein's philosophy of history does not encourage him to conclude that there is a necessary and rational direction to history. 'It is simply not true', he has argued, 'that capitalism as a historical system has represented progress over the various previous historical systems that it destroyed or transformed' (1983, p. 98) But Wallerstein does not thereby imply that history is leading us on an inevitable downward track, to our eventual destruction. Such an outcome is possible. But Wallerstein believes that although we operate within severe structural constraints the potential exists to nudge the world system in a more just and equitable direction. Critics have argued, however, that Wallerstein has given us very few clues about what the new system would look like or why we should accept that it will be any improvement over the existing order.

Setting this criticism to one side, for the moment, Wallerstein argues that to realize the potential for change within a system, we must understand first how world systems operate, and this, he believes, involves working within the context of world history, although in practice he has devoted almost all of his own efforts to examining the emergence of the contemporary world system which, in his framework, has evolved over the past five hundred years. As a consequence, his view of world history, described by three main phases, has been sketched in only the broadest of outlines. Before identifying these historical phases, however, it is necessary to present his major theoretical building blocks.

He starts from the premise that the basic unit of analysis for social scientists is the social system. The systemic perspective presupposes that human beings cannot survive on their own and that they must rely on a division of labour which establishes a network or grid of interdependent human beings. The division of labour defines the smallest grid within which the basic needs of the component members can be met. If individuals within the grid start to rely on external parties for the satisfaction of their survival needs, the division of labour extends, and with it the boundary of the system. During the first phase of human history, the period prior to around 10,000 BC, divisions of labour never extended beyond the bounds of a common culture, establishing what Wallerstein refers to as mini-systems. Thereafter, the division of labour often embraced divergent cultural groups and mini-systems start to give way to world systems.

Wallerstein argues that, logically, there can be only two types of world system: one with a common political framework identified as a world empire and the other without such a framework, identified as a world economy. In a world empire, political power is concentrated at the centre of the system and is used to control and regulate divergent cultural groups both economically and politically. On the economic front, tribute and tax are extracted from the periphery and then used on the political front to provide order and security across the empire. The boundary of a world empire is determined, therefore, by how far political power can be extended from the centre. During the second phase in world history which extends from 10,000 BC to AD 1500, mini-systems, world empires and world economies are seen by Wallerstein to have co-existed. But throughout this period the dominant and most successful system was the world empire. Throughout this second phase, the globe, according to Wallerstein, was divided into a number of autonomous world systems. He acknowledges that there was some contact between these systems, but he insists that the contact was so limited in character that it did not affect the working of these independent systems.

The third phase in world history, the one in which we are still operating, marks the period when a capitalist world economy takes shape and eventually absorbs all the other existing world systems. World economy is an unfortunate label because it has led some critics to accuse Wallerstein of economic reductionism, whereas an evaluation of his overall framework reveals that culture and politics provide the starting points of his theoretical analysis. But it is true that in a world economy the division of labour is defined only in economic terms. The boundary of a world economy is determined not by the reach of political power, but by the limits set by the trade in essential goods. For most of world history, Wallerstein argues, the disjunction between economic and political structures rendered world economies highly precarious; they displayed a persistent tendency either to disintegrate or to be amalgamated into a world empire. His major preoccupation over the past twenty years has been to understand why the world economy which emerged in north-west Europe at the start of the sixteenth century followed such a different and distinctive trajectory.

Wallerstein defines this world economy as capitalist in form. But, in fact, he tends to see capitalism and world economies as 'obverse sides of the same coin' (1979, p. 6). It follows that the world economies which existed in the previous historical phase can be represented as incipient or proto-capitalist systems. Certainly Wallerstein is quite clear that only world economies carry the potential to develop into capitalist systems. In developing this line of argument, it is clear that Wallerstein is adhering to a very distinctive conception of capitalism. He does not think that capitalism can be related in the first instance to industrialization, for example, or a particular form of class formation or mode of production. For Wallerstein, capitalism is quintessentially concerned with the production of goods to trade in a market 'in which the object is to realize the maximum profit' (1979, p. 15). Capitalism is associated with the process of capital accumulation. Wallerstein does not doubt that trading for profit took place in world empires but he insists that it was not a dominant or defining feature of the system. By the same token, trading connections broke down in previous world economies because the systems themselves collapsed. Only after AD 1500, he insists, did profit-maximization manage to become a stable and enduring feature of trading relations in a world system. Capitalism at that juncture became firmly rooted in a world system and with the expansion of this system, by the nineteenth century, capitalism finally triumphed at a global level.

From Wallerstein's perspective, then, capitalism cannot be defined in terms of economic organization within the state; it is necessarily an international (although Wallerstein dislikes this term) phenomenon. It is not possible to give a detailed account of Wallerstein's analysis of how the modern world economy came into existence and why it has flourished. But at the heart of the explanation lies the essentially realist notion that the competition among strong states at the core of the system ensured the survival of an independent market-place and thereby prevented the emergence of a world empire. The disjunctive economic and political structures which had in the past been a source of weakness now reinforced each other and thus helped to consolidate the system. The strong states were able to ensure high rates of profit, thereby enhancing their own strength and simultaneously reproducing the system.

In contrast to realists, however, Wallerstein does not measure the strength of states in terms of their military capabilities but in terms of their capacity to control and regulate the economic market. The consequence of this orientation becomes most apparent when we examine the Cold War era. In contrast to the vast majority of analysts, Wallerstein never defined this era in bipolar terms. In 1945 the US is clearly seen to have had a hegemonic status in the world economy. The Soviet Union, by contrast, is not seen even to occupy a position at the centre of the world economy. Wallerstein does not locate the Soviet Union in the periphery of the world economy because its vast internal resources and its military grip on Eastern Europe gave it a degree of autonomy. Instead, the Soviet Union is located in an area identified as the semi-periphery of the world economy. The Soviet Union, therefore, is seen to have occupied a vulnerable and ambiguous position in the world economy. Although there are difficulties with the idea of a semi-periphery, the fact remains that Wallerstein's framework does generate an assessment of the relationship between the US and the Soviet Union which is very different from the bipolar relationship identified in much of the more conventional international relations literature but which makes just as much sense.

From Wallerstein's perspective, then, the demise of communism cannot be construed in terms of the triumph of capitalism, neither can it be seen to have precipitated any dramatic change in the structure of the world economy. But Wallerstein does accept that the demise of communism will have an effect on the world economy. To comprehend the effect, however, it is necessary to highlight three of the dynamic features of the world economy identified by Wallerstein in his theoretical framework. In the first place, Wallerstein argues that the capitalist world economy has gone through regular cycles of expansion and contraction during its history. Although some world systems theorists consider that Wallerstein has adopted an overly mechanistic attitude to the regularity of these cycles (Abu-Lughod, 1989, p. 356), it is difficult to deny either that the world economy has gone through recurring periods of expansion and contraction or that the system is currently in an era of contraction. Second, Wallerstein notes that the degree of power concentration also passes through cycles, with periods of hegemony giving way to periods of multipolarity. He argues that there was a period of American hegemony after 1945 but that it lasted only until about 1967 and that we are now entering a phase of increasing competition between the US, Japan and Western Europe which can only intensify in a period of economic contraction. Wallerstein's belief is that the competition at the centre of the world economy will become increasingly unfettered now that the collective fear of the Soviet Union can no longer be played upon. He argues that the demise of communism represents a 'geopolitical catastrophe' for the US because it 'eliminates the only ideological weapon the USA had to restrain the EC and Japan from pursuing their self-defined objectives'. But more important, Wallerstein considers that the capitalist world economy as a historical system is entering a period of acute crisis since the end of communism has removed the long-standing 'justification of the status quo without replacing it with any viable substitute' (1993, p. 4; 1992b, 1992c).

Against this background of crisis, Wallerstein and his colleagues have also identified the emergence of what they call 'antisystemic movements'. Throughout history, there has always been sporadic opposition to oppression. But world systems theorists insist that one of the contradictions which has emerged as a consequence of the 'integrating tendencies' associated with the development of capitalism was the 'institutionalization' of anti-systemic movements; a development which occurred during the course of the nineteenth century (Arrighi, Hopkins and Wallerstein, 1989, p. 30). Opposition to the status quo thereafter tended to crystallize in the form of institutional organizations which aimed to establish political power. The record of social-democratic groups at the centre of the system and nationalist movements on the periphery have, according to Arrighi and his colleagues, been 'impressive' (p. 33). In the process, however, these anti-systemic forces have been co-opted into the state system, reinforcing the hegemonic influence of liberal ideology, and thereby truncating their ability to precipitate radical change. As a consequence, at both the centre and the periphery of the capitalist world economy there remains a strong sense of an 'unfulfilled revolution' (p. 34). Anti-systemic movements, as a consequence, have turned away from the strategy of attempting to capture state power. A concern with geopolitics is seen to be giving way to what Wallerstein calls 'geoculture'. As he sees it, 'disillusionment with the efficacy of transforming the world by altering its economic and political forms' (1991, pp. 11–12) is leading new social (anti-systemic) movements to focus on culture. This is revealed in the creation and emphasis laid on the concepts of racism and sexism.

In his more polemical writings, Wallerstein has insisted that since we are now moving into an 'era of disintegration of the capitalist world-economy' (1992a, p. 107) in which 'the final collapse of liberalism as a hegemonic ideology' (1992a, p. 104) has taken place, the opportunity now exists to influence the shape of a new world system. In developing this thesis, Wallerstein has been influenced by the writings of the Nobel-winning scientist Ilya Prigogine, who has argued that we are passing through an era of scientific revolution which has profound consequences for our understanding of both the natural and social world. Modern science, he argues, has undermined the 'vision of classical physics' which asserted that 'the future is determined by the present' because of the existence of the 'irreversible laws' of nature (1980, p. 214) It is now recognized that the idea of 'irreversible laws' is an illusion. Wallerstein quotes with some satisfaction:

> The ways of nature cannot be foreseen with certainty. The elements of accident therein cannot be eliminated, and it is far more decisive than Aristotle himself understood. Bifurcating nature is that in which small differences and insignificant fluctuations can, provided they occur in opportune circumstances, spread out through the whole system and bring into being a new mode of functioning. (Prigogine and Stengers, 1979, p. 271, cited in Wallerstein, 1991, p. 230)

Wallerstein believes that we have come to a juncture where there are 'opportune circumstances' to change the way in which the world system operates. The real problem is that the advocates of change have no effective strategy for intervening and he sees the formation of such a strategy as the major task confronting those who wish to operate in a more egalitarian world.

Wallerstein, like Fukuyama, therefore, carefully avoids presenting his philosophy of history in deterministic terms. For Wallerstein, socialism is an option which may or may not be realized. The future remains open. The past, on the other hand, is closed and yet Wallerstein's historical analysis is just as controversial as his views about the future. At the heart of the criticism lies the notion of the world system. Critics strenuously deny that the modern world system operates in the way Wallerstein suggests. States possess, and have always possessed, far more political and economic autonomy than Wallerstein acknowledges. States do not operate at the mercy of the structures of the system. The grandiose, holistic picture painted by Wallerstein simply fails to take account of the importance and determining influence of local conditions within the system (Skocpol, 1977; Stinchcombe, 1982). The speed with which the Soviet Empire collapsed provides some powerful evidence in favour of this view. More sympathetic critics, however, have acknowledged that large-scale structures do play a significant role in complex events and help to tell part of the story (Deudney and Ikenberry, 1991).

CONCLUSION

Mainstream theorists readily acknowledge that the international system is in the throes of major structural change and that the tools used to analyse international politics in the bipolar era are now 'antique', as Blight and Weiss put it (1992, p. 229). Although there is little agreement about the nature of the structures which will finally replace bipolarity, these theorists are generally agreed that major structural differentiation within the system will persist. One model around which some consensus is beginning to emerge establishes an ideological divide between a peaceful core of states which adhere to a common ideology identified as liberal capitalism, and an unstable periphery made up of ideologically divergent states (Buzan, 1991; Goldgeier and McFaul, 1992). Given this model, the established division of labour in the mainstream study of international relations can persist, with realists, in the first place, exploring power relationships at the centre, conflict in the periphery and the potential role of force in the relationship between the centre and the periphery. Pluralists can at the same time continue to examine those forces of capitalism at the centre and periphery of the contemporary world which are eroding the independence of the state. There is little evidence that the resulting tension between the pluralists and the realists will disappear.

For very different reasons, neither Fukuyama nor Wallerstein is likely to find the emerging mainstream model either persuasive or useful. Fukuyama believes that historical forces are moving us towards the point where capitalism and liberal democracy have been universally accepted. It becomes important and relevant, therefore, to examine how international relations will look in a world of liberal democratic states. Wallerstein, adopting an even more radical position, asserts that the forces of capitalism extend across the globe, shaping and moulding the way agents can operate at the local level. Although he also talks explicitly in terms of a centre and periphery, this division reflects a structural rather than an ideological divide within the world system and his intention is to work towards a theory which will reveal how the global dominance of capitalism can be overcome.

The keen interest expressed by both Fukuyama and Wallerstein in the direction that history will take is closely related to a common interest in attacking mainstream theory and revealing its disfunctional character. As noted earlier, Wallerstein focuses, for example, on how modernization theory, although built on false premises, has had a very significant and negative effect on Third World economies. And, by the same token, Fukuyama asserts that realism has shaped the thinking of foreign-policy decision-makers not only in the US but also around the world. A self-fulfilling prophecy is thereby established, with foreign-policy makers assuming that the world is hostile and then acting in a way which justifies and reinforces this assumption.

Wallerstein and Fukuyama, therefore, both set themselves apart from mainstream theorists and can be characterized as critical theorists rather than problem-solving theorists. They see mainstream theorists operating as natural scientists do, observing the social world and then forming empirical theories which correspond to their observations. Critical theorists, by contrast, are seen to recognize that theorizing is not a neutral activity but can have very significant social consequences. By failing to acknowledge the social impact of theorizing, therefore, mainstream thinkers are unintentionally formulating theories which help to reproduce the status quo. This division between problem-solving theorists and critical theorists has been observed throughout the social sciences (Bernstein, 1976).

How seriously does the challenge offered by Fukuyama and Wallerstein have to be taken by mainstream theorists? To some extent it can be absorbed with relative ease. Fukuyama, in the first instance, can readily be located within the long-established debate between idealists and realists. Idealists have often traced their antecedents back to Kant and so the link which Fukuyama establishes between liberal democracies and the emergence of a pacific union is very familiar. His position, moreover, can relatively easily be attacked by both the pluralists and the realists. From a pluralist perspective, Fukuyama looks much too state-centric. He simply fails to take account of the complex forces within capitalism which pluralists claim are successfully challenging and undermining the authority of the state. By arguing that the discipline has been dominated by the realists, therefore, Fukuyama neatly avoids exposing his own analysis to the sceptical gaze of the pluralists.

But his position is also susceptible to attack from the realists. They can point, in the first place, to an internal contradiction in his thesis. The argument that foreign-policy makers are realists undermines his argument that liberal democracies have managed to evolve peaceful relations among themselves. Within Fukuyama's frame of reference, this could have happened only if the realist decision-makers in liberal countries had come to share the views being propagated by Fukuyama himself. Even more significant, mainstream theorists who have examined the thesis linking peace to democracy are highly sceptical about the kind of evidence used by Fukuyama. Cohen (1994), for example, not only points to the very limited number of stable democracies which exist in the contemporary international system, but also demonstrates that although South America cannot be defined as a region of democracies, it has managed to form one of the very few pacific unions in the international system.

Of course, the centre–periphery model established within the mainstream to characterize developments since the demise of the Soviet Union is also vulnerable to this criticism. It too assumes that relations among democratic states at the centre of the system will be peaceful while those among the non-democratic periphery will be unstable and potentially violent. But this does not alter the fact that much of Fukuyama's assessment of international relations is both familiar and highly contestable within the mainstream perspective. But Fukuyama does score palpable hits, with his arguments that realist scholarship is ahistorical in character, and that the structural framework used is incapable of looking at the evolving structure of states. Although he circumvents the work of the pluralists, it can also be argued that they fail to fit the evolution of capitalism into a broader or trans-historical framework.

Wallerstein and the world systems approach is less easy to absorb into the mainstream. Instead, it has come under fundamental attack from mainstream theorists for failing, in particular, to recognize that states have access to political power which enables them to act independently of the economic structures established by the capitalist world economy (Gourevitch, 1977–8; Zolberg, 1980–1). But world systems theorists can argue with some force that in practice their conception of a global capitalist system accommodated the demise of the Cold War much more effectively than did the approaches used by either the realists or the pluralists. As was shown earlier, world systems theorists never saw the Cold War period in bipolar terms and, indeed, the Soviet Union was considered to occupy a marginal position in Wallerstein's model. World systems theorists could well argue that this reflects the fact that their analysis has a more effective historical grounding than either realism or pluralism. In contrast to Fukuyama, who works within the familiar framework of an anarchic system of independent states, Wallerstein provides a distinctive picture of how the world system has evolved historically. Other members of the world systems school, moreover, have challenged Wallerstein's account and there is now an active debate about how the world system evolved (Abu-Lughod, 1989; Frank, 1990; Gills and Frank, 1992). By contrast, in mainstream international relations, the analysis has been overwhelmingly ahistorical and Eurocentric.

Although mainstream theorists readily acknowledge that the international system is undergoing change and can, from very different perspectives, criticize details of the theories advanced by Fukuyama and Wallerstein, neither pluralists nor realists can begin to interpret developments in the international system from the perspective of the trans-historical frameworks provided by Fukuyama and Wallerstein. Although both Fukuyama and Wallerstein are open to criticism, at least they have developed approaches which allow them to locate capitalism and its effect on international relations within a trans-historical framework. This represents the critical challenge to mainstream theorists in the study of international relations. Because of a general antipathy to any kind of philosophy of history, it is unlikely that many pluralists will wish to meet this challenge. And neo-realists, accepting Waltz's ahistorical framework, continue to deny the need for such a perspective. But structural realists are beginning to move in this direction (Buzan, Jones and Little, 1993; Buzan and Little, 1994). The image of autonomous units interacting in an anarchic arena is no longer accepted as an adequate way of characterizing the international system. Indeed, it is insisted that such a characterization holds only for a very brief period in the history of the system. Units and system are seen to be mutually constituted, so that as the nature of the units changes; so too does the nature of the international system. In contrast to Waltz, who argues that the units have been undifferentiated throughout the history of the system, structural realists are exploring the extent to which the units have been differentiated and the effect that this has had on the structure of the international system. The neo-realist emphasis on autonomous states makes it impossible to understand the nature of international relations in the feudal period, for example, when there was substantial variation in the degrees of autonomy possessed by the units in Europe. These variations in the degree of autonomy give a measure of the functional differentiation within the system. The neo-realist conception of undifferentiated units also makes it impossible to examine the role played by nomadic tribes which had such a dramatic impact on the course of world history. Structural realists, therefore, recognize the need to take account of structural differentiation between units. The work of both Fukuyama and Wallerstein is compatible with this undertaking. But whereas international relations is of tangential interest to both these theorists, activity within the international system provides the focal point of attention for structural realists.

Note

The author wishes to thank Barry Buzan, Nick Rengger and the editors for their comments on earlier drafts of this chapter.

References

Abu-Lughod, J. L. 1989: *Before European Hegemony: the world-system A.D. 1250–1350*. Oxford: Oxford University Press.

Arrighi, G., Hopkins, T. K. and Wallerstein, I. 1989: *Antisystemic Movements*. London: Verso.

Bernstein, R. J. 1976: *The Restructuring of Social and Political Theory*. Oxford: Basil Blackwell.

Blight, J. G. and Weiss, T. G. 1992: Must the grass still suffer? Some thoughts on Cold War conflict after the Cold War. *Third World Quarterly*, 13, 229–50.

Buzan, B. 1991: New patterns of global security in the twenty-first century. *International Affairs*, 67, 431–52.

Buzan, B., Jones, C. and Little, R. 1993: *The Logic of Anarchy: Neorealism to Structural Realism*. New York: Columbia University Press.

Buzan, B. and Little, R. 1994: The idea of international system: theory meets history. *International Political Science Review*, 15(3), 23–56.

Cohen, R. forthcoming: Pacific unions: a reappraisal of the democratic peace theory. *Review of International Studies*, 20, 207–223.

Cox, R. W. 1981: Social forces, states and world orders: beyond international relations theory. *Millennium: Journal of International Studies*, 10, 126–55.

DePorte, A. W. 1986: *Europe Between the Super-Powers: the Enduring Balance*, 2nd edn. New Haven and London: Yale University Press.

Deudney, D. and Ikenberry, G. J. 1991: Soviet reform and the end of the Cold War: explaining large-scale historical change. *Review of International Studies*, 17, 225–50.

Frank, A. G. 1990: A theoretical introduction to 5000 years of world system history. *Review*, 13, 155–248.

Fukuyama, F. 1992: *The End of History and the Last Man*. London: Penguin Books.

Gaddis, J. L. 1987: *The Long Peace: Inquiries into the History of the Cold War*. Oxford: Oxford University Press.

Gills, B. K. and Frank, A. G. 1992: World system cycles, crises and hegemonial shifts: 1700BC–1700AD. *Review*, 15, 621–87.

Goldgeier, J. M. and McFaul, M. 1992: A tale of two worlds: core and periphery in the post-Cold War era. *International Organization*, 46, 467–91.

Gourevitch, P. 1977–8: The international system and regime formation. *Comparative Politics*, 10, 419–38.

Halliday, F. 1992: An encounter with Fukuyama. *New Left Review*, 193, 89–95.

Jones, R. E. 1993: Thinking big. *Review of International Studies*, 19, 201–12.

Kratochwil, F. 1993: The embarrassment of changes: neo-realism as the science of *realpolitik* without politics. *Review of International Studies*, 19, 63–80.

Kumar, K. 1992: The revolutions of 1989: socialism, capitalism and democracy. *Theory and Society*, 21, 309–56.

Prigogine, I. and Stengers, I. 1979: *La Nouvelle Alliance*. Paris: Gallimard.

Prigogine, I. 1980: *From Being to Becoming: Time and Complexity in the Physical Sciences*. San Francisco: W. H. Freeman and Co.

Shannon, T. R. 1989: *An Introduction to the World-System Perspective*. Boulder, Colorado: Westview Press.

Skocpol, T. 1977: Wallerstein's world capitalist system. *American Journal of Sociology*, 4, 217–22.

Stinchcombe, A. L. 1982: Review essay: the growth of the world system. *American Journal of Sociology*, 87, 1389–95.

Suganami, H. 1990: Bringing order to the causes of war debates. *Millennium Journal of International Studies*, 19, 19–36.

Therborn, G. 1977: The rule of capital and the rise of democracy. *New Left Review*, 103, 3–41.

Tyrrell, I. 1991: American exceptionalism in an age of international history. *American Historical Review*, 96, 1031–72.

Wallerstein, I. 1979: *The Capitalist World-Economy*. Cambridge: Cambridge University Press.

Wallerstein, I. 1983: *Historical Capitalism*. London: Verso.

Wallerstein, I. 1991: *Geopolitics and Geoculture: Essays on the Changing World-System*. Cambridge: Cambridge University Press.

Wallerstein, I. 1992a: The collapse of liberalism. In R. Miliband and L. Panitch (eds), *Social Register: New World Order?*, London: Merlin, 96–110.

Wallerstein, I. 1992b: The West, capitalism and the modern world-system. *Review*, 15, 561–620.

Wallerstein, I. 1992c: America and the world: today, yesterday and tomorrow. *Theory and Society*, 21, 1–28.

Wallerstein, I. 1993: The world-system after the Cold War. *Journal of Peace Research*, 30, 1–6.

Waltz, K. N. 1979: *Theory of International Politics*. Reading, Mass.: Addison-Wesley.

Zolberg, A. R. 1980–1: Origins of the world system. *World Politics*, 33, 253–81.

4

International Political Theory and the Idea of World Community

Chris Brown

'Community' is a deceptive and different notion to employ. It is one of Raymond Williams's *Keywords*. Having noted its reference to a sense of common interests and common identity – and the classical contrast with 'society' formalized by Tönnies (1963) as a contrast between *Gemeinschaft* and *Gesellschaft* – he remarks that it is a 'warmly persuasive' word, whether used to describe an existing or alternative set of relationships: 'What is more important, perhaps, is that unlike all other terms of social organisation (state, nation, society, etc.) it never seems to be used unfavourably, and never to be given any positive opposing or distinguishing term' (Williams, 1976, p. 66). Much the same could be said of the use of the term 'world community' – it is never employed with pejorative connotations. It may not be entirely clear what is, or should be, meant by the term, but it is clear that those who use it believe that the world would be a better place if it could be described as a community. As with the diplomatic use of 'international community' – a related but, in contrast to world community, essentially state-centric term – it is always employed persuasively.

Unanimity of this kind is often a matter for suspicion, and, sure enough, further investigation does reveal that all is not as it seems. First, the uniformly positive connotations of the term community in ordinary political discourse are achieved at the expense of content. Even the Thatcher government in Britain, whose leader famously held that there was no such thing as society, employed the term community quite readily, as with the community charge (alias the poll tax) and, most egregiously, in the 'Care in the Community' policy, which involves emptying psychiatric hospitals of as many of the mentally ill as could with some plausibility hope to survive in the wider world. As a journalist on the *Independent on Sunday* noted, after one appalling incident consequent on this policy, community is a 'nice homely word', invoking images of responsible folks looking after one another but, in this context: 'In reality, "community" means virtually anywhere that is neither a hospital nor a prison' (Jones, 1993, p. 17).

Conversely, and contrary to Williams's generalization, in contemporary political theory, community (or at least a word derived from it) *is* sometimes used unfavourably and *is* given an opposing term. 'Communitarian' approaches to political theory – the term is Sandel's (1982) but, of course, the idea is much older – identify the community as a major, or the only, source of value in social life. Such approaches are clearly controversial and are opposed by 'individualist' and 'cosmopolitan' perspectives (Avineri and de-Shalit, 1992; Brown, 1992; Mulhall and Swift, 1992). Since community in this context suggests that values are necessarily particularistic, it would seem to follow with only an apparent paradox that it would not be possible to mount a 'communitarian' defence of the idea of world community – or, better, that on communitarian lines a world community could not exist in the first place. This view is indeed supported by communitarian thinkers. Hegel's scepticism towards the notion is expressed throughout the sections on international law and world history to be found in *Philosophy of Right* (1991: pp. 366–80), while a modern, indeed postmodern, communitarian writes that there is nothing 'that stands to my community as my community stands to me . . . [no] larger community called 'humanity' that has an intrinsic nature' (Rorty, 1989, p. 59). These ideas will be followed up in a later section but, for the time being, it is sufficient to note that when the language of 'world community' is used in such a way as to convey something of substance it is quite likely to generate opposition and controversy.

With these points in mind, it is now possible to turn to the subject of this chapter: a critical examination of the prospects for the emergence of a world community. The existence of such a community would be signalled by the development not just of global common interests but also of a worldwide consciousness of common identity. A number of countervailing forces in the modern world – in the realms of ideas, or of technology broadly defined, or of social and political action – appear to act either to promote or to hinder this development but, crucially, behind the struggle between these forces it is, I suggest, generally assumed that there is an underlying trend guaranteeing, or at least making very likely, a victory for the promoters of community. The assumption that universal norms and values will triumph over those based on particular local contexts is a feature of contemporary liberalism in almost all its forms – indeed is termed the 'liberal expectancy' by Milton Gordon (cited from Moynihan, 1993, p. 27) – but draws support equally from Christian, eschatological, Enlightenment, Marxist and Western progressivist thinking in general. The premise is that the world is moving in the direction of community, albeit with a faltering step because of the contest between forces representing common interests and common identity and those representing the old, particularistic, order. In what follows these claims will be set out in greater detail and, in the process, subjected to criticism. Eventually, this way of looking at things will be challenged *in toto*.

THE UNDERLYING TREND

On what basis can it be argued that there is a trend towards the development of ever-wider common interests and a deepening sense of common identity? Clearly, it is important at the outset to make a distinction between a trend towards the creation of *community*, and trends which, simply, point towards the emergence of 'one world' – failure to make this distinction bedevils a great deal of thought on the subject of world community. An illustration of this point, important in its own terms, can be found in readings of the significance of the emergence in the twentieth century of a genuinely global economy.

Looking, for example, at radical writing on the world economy, it may well be the case that, in Wallerstein's terminology (1974, pp. 3–11), the 'modern world-system' is now a world system not simply in social but in geographical terms. But as he, and other structuralist theorists, would insist, this world system is based on a fundamental *disharmony* of interests between the peoples of its component core, semi-periphery and periphery. For the time being, there is no world community here. Similar points can be made of more orthodox Marxist accounts of the emergence of a world economy, although here cross-national class solidarities are easier to find (Brewer, 1980), and of the non-economistic but equally radical investigations of world order by the World Order Models Project or WOMP (Falk, 1971, 1987; Mendlovitz, 1977). Each of these radical positions envisages the eventual emergence of community on a world scale but only after the revolution, or the transformation of values envisaged by WOMP. For these writers 'one world' will equate to a world community only after the destruction or transcendence of the existing order.

Less radical theorists of the political implications of a world economy have created the pluralist model of 'complex interdependence' to describe the existing order, with non-state actors, economic and social, as well as states engaging in the exercise of power, regime building, agenda setting, and so on (Keohane and Nye, 1977; Krasner, 1983); with greater emphasis on non-state actors and less on economic transactions a similar model is described by 'world society' theorists (Burton, 1972; Banks, 1984). Unlike accounts produced by radical readings of the world economy, there is nothing in these accounts of the world that *precludes* the existence of community in the here-and-now, but, equally, there is no *necessity* for complex interdependence to lead in this direction. Thus, while Beitz (1979) based his cosmopolitan critique of realism, and his advocacy of international distributive justice, on the proposition that interdependence would create community, he later (1983) acknowledged the force of critiques of precisely this assumption by Barry (1982) and Richards (1982). Given the one-sidedness of many economic relationships, especially but not exclusively between rich and poor countries, it cannot be assumed that a trend towards a complexly interdependent world will, of its own accord, create community.

There is a more general point to be made here. For community to begin to emerge there has to be a growing awareness of common interests and identity; the creation of 'one-world' is a necessary condition for the emergence of a world community but it is not, of itself, sufficient. This is clearly so with regard to the unifying forces of global economic interdependence but, perhaps less intuitively obviously, the point also applies when it comes to other unifying forces, including material factors such as common consumer goals and non-material factors such as the global spread of common notions of scientific method and, possibly, common standards of rationality. The fact that young people everywhere desire the same jeans, trainers and electronic games, or that contemporary technology seems to work better when based on Western science rather than, say, the Hindu scriptures is, obviously, something that is useful to know about the world, but something further is needed if an essentially *empirical* account of an increasingly unified world is to be accompanied by an essentially *normative* account of the emergence of a world community.

Returning to square one, the 'something further' required is the moral impulse which creates a sense of common interests and identity. The aim of this detour has been to drive home the point that this is not something that can be expected to emerge simply as a result of individuals and peoples coming to have more contact with one another, because such contact need not generate the essentially moral consciousness of common identity that is required. It could, instead, generate incomprehension or hatred – as seems to have been the case with initial contacts between Europeans and Aztecs (Todorov, 1987). The question is, are there good reasons for thinking that the gradual, recently quite rapid, widening of the range and scope of contacts between individuals, groups and peoples has been accompanied by some kind of corresponding recognition of common interests and a common identity?

As a first approximation, it would seem that there is good reason to answer this question in the affirmative. *Prima facie* it does seem that there has been an 'expanding circle' of concern (Singer, 1981) and that the extension of the range and scope of political reference groups from kin to tribe to city to state *has* been accompanied by something like an equivalent extension of moral concern. Within the scope of this chapter such a proposition cannot be defended, only illustrated: thus, Greeks of the age of Pericles identified with their kin, tribe and city, to a lesser extent with Hellas but not at all with 'barbarians' – those who did not speak Greek. Roman thinking was politically universalist, but morally orientated only to fellow citizens. Christendom offered a wide moral identity, but one explicitly achieved by the exclusion of Slavs, Saracens, Jews and 'others' generally. In contrast, in the world today, modern nation-states involve tens, even hundreds, of millions of people who believe one another, in principle at least, to be fellow citizens and are prepared to accept obligations to one another – through, for example, redistributive taxation – which give substance to this belief. Moreover, the growth of voluntary aid organizations such as Oxfam and human rights groups such as Amnesty International suggests that some concern for the interests and rights of citizens of other states is quite widely accepted. This loosely delineated temporal sequence – which could be replicated for other cultures – supports the view that on the whole, and so far, a widening sense of identity has accompanied the growth of ever larger networks of interdependence. It is not totally implausible to hypothesize that this process will continue until a world-wide community becomes a reality.

Of course, the fact that the circle of concern has expanded in the past does not mean that it will continue to do so in the future. Certainly there are forces working towards both the expansion and the contraction of common identity in the modern world, and it is quite possible that the latter will prove more effective than the former. These are issues that will be examined in the next section of this chapter, but before taking this step it is necessary to address some ways in which the idea of a trend towards world community might be damagingly misunderstood.

First, it should be stressed that the notion of a secular trend implies movement in a particular direction, but not necessarily on a smooth, untroubled curve. There are always likely to be setbacks as well as advances – witness, for example, the loss of Latin as the universal medium of communication among the educated elite of Europe as a consequence of the employment of vernacular languages in the construction of wider and deeper national communities. Great historical changes will never work in such a way that all the relevant indicators will always point in the same direction.

A more important point concerns the competing claims of different kinds of community. Some writers of a cosmopolitan disposition seem to assume that an emerging world community would require of its members an implausibly high level of loyalty, overriding all other obligations. Singer, for example, espouses a variety of utilitarianism which requires that need be assessed impersonally and without reference to factors such as distance or nationality. Thus, we should support transfers of wealth and income to relieve poverty and need up to the point where the marginal utility of any extra sum is the same to us as it would be to the putative recipient (1985, p. 252). This is an incredibly demanding requirement but it stems not from the needs of community as such, but from Singer's version of utilitarianism; it is perfectly possible to promote the desirability of world community without espousing such an impersonal account of the requirements of morality.

Similarly, Beitz's (1983) opposition to the 'priority principle' – that the needs of one's fellow nationals take priority over the needs of others – is unnecessarily strong. Such opposition might make sense if the only choice were to be between total loyalty towards one's fellow citizens on the one hand, and a complete disregard of such identifications on the other. But this is not how the world works nor is there any reason that it should work in this way. In practice, and quite sensibly, we recognize degrees of obligation towards family, friends, acquaintances, fellow citizens, and so on, and as long as this recognition does not lead us to disregard the interests of those in the outer circles of our concern there is no reason to see this as immoral. Priority to fellow nationals becomes contrary to the requirements of world community only if it is pushed beyond the bounds of the quite defensible view that those nearest to us have the first, but not an exclusive, call on our sympathies.

So, perhaps fortunately, a belief that world community is emerging need entail neither adherence to a facile progressivism of the 'ever onwards, ever upwards' variety, nor the belief that a saintly, self-sacrificing altruism is, will be, or should be rife among the peoples of the world. The sense of common identity that *is* required is more down to earth and practical, closer to Nagel's (1986) requirement that we should not be indifferent to the suffering of others than to Singer's or Beitz's requirement that we give the interests of others equal weight with our own. However, even in this less ambitious form, there are still reasons to doubt whether this sentiment will, or could, come to dominate – and it is to this issue that we now turn.

IMMOVABLE OBJECTS, IRRESISTIBLE FORCES

Assuming for the sake of argument that there is a trend towards the emergence of world community, which are the forces in the modern world that promote and enhance this trend, and which are those that obstruct or block its operation? And can a judgement be reached on the relative strength of these forces? As at the beginning of the previous section – but here the point can be made more simply – it must be stressed at the outset that forces which simply promote or obstruct the integration of the world as a system are not, taken on their own terms, critical to these judgements. At least as a first approximation, what is of interest is the clash between forces articulating global solidarities and forces expressing particularistic loyalties – although these normative positions may be related to empirical trends they are clearly distinguishable from them, and should be so distinguished.

Global solidarities clash with particularistic loyalties in a number of different contexts, but at the heart of each such clash is a contest between differently based normative claims on the individual, often reaching to critical questions concerning his or her sense of identity. Ought women in countries where Islamic law is in force see themselves as victims of discrimination – as the international women's movement would have it – or as participants in a living and sacred culture, as their co-religionists see the matter? How is a Brazilian environmentalist to reconcile within his or her own mind the claims of national development with the need to protect the common heritage of humanity? What is the mechanism by which those who seek social justice in the advanced industrial world choose between the claims of their disadvantaged fellow nationals and the usually greater, but always more distant, poverty of the dispossessed of the less developed countries? In each case, the real question is not so much 'What should I do?' but, rather, 'Who am I?' – because what I do will depend on who I think I am.

As the examples above suggest, the contest here is often cast in terms of an opposition between the different conceptions of moral identity offered by: 'new social movements' – on which see Mendlovitz and Walker (1987), Scott (1990) and Pakulski (1991); the women's movement – see Enloe (1989), Grant and Newland (1991), Peterson (1992) and, particularly relevant in this context, Sylvester (1993); universalist conceptions of human rights – see, for an emphasis on economic rights, Shue (1980), for political and general dimensions, Donnelly (1985, 1989) and Vincent (1986) and, for an attempt to find anthropologically based cross-cultural rights, Renteln (1990); and, in apparent contrast with all of the above, 'traditional' forces such as religion, ethnicity and nationalism – from a very long potential list, see Mayall (1989) and Anderson (1983) on nationalism, Piscatori (1986) and Esposito (1983, 1992) on Islam, and, on ethnicity and identity, Smith (1991) and, a brilliant if at times somewhat wayward essay, Moynihan (1993). The problem is that this way of setting up the issue is based on the assumption that these different packages of ideas are internally consistent, which often they are not.

Thus, some of the new social movements have particularistic as well as global implications. For example, it is a matter of some debate among different wings of the feminist movement as to whether gender should be seen as the basis of a new division of the world or, alternatively, as a force which overcomes divisions and creates, for the first time, the basis for a genuine worldwide common identity – on which see classifications of feminist thought such as Zalewski (1993) as well as the works cited above. This situation is similar in structure and in its general implications to one that appears with some regularity in all variants of Marxism, with, of course, gender replacing class. In principle, the aim of revolutionary action on behalf of the working class/women is to create a world in which class/gender no longer matters – a genuine global community – but in the unredeemed time in which the struggle takes place, the effect of this worldwide contest is to intensify divisions, not to heal wounds, and, indeed, if the injuries of class/gender come to seem to be untreatable in the present system, so much the better. Thus, even on the assumption that the new social movements such as feminism aim eventually to promote global solidarity, they may do so via the indirect route of increased tension and a heightened sense of disunity.

In much the same, rather confusing, way, some of the forces which appear to have the effect of promoting particularistic loyalties do so from a basis that can plausibly claim to offer an alternative conception of global solidarity. Some, but not all, world religions can be seen in this light. For example, the occasionally quite virulent clash between Islam and the West (often in this case represented by the new social movements, or by human rights pressure groups such as Amnesty International) is generally seen by the latter as a clash between the universal values of enlightenment, science and rationality and the mores generated by a particularistic, culture-specific vision of the world. Unsurprisingly, this is not how radical Islam sees itself. This proselytizing religion regards its message as of universal import for humanity, and its goal is a world community in which all have submitted to this message – in this respect resembling Christianity in contrast to, say, Hinduism, where, in principle, the only way to possess a caste identity is to be born to it.

The purpose of this discussion is to suggest that setting up the issue of world community in terms of a contrast between the forces of globalism and localism, solidarity and particularism, may be less helpful than, at first glance, it seems to be. Clearly there *are* circumstances where this way of seeing things does approximate to reality. Secularists in India who oppose Hindu 'fundamentalism' can reasonably see themselves as representing a global solidarity as opposed to local particularism – although whether this status conveys moral superiority will, of course, be a matter of opinion. Nationalism and racism are self-evidently not dead forces in the modern world, and those who oppose their local manifestations in the name of universal human values are not misleading themselves or others – there is a real struggle here which is not lightly to be explained away. However, some of the most interesting of contemporary contests are *not* of this form: instead of pitting local norms against global, universal values, they take the form of a contest between different conceptions of what is or should be universal. What is at issue in these cases is not whether or not there should be a world community but, rather, which of several possible world communities will emerge.

For this reason it is difficult, if not impossible, to see which way the wind is blowing when it comes to assessing the prospective growth of common interests and identities in the world today. In most parts of the world genuinely local forces such as nationalism and ethnicity may be under pressure but they are fighting back and, in any event, their opponents are as varied as they are and engaged in equally fierce contests with one another. This complex, multidimensional reality cannot be simplified into a straightforward contest between world community and its opponents: in different concrete contexts, apparently particularistic 'immovable objects' can become 'irresistible forces' based on universal values, as witness the role of Islam, anti-secularist in its relations with the West, but aligned with secularism in India in opposition to Hindu particularism.

Of all the forces allegedly pushing in the direction of universal values, perhaps only environmentalism is at least partly immune to a particularist interpretation. Although the politics of environmental protection are clearly based on a clash between global and local interests (Hurrell and Kingsbury, 1992) environmental ethics are much more unambiguously universalist, since it is difficult to see how a local community could rationally and ethically claim, much less exercise, a right to inflict irreversible damage on a world it shares with others. The key issues in environmental ethics do not centre around claims to such a right, but instead focus on the question of collective responsibility for environmental degradation and, in particular, whether, and on what basis, the world community ought to be expected to compensate states for not exercising their ability to destroy the environment in circumstances where there are clear short-term gains from such actions – obviously a key issue in many developing countries (McCleary, 1991; Engel and Engel, 1992). Here it *is* possible to identify a global force which is incontrovertibly based on common interests, and promotes a common identity shared by all who desire that they themselves and their descendants should be able to continue to live on the planet.

However, what sets environmentalism apart from other superficially similar movements is precisely the fact that the common identity it promotes is based on biological factors, and translating this identity into cultural, social or political terms seems to present real problems. It may be that, in the long run, global environmental change will force a radical shift in the way of life of all the inhabitants of the planet – especially those in the advanced industrial world – but, for the time being, claims of this sort made, for example, by 'deep ecologists' such as Arne Naess (1992), do not have the political purchase required to create a genuinely universalist political practice.

If these judgements approach in some measure the truth – and, obviously, in a chapter of this length approximation is all that can be expected – it would seem that there is very little that can be said about the probability that some kind of world community is emerging: the complex interplay of forces in the modern world simply do not readily sort themselves into those supporting and those opposing such a development. This degree of indeterminacy is not exactly unusual in contemporary political theory and it may be that there is not much else to be said on this matter – the hypothetical trend towards world community identified in the previous section will simply have to be left, as it were, in the air. However, there is another possibility, namely that the indeterminacy of this issue has a direct bearing on the very idea that there could be a secular trend towards world community – a re-examination of the root idea of community seems called for.

THE LIMITS OF COMMUNITY

It was suggested above, first, that a trend towards the emergence of an ever wider sense of community could be identified as a complement to the development of larger political units, and, second, that it is reasonable to hypothesize that this trend would continue – that the sequence 'kin, tribe, city, state' would, eventually, be completed by 'world'. However, the burden of the previous section of this chapter is that it is difficult to read the contemporary world in this light – the signs are simply too confusing to convey any clear sense of which way the world is going. It seems possible that something has gone wrong with the argument somewhere along the line – and there are at least two points at which error might have crept in.

First, it might be that the very idea of a historical trend towards *anything*, much less an ever widening sense of community, is mistaken. The idea that it is possible to find patterns of meaning in history has a very long heritage in Western thought and not simply in the Enlightenment and post-Enlightenment eras – the biblical and Christian roots of this idea are brilliantly reviewed by Karl Löwith in his *Meaning in History* (1949) – but has been put under question from a number of directions in recent years. The radical approach to the history of ideas associated with Quentin Skinner (Tully, 1988) denies the existence of a common set of 'problems of politics' persisting over time in different contexts; such a denial necessarily undermines the idea that trend lines can be identified on any long-term cross-cultural basis. The postmodern 'turn' in social thought offers an even more radical 'scepticism towards metanarratives' (Lyotard, 1986, p. xxiv) such as the metanarrative of 'community'. Moreover, outside the academy, the obvious failures of Marxism–Leninism – and, less dramatically, of the sort of programmatic liberalism associated with Hayek (1960) – seem to have led to a widespread public mood of disillusionment with grand political ideas, a position which endorses this postmodern scepticism, albeit not in so many words.

However, on closer inspection, this pervasive scepticism seems overblown. Clearly it is good to get away from the sort of facile Victorian progressivism which portrays the history of ideas in such a way that our predecessors are seen as inadequately addressing our agenda rather than doing their best to cope with their own, and, equally clearly, it is good that the spirit of the age is unwilling to allow itself to be conscripted into the armies of the oversimplifiers, but these healthy tendencies should not be allowed to underwrite a self-destructive nihilism. To suggest that the political problems of the past have *nothing* to do with modern man, or that *all* ideologies and general perspectives on life are equally distorted would be to turn a serious point of view into an affront to common sense. It is perfectly possible to defend the idea that we have today a wider sense of political community than that of our forebears without falling into irredeemable naivety. Modern states clearly have not solved the problems of community but to recognize that this is so need not involve a denial that considerable progress has been made or a refusal to recognize the real virtues possessed by contemporary liberal democratic states.

There is, then, no good *a priori* reason to deny that within the sequence 'kin, tribe, city, state' can be found a widening and deepening of community, but a second possibility – namely, that there are good and substantial reasons that this sequence cannot be completed by 'world' – is less easily disposed of. At its simplest, it might be the case that a sense of common identity actually *requires* the existence of 'others' with whom one does not identify. This is a commonplace and seductive point of view, nicely expressed in 1972 by Daniel Bell: 'It is always possible to bind together a considerable number of people in love, so long as there are other people left over to receive the manifestations of their aggressiveness' (cited from Moynihan, 1993, p. 61). But, although seductive, such an argument is ultimately unconvincing, not just because it offers such a bleak view of human nature, but also because it denies without good reason the possibility that this nature might change. More plausible are those arguments for pluralism which rest upon a specific idea of community, one rather less loosely defined than that upon which this chapter has, so far, rested. The *locus classicus* for such an idea is to be found in the writings of the communitarian tradition referred to in the introduction to this chapter, and particularly, but not exclusively, in the work of modern neo-Hegelians such as Charvet (1981), Sandel (1982) and Frost (1986).

In order to understand this position it is necessary to backtrack somewhat, and ask *why* the growth of a sense of community has, apparently, accompanied the growth of networks of communication and interdependence signalled by the sequence from kinship group to state referred to above. From some perspectives, this is not a very interesting question. If, for example, in the best liberal tradition, society is a 'co-operative venture for mutual advantage' (Rawls, 1971, p. 4) then a degree of identification with fellow co-operators is unsurprising, and, equally, there is no reason to look for a deep explanation to account for the fact that as the scope of the venture becomes more extensive so the number of co-operators who identify with one another is also likely to increase. By the same token, as this co-operative venture becomes worldwide in scope, so one might expect the emergence of a worldwide sense of community – hence the attempts by Beitz (1979) and Pogge (1989) to apply Rawlsian notions of social justice to a global definition of society.

But from a communitarian perspective, this account of the growth of society and community is highly misleading because it rests on the characteristically liberal assumption that the individual co-operators who venture together for mutual advantage have a pre-social existence, and pre-social interests and values, that they bring with them to the process. By contrast, the communitarian perspective suggests, first, that human beings become 'individuals' only by the process of relating to one another in societies and, second, that, by extension, the kind of individuals they become will be a product of the kind of society within which this takes place. Thus, the sense of community that emerges from kinship group or tribe is not simply quantitatively different from that which is shaped by the modern state. There is a qualitative difference here. By situating the family within the context of civil society – a location within which the individual learns to make his or her way in the world – and by situating civil society within a constitutional context wherein law is seen as ultimately self-created rather than an external, alien force, the modern state makes possible the creation of individuals whose potentiality is far greater than that possessed by those whose individuality is constituted by societies in which these institutions are not differentiated – such at least is the position of communitarians of a Hegelian disposition.

From this perspective the sequence 'kin, tribe, city, state' is not simply a sequence of ever larger political and social units: it is a sequence of progressively differentiated entities, each adding something to the constitution of human beings that its predecessor could not offer. At this point, the obvious next step is to ask whether a *world* community would continue this process by providing something that the modern state does not – and the classic communitarian answer, given by Hegel and Rorty in the introduction to this chapter in statements which could be replicated from a variety of other sources, is that it would not. From the communitarian perspective, the modern state could already provide the individual with the basis for a life lived in freedom, dealing justly with all, and there is, thus, no necessity to go beyond this to any allegedly higher form of community, even if such a move were possible. World community cannot be seen as a *necessary* step, because it could not provide any resource for the creation of individuality and personality on top of those already to hand in the modern state. However, and this point cannot be stressed too strongly, the fact that these resources are to hand does not mean that they are actually employed, and the perspective outlined here does *not* underwrite a conservative acceptance of the status quo; indeed, the fact that a rational, ethical community is possible yet nowhere exists signposts the imperative need for a change in the way we live.

Thus, communitarians of this Hegelian or neo-Hegelian persuasion have no difficulty in explaining the indeterminate nature of the struggle between the forces of global solidarity and those of local particularism. This global struggle has no obvious shape and is leading in no clearly defined direction because the underlying logic which created community at 'lower' levels of social organization does not operate on this terrain. Local struggles *can* be understood in communitarian terms, and neo-Hegelians *do* believe that the modern state is a superior form of social organization to its alternatives but even here, without the metaphysical assurance provided to their predecessors by the notion of *Geist*, there can be no guarantee that the good will in the end drive out the bad. In any event many modern communitarians would be less willing than the neo-Hegelians to make this kind of comparative judgement, believing that different political forms will be appropriate to different communities (Walzer, 1983).

For many, the difficulty with this latter form of communitarianism is that it tends in the direction of relativism, and an apparent refusal to judge and condemn in circumstances where judgement and condemnation seem mandatory – for example, in assessing the policies of genocidal leaders such as Hitler or Pol Pot. There is some justice to the general charge of relativism, and Walzer attempts to meet it by positing a kind of 'minimal and universal moral code' (1987, p. 24), which, while not sufficient for human beings to live by, is specific enough to allow us to say that some ways of life – those based on large-scale human sacrifice is the example he offers – are clearly wrong. But in any event, even a relativist who does not endorse such an escape clause (Rorty, for example) need not feel obliged to refrain from condemning genocidal maniacs. Relativists do not believe that social practices can be considered in isolation; their belief is that 'forms of life' taken as wholes cannot be judged against criteria drawn from one another or from some universalist 'view from nowhere' (Nagel, 1986; see also the discussion in Part II of Nussbaum and Sen,

1993). There is no reason to see this position as providing cover for the activities of, for example, the Khmer Rouge or the Nazis, because there is no reason to believe that these groups are or were authentic representatives of their cultures or forms of life. Pol Pot's position was, and is, explicitly to reject Cambodia's past, while the version of Germany's history promulgated by Hitler was largely spurious.

Clearly, it *is* possible that there will be cases where social practices which appear to be authentically grounded in a locally approved way of life *do* offend moral standards which most modern Westerners want to preserve – the case of the treatment of women in Islamic societies comes to mind – and here there is a genuine dilemma for the communitarian relativist whose personal values and sympathies are, broadly, liberal. For such a person, the hope is that, since no long-lived and complex culture is monolithic, made up of social practices which always in all circumstances work in the same direction, the effect of social criticism from critics working *within* the culture in question and teasing out its contradictions will be, in the end, subversive of the undesirable practice. A model here is provided by the way in which (eventually) slavery of – and (much later) legal discrimination against – non-Westerners has come to be seen by Western societies as contrary to Western values. It is only a 'hope' that this process will work in any particular situation, but from the perspective of the communitarian relativist the alternative of intervention to bring about change constitutes an act of cultural imperialism which will almost always be unjustifiable.

The point of this, perhaps overlong, digression has been to show that there are different kinds of communitarian theory ranging from the Hegelian 'metanarrative' of *Geist*, via the quasi-relativism of a Walzer, to the out-and-out postmodernism of a Rorty. However, each approach holds this in common: that there is no sufficient reason to believe that a world of communities will be, or even could be, transcended by a world community.

CONCLUSION – INTERNATIONAL SOCIETY AND WORLD COMMUNITY

The line of argument espoused here clearly flies in the face of a great deal of conventional rhetoric, and seems in particular to contradict socialist, communist and (some) liberal hopes for the emergence of a universal commonwealth, a solidarity which encompasses the whole of humanity. However, it needs to be asked whether the values articulated by such aspirations might not find expression in different forms, and, indeed, a refusal to think in universalist terms opens up the possibilities of a pluralistic conception of world order, an openness to the recognition and acceptance of difference, which may actually signal a more practical and less ethnocentric understanding of human solidarity than conventional radicalism has to offer – such, at least, is the promise of late modernist thinkers such as Connolly (1991).

It is here that the notion of international society becomes important, because it is plausible to suggest that many of the positive features that a putative world community might provide could be found within the scope of an association of communities founded on the rule of law but not united in any global project – international society as a practical association, in the terminology of Nardin (1983). Such an association could be based on the recognition of a general duty to relieve suffering by mutual aid and assistance and, thus, would mandate substantial redistributions of income and wealth, but the basic premise would be that the pursuit of social justice and a deeper sense of community is something that makes more sense locally than on a global scale – that the most important 'spheres of justice' are those which are internal to particular societies rather than cross-cultural in aspiration (Walzer, 1983). The goal would be an association of socially just communities which was, itself, constructed on socially just lines. In so far as this notion involves the setting of standards that can serve as goals of political change in a non-ideal world it is as much a product of 'ideal theory' (Beitz, 1979, p. 156) as the notion of a world community with its own substantive ends – but the ideal of a plurality of morally autonomous, just communities relating to one another in a framework of peace and law seems rather more appropriate to today's world than does its alternative.

References

Anderson, B. 1983: *Imagined Communities*. London: Verso.

Avineri, S. and de-Shalit, A. (eds) 1992: *Communitarianism and Individualism*. Oxford: Oxford University Press.

Banks, M. (ed.) 1984: *Conflict in World Society*. Brighton: Wheatsheaf Press.

Barry, B. 1982: Humanity and justice in global perspective. In J. R. Pennock and J. W. Chapman (eds), *Nomos XXIL: Ethics, Economics and the Law*, New York: New York University Press, 219–520.

Beitz, C. R. 1979: *Political Theory and International Relations*. Princeton, N.J.: Princeton University Press.

Beitz, C. R. 1983: Cosmopolitan ideals and national sentiment. *Journal of Philosophy*, 80, 591–600.

Brewer, A. 1980: *Marxist Theories of Imperialism*. London: Routledge and Kegan Paul.

Brown, C. 1992: *International Relations Theory: New Normative Approaches*. Hemel Hempstead: Harvester Wheatsheaf.

Burton, J. W. 1972: *World Society*. Cambridge: Cambridge University Press.

Charvet, J. 1981: *A Critique of Freedom and Equality*: Cambridge: Cambridge University Press.

Connolly, W. E. 1991: *Identity/Difference: Democratic Negotiations of Political Paradox*. Ithaca N.Y.: Cornell University Press.

Donnelly, J. 1985: *The Concept of Human Rights*. London: Croom Helm.

Donnelly, J. 1989: *Universal Human Rights in Theory and Practice*. Ithaca N.Y.: Cornell University Press.

Engel, R. E. and Engel, J. G. (eds) 1992: *Ethics of Environmental Development: Global Challenges and International Responses*. London: Belhaven.

Enloe, C. 1989: *Bananas, Beaches and Bases: Making Feminist Sense of International Politics*. London: Pandora Books.

Esposito, J. L. (ed.) 1983: *Voices of Resurgent Islam*. Oxford: Oxford University Press.

Esposito, J. L. 1992: *The Islamic Threat: Myth or Reality?* Oxford: Oxford University Press.

Falk, R. A. 1971: *This Endangered Planet: Prospects and Proposals for Human Survival*. New York: Vintage Books.

Falk, R. A. 1987: *The Promise of World Order*. Brighton: Wheatsheaf.

Frost, M. 1986: *Towards a Normative Theory of International Relations*. Cambridge: Cambridge University Press.

Grant, R. and Newland, K. (eds) 1991: *Women and International Relations*. Milton Keynes: Open University Press.

Hayek, F. A. 1960: *The Constitution of Liberty*. London: Routledge and Kegan Paul.

Hegel, G. W. F. 1991: *Elements of the Philosophy of Right* (first published 1821) (trans. H. B. Nisbet, ed. A. Wood). Cambridge: Cambridge University Press.

Hurrell, A. and Kingsbury, B. (eds) 1992: *The International Politics of the Environment*. Oxford: Oxford University Press.

Jones, J. 1993: 'Care in the community'. *Independent on Sunday*, 10 January.

Keohane, R. O. and Nye, J. S. 1977: *Power and Interdependence*. Boston: Little, Brown & Co.

Krasner, S. (ed.) 1983: *International Regimes*. Ithaca N. Y.: Cornell University Press.

Löwith, K. 1949: *Meaning in History*. Chicago: University of Chicago Press.

Lyotard, J. – F. 1986: *The Postmodern Condition: A Report on Knowledge* (trans. G. Bennington and B. Massumi). Manchester: Manchester University Press.

Mayall, J. 1989: *Nationalism and International Society*. Cambridge: Cambridge University Press.

McCleary, R. M. 1991: The international community's claim to rights in Brazilian Amazonia. *Political Studies*, XXXIX (4), 691–707.

Mendlovitz, S. (ed.) 1977: *On the Creation of a Just World Order: Preferred Worlds for the 1990s*. New York: Free Press.

Mendlovitz, S. and Walker, R. B. J. (eds) 1987: *Towards a Just World Peace: Perspectives from Social Movements*. London: Butterworths.

Moynihan, D. P. 1993: *Pandemonium: Ethnicity in International Politics*. New York: Oxford University Press.

Mulhall, S. and Swift, A. 1992: *Liberals and Communitarians*. Oxford: Blackwell.

Naess, A. 1992: *Ecology, Community and Lifestyle*. Cambridge: Cambridge University Press.

Nagel, T. 1986: *The View from Nowhere*. New York: Oxford University Press.

Nardin, T. 1983: *Law, Morality and the Relations of States*. Princeton, N.J.: Princeton University Press.

Nussbaum, M. and Sen, A. (eds) 1993: *The Quality of Life*. Oxford: Clarendon Press.

Pakulski, J. 1991: *Social Movements: The Politics of Moral Protest*. Melbourne: Longman Cheshire.

Peterson, V. S. (ed.) 1992: *Gendered States: Feminist (Re)Visions of International Relations Theory*. Boulder, Colorado: Lynne Reinner Press.

Piscatori, J. 1986: *Islam in a World of Nation-States*. Cambridge: Cambridge University Press.

Pogge, T. 1989: *Realizing Rawls*. Ithaca N.Y.: Cornell University Press.

Rawls, J. 1971: *A Theory of Justice*. Oxford: Oxford University Press.

Renteln, A. D. 1990: *International Human Rights*. London: Sage Publications.

Richards, D. 1982: International distributive justice. In J. R. Pennock and J. W. Chapman (eds), *Nomos XXIL: Ethics, Economics and the Law*, New York: New York University Press, 275–99.

Rorty, R. 1989: *Contingency, Irony and Solidarity*. Cambridge: Cambridge University Press.

Sandel, M. 1982: *Liberalism and the Limits of Justice*. Cambridge: Cambridge University Press.

Scott, A. 1990: *Ideology and the New Social Movements*. London: Unwin Hyman.

Shue, H. 1980: *Basic Rights*. Princeton, N.J.: Princeton University Press.

Singer, P. 1981: *The Expanding Circle: Ethics and Sociobiology*. Oxford: Clarendon Press.

Singer, P. 1985: Famine, affluence and morality. In C. R. Beitz et al. (eds), *International Ethics*, Princeton, N.J.: Princeton University Press, 247–61.

Smith, A. D. 1991: *National Identity*. Harmondsworth: Penguin.

Sylvester, C. (ed.) 1993: Feminists write international relations. *Alternatives*, 18(1.) (special issue).

Todorov, T. 1987: *The Conquest of America* (trans. R. Howard). New York: Harper Torchbooks.

Tönnies, F. 1963: *Community and Association* (trans. C. P. Loomis). New York: Harper and Row.

Tully, J. (ed.) 1988: *Meaning and Context: Quentin Skinner and his Critics*. Cambridge: Polity Press.

Vincent, R. J. 1986: *Human Rights and International Relations*. Cambridge: Cambridge University Press.

Wallerstein, I. 1974: *The Modern World-System I: Capitalist Agriculture and the Origins of the European World-Economy in the Sixteenth Century*. New York: Academic Press.

Walzer, M. 1983: *Spheres of Justice: A Defence of Pluralism and Equality*. Oxford: Martin Robertson.

Walzer, M. 1987: *Interpretation and Social Criticism*. Cambridge, Mass.: Harvard University Press.

Williams, R. 1976: *Keywords: A Vocabulary of Culture and Society*. Glasgow: Fontana.

Zalewski, M. 1993: Feminist theory and international relations. In M. Bowker and R. Brown (eds), *From Cold War to Collapse: Theory and World Politics in the 1980s*, Cambridge: Cambridge University Press, 115–44.

5

The Political Theory of International Society

Robert H. Jackson

THE IDEA OF INTERNATIONAL SOCIETY

That international relations ought to be portrayed as a society of states has long been the view of certain international relations scholars. The writings of Martin Wight (1977) and Hedley Bull (1977a) are closely associated with this view and it is with their ideas that I will be mainly concerned in this chapter. The intimate association between the idea of international society and that of statecraft will also be discussed. Later in the chapter I glance briefly at the conflicts in the Persian Gulf, Somalia and Bosnia-Herzegovina to see what they tell us about international society at the end of the twentieth century.

The idea of 'international society' requires clarification in several respects. First, it should be noticed that its members are exclusively sovereign states. This goes back to a time in European history when sovereigns were a class of persons – rulers – with equal rights (sovereignty) that distinguished them from their subjects, who had no international legal standing as such. Sovereigns could deal with others of similar status, and their relations are the beginning of international society. That same principle of membership continued after sovereigns became states, and even after states became nation-states. International society therefore began its history as a society of princes which, with the spread of nationalism and the rise of democracy, was later transformed into a society of nation-states. By membership it is a very small society – with fewer than 200 members – but one that nevertheless encompasses virtually every man, woman and child on earth. Citizens of states are members of international society only indirectly through their national governments; they are not members on their own. And all other social, economic or political organizations are also excluded from membership, which is merely another way of saying that each and every one of those organizations is subordinate to a particular state.

Second, international society theorists also refer to 'world society', which they see as an alternative to international society or the society of states. They have in mind every member of the world's population conceived as possessing equal rights as human beings – human rights – regardless of the country they happen to live in. But they also see human rights at the present time as still subordinate to the rights of sovereign states. Today the legal status of human beings in international law, as expressed by the law of human rights, is something that has been erected by sovereign states and could also, at least in principle, be dismantled by them. World society is thus a client of the society of states rather than the reverse.

Third, these same theorists distinguish between 'international system' and 'international society': the latter involves mutual obligations between states, whereas the former merely supposes contacts and interactions between them. Thus, the degree of society between states can be conceived as a continuum, from mere awareness and very limited and intermittent contact at one extreme, to extensive and continuous interaction through a highly developed institutional framework of international relations at the other. The closer international relations come to the latter pole, the more developed will international society be. Finally, the notion of an 'international society' presupposes persons who act in behalf of states: statesmen – or, in other words, presidents, chancellors, prime ministers, foreign ministers, ambassadors, and the numerous other representatives and agents of independent countries. Their conduct is central to the theory of international society although this is not always made explicit by the theorists who frequently refer to 'states' when they really mean the representatives and agents of states: 'statesmen'. I develop this point later in the chapter, where attention is given to international society theorists who focus on the ethics of statecraft.

International society can easily be conceived as a structure apart from the conduct of statesmen. But that would be a misunderstanding. Bull's (1977a, pp. 13–14) distinction between 'system' and 'society' contributes to this misunderstanding because 'system' is a term that invites the positivist billiard ball image of international relations as a 'clash of forces'. The focus is on the balls moving and colliding on the table, and any explanation of their motions and collisions has something to do with the nature or 'structure' of the system of which they are a part (Waltz, 1979). The focus is not on the rules, stratagems, plays, players and – most important – what might be going on in the minds of statesmen (ideas, interests, expectations, calculations, values, beliefs, attitudes, etc.) as they contemplate their next foreign policy move. Yet it is this latter way that international society theorists conceive of international relations. They see international society as an association of states: a volitional arrangement between people who act on behalf of political collectivities called sovereign states. They do not see it as an involuntary structure or a functional system that somehow exists independent of those actors.

This distinction marks an academic rift which runs down the middle of international studies dividing (normative) international society theorists, such as Martin Wight and Hedley Bull, from (positivist) international system theorists, such as Kenneth Waltz. To avoid any misunderstanding on this point, Bull's distinction between system and society should probably be abandoned. Because all relations between human beings – including people who speak and act in the name of states – necessarily rest on mutual intelligibility and communication, however minimal, they are social at least in a minimal sense. The distinction is better conceived in terms of two types of human conduct: 'instrumental' and 'noninstrumental' (Oakeshott, 1983). The former refers to maxims, stratagems, tactics, and other pragmatic considerations or expedients which express the idea of an actor's endeavours to respond successfully to the anticipated or actual decisions and actions of other actors. If the actor is a statesman, that endeavour involves a distinctive political art: the art of power politics or, in other words, that element of statecraft concerned with the national interest and ultimately national security and survival. The latter refers to legal and moral requirements and entitlements – norms – which express the idea of conduct befitting a recognized, respected and equal member of a collectivity. If the member is a state represented by a statesman the required behaviour involves a distinctive political art: the art of civilized conduct or, in other words, that element of statecraft that is concerned with diplomatic dialogue, the rule of international law, and international ethics between states. Both elements are essential to the art of statecraft and both are evident in the actual foreign policies of states. The international society approach thus embraces power politics, international law and civility, universal morality and any other way of thinking about international relations as a distinctive sphere of human conduct. It is thus a holistic and pluralistic theory which seeks to contain within its compass the diversity of human relations in the international sphere.

THE ANALYSIS OF INTERNATIONAL SOCIETY

The foregoing discussion is scarcely anything more than the briefest introduction to an idea. The theoretical challenge is to construe international society not merely as an abstract concept but as an empirical reality: the handiwork of real people engaged in ongoing activities that we identify with the subject of international relations. With this aim in mind Martin Wight singled out 'norms and values' and 'institutions' as giving expression to international society over historical time and geographical space (Bull, 1977b, p. 17). This led him into a historical and comparative study of cultures, religions, cults, oracles, ideologies, political philosophies, ethical ideas, laws, customs, linguistic usages, public opinion, propaganda and whatever else shaped human outlooks and provoked human activities beyond the boundaries of domestic jurisdiction. These features of international society were explored not as stated here – i.e. in the abstract – but in rich, historical detail, i.e. in the flesh. In many places this account came close to being an international anthropology.

Hedley Bull's main emphasis was on order, which derived from 'a sense of common interests in the elementary goals of social life', the prescriptive rules 'that sustain these goals', and the 'institutions that help to make these rules effective' (1977a, p. 65). The jurisprudential assumption that human behaviour is based on rules conceived as standards of conduct is fundamental to Bull's international political theory. Bull went on to explore the way that modern international society came into existence and spread around the world (Bull and Watson, 1984). He also considered the alternatives to international society – such as a world society in which sovereign states were of less moment – and whether there was any evidence for the claim that these alternatives were coming into historical existence (Bull, 1977a, 1984). In many places his account came close to being a historically grounded international jurisprudence.

Martin Wight (1987, 1991) was persuaded that human relations in the world beyond the boundaries of the state could be theorized in terms of three rival traditions of thought: realism (or Machiavellism), rationalism (or Grotianism) and revolutionism (or Kantianism). These are, for Wight, the paramount ideas in the history of international political thought. Each of these 'patterns of thought' rests fundamentally on a distinctive assumption about human relations. Realism assumes an international anarchy of self-regarding and self-interested agents of power – states – whose relations are regulated ultimately by war. Realism taken to extreme is a denial that an international society exists; what exists is a Hobbesian state of nature. The only political society and, indeed, moral community is the state; there are (domestic) obligations between the state and the citizen but there are no (international) obligations between states. Rationalism assumes a world of habitual diplomatic and commercial intercourse between independent states which are legal persons connected by international law and civility. Rationalism taken to extreme – if it is possible to push to the limit that which claims to be the soul of moderation – is a perfect world of mutual respect, concord and the rule of law between states. Revolutionism assumes a world society in which states, while still present, nevertheless are subject to certain moral obligations to human beings, who in some fundamental respects are prior to them. Revolutionism taken to extreme is a claim that the only real society on earth is a world society consisting of every human being, that is, humankind.

Wight sees social and political ideas as the medium by which we define ourselves and our relations with others: one such idea is the state; another is the society of states; still others – in no particular order – are sovereignty, humanity, international legitimacy, the law of nations, the balance of power, war and peace, trade and commerce, revolution, imperialism, colonialism, and so forth. Leading theorists seek to weave such ideas into a theoretical account which authentically and conclusively interprets the world. The three traditions identified by Wight are presented as rival attempts to do this. Although at the end of his last (posthumous) book Wight (1991, p. 268) confesses (reluctantly it seems) that his 'prejudices are Rationalist', elsewhere he also says (1987, p. 227), 'when I scrutinize my own psyche I seem to find all these three ways of thought within me'.

Hedley Bull wrote a series of lectures on international justice – the Hagey Lectures (1984) – which he delivered at Waterloo

University in Canada only months before he died. Bull took notice of a continuing underlying tension between conceptions of justice in international relations and the requirement of order. The ghost of Martin Wight still haunts his discussion where he remarks that liberal (rationalists) 'refused to accept that order and justice in international relations are necessarily at loggerheads' and that they preferred 'to believe that order in international relations is best preserved by meeting demands for justice, and that justice is best realized in a context of order'. Yet he concludes by detecting 'a deeper wisdom in the recognition, common to conservatives [realists] and . . . revolutionaries [revolutionists], that terrible choices have sometimes to be made' (1984, p. 18). These comments could easily be read as the uncertainty in Bull's mind on this profoundly important issue. But that would probably be a misreading, for what Bull is really acknowledging here are the difficult normative decisions that statesmen must sometimes make when they engage in foreign affairs.

RESPONSIBILITY IN INTERNATIONAL RELATIONS

The Wight–Bull approach leads to the analysis of moral choice in foreign policy, which is that part of the political theory of international society that still requires a good deal of work. One can discern at least three distinctive conceptions of responsibility which correspond to Wight's three traditions noted above: devotion to one's own nation and the well-being of its citizens; respect for the legitimate interests and rights of other states and for international law; and respect for human rights and for common morality. Of course, one could add the demand for distributive justice and the global environmental ethic and perhaps other normative considerations as well, but I will confine myself to these three.

National responsibility

According to this conception, the only fundamental standard of conduct that statesmen must adhere to in their foreign policies is that of national self-interest and specifically national security – the latter being the foundational value that statesmen are duty-bound to protect. This normative benchmark for evaluating foreign policies gives rise to Machiavellian precepts such as: always put your nation and its citizens first; avoid taking unnecessary risks with their welfare; collaborate with other countries when it is advantageous or necessary but avoid needless foreign entanglements; do not subject your population to war unless it is absolutely necessary; avoid putting your own soldiers in harm's way if it is not absolutely necessary; ensure they are well trained and well equipped before they are sent into combat; and so forth. These normative considerations obviously are characteristic of a world of separate states in which statesmen's responsibilities are determined exclusively by the national interest and by obligations to the citizens of their own country.

These *dicta* are not an international ethic, strictly speaking, because there is no external obligation; there is only foreign interest, concern or entanglement. What is the normative basis for claiming that statesmen are responsible only for their own country? The answer can be derived from a familiar theory of political obligation: the state – whether it is formed by a social contract, by historical evolution, by conquest or by any other method – is a self-contained political community that is prior to any international associations it may subsequently join. International law and international organization are merely instrumental relations. Human beings have positive rights – civil and political – only by virtue of being citizens of states: statesmen are responsible for defending their own citizens but not the citizenries of other states.

International responsibility

According to this conception, statesmen have external obligations that derive from their state's membership of international society, which brings with it not only benefits but also rights and duties as defined by customary international law, by the UN Charter, and by any other international agreements states enter into. This normative benchmark for evaluating foreign policies gives rise to Grotian precepts such as: be a good citizen of international society; recognize that other states have equal rights with your own and legitimate interests which deserve respect even if they may conflict with the interests of your own state; act in good faith; observe international law; punish aggressors; observe the laws of war; be magnanimous in victory; and so forth. These normative considerations are characteristic of a society of states in which responsibility is determined by international law and by underlying norms of amity, reciprocity and dialogue between states.

This criterion of responsible statecraft is a bona fide international ethic that stems from the fact that states are members of international society, from which they derive important rights and benefits. What is the normative basis for believing that statesmen have a separate responsibility to international society and its members? The usual answer comes from a theory of political obligation: states have foreign obligations to other states and to international society as a whole owing to their membership in that society, which can be conceived as based on a covenant between states. That covenant and the external obligations defined by it are independent of national covenants between sovereigns and citizens and thus independent of the domestic obligations of statesmen. There are human rights but they are established by the international agreements of sovereign states and thus being a good international citizen neccesarily involves respecting human rights.

Humanitarian responsibility

According to this conception, statesmen first and foremost are human beings and as such they have a fundamental obligation not only to respect but also to defend human rights around the world. This normative benchmark for evaluating foreign policies gives rise to Kantian precepts such as: always remember that people in other countries are human beings just like yourself; observe common morality; respect human rights; assist those who are in need of material aid which you can supply at no sacrifice to yourself; in waging war spare non-combatants; and so forth. These normative considerations are characteristic of a world society in which responsibility is defined by one's membership in the human race and thus by common morality.

This cosmopolitan criterion of responsible statecraft goes well beyond international responsibility. It derives not only from the fact that statesmen are human beings themselves but also from the fact that they are in a better position than anyone else to help or hinder their fellow humans in other countries. What is the normative basis for believing that statesmen are responsible for human rights around the world? The usual answer derives from a theory of political obligation: before one can be a statesman or a citizen of a state one is a human being. This naturally entails fundamental human obligations that everyone must observe. The traditional way of expressing one's obligations as a human being is by claiming that there is a natural law, a universal law of reason and of conscience, and natural rights which statesmen no less than anyone else are duty bound to respect.

If these foregoing criteria and the precepts they give rise to are operative norms and not merely academic speculations it becomes clear that we should expect normative dilemmas and conflicts to be a feature of contemporary international relations. Any normative analysis of international relations must consider all three of these dimensions of responsibility and any others which may be operative: to consider only one or two of them is to carry out at best a part analysis and at worst a biased account which would underestimate the normative complexity of international relations and consequently the actual difficulty of making normatively defensible choices in foreign policy. No criterion can predictably trump all other considerations in all circumstances. There is an underlying normative pluralism which statesmen cannot escape from, which scholars should not ignore, and which perhaps is what Martin Wight is referring to when he said he encountered all three perspectives when he canvassed his own mind on such questions.

CONTEMPORARY INTERNATIONAL SOCIETY: THREE EPISODES

One way to test the foregoing conceptions of responsible statecraft is to see whether they help to shed light on international society at the end of the twentieth century. For example, would they be useful for understanding the conflicts in the Persian Gulf, the horn of Africa and the Balkan peninsula which preoccupied statesmen in the early 1990s? I cannot go into the details of these episodes, the second and third of which were still unfolding at the time of writing. I can only make a few brief passing remarks on some of their implications for the international society approach.

Iraq–Kuwait

Many people would probably say that the West's vital interest in an interrupted supply of Middle East oil or, in other words, national security was uppermost in the minds of President George Bush and other Western leaders when in January 1991 they embarked upon a course of war to evict Saddam Hussein's armed forces from Kuwait. But is that an adequate account of their responsibilities in the matter? The nearly universal condemnation of Iraq's invasion and occupation of Kuwait indicates that most statesmen nowadays expect their fellow statesmen to respect the UN Charter and not to threaten international peace and security. In other words, the norm of international responsibility was applied to Iraq's conduct in this episode, which was generally construed as an act of aggression and thus a violation of the Charter.

Another aspect of this case deserves comment: the international military intervention in northern Iraq in the immediate aftermath of the Gulf War to establish 'safe havens' to protect the Kurdish minority from the Iraqi army. 'No-fly zones' were also created in both northern and southern Iraq. These actions authorized by the UN Security Council could be construed as a strengthening of humanitarian responsibility in contemporary international relations. But a fundamental feature of this episode cannot escape notice: it is the sort of action one would expect in the aftermath of a war in which the victors – in this case the UN Security Council and the 'coalition' states acting on its behalf – could claim military rights to intervene in the territory of the defeated state. The 'coalition' intervened elsewhere in Iraq for military purposes. Iraq was deemed to be an aggressor and in losing the Gulf War it could be considered to have relinquished (at least for the time being) its right to control all its territory. This interpretation makes the intervention in northern Iraq less exceptional and perhaps not fundamentally different from humanitarian actions by the allied powers in Germany at the end of the Second World War. On the other hand, it was followed by Security Council steps to create 'safe havens' in Bosnia-Herzegovina and may in this respect turn out to be an important precedent rather than a one-off action.

Somalia

In 1991–2 the state of Somalia ceased to exist in any empirical sense and whatever political control that did exist in that east African country fell into the hands of warlords of the rival clans into which the population was divided. The country was also in the grip of a severe drought, thousands of Somalis were starving to death, and thousands more were suffering from starvation or malnutrition and would perhaps also die if the anarchy and violence of clan warfare continued to interrupt the distribution of food imported by voluntary aid organizations. In late 1992 the Security Council sanctioned an international military intervention in Somalia to distribute food to the starving. The US provided the bulk of the armed forces and other Western and non-Western countries contributed small military contingents. The intervention made it possible to deliver food and thus bring an end to starvation in most parts of the country. In the spring of 1933 the UN took military action against one of the clan warlords whose forces had attacked and killed UN troops. In this UN action some civilian Somalis were killed or wounded and questions were raised about the UN's mandate and particularly whether it extended to the business of getting directly involved in the civil war. But by that time Somalia was already more or less under UN authority with no sign that the Somali state would be back together very soon.

Commentators took notice of the fact that Somalia had become a UN protectorate in everything but name. Thus, not only did the international community intervene militarily in Somalia but the UN effectively took over the responsibility of governing the country until such time as a new Somali state could be built to take the place of the one that had been destroyed by the clan warlords. This internationalization of the Somali state is reminiscent of an earlier colonial era of League mandates and UN trusteeships. The case discloses a strong element of international paternalism which perhaps marks a departure from the post-colonial era in which the rule of non-intervention was an absolute international prohibition. There were no national security reasons for intervening in Somalia: no oil or other security concerns comparable to those in the Iraq–Kuwait case. The overriding concern was humanitarian.

Bosnia-Herzegovina

Perhaps the most perplexing post-Cold War conflict to date is that in the former Yugoslav republic of Bosnia-Herzegovina. The Security Council, the European Community and major outside powers have been reluctant to intervene militarily beyond a more intrusive version of peacekeeping. The wars in Bosnia-Herzegovina took place within what recently had been the state of Yugoslavia. Some of the international uncertainty and hesitation regarding direct military intervention in Bosnia-Herzegovina stemmed from a widespread perception of the conflicts as popular wars of ethnic self-determination by the rival Muslim, Serb and Croat communities into which the population was divided. At one point the main argument against intervention was the claim that it was essentially a civil war. On the other hand, Bosnia-Herzegovina became a sovereign state as a direct result of recognition by member states of the European Community and the United Nations, which thereby bear a crucial responsibility for its independence. Furthermore, the international community had already intervened massively by imposing an arms embargo which put the government at an enormous military disadvantage since the Serbian and Croatian minorities were supplied with arms by their kindred states. Many observers claimed that this made it possible for the Serbian and the Croatian militias to conquer most of the country and set in motion its eventual partition. The UN and the EC tried to prevent this from happening by sponsoring a plan to give local autonomy to ten separate regions of the country without partitioning it. But this plan came to nothing.

The protracted and tortured international debate concerning the 1992–3 wars in Bosnia-Herzegovina indicates that contemporary statesmen are concerned about human rights but are reluctant to become involved militarily if there is no evidence of a clear national interest to intervene with armed force or of a clear breach of international peace and security and if there is also a high risk of harm to their own troops and a low prospect of success. The length, intensity and circuitous course of that debate did not indicate any lack of humanitarian concern. What it indicated was the absence of confidence among most statesmen that military intervention in Bosnia-Herzegovina would be successful; on the contrary, many feared that it would actually make the problem worse than it was. Concern about the chances of success is a well-founded moral consideration. Thus in certain circumstances caution will have to override compassion in international relations. But this is fundamentally a question of judgement, with compelling normative considerations on both sides, as indicated by the comment of US Senator Daniel Patrick Moynihan in an interview on television: 'the world that watched has committed a grave sin'.

What do these three episodes tell us about international norms and the ethics of statecraft today? Arguably the Iraq–Kuwait case illustrates the following normative reasoning about international armed intervention: if there is a clear national and international responsibility to intervene on the part of powers which are in a position to do so, such intervention is justified. Suppose military intervention is justified on such grounds: that would mean that statesmen would have a right to intervene. But they would still bear the heavy responsibility of deciding whether or not they ought to intervene. Such a decision could not (and should not) avoid the question of prudence: would it be wise to embark on war to evict Iraq from Kuwait even if it could be justified on those grounds? The first duty of a government is to protect its own people. After that it can try to help whomever else it can. Evidently in this case it was decided that the threat to world oil supplies was sufficiently great, there was a clear violation of international law by Iraq, the risk of harm to their own troops was sufficiently low, and the chances of success were sufficiently high for the US and other UN military powers to justify taking that military action. Events proved the soundness of this judgement but the decision-makers did not know that at the time.

What does this same normative reasoning suggest about the cases of Somalia and Bosnia-Herzegovina? Common morality and international humanitarian law tell us that if possible something should be done to stop human suffering on a mass scale wherever and whenever it occurs. Evidently in the Somali case it was decided that the risk of harm to their own troops was sufficiently low for the US and other UN military powers to justify intervening on humanitarian grounds. Events up to spring 1993 proved the soundness of this judgement although again the decision-makers did not know that at the time they decided to intervene. Evidently in the case of Bosnia-Herzegovina it was difficult for most statesmen to avoid the conclusion that the risk of harm to their own troops was too high and the chances of success were too low to justify intervening even though there were more than sufficient humanitarian grounds for doing so. Events up to spring 1993 proved very little: it was impossible to know whether more lives were lost or saved, and whether more or less suffering was caused by the policy followed to that point. These two cases suggest that norms of humanitarian intervention are operative in contemporary international society, but only in certain circumstances: those circumstances are usually defined in prudential terms as presenting low military risk and a good or at least a reasonable chance of success.

The Bosnia-Herzegovina case illustrates the deeply troubling moral choices confronted by statesmen in a world divided into independent states in which their foremost responsibility is to ensure the well-being of their own country and its citizens but at the same time a world that is beginning to move beyond strict sovereignty in international relations. In other words, it is becoming a world in which statesmen have international and humanitarian responsibilities as well as national responsibilities. Political virtue in such circumstances involves the willingness not only to recognize that these diverging responsibilities exist but also to make decisions in which due regard is paid to all of them. But any decision would have to pay final respects to national responsibility. Here is the operational dilemma confronting a responsible statesman in an international community which recognizes a right of humanitarian intervention in appropriate circumstances but does not (and could not) make it a duty.

Thus, in all these cases the 'bottom line' is national responsibility. This could be interpreted as meaning that the other two normative considerations are merely disguises and the real norm which drives international relations is national interest and national security: power politics. That is the classical realist view. An alternative view associated with the international society theorists is the following: statesmen have international and humanitarian responsibilities which they should endeavour to respect whenever and wherever they have an opportunity to do so without sacrificing their national responsibilities. If national responsibility was all that mattered in international relations the Somalia and the Bosnia-Herzegovina problems would be left to the people who live in those countries to sort out themselves. In brief: to construe these three episodes in the correct light it is necessary to adopt an approach which takes account of all dimensions of responsible statecraft. Realism is necessary but it is not sufficient to account for the normative complexity of international relations today. Rationalism and revolutionism are also required.

To sum up: because international relations is subject to diverging and even conflicting moral and legal considerations, what the most responsible choice would be in any particular case is not something that can be determined in principle or in advance. There are no moral philosophies that we can bring to bear in the confident expectation of arriving at a clear decision one way or the other. Any normative political theory of international relations must be open to the real likelihood and indeed near certainty of moral dilemmas, which means that it must be pluralistic in its orientation.

SITUATIONAL ETHICS

All normative political theories rest ultimately on a conception of ethics. The political theory of international society is no exception but its ethical foundations are only implicit in the writings of Martin Wight and Hedley Bull. However, Arnold Wolfers (1965) and Stanley Hoffmann (1981) have written explicitly on the subject. Their work provides a springboard into the applied ethics of statecraft which lies beneath the foregoing analysis.

The applied ethics of statecraft is an awkward subject. Scholars can second-guess the normative choices of statesmen at the time or judge their decision after the event knowing how it turned out. But that is not the same as having to make the choice themselves. Probably the best the scholar can do is try to grasp the roles and the situations of the people involved: to imagine what it must be like to be in the circumstances of a president or a prime minister at the time that decisions are confronted and taken. In other words, if we hope to understand normative choices in international relations we must try to put ourselves in the shoes of the actors before making any pronouncements about their conduct. In doing this scholars are doing justice to the people they are studying. That might be a preliminary definition of the ethics of scholarship. About the last thing scholars should do is look down upon statesmen from some Olympian heights of abstract political and moral philosophy. I agree with Stanley Hoffmann (1981, p. 189) that the study of international ethics is an 'applied ethics' which 'is not the province of the ethical philosopher' but, rather, that of the international relations scholar who takes an interest in normative questions.

Statesmen almost by definition are people who have to make tough choices which they cannot pass on to someone else; the responsibility goes with the territory. This circumstance sets them apart from private citizens, who may very well face difficult choices but whatever they decide it cannot affect the well-being of anything like the same number of people: there is an important distinction between public and private responsibility. One is here reminded of De Gaulle's definition of a statesman 'as somebody who takes risks, including moral risks' (Hoffmann, 1981, p. 18). Presidents and prime ministers – as a condition of their offices – hold the well-being and sometimes, for example during war, even the lives of many other people in their hands. In making foreign policy choices they can consult whomever they wish. But in the final analysis they are still the ones who must decide. One is here reminded of a well-known slogan that was prominently displayed on President Truman's desk in the Oval Office of the White House: 'the buck stops here'. And if a decision is taken they must then act never knowing what the ultimate consequences of those actions will be. Perhaps the most extreme example in international history is Truman's decision to drop atomic bombs on Hiroshima and Nagasaki in August 1945.

Since the decisions and actions of statesmen are always made in concrete circumstances of time and of place, scholars who seek to understand them are obliged to adopt some version of situational ethics. One international relations theorist who consistently tries to do exactly that is Arnold Wolfers (1965, p. 51), who identifies 'the best moral choice that circumstances permit' as the ethics of statesmen: 'nonperfectionist ethics'. This conception is a good starting point for studying normative choices in international relations but it leaves out a crucial element: the actors and their conduct. For once we bring circumstances into the picture we must also bring the actors and their conduct equally into that picture. What can we reasonably expect of statesmen and other international actors in the circumstances of foreign affairs in which they find themselves? We can answer this question only if we have some realistic and reasonable way of judging their conduct.

I am convinced that the best way of appraising the conduct of statesmen in the demanding circumstances in which they find themselves is by returning to the classical idea of the virtues, and specifically civic or political virtue. By the 'virtues' I refer to the dispositions and disciplines that are required to make the best choice that circumstances permit, or the least bad choice if all choices are harmful to a certain degree. The latter is not uncommon in international relations, particularly during war. Thus, when we judge human conduct by reference to the virtues we are not judging it by reference to a rule or to a consequence. Instead, we are judging it in relation to what we could reasonably expect of a person of sound mind and good character in such circumstances. To act virtuously in the circumstances is to stick to one's post and discharge one's duty despite the difficulties involved and the temptations to do otherwise. Thus, we expect responsible statesmen to base their policies on correct information and to conduct them with due care and attention to the situation at hand. That is what statesmanship involves. In other words, we could justifiably condemn a statesman for failing to be informed and for failing to be prudent.

Because statesmen hold the welfare of so many others in their hands and at the same time have at their disposal greater destructive power and corresponding responsibility than anyone else, a necessary political virtue is undoubtedly prudence, which has been called 'the centre of gravity' around which the entire scheme turns (Beiner, 1992, p. 153). Thus recklessness and miscalculation are among the greatest political vices. One could readily identify other political virtues: loyalty, good faith, resolve, courage, compassion, even-handedness and, above all, justice. The importance of any one of these virtues would depend in part on the situation being confronted by the actor. Churchill (1953, p. vii) identified the following: 'In war: resolution; in defeat: defiance; in victory: magnanimity; in peace: goodwill.' The point here is not to enumerate the political virtues but merely to emphasize that when we begin to view international relations from the angle of situational ethics we are led by this kind of analysis to adopt an approach which emphasizes the virtues. Because the virtues oblige us to look directly at the conduct of actors in their situations I believe that this approach to the applied ethics of statecraft is more pertinent and realistic than any other.

CONCLUSION

Hedley Bull (1969, p. 20) once defended the 'classical approach' to theorizing which derives from 'philosophy, history and law' and 'is characterized above all by explicit reliance upon the exercise of judgement'. That pretty well sums up the political theory of international society. The political theorist who seeks to understand the statesman and reflect intelligently on his or her distinctive moral predicament must become schooled in the exercise of judgement. This scholarly faculty is more likely to be honed by reading history and looking at contemporary events with an eye for the difficult moral choices they present to those involved than by mastering abstract political and moral philosophy. We arrive at what I am tempted to say is the fundamental problem of political theory which goes right back to its beginnings: what moral qualities should a statesman possess? This ancient question is at the heart of international political theory. The question obviously cannot be answered to everyone's satisfaction. But the question is more important than the answer, for it recognizes a fundamental truth: that those who wield power which affects the lives of many other people bear heavy responsibilities – perhaps the heaviest that any human beings can bear.

Note

I am grateful to Terry Kersch, Nicholas Wheeler and the editors for helpful comments on an earlier draft of this chapter. I also wish to acknowledge the financial support of the Social Sciences and Humanities Research Council of Canada.

References

Beiner, R. 1992: The moral vocabulary of liberalism. In J. W. Chapman and W. A. Galston (eds), *Virtue: Nomos XXXIV*, New York and London: New York University Press, 145–84.

Bull, H. 1969: International theory: the case for a classical approach. In K. Knorr and J. N. Rosenau (eds), *Contending Approaches to International Politics*, Princeton, N.J.: Princeton University Press, 20–38.

Bull, H. 1977a: *The Anarchical Society: A Study of Order in World Politics*. London: Macmillan.

Bull, H. 1977b: Introduction: Martin Wight and the study of international relations. In Wight (1977), 1–20.

Bull, H. 1984: *Justice in International Relations* (The Hagey Lectures). Waterloo, Ontario: University of Waterloo Press.

Bull, H. and Watson, A. 1984: *The Expansion of International Society*. Oxford: Oxford University Press.

Churchill, Winston S. 1953: *The Second World War: Triumph and Tragedy*. Boston: Houghton Mifflin.

Hoffmann, S. 1981: *Duties Beyond Borders*. Syracuse, N.Y.: Syracuse University Press.

Oakeshott, M. 1983: The rule of law. In M. Oakeshott, *On History and Other Essays*, Oxford: Blackwell, 119–64.

Waltz, K. N. 1979: *Theory of International Politics*, Reading, Mass.: Addison-Wesley.

Wight, M. 1977: *Systems of States* (H. Bull ed.), Leicester: Leicester University Press.

Wight, M. 1987: An anatomy of international thought. *Review of International Studies*, 13, 221–7.

Wight, M. 1991: *International Theory: The Three Traditions* (G. Wight and B. Porter eds), Leicester: Leicester University Press.

Wolfers, A. 1965: *Discord and Collaboration*. Baltimore: The Johns Hopkins University Press.

6

International Political Theory and the Global Environment

Andrew Hurrell

This book is concerned with the proper scope of international political theory, with the identification of the major issues which contemporary international political theory needs to address, and with the ways in which the complexities of world politics can best be conceptualized. The fragility of international society and the propensity of international relations to frustrate hopes for progress make it important to adopt a broad definition of the scope and purpose of political theory and to insist at the outset that normative conceptions of how we should tackle the environment challenges facing us be firmly anchored in a realistic appreciation of the possibilities of effective political action. As John Dunn puts it:

> The purpose of political theory is to diagnose practical predicaments and to show us how best to confront them. To do this it needs to train us in three relatively distinct skills: firstly in ascertaining how the social, political and economic setting of our lives now is and in understanding why it is as it is; secondly in working through for ourselves how we could coherently and justifiably wish that world to be or become; and thirdly in judging how far, and through what actions, and at what risk, we can realistically hope to move this world as it now stands towards the way we might excusably wish it to. (1990, p. 193)

WHY THE ENVIRONMENT IS AN ISSUE

Why should we be led to consider environmental problems and the prospect of global environmental change at all? Part of the answer rests on our growing awareness of the material limits to the kinds of progress and development around which Western political theory has traditionally been constructed, and on the real possibility that our dominant forms of political organization may be inadequate to manage the relationship between humankind and the natural environment on a lasting and sustainable basis. The international political salience of environmental issues has increased enormously over the last two decades. This has been the result of accelerating rates of environmental degradation, improved scientific knowledge and heightened popular awareness of the seriousness of the ecological challenges facing humanity. Whilst much of the picture remains obscure and whilst the claim that we are already 'beyond the limits' is much contested, there is growing evidence that human social and economic activity is placing excessive strains on the physical limits of the ecosphere and that, in a crude but real sense, we are filling up the ecological space available to us (Daly and Cobb, 1990; Meadows, Meadows, and Randers, 1992). This, it should be noted, means that a political theory of the environment is concerned not simply with the ideas of the 'good life', but also with the means to ensure human survival best, thereby overcoming what has often been taken to be one of the critical distinctions between domestic and international political theory (Wight, 1966).

A further part of the answer concerns the inherently transborder, and increasingly global, character of contemporary environment issues, and it is this which takes us directly into the realms of international political theory. There are three senses in which the environment has become a global issue. First, and most obviously, humanity is now faced by a range of environmental problems that are global in the strong sense that they affect everyone and can be effectively managed only on the basis of co-operation between all, or at least a very high percentage, of the states of the world: controlling climate change and the emission of greenhouse gases, the protection of the ozone layer, safeguarding biodiversity, protecting special regions such as Antarctica or the Amazon, the management of the sea-bed and the protection of the high seas are among the principal examples.

Second, the scale of many originally regional or local environmental problems, such as extensive urban degradation, deforestation, desertification, salination, denudation, or water or fuel-wood scarcity, now threatens broader international repercussions: by undermining the economic base and social fabric of weak and poor states, by generating or exacerbating intra- or inter-state tensions and conflicts, and by stimulating increased flows of refugees. Moreover, although many such problems are 'localized' in that their *effects* are felt locally, their causes often lie far beyond national borders, as local ecosystems are tied into transnational structures of production and exchange.

This leads to the third, and in many ways most important, aspect of globalization, which derives from the complex but close relationship between the generation of environmental problems and the workings of the now effectively globalized world economy. On the one hand, there is the range of environmental problems caused by the affluence of the industrialized countries; by the extent to which this affluence has been built upon high and unsustainable levels of energy consumption and natural resource depletion; and by the 'ecological shadow' cast by these economies across the economic system. On the other, there is the widely recognized linkage between poverty, population pressure and environmental degradation, a linkage which was given prominence by the Brundtland Commission in 1987 and which emerged as the central theme of the Earth Summit in Brazil in June 1992 (World Commission on Environment and Development, 1987). Sustainable development is an inherently global issue both because of the high levels of economic interdependence that exist within many parts of the world economy and because it raises fundamental questions concerning the distribution of wealth, power and resources between North and South.

Perhaps the most important shift to have taken place in the twenty years that separate the UN Conference on the Human Environment held in Stockholm in 1972 from the UN Conference on Environment and Development (the Earth Summit) held in Rio de Janeiro in 1992 concerns the emergence of a paradigm of global environmental change and a sense of global crisis. Dominant understandings of the most pressing environmental problems have moved from the discussions of the 1970s about the impact of localized pollution and the limits to natural resources (the predictions of the Club of Rome, the emergence of the idea of 'limits to growth', the shock of the OPEC price increases, etc.) to an increased emphasis on the notion of 'global environmental change' and on the limited capacity of the planet to absorb the wastes produced by economic activity: in shorthand, a shift from 'resource limits' to 'sink limits'. Of course definitions of 'global' are politically constructed and hence politically contested. How many millions of people have to be affected by water scarcity before it qualifies as a global problem? Moreover, to talk of the environment as a global issue is certainly not to imply that all environmental problems have global repercussions, still less to argue that all problems need to be managed on a global basis. Rather, it is to argue that the material foundations of international political theory are necessarily limited by the carrying capacity of the earth as a whole and that the ways in which politics is organized globally have become a critical factor influencing the long-term sustainability of the relationship between human beings and the natural world.

Above all, the emergence of a new and unprecedented set of environmental challenges has highlighted the disjuncture between a single integrated, enormously complex and deeply interdependent ecosystem and the still dominant form of global political organization: a fragmented system of sovereign states, normatively built around the mutual recognition of sovereignty, and politically forming an anarchical system in which co-operation has historically been limited and in which war and conflict are deeply rooted, and for many an inherent feature.

How has international relations theory responded to the issues raised by the problems of global environmental change? What sorts of questions does it ask? What kinds of answers might it provide? Very broadly, two clusters of theories can be identified.

INTERNATIONAL POLITICAL THEORY AND THE ENVIRONMENT: THE TRADITIONAL AGENDA

The first cluster of theoretical approaches stays close to the 'traditional' concerns of international relations theory: the belief that states remain the primary actors in world politics; that international relations constitutes a largely autonomous sphere of political action; and that the central focus of enquiry should be on the power and interests of states competing in an anarchical international political system and on the identification and explanation of patterns of conflict and co-operation between states.

From this perspective, the emergence of environmental issues raises a number of pressing, but essentially familiar, questions, of which three are especially important. First, in what ways do environmental issues affect the distribution of power and give rise to new patterns of alignment and antagonism? To what extent, for example, have environmental concerns rekindled a structural conflict between rich and poor states, between North and South? Second, to what extent do environmental issues threaten new sources of violent conflict between states? And third, how do the institutions of international society and existing mechanisms for inter-state co-operation facilitate (or hinder) the identification and management of environment problems?

It is with this last question that international relations theory has been most centrally preoccupied. Feeding directly into the debates of the 1980s between neo-realists and neo-liberal institutionalists, much work has been done on inter-state environmental co-operation, on the politics of regime formation, and on the theories that best explain how and why such co-operation is possible. (For samples of a voluminous literature see Young, 1989; Hurrell and Kingsbury, 1992; and Haas, Keohane and Levy, 1993). Within the somewhat narrow confines of political science (and particularly US political science) the dominant focus has been on the role of 'international regimes' in managing conflicts and in solving collective action problems. More generally, however, the study of inter-state environmental co-operation has also encompassed a large amount of work within international law – at the level of academic analysis but also, very importantly, involving diplomatic practice. (See, for example, Kiss and Shelton, 1991; Birnie and Boyle, 1993.)

This work has provided an invaluable framework for analysing the politics of regime formation and isolating the most important variables that affect that process. Yet, as the discussions of the Earth Summit illustrate all too clearly, there is little consensus on how the growing number of international environmental agreements, negotiations and institutions should be understood or evaluated. Liberals remain inclined to believe that the reality of ecological interdependence will create problems that can be solved only by new and more far-reaching mechanisms of co-operation. Radical environmental degradation of the planet will involve losses for all and, more so than in the case of economic interdependence, states are locked into a situation from which they cannot escape and about which they will be forced to co-operate. Moreover, for the liberal, increased scientific understanding of environmental problems will work to redirect state interests and to facilitate international co-operation. On this optimistic view, we are already witnessing the emergence of a complex structure of global environmental governance with new sets of institutions and an array of new legal concepts. Indeed, for the optimists, the effectiveness of many environmental regimes does not derive solely from their individual strengths but, rather, from the extent to which they tie states into a continuing and institutionalized process of negotiation: hence the importance of provisions for regular meetings and for the generation and dissemination of information; hence the view of regimes as frameworks around which political pressure on states can be effectively mobilized. Building on these ideas, positive interpretations of the 1992 Earth Summit highlight the importance of the institutions that were created (most importantly the Commission for Sustainable Development (CSD) and an enhanced role for the Global Environmental Facility (GEF)) and the fact that the framework conventions on biodiversity and global climate change establish institutionalized procedures for further negotiation. (For an assessment of the Earth Summit, see Grubb *et al.*, 1993.)

Sceptics, on the other hand (who include both realists and many environmentalists), continue to highlight the many obstacles to co-operation: the weakness of most international institutions and the absence of sanctioning power; the unprecedentedly high levels of co-operation and policy co-ordination required to deal with many of the most pressing environmental issues; the pressures on states and state representatives to place a high priority on their immediate short-term interests and on the protection of political autonomy; the mismatch between the time horizons of politicians and political processes on the one hand and the extended time frames needed to address and deal with many of the most serious environmental problems on the other; the fact that there is no easy link between increased scientific knowledge and the growth of international co-operation; the extent to which the loose rhetoric of 'interdependence' disguises a wide variety of problems whose specific dependence structures may sometimes work to promote co-operation (as in the case of ozone) but may also militate against it (as in the case of global climate change); and, finally, the extent to which these difficulties have to be set against the large number of deep-rooted historical conflicts that exist between states and the cultural, political and economic heterogeneity of the international system.

These traditional questions are, and will remain, fundamental to the international politics of the environment, and hence to international political theory. For better or worse, environmental issues have to be managed within the constraints of a global political system in which states continue to play a major (although by no means unchallenged) role. Moreover, the issue of how the biosphere can be protected within a fragmented and historically relatively unco-ordinated political order brings the traditional and distinctive concerns of international relations very much to centre-stage. International relations has often been viewed as on the margin of the core concerns of political theory – either because political theory was concerned essentially with ideas of furthering the good life within the state (the dominant attitude of Western political theory), or because the conditions of anarchy that existed between states were deemed tolerable and posed no particular challenge (the position of Hobbes and Pufendorf), or because international life was viewed as not amenable to change and improvement (the position of both realists and despairing liberals such as Rousseau). In considering the problems of the global environment, however, 'political theory in one country' is no longer an intellectually adequate option. Having moved centre-stage, it is very important that international political theory does not lose or forget the distinctive insights of its past.

At the same time, it is difficult to see how international political theory can make much sense of our environmental dilemmas if it remains confined to its traditional domain and to its traditional discourse. The traditional agenda, as sketched out above, is too narrow in its conceptualization of the processes by which environmental problems are generated, in its appreciation of the political forces that impact on environmental issues, and in its treatment of the normative dimension.

INTERNATIONAL POLITICAL THEORY AND THE ENVIRONMENT: TOWARDS A NEW AGENDA?

A second cluster of writings has therefore tended to view the problems associated with global environmental change from a broader, and often more radical, perspective and to identify a number of developments that challenge the adequacy of traditional ways of thinking about international political theory. Indeed, of all contemporary claims that traditional conceptualizations of world politics need recasting, those relating to the impact of global environmental change are perhaps the most resonant and the most intuitively plausible.

The most important thread running through these diverse arguments is their questioning of the empirical and normative basis of state sovereignty – the central, if all too easily unexamined, concept around which international relations as a discipline has traditionally been organized. Ecological challenges force us to reopen questions about the nature and limits of state sovereignty. Claims to sovereignty are being called into question by the limited capabilities of states to deal with environmental threats (both locally and globally), by the mobilization of new social actors around environmental issues, by the loss of state control of the workings of the global economy, and by the increasingly dense set of international institutional arrangements designed to manage environmental problems. Moreover, for some writers, growing awareness of environmental problems and of environmental interdependence has created a new sense of planetary consciousness which is leading to new forms of non-territorially based political identity and to new mechanisms of political organization and action. The remainder of this chapter will examine five sets of arguments about the ways in which international political theory might need to be broadened, recast or transformed in order to understand global environmental problems and the ways in which these can, or should be, tackled.

The Erosion of Sovereignty from Above

The first set of arguments builds directly on the traditional agenda but claims that the creation of a dense and wide-ranging juridical and institutional structure of environmental agreements in itself represents a fundamental challenge to sovereignty and to our understandings of the dynamics of world politics. On this quintessentially liberal view, the global environmental challenge and the consequent process of 'institutional enmeshment' are leading to a 'fading away of anarchy' at the inter-state level and to a 'denationalizing' or 'internationalizing' of the state.

> Basically, it is no longer accurate to conceptualize states as having their traditional degree of autonomy because of the network of formal and informal regimes in which they are becoming increas-

> ingly involved, and this process of enmeshment is likely to progress (albeit in fits and starts) throughout the coming century. (Zacher, 1992, p. 60)

On this view power is shifting to institutions above the level of the state, driven by the need to solve common problems in an increasingly interdependent world. As a result we are seeing a fundamental shift in the balance of rights and duties between the particularist claims of nominally sovereign states on one hand, and the authority of international society on the other. Regimes and international institutions are coming to form new centres of authority that challenge the authority of national governments (Schachter, 1991; Held and McGrew, 1993). Increased levels of institutionalization are therefore placing growing constraints, practical and normative, on the sovereignty of states. States are constrained by an ever denser set of international principles, rules, norms and institutions, and by fact that, in an interdependent world, even the 'powerful' rely on co-operative arrangements that restrict their power and give influence to others.

Yet, whatever its weaknesses in providing a full account of inter-state environmental politics, realism provides powerful grounds for questioning the extent to which these processes have thus far eroded or undermined state sovereignty. It is certainly true that the number of environmental agreements has increased very significantly. It is also true that attitudes to sovereignty, particularly in the developing world, have shifted very substantially since the Stockholm Conference in 1972. Developing countries such as India or Brazil have moved away from the rigid dichotomy between environment and development visible at Stockholm. They have come to lay greater weight on the importance of protecting the environment and on moving towards more sustainable patterns of economic development. There is, then, increasing consensus on the ways in which environmental protection can reinforce economic development. There is also increased awareness of the threats posed to the South by unchecked environmental degradation. Indeed, the persistent poverty in many parts of the developing world means that the South is less able to afford to put right reversible damage to the environment and also less able to manage the process of adaptation to whatever global environmental changes do occur. In addition, the South has come to accept that environmental degradation within states is a matter of legitimate interest to the outside world, being both of 'international concern' (suggesting that it is legitimate for other states to become involved), and of 'common concern to humankind'.

Yet the concern for sovereignty remains a fundamental factor in global environmental politics in both North and South and the political acceptance of the erosion of sovereignty is less apparent than legal declarations would tend to suggest. This is well illustrated by the impasse at the Earth Summit on those critical issues that threatened to bite really deeply into the sovereign prerogatives of governments: the near absolute refusal of the North to accept that sustainability might require a change in its consumption patterns and resource use; or the bitter resistance of developing states to the negotiation of a convention on the protection of forests.

The idea that we may be witnessing a fading away of anarchy is also called into question by the continued obstacles to international environmental co-operation noted earlier and by the limited scope of most existing environmental agreements. The number of agreements may well be large but sanctions for compliance are weak. There is a marked preference for non-binding targets/guidelines which states are free to implement at whatever pace they see fit rather than the acceptance of firm and unambiguous obligations. Indeed, the agreements negotiated at Rio on global climate change and biological diversity are peppered with caveats, ambiguities and qualifications. No existing environmental treaty contains inescapable requirements that states resort to binding third-party procedures for settlement of disputes. States remain extremely keen to maintain firm control over reporting, monitoring and inspection procedures. And although much is made of the increased willingness of states to co-operate with non-governmental organizations (NGOs), it is interesting to note that the newly created Commission on Sustainable Development has an exclusively inter-governmental membership (partly balanced by its mandate to enhance co-operation with NGOs, and by the creation of a high-level advisory board which will include experts drawn from the NGO community).

Finally, claims about the 'internationalization' of the state are misleading in that they underplay the extent to which global problems and global processes can often work to reinforce the centrality of the state. Thus, the proliferation of environmental regimes can be seen as evidence of the way in which state authority is being extended and reasserted in the face of new challenges and of how states are willing to trade a degree of legal freedom of action on a particular issue in return for a greater degree of practical influence over the policies of other states and over the management of common problems.

To argue in this way is certainly not to claim that nothing has changed or that realism is capable of providing an adequate account of the historically remarkable degree of international environment co-operation. There has indeed been a most important shift in emphasis away from the individual rights of states and towards an acceptance of common duties. We have seen a very important change in the character and goals of international society: away from minimalist goals of co-existence towards the creation of rules and institutions that embody notions of shared responsibilities, that impinge heavily on the domestic organization of states, that invest individuals and groups within states with rights and duties, and that seek to embody some notion of the planetary good. Yet the still evident limits to these changes (certainly within the area of environmental issues) undermine arguments that increased institutionalization and enmeshment should force us to recast completely traditional accounts of the nature of international political theory. Indeed many of the arguments that we are moving 'beyond Westphalia' overlook the extent to which sovereignty was always a socially constructed right: not something that could be claimed solely on the basis of power, but a quality grounded in a common and evolving set of understandings between a group of states.

Eroding the distinction between the 'domestic' and the 'international'

Many of the most important traditions of thought in international relations have been built on the claim that international relations represents a distinctive sphere of political activity that can be studied within its own terms. This is most obviously the case with realism/neo-realism. But it is also true of more recent forms of neo-liberal institutionalism which (leaving behind their roots in theories of interdependence and transnationalism) have sought to explain inter-state co-operation on the basis of realist premises and assumptions. And it is also true of those who have sought to explain international relations in terms of the existence of international society, a form of society that is seen to be different in scope and character from that which exists within states. A second set of arguments points to the extent to which the complexities of the international politics of the environment are eroding the analytical validity of this kind of distinction.

One example has already been mentioned, namely the link between environmental degradation and violent conflict. It is certainly possible to conceive of such conflict in traditional realist terms – the image of 'resource wars' occurring between states (for example, over water resources in the Middle East); or the possibility of inter-state conflict resulting from the impact of environmental degradation on the balance of power or from a failure to agree on the management of a particularly important environmental problem (Myers, 1989; Deudney, 1992). But such a perspective runs the risk of missing the most important dimensions of environmental security: the (already apparent) risk of environmental degradation undermining the social fabric of weak states and provoking internal social disruption and violence. In other words, ideas of environmental security cannot be usefully conceptualized in terms of a clear-cut distinction between domestic and international conflict or between military threats and other forms of insecurity.

A second example concerns the identification of state interests. The realist assertion that interests can be derived principally in terms of the relative power position of a state has always been fragile. But it is impossible to understand the identification of state interests on environmental matters in such terms. It is for this reason that analyses of environmental politics have come to lay greater stress on the relationship between science and policy; on the role of scientific knowledge in shaping state interests and fostering processes of 'environmental learning' by states; and on the role of domestic actors and domestic values in shaping foreign environmental policy objectives (Caldwell, 1992; Haas, 1990, 1992).

A third example that goes to the heart of the traditional agenda concerns the effectiveness of international environmental institutions. Within the traditional agenda, a great deal of intellectual effort has been devoted to the issue of regime formation, to links between regimes and power, and to the factors that explain the durability of regimes. The question of implementation, of whether and how regimes actually affect state behaviour, has been far less directly examined. Yet the weakest link in the chain of international environmental co-operation may well not lie in the difficulties of negotiating formal agreements but, rather, in ensuring that those agreements are effectively implemented. It is already very clear that many of the most serious obstacles to sustainability have to do with the domestic weaknesses of states and state structures. Providing a convincing account of the effectiveness of environmental regimes therefore involves paying far closer attention to the problems of implementation and this, in turn, forces the theorist to consider the impact of a wide range of domestic factors.

These three examples provide a powerful argument that international political theory needs to focus far more intensively on the interactions between domestic and international politics. But they also raise a nagging and more subversive doubt. To what extent can states implement effective environmental policy within their own borders? To what extent do the declining domestic capacities of states suggest an erosion of sovereignty from below? To what extent are the empirical claims to statehood of many 'quasi-states' being gutted of any real meaning – partly as a result of the difficulty of managing environmental degradation, but also of chronic economic failure and the loss of political legitimacy (Jackson, 1990)? An affirmative answer to these questions would undoubtedly undermine the validity of building international political theory around the claims to effective authority and legitimacy implicit in the idea of sovereignty.

It is certainly plausible to interpret what is happening in many parts of the world in precisely these terms. The traditionally clear distinction between 'international anarchy' and 'domestic order' has been blurred in many parts of the world. The difficulty, however, comes in knowing how general trends towards the erosion of statehood from below actually are, or are likely to become. If, as seems likely, their impact is partial and uneven, the result will not be a move towards a neo-medieval world in which sovereignty ceases to be a central organizing principle. Rather, it will reinforce the already marked inequality that has become such a central feature of the post-Cold War international system and lead to new patterns of dominance and dependence.

The 'environment' and the global economy

The greatest difficulty of discussing international political theory in relation to the environment comes from the impossibility of treating the 'environment' as if it were a discrete aspect of human life. As has often been remarked, the environment is everywhere and nowhere, and there are no obvious or uncontested boundaries.

This problem is well illustrated by examining debates about the nature of sustainability and sustainable development. Definitions of sustainability are necessarily concerned with the interaction between human beings and the natural world. Whilst they might begin with a narrow view of such interactions (for example, protecting particular kinds of natural resources), they tend to move rather quickly to a broader analysis of the kinds of societies and forms of political and economic organization that would balance economic development with the carrying capacity of the planet. For this reason many argue that sustainable development is a multidimensional concept: a pattern of development that maintains the integrity and long-term viability of the biosphere, but that is also sustainable in economic, social and political terms. According to one formulation it is a pattern of development that is sustainable in terms of biological system goals (genetic diversity, resilience, biological productivity), economic systems goals (stabilizing production of goods and services whilst satisfying basic needs and reducing poverty) and social system goals (cultural diversity, social justice, gender equality, participation) (Holmberg, 1992).

Sustainability remains an essentially contested concept in both the philosophical and political senses and it is impossible to examine the debate in any depth here. But even to raise the issue is sufficient to underline the very close linkages that exist between the various structures and systems that together comprise the world system. In particular, any discussion of international political theory in relation to the environment is likely to be very deeply concerned with the workings of the international economic system and with theories of international political economy.

In terms of the traditionalist agenda, this means that it is no longer possible to treat ecology and international political economy as separate spheres. For example, the institutions that matter cannot be confined to those that have a specifically 'environmental' label (such as the UN Environment Programme (UNEP), the CSD or the GEF), but, rather, are the core institutions that manage (or at least seek to manage) the world economy (the World Bank/International Monetary Fund (IMF), the GATT, the Group of Seven). In addition, these interconnections place the dominant techniques of international environmental co-operation under increasing strain. International environmental regulation (especially legal regulation) has traditionally relied on separating issues and negotiating particular agreements to deal with particular problems. Yet attempting to give meaning to sustainability at the international level is necessarily about managing the environmental implications of a diverse and highly politicized set of relationships (for example, links between trade and environment, between debt and environment, between military spending and environment). Unsurprisingly international society has found this task to be a daunting one and the most notable step in this direction (the negotiation at the Earth Summit of an 800-page international programme of action for achieving sustainable developments entitled *Agenda 21*) was marked by omissions, by lack of overall coherence, and by a reluctance to prioritize and to specify any too clear link between impressive aspirations and effective action.

Yet exploring these linkages also raises further nagging doubts about the adequacy of the traditional agenda. If it is indeed the case that power in the global economy is exercised increasingly by non-state actors and, in particular, by transnational companies, the utility of a predominantly state-centred approach to international political ecology is also likely to be limited. Many of the most important environmental policy 'decisions' are not taken by states, but emerge out of the production, technological and trading strategies of a relatively small number of powerful transnational companies. Equally, both the generation of many 'local' environmental problems and the capacity of states to deal with those problems are heavily influenced by the pressures and constraints of an increasingly globalized world economy (for example, linkages between structural adjustment policies and environmental degradation or, more broadly, the transmission via the market of Western lifestyles, of a particular vision of modernity and progress, or of particular kinds of environmental knowledge).

Conclusions about the proper scope of policy co-ordination and global environmental governance are likely to be very heavily influenced by assessments of the character of the global political economy and by one's views of the adequacy of market-based approaches to environmental problems. Indeed, it is precisely doubts about the compatibility of an increasingly globalized world economy with any notion of global ecological rationality that have given rise to an emerging radical ecological critique of the world economy. This has very important implications for international political theory. For a long time International Relations has debated the merits of dependency and world systems approaches that posited a clear link between global capitalism and structural inequality. Justifiably or not, much of the force of such radical arguments has been removed by the widespread move to market liberalism and by the alleged triumph of neo-classical economics. Although containing many disparate strands, ecological critiques of the global economy throw up a new and equally important set of questions that challenge the predominantly market-liberal assumptions that characterize Northern policies and attitudes (Daly and Cobb, 1990; de la Court, 1990; Goodland, Daly and El Serafy, 1991; Ekins, 1992).

In the first place, these critiques challenge the dominant reformist liberalism that has characterized so much international thinking on the environment – the idea that a revitalization of global growth (albeit of a more sustainable character) is an essential part of averting future environment catastrophe and of securing some form of 'global bargain'. For those who see a deep contradiction between this continued emphasis on growth and the finite nature of the earth's ecosystem, the distributional conflicts, above all between rich and poor, are likely to be far more intense and politically significant than the comforting rhetoric of 'Brundtlandism' and 'sustainable development' would suggest.

Second, the critics argue that the existing global economy works to intensify environmental degradation, to undermine the effective authority of states, and to frustrate efforts at effective environmental regulation. From this perspective the choice is a stark one: either to 'bring the world economy under control' and to move to more centralized political co-ordination, or to try to reverse the powerful contemporary pressures towards integration and globalization, to decentralize economic and political power, and to build a sustainable future around grassroots democratic participation and locally generated economic transformation. Indeed, the attenuation of sovereignty as part of a project of radical decentralization forms a common plank of much of the environmentalist agenda.

The emergence of 'transnational civil society'

The fourth set of arguments attacks the state-centredness of traditional international political theory from a related, but distinct, perspective. The focus here is on the increased role of specific sets of transnational actors and NGOs, loosely collected under the broad heading of the 'environmental movement'. This encompasses both the scientific community and transnational environmental pressure groups concerned with the interlinked issues of sustainable development, the promotion of grassroots democracy, and the protection of indigenous peoples. The strength of such groups rests on their ability to develop and disseminate knowledge, to articulate a powerful set of human values, to harness a growing sense of cosmopolitan moral awareness, and to respond to the multiple weaknesses of the state system, both local and global. As a result we are seeing the 'emergence of a parallel arrangement of political interaction ... focused on the self-conscious construction of networks of knowledge and action, by decentred, local actors' (Lipschutz, 1992, p. 390). This set of arguments is related to the previous claim in that the increased level of economic globalization provides the 'infrastructure' for increased social communication – the role of communications technologies in facilitating the flow of values, knowledge and ideas and in allowing like-minded groups to organize across national boundaries.

One line of enquiry is to consider the impact of such groups on the ways in which states deal with environmental problems, to maintain the traditional agenda but to broaden its focus. One approach looks at the particular role of what Peter Haas has called epistemic communities: 'networks of knowledge based communities with an authoritative claim to policy relevant knowledge within their domain of expertise' (1992, p. 3). Here understandings of the 'problem to be solved' and definitions of state interest are influenced by the existence of transnational coalitions based on technical knowledge of a particular set of environmental issues.

Another approach, still predominantly within the traditional agenda, is to examine the impact of the environmental movement on international environmental co-operation. On many accounts environmental NGOs have played a major role in shifting public and political attitudes towards the environment and placing environmental issues high on the political agendas of an increasing number of states: in publicizing the nature and seriousness of environmental problems; in acting as a conduit for the dissemination of a scientific research; in organizing and orchestrating pressure on states, companies and international organizations; and in providing one of the most important mechanisms for helping to ensure effective implementation of environmental agreements. Certainly environmental NGOs have been able to harness an impressive array of resources (financial, technical, legal and scientific) and the role of the 1,500 or so NGOs at the Earth Summit was one of the most commented-upon aspects.

Yet, the emergence of 'transnational civil society' is also held to have subverted the traditional agenda: by challenging the hegemony of statist world politics; by establishing a non-territorially based focus of political identity (Ruggie, 1993); by creating new forms of political organization, particularly in areas where the writ of the state has quite literally ceased to run; and, perhaps most importantly for our purposes, by giving concrete embodiment to the idea of a global moral community. The sceptic has traditionally denied the importance of the idea of a global community by claiming that it is no more than the figment of the theorist's imagination. Attempts to root such a community in the workings of the global economy drastically underplayed the difference between being part of a common (and often exploitative) system and having a real sense of belonging to a single community (Beitz, 1979). The notion that the environmental movement can give concrete political expression to the idea of a global community is therefore one which carries particular resonance.

Speculations of this kind certainly provoke many questions and provide fertile ground for further research. One problem, however, is that the empirical evidence to support such claims is not yet available. The literature on environmental movements – above all, outside the industrialized world – is limited and uneven, and work that focuses in detail on their transnational character is even more limited. What we do know suggests that the influence of environmental groups is uneven, that it has probably risen in aggregate, but that it can also recede quite dramatically. Another problem concerns the criteria for evaluation. Should we focus merely on the capacity to mobilize concrete resources ('resource mobilization theory') or should we try to assess the power of ideas and the importance of attempts to reconstruct or re-imagine world politics?

Finally, there may be a degree of romanticization about the potential capabilities of such movements to define a new pattern of politics: both within states, where the undoubted retreat of the state that is occurring in many parts of the world can all too easily lead to the breakdown of all political order; and, even more, at the 'international' level. Those who see in the spread of such movements a new non-exploitative and inherently co-operative pattern of environmental action have yet to explain in detail how or why the many conflicts that surround environmental issues will be resolved. Is it not possible, for example, that the persistent calls from the environmental movement for 'global democratization' will in fact sharpen distributional conflicts between the industrialized and non-industrialized world? How compatible are the projects of radical decentralization on the one hand and calls for a fairer distribution of the world's resources on the other? Given the extent of existing global inequality, is there not a risk that decentralization will in fact result in a reduced capability to protect weak communities from external pressures? (For a strong claim of the potential transformatory impact of new forms of political action, see Ekins, 1992, especially chapter 9.)

The State System as an Obstacle to Managing the Global Environment

Whatever the difficulties of establishing that the central theoretical category of sovereignty has in fact been eroded, the increased seriousness of environmental problems, the emergence of a stronger planetary consciousness, and the manifold obstacles to effective international co-operation have undoubtedly strengthened the arguments of those who believe that sovereignty ought to be restricted, if not reconsidered. As we have seen, the emergence of global environmental issues is held to have undermined the assumptions on which ideas of sovereignty and non-intervention previously depended. The state is both too big and too small to deal with many of the most pressing environmental challenges: too big for the task of devising viable strategies of sustainable development, which can be developed only from the bottom up; and too small for the effective management of global problems, which by their nature demand increasingly wide-ranging forms of international co-operation. On this view, the fragmented system of sovereign states has become a fundamental obstacle to the effective and equitable management of an interdependent world in general and of the global environment in particular.

More abstractly, the emergence of global environmental problems and the greatly strengthened awareness of a global common interest among all peoples in protecting the environment and safeguarding the future of humanity have provided a powerful stimulus to the growth of a cosmopolitan moral consciousness. The notion of sharing a world, the essential interconnectedness and interdependence of the global environment, and the scarcity of the resources available to the humanity that need to be distributed both within and between generations all create conditions within which it becomes much harder than in the past to accept that consideration of justice in general, and of distributive justice in particular, end at the borders of states. For many people, then, global environmental interdependence has given greater plausibility to visions of a cosmopolitan global community, to what Locke once called 'the great and natural community of the species'.

Such arguments lead to two sorts of demands for the restriction of state sovereignty in the interests of environmental management or stewardship. On the one hand, the emerging sense of a global moral community strengthens the duty of all states to protect the rights of individuals and groups within states and to ensure a more equitable distribution of wealth as part of the promotion of sustainable development. On the other, such considerations increase the legitimacy of calls to curtail the sovereignty of states as part of the common management of the global ecosystem, for example by restricting fossil fuel consumption, controlling the use of ozone-depleting substances, or limiting the destruction of tropical rainforests.

It is impossible to debate these claims in any detail in a short chapter of this kind. But is it important to highlight the tensions and dilemmas around which this kind of explicitly normative political theory is likely to revolve. In the first place, there is the tension between the use of centralized power by the international community to promote sustainability from 'above' or from 'outside' and the growing recognition that sustainability must also be built from 'below', on the basis of local knowledge, local values and the direct involvement and empowerment of local communities – a tension between globalism and parochialism. Such a tension feeds into the now well-established debate in normative theory between cosmopolitan and communitarian approaches (Brown, 1992).

Both sides can claim that environmental dilemmas strengthen their case. We have already noted the increased urgency of cosmopolitan claims. Yet one can also argue that the general communitarian argument in favour of pluralism and diversity assumes particular importance in the environmental field. The relationship to nature and the natural world is often a defining feature of a community's sense of itself. Moreover, there can be no universal definition of sustainable development that can be applied in a mechanistic fashion in all parts of the world. Environmental policies and priorities will inevitably and legitimately vary from one country (and from one community) to another. This reflects the immense variation that exists in the physical world, in the nature and scope of environmental challenges, and in the different perspectives on environmental problems that come from different levels of economic development. There is certainly a good deal of room for positive reinforcement between different goals and priorities. But sustainability is unavoidably about making trade-offs between different priorities: between the maximum preservation of the natural environment and the pursuit of continuously high levels of economic development; between rapid economic growth and the protection of traditional cultures or improvements in equity and the social justice; or between importing the latest technology and safeguarding traditional practices and cultures.

Similarly, differing cultural and historical circumstances will influence the allocation of environmental values. Definitions of sustainability are inextricably bound up with the allocation of values and the distribution of costs and benefits between individuals and groups both within this generation and across time. Whilst there is widespread agreement that the benefits of environmental protection and the costs of environmental damage need to be made far more explicit and internalized within both markets and government policy-making, there can be no 'objective' and universal way of determining these costs and benefits. This is especially so when it comes to assessing the intrinsic value to be placed on the natural world and its preservation, the idea that what makes nature valuable to human beings is its very 'naturalness' and irreplaceability (Goodin, 1992). The importance of subjective and culturally determined judgements also arises because of the need to make assumptions about the needs and desires of future generations.

The second source of tension takes us back to the view of political theory with which this chapter began, a definition which stressed the need both to delineate a vision of the good life and to show, in principle at least, how such improvements might be achieved. Universalist claims that ideas about sovereignty are outmoded and obstructive can easily overlook the extent to which the new moral cosmopolitanism is still frail. The idea of a functioning global moral community is still largely a rhetorical construct, particularly when seen in terms of the political institutions by which the emerging idea of a global community could be given concrete and practical expression. The principles of global justice remain tentative and uncertain: at the level of theory but even more of practice. More important, the distribution of the costs and benefits of managing the global environment will continue to be determined, not by principles of justice, but by unequal political bargaining between states and by the operation of global markets over which the most powerful states continue to exercise a significant degree of authority. The negotiation of environmental agreements in a profoundly unequal world will affect both the distribution of costs and benefits and the degree to which sovereignty and autonomy are in practice restricted.

Given these circumstances, there is a very real danger that proposals to restrict sovereignty will reinforce an unequal sharing of the burdens of moving towards sustainability which will continue to be characterized by a lack of reciprocity between rich and poor. The coercive restriction of sovereignty may therefore easily become a lever used by Northern governments to press for changes in the environmental policies of developing countries, whilst they themselves are subject to no such constraints. It may also become a way of shifting the focus of the environmental debate: towards those issues in which Northern countries have a particular interest (biodiversity, climate change, tropical deforestation) or which particularly engage the emotions of Northern publics; and away from often less headline-grabbing problems that are of the greatest concern to the peoples of the South (desertification, water and fuel-wood scarcity, lack of access to safe drinking water, clean air and decent sanitation) and, above all, from the pressing need for continued economic development. It may thus divert attention away from the grave need for the industrialized world to adopt changed patterns of economic development involving lower resource use, the full internalization of environmental externalities, strict pollution-abatement measures and a lower relative share of both the earth's resources and its 'sinks'. Finally, increased levels of external involvement in determining the domestic priorities of states runs the risk of undermining the importance of accountability and representation. How can governments be held accountable for policies and priorities over which they have only limited control or authority?

The drama of global environmental change and the extent to which environmental problems threaten to overwhelm our existing forms of political and economic organization make it particularly tempting to devise new schemes of how the world ought to be organized: to put forward arguments about desirable reforms in the way in which states negotiate and co-operate; to argue that sustainability requires both a radical redistribution of the world's wealth and a new form of global democratization. Yet, however impressive the abstract principles on which such schemes or proposals may be based, they will be of limited utility unless related to the actual process of social and political change by which they might plausibly be implemented and to the existing institutions of international society.

The challenge posed by Martin Wight's seminal paper 'Why Is there no International Theory?' (1966) is not that it opens the door to a blank wall of necessity and despair, nor that it forces us to be content with an introspective and egotistical ethic of responsibility. Rather, it (and the tradition of prudential ethics of which it is representative) reminds us of the fragility of international society and of our ideas about what it may be reasonable to expect. Within states we can identify how ideas of order and justice have historically been established, however imperfectly. Between states political theory cannot ignore the fact that the very possibility of a sustained co-operation (and certainly of the kinds of highly extensive co-operation around which much of the environmental debate revolves) has never been firmly established. Hence, at a minimum, we need to anchor ideas of the good life in an understanding of the social, political and economic forces that could plausibly explain how such improvements could be achieved.

CONCLUSIONS

This chapter has sought to draw a distinction between two ways of thinking about the relationship between international political theory and the global environment. As John Ruggie has argued, there is a striking gap between the traditional and dissenting accounts.

> The global ecological implosion inherently invites epochal thinking, yet analytically informed empirical studies of 'ozone diplomacy' or of attempts to save the Mediterranean invariably focus on negotiations processes and the dynamics of regime construction, as

opposed to exploring the possibility of fundamental institutional discontinuity in the system of states. (1993, p. 143)

This chapter has examined five sets of arguments which suggest that the traditionalist account of the scope of international political theory provides an inadequate basis for understanding the problems of global environmental change, and which, in different ways and to a varied extent, do indeed open up the possibility of a 'fundamental discontinuity in the system of states'. The central argument of this chapter has been that detailed consideration of these arguments is necessary *both* to understand and illuminate the still very important state-centred agenda of 'traditional' international political theory *and* to understand the ways in which environmental problems and politics may be altering dominant frames of reference and suggesting a broader, if murkier, scope for international political theory. Rather than be seen as two different kinds of project, a great deal of international political theory in the future is likely to be concerned with the complex ways in which these two agendas relate and interact.

References

Beitz, C. 1979: *Political Theory and International Relations*. Princeton, N.J.: Princeton University Press.

Birnie, P. and Boyle, A. 1993: *International Environmental Law*. Oxford: Oxford University Press.

Brown, C. 1992: *International Relations Theory: New Normative Approaches*. Hemel Hempstead: Harvester Wheatsheaf.

Caldwell, L. K. 1992: *Between Two Worlds. Science, the Environmental Movement and Policy Choice*. (Paperback ed.). Cambridge: Cambridge University Press.

Daly, H., Daly, E. and Cobb, J. B. 1990: *For the Common Good*. London: Green Print.

de la Court, T. 1990: *Beyond Brundtland. Green Development in the 1990s*. London: Ned Books.

Deudney, D. 1992: The mirage of eco-war. In I. H. Rowlands and M. Greene (eds), *Global Environmental Change and International Relations*, London: Macmillan, 169–91.

Dunn, J. 1990: *Reinterpreting Political Responsibility*. Cambridge: Polity Press.

Ekins, P. 1992: *A New World Order. Grassroots Movements for Global Change*. London: Routledge.

Goodin, R. E. 1992: *Green Political Theory*. Cambridge: Polity Press.
Goodland, R., Daly, H. and El Serafy, S. 1991: *Environmentally Sustainable Development: Building on Brundtland, World Bank Working Paper*, July.
Grubb, M., Koch, M., Munson, A., Sullivan, F. and Thomson, K. 1993: *The Earth Summit Agreements. A Guide and Assessment*. London: RIIA/ Earthscan.
Haas, P. M. 1990: *Saving the Mediterranean*. New York: Columbia.
Haas P. M. (ed.) 1992: Knowledge, power and international policy coordination. *International Organization*, 46(1) (special issue).
Haas P. M., Keohane, R. O. and Levy, M. A. (eds) 1993: *Institutions for the Earth*. Cambridge: MIT Press.
Held, D. and McGrew, A. 1993: Globalization and the liberal democratic state. *Government and Opposition*, 28(2), 261–88.
Holmberg, J. 1992: *Policies for a Small Planet*. London: Earthscan.
Hurrell, A. and Kingsbury B. (eds) 1992: *The International Politics of the Environment*. Oxford: Oxford University Press.
Jackson, R. H. 1990: Quasi-States: Sovereignty, International Relations and the Third World. Cambridge: Cambridge University Press/BISA.
Kiss, A. and Shelton D. 1991: *International Environmental Law*. New York: Transnational Publishers.
Lipschutz, R. D. 1992: Reconstructing world politics: the emergence of global civil society. *Millennium Journal of International Studies*, 21(3), 389–420.
Meadows, D. H., Meadows, D. L. and Randers, J. 1992: *Beyond the Limits. Global Collapse or a Sustainable Future*. London: Earthscan.
Myers, N. 1989: Environment and security. *Foreign Policy*, 74, 23–41.
Ruggie, J. G. 1993: Territoriality and beyond. *International Organization*, 47(1), 139–74.
Schachter, O. 1991: *International Law in Theory and Practice*, 2nd edn. Dordrecht: Martinus Nijhoff.
Wight, M. 1966: Why is there no international theory? In H. Butterfield and M. Wight (eds), *Diplomatic Investigations: Essays in the Theory of International Politics*, London: Allen & Unwin, 17–34.
World Commission on Environment and Development 1987: *Our Common Future* (The Brundtland Report). Oxford: Oxford University Press.
Young, O. 1989: *International Regimes for Natural Resources and the Environment*. Ithaca N.Y.: Cornell University Press.
Zacher, M. W. 1992: The decaying pillars of the Westphalian temple: implications for international order and governance. In J. N. Rosenau and E. O. Czempiel (eds), *Governance without Government: Order and Change in World Politics*. Cambridge: Cambridge University Press, 58–101.

7

Political Economy and International Relations

Susan Strange

It is now more than twenty years since I and others first pleaded for an end to the long and harmful divorce of politics and economics in the study of the world system (Strange, 1970, 1972; Kindleberger, 1970; Baldwin, 1971; Keohane and Nye, 1972; Morse, 1976). In one way, the subsequent development of international political economy as an accepted academic field has been highly satisfactory. Many universities have established courses in the subject. Doctorates have been awarded. Teaching positions have been advertised and filled. It has become an area of rapid growth, now slowing perhaps, but certainly occupying a much more salient part in international studies than it did at the start of the 1970s.

Success – if that is what it is – is not, however, the result of some great intellectual breakthrough. It owes little to the arguments made by myself and other pioneers like Robert Gilpin, Ed Morse, David Baldwin, Robert Keohane and Joseph Nye that the focus of work in international relations was devoted too much to what the dominant realist school called 'high politics' – foreign and defence policies and issues of international order and security – and too little directed at the 'low politics' of the management of the international economy.[1]

INTERNATIONAL POLITICAL ECONOMY: THE ECHO OF EVENTS

The boom in international political economy (IPE) as an area of specialization has reflected not ideas but events. It was pure coincidence that President Nixon decided unilaterally to float the dollar, close the gold window and effectively write the epitaph of the Bretton Woods rules on exchange rates between the major currencies only eighteen months after an article of mine in *International Affairs* (Strange, 1970) had called for an end to the long separation of politics and economics. His action galvanized thought and discussion on the politics as well as the economics of the international monetary system. Within another two years, the OPEC countries had seized the golden opportunity of a booming commodity market – and therefore strong demand for oil – coinciding with the 1973 Arab–Israeli war to quadruple the asking price for their oil. Their success – however short-lived, since inflation in the US rapidly devalued the real price of the same oil – put new life into the demands of developing countries for economic justice and a better deal from the rich, industrialized countries in matters of trade and aid. All this was only the beginning of a period in which headlines in the newspapers and the agendas of politicians came, more and more, to be dominated by issues that were superficially economic – but also fundamentally political in the sense that outcomes were the product of changing policies as well as of changing markets.

The long debt crisis of the 1980s was just one more example among many of how economic events have both been triggered by political decisions and had highly political consequences, so that the dividing lines collapsed – both those that separated politics and economics and those that separated domestic political economies from the international political economy. It was a change in US monetary management in 1981 that set off the 1982 rise in interest rates worldwide. This in turn increased the burden of debt-servicing for Mexico, Poland and many developing countries which had borrowed through the banks, threatening the banks with a dangerous burden of bad debts, euphemistically called 'non-performing loans'. Two highly political issues resulted: one concerning the creditors, the others the debtors. First, how was the threat to the big international banks which had imprudently made such loans to be averted for the sake of the stability of the whole world market economy? Second, how were the debtor countries to be treated and how could their economic development plans, predicated as they were on a continued flow of foreign capital, be sustained? To cut a long story short, the political decisions were taken that the lending banks would have to write off some loss, but not so much that the system would collapse;

and that the indebted governments – as in the 1930s – would not be allowed to default, and would suffer a continuing dearth of credit, obliging them to sacrifice investment in growth for the sake of repaying their debts as and when they were able.

Thanks to these and other events, it was only natural that politicians, the media and the academics should develop a strong interest in IPE. Governments and banks were under pressure from events. They could not avoid taking decisions that affected the distribution of costs and benefits, of risks and opportunities, not just within states but across national frontiers. Also at stake was the stability and soundness of the capitalist system of production and distribution and who should exercise power over these economic outcomes.

Yet while increasing attention has been given to the public policy issues of IPE, the intellectual problem of synthesis has still not been solved. International relations people have studied economic phenomena and have made use of concepts and even methods of argument borrowed from economics. Economists, by contrast, have largely ignored the literature of international relations. Where they have ventured into IPE, either they have done so on their own terms and in virtual isolation from all other disciplines or, sometimes, they have started with international economic history and used comparative historical methods to draw their conclusions. A good example is the work of Barry Eichengreen (1992) on inter-war monetary relations, on the gold standard and other historical case-studies. This has been the basis for informed judgements on contemporary issues of monetary management and policy co-ordination. Mostly, though, economists have been reluctant to abandon or even modify the assumptions underlying the basic theories and axioms of neo-classical economics. For the economists, efficiency in the creation of wealth, the maximization of benefits and the minimization of costs – both calculated in purely economic terms – still constitute the prime criterion of good policy, whether applied at the national or the global level. Only the practical economists engaged in management studies – because they are necessarily in close touch with the realities of international business – have moved decisively beyond the single criterion of profit-maximization at the level of the enterprise to a more pluralistic 'political economy' form of analysis. One example of this is the attention now given in business schools and management journals to the ethical dilemmas of corporate management. Very likely, this is a response, again, to events: to the recent spate of cases of individuals accused of business and financial crimes – Maxwell, Nadir, Milken, Trump – not to mention the business scandals affecting Italy and Japan. The point here is that the management economists' rising concern with moral issues is not matched by a similar concern among most mainstream economists.

The result of this persisting gap between international relations and international economics is that there is an unresolved disarray in the study of IPE. There is a kind of malaise, a sense of uncertainty about where to go from here, even of confusion about where we have reached so far, prevailing among the rather large number of people engaged in the field.

In my view this goes further than the observation made by Murphy and Tooze in their introduction to a recent collection of essays on the subject: 'International political economy', they remark, 'has developed as a field defined more by agreement among scholars about what to study than by agreement about how to study it' (1991, p. 1). Of course, it is undeniable that there are certain commonly agreed 'areas of investigation' which are accepted as 'belonging' to IPE. Reflecting the concerns of governments, these include the management of world trade, of exchange rates, of foreign debt, of foreign investment and notably the multinational corporations. These topics make up a certain core, a kind of lowest common denominator, for the subject, reflected both in the ever growing literature and the topics discussed at conferences on international studies.

It is more doubtful, in my opinion, that beyond that core, there is any real agreement about what else should be discussed – about the further extent of the subject and the rationale behind it. Is the subject to be limited to those questions that make newspaper headlines, that reflect 'events', and that involve governments of states when they conflict or co-operate with one another? Or should it aspire to go further into the fundamentals of how the multiple authorities in the world market economy and society allocate values among classes, generations, genders and other social groups? In other words, should it translate into global terms the original remit of *oikonomia*, the study of the management of all aspects of the household, recognizing that instead of the extended-family homestead of ancient Greece, we are all living, to some extent, in a global houschold? But if it were to be extended in this way, how are such broader questions to be analysed? Uncertainty reigns not only over the limits to the subject but also over the legitimate methods to be employed. No wonder there is no clear explanation of how and why the particular set of questions that interest scholars in the field has been selected. No wonder there is a particularly striking absence of a general theory, or even of an agreed methodology.

A STATE OF CONFUSION

Just as the study of international political economy was triggered by developments in the world at large, and its development favoured by the succession of events briefly sketched above, so some more recent real-world developments have contributed to an increased confusion about what the subject is and where it should be going.

One such event, obviously, is the end of the Cold War. A very early pioneer in IPE was the American economist, Richard Cooper. His argument was that the Atlantic Alliance, to which the US looked to help it resist the perceived threat from the Soviet Union, was under threat unless the economic policies of its member states were better co-ordinated (Cooper, 1968). As trade barriers and exchange controls came down, the resulting economic integration – the interdependence, to use his suggestive euphemism that soon became common usage – required a positive effort on the economic front as well as on the military one. In short, the need to fight the Cold War justified an intellectual investment both in the diplomacy of trade and money and in the academic analysis of the economic issues that threatened to divide and therefore weaken the affluent capitalist alliance. IPE was thus just one more weapon in the contest between capitalism and socialism.

Now, with the Cold War over, why should Europeans or Japanese – not to mention poor Africans, Asians or Latin Americans – continue to worry about the need for policy co-ordination? Another American economist, Marina Whitman, had characterized the management of the international economic order during the cold war as 'an implicit bargain' in which the affluent allies forbore to contest US hegemonic leadership – unilateralism, even – in matters of trade and money. This was the price they paid for their security under the American nuclear umbrella (Whitman, 1984).

That there was much truth in this notion of an implicit bargain could be seen in the monetary history of the 1960s. Politicians in West Germany – the affluent European ally most exposed to a Soviet threat – repeatedly swallowed their criticism of the conduct of US economic and fiscal policies as they remembered (or Americans reminded them of) their dependence on US troops deployed in their country as a tripwire against invasion. Their self-restraint contrasted sharply with De Gaulle's outspoken attacks on a system which preserved the exorbitant privileges of the US dollar. Clearly, the different reactions of the French and Germans could be better explained by their unequal dependence on the Americans keeping their side of the implicit bargain – in short, by military rather than by purely monetary factors.

Circumstances alter political attitudes. Democratic societies, for example, will tolerate restrictions on free speech or a free press in time of war, but will quickly reclaim these political freedoms in time of peace. Similarly, America's allies might be expected to reclaim their right to pursue divergent policies from those of the US as soon as the fall of the Berlin Wall reduced the perceived threat to their security. The global contest between the market or capitalist way of running the economy and the state-capitalist way being at an end, the more complex competition between the industrialized economies took over. Even in the US the political debate quickly shifted from how to impose more effective conformity on the other allied countries to how the American economy could best compete against Japan.

This shift in political attention in the US is already having its academic repercussions. In the past, concern with maintaining maximum economic order in the Western alliance had lent drive and purpose to the academic discussion of international regimes – to regime formation and regime change. It is even fair to guess that the great bulk of analytical work in international political economy, following the Nye and Keohane lead, had concentrated on the area of regimes – regimes for trade, for exchange rates, for the management of foreign debt and foreign investment, for environmental protection, for the regulation of air and sea transport, etc. Now, external change in the security structure was pulling a substantial part of the political rug from under this concern with regimes. The study of regimes had always been vulnerable to the criticism that it was value-loaded in favour of order over justice or autonomy (Strange, 1983). The definition of order, moreover, was contestable; it was often automatically assumed by Americans to coincide exactly with the perceived national interests of the US. A 'level playing field' was one seen from the US goalposts.

Probably, none of this will entirely dampen the interest of the hard-core neo-functionalist scholars in the study of international regimes. It was not the US government or the CIA but their own idealistic belief in the potential of international institutions to undermine the wayward self-serving behaviour of nation-states that inspired their work. Ernst Haas was a follower of David Mitrany; Keohane, Ruggie and others were his students; a younger generation in turn followed their lead, and not only in America but also in Europe.[2]

My point is only that the political tides that gave legitimacy to a great deal of this work in IPE and which kept it financially afloat are already receding and may do so still further in the future. An alternative focus on the bargains – domestic and international, political and economic, corporate and inter-state – underlying the regimes, rather than the regimes themselves would give better results. Focusing on the regimes comes naturally to students of international organization. But the inevitable bias is towards order over equity and other values, and towards inter-government bargaining to the exclusion of other bargains, either those within states or those between governments and enterprises or other social groups. There is also in regime analysis a certain bias towards static analysis of organizations which may remain in being long after their sustaining bargain has collapsed. Since it is obvious that the balance of bargaining power is apt to shift over time and that the objectives of those doing the bargaining are also apt to change, an analytical method based on bargains is more likely than regime analysis to take dynamic factors into account.

Besides the end of the Cold War, there is a second, longer-term, development which has played a part in the current state of confusion in the study of IPE. It is the increased integration of national economies in the world market economy. The change affects states but originates outside the state – in all four of the basic structures of the international political economy, but mostly in the increasingly integrated structure of credit and finance and in the increasingly transnationalized structure of production (Strange, 1988; Stopford and Strange, 1991). The result is a marked reduction in the autonomy of the state, a reduction that other social scientists – the anthropologists, the sociologists, even the geographers – have shown themselves rather more aware of than either the economists or most political scientists (Dicken, 1986; Mann, 1986; Giddens, 1990; Sklair, 1991; Corbridge and Thrift, 1994).

The evidence is there for all to see. No longer can any state today afford to opt out of the global market economy. The successor states of the old USSR, Burma (now Myanmar), the People's Republic of China, India, Iran, Vietnam and South Africa have with more or less reluctance accepted the fact and acted accordingly to invite foreign-owned firms to invest in their economies, to liberalize their protected national markets in order to make producers more competitive and to allow world market prices to act as realistic signals to the private sectors. It can only be a matter of time before Cuba and North Korea also give in. But the consequences of opting in, of acknowledging the constraints of opting in, so to speak, are fundamental and for the foreseeable future, irreversible. Competing for world market shares, whether oil or semiconductors or air travel, means accepting the established structures and customs of those markets. Competing for foreign capital means accepting the terms and conditions set by the major financial centres and the major international banks, insurance firms, law firms and accountants. It means becoming vulnerable to the ups and downs and the consequent risks of an intrinsically volatile and not particularly rational market. It means accepting the imperative of negotiating with foreign firms which have more control than national governments over access to major world markets, and have ownership of and control over advanced technologies; and whose co-operation can also gain access to the foreign human and financial capital necessary for economic growth and a secure balance of payments (Stopford and Strange, 1991, chapter 2). Out of the window have gone most of the policy options that it used to be assumed were open to the governments of sovereign states. Which specific options are still open is a matter over which most states now have very little control.

Thus, if the state can no longer exercise control over the domestic economy – no matter that, in self-defence, politicians will go on claiming that their decisions for growth, inflation and employment are significant – and if it is unable to opt out of a world market economy which imposes its own independent imperatives, then it is hard for international relations scholars to insist that the state is still the primary unit of analysis in international politics. That it is a unit of analysis, and that the decisions of states can affect outcomes, is not in question. But the invasion by transnational structures of the prerogatives formerly associated with the state means that the state shares its role as a unit of analysis with others – other states and other non-state authorities. It can affect outcomes – though its ability to do so is increasingly asymmetrical – but it can no longer claim to determine them, even within its own territorial borders.

One rather striking example of the increasing vulnerability of states to global economic structures is to be found in the experiences of France over the past decade. This was a country which in the 1960s and even the 1970s was lauded as a model of economic planning and management in a democratic political system.[3] It even claimed the independence of a *tous-azimuths* defence policy, and opted out of NATO. But when it elected a socialist president in 1982, he was quickly obliged *by the markets* to make a U-turn in economic strategies. And in defence, because of rising costs of production in defence weaponry, France was also obliged increasingly to compromise with NATO and the Germans in matters of national security. The Gaullist pretence to autonomy had quite vanished by 1992 when the *franc fort* was maintained only with the support of the German Bundesbank.

A third main source of academic uncertainty and confusion, it seems to me, has been the collapse of the Third World coalition of less developed countries. One of the largest constituencies of the IPE academic community, even before the subject was recognized in the rich, industrialized world, was persuaded neither by the ideology of liberalism and free markets nor by that of nationalism. Robert Gilpin (1987, chapter 2) describes it as 'Marxist' and criticizes it as such. But in reality, although some of the values and concepts of this constituency owed a lot to Marx, it was not limited to marxists. It comprised all those who saw the capitalist market economy as fundamentally unjust and therefore flawed. It was not only marxists who rejected the liberal claim that the benefits of free markets would eventually trickle down from the rich to the poor; who harboured doubts whether the latecomers to industrialization would eventually enjoy the same improvement in living standards that the firstcomers had experienced; who wondered whether everyone would, one fine day, reach Walt Rostow's point of take-off into economic growth and development.

This critical, or structuralist, constituency also included all those who thought that the faults of the capitalist system could be redeemed by political intervention on a global as much as on a national scale. Its inherent asymmetries of distribution could be made good by more aid and more sympathetic trade policies, and by changes in the role of transnational enterprises based in the rich countries. They included not only all the Latin Americans, Asians and Africans who subscribed to the analysis and prescriptions of Raul Prebisch, but also many Europeans and others who welcomed the message of the Brandt Report. Prebisch had used his position as head of the UN's Economic Commission for Latin America to expound an intellectual argument for a better deal on trade and aid for developing countries. A similar concern had inspired Willy Brandt's independent Commission on Economic Development, which had argued the welfare ideals of Europe should be applied to the relations between the rich North and the poor South (Brandt, 1980). But in America there was no such social-democratic tradition and the Brandt Report, and Prebisch, received a cool reception. By the early 1990s, all talk of a new international economic order, of an integrated commodity stabilization programme and other reformist ideas, was over. The Brandt Report was forgotten. Even the UN's Centre for Transnational Corporations, originally established in New York as the hammer of the multinationals, had changed its tune. Its message now was to co-operate, to bargain constructively, with the multinationals, not to oppose, confront or nationalize them.

The fact was that the structuralist analysis that condemned all developing countries to chronic underdevelopment as a result of integration in the world market economy had been shown to be wrong. The world system structuralists like Andre Gunder Frank, the neo-marxists like Samir Amin, and with them the politicians who had negotiated the Andean Pact or who had pushed for a bigger role for the UN Conference on Trade and Development (UNCTAD) and a new deal on trade and aid were confounded by the successors of the NICs (newly industrialized countries) of East Asia. If they could register whole decades of annual growth rates between 7 and 10 per cent despite the handicaps imposed on them by the capitalist system, others could surely do the same. In place of the coalition strategies of the Group of 77 developing countries – actually they numbered well over a hundred – there was a Hobbesian scramble to find new allies, either neighbouring states as in the Association of South East Asian Nations (ASEAN) and other regional groups, or among foreign firms, banks and consultants. And while some writers alert to these changes kept up with the times, some (older ones usually) held to their old views, arguing that it had been a special coincidence of circumstances that had allowed the Asian Tigers to follow the Japanese model.[4]

DIVERGING PERCEPTIONS

Many American readers will already have been puzzled by my characterization of the current state of IPE. 'What disarray? What confusion?' they may ask. For it is surely the case that there is little reflection of disarray or confusion in the pages of current issues of *International Organization*, the flagship of American IPE.

There are two possible explanations for this divergence between American and non-American perceptions. One is that most American scholars have understood the field as it is reflected in the title of Gilpin's (1987) popular text *The Political Economy of Inter-national Relations* (my hyphen), and in earlier texts by Spero (1977) and Blake and Walters (1976) (PIER). They believe it to be concerned primarily with the political aspects of those broadly economic issues that figure on the agendas of governments of nation-states. Indeed, many taught courses are still called 'The politics of international economic relations'. And even when they claim to be about IPE, it is narrowly construed as a branch, almost, of foreign-policy studies – but foreign economic policy as distinct from defence policy or bilateral or multilateral alliance-building. The recent interest in 'strategic trade policy' – often a euphemism for protectionist targeting of trade rivals – in the US is only a reflection of this narrow concept of what IPE is about.

The other explanation is that it has fallen victim in the US to the imperialism of the economics profession. IPE has been 'taken over' by economists, or at least by their way of looking at issues, and by their most favoured concepts and methodologies. A great many younger American scholars have come to believe that the one sure path to promotion, respectability and fame is to ape the economists by resorting to game theory as an explanation of behaviour, by subordinating – as they habitually do – realism to rigour, and consequently being prepared to make rather extravagant and even bizarre assumptions about motivations and objectives (Cole, Cameron and Edwards, 1983; Hodgson and Screpanti, 1991; Colander and Brenner, 1992).

The two explanations are not necessarily mutually exclusive. And both or either may be reinforced by the observable introversion of American perceptions. Just as newspapers and TV news programmes in the US display an almost total lack of interest in 'foreign' news – unless, of course, US troops are, or may be, involved – so academic writing by the great majority of American scholars is blissfully and habitually deaf and blind to the ideas and perceptions of the outside world. I am not alone in noticing and complaining about this; Kal Holsti teaching in Vancouver has commented on it and so has Richard Higgott (Holsti, 1985; Higgott, 1991).

But indifference to the outside world – what in industry is known as the NIH (not invented here) syndrome – is not a new phenomenon. The tendency to stick doggedly with the PIER definition of the content of IPE, and the prominence of economics in specifying how to do it, are both fairly recent. Both have broader implications for the content and the methods of the subject.

By 'sticking with the PIER definition', I mean that the pluralist or interdependence school that started with Keohane and Nye's (1972) edited collection of essays on transnational relations went only part of the way to a radically new study of the political economy of world society and economy. It is true that they added entities other than states as actors and issues other than peace and war to the agenda. Where this school stopped short – and still stops short – is in thinking of 'structure' only in political terms: that is, in terms of the power structures between states, of the hierarchy of superpowers, great powers, middle powers and others. Hence the common concern with the decline of the power of the US. Outcomes are affected, in this perception of IPE, by the geometry of power – bipolar, multipolar or hegemonic, for instance. It is this which determines the way in which the system functions or malfunctions. Economic processes are conceived as taking place within the political structure.[5] It does not admit of the reverse process – of political processes taking place within the existing economic structure. It does not perceive the economic and social structures co-existing side by side with the political structure, the international system of territorial states. It cannot conceive that economic structures can and do generate their own kinds of power over outcomes. Giddens, who uses the ungainly word 'structuration' to make just such an argument, is totally ignored. And in denying these parallel structures, the PIER perspective tends to limit its questions of 'Who gets what?' in the world system to the distributive consequences between states or between national economies. It too easily becomes just an exercise in national public policy analysis. In situation X or Y, how should the US (or any other country) react in defence of its own self-interest? What policies should Washington, or Bonn or Moscow, adopt?

This weakness was the main target of the analytical framework I outlined in *States and Markets* (Strange, 1988). It was suggesting that the 'bottom line' of judgment was how the system, not its components, was responding, and with what distributive consequences among all kinds of individuals and social groups. These outcomes, it further suggested, reflected various kinds of structural power; power over outcomes was derived not from one but from all of the four primary structures of the global political economy: the security structure, the production structure, the financial structure and the knowledge structure. In each of these, markets as well as states determined processes. Although some states could shape, or later could change, the way in which a market – whether for wheat or oil or Eurocurrency loans – operated, the market, once set up, put constraints, imposed risks or offered opportunities to all those who entered it. Even in the security structure, which states (because of their monopoly of legitimate violence) appeared to dominate, the structure of the market increasingly affected security outcomes. Market access to nuclear weapons and nuclear technology was at least partly restricted. But access to even the most advanced 'conventional' weapons was open and state-supported enterprises were fiercely competitive for market shares; access to small arms was virtually unregulated. The results of this market structure can be plainly seen in recent times in the *in*security of families in Northern Ireland, in US inner cities, in Bosnia or in Bombay. It could not be explained simply by the structure of power in the inter-governmental political system.

The same is true of the financial structure through which credit is created, or of the production structure through which the nature, location and processes of production of raw materials, manufactures and services are determined – largely by decisions taken by the managers of enterprises rather than the ministers of governments. It is also true of the knowledge structure through which choices are made about the kind of knowledge created and respected, the manner and modes of its accumulation, storage and communication. Though states as the major legitimate authorities in society have made important choices in each of these, the resulting structures then assume an influence and a logic of their own within which governments, enterprises, social movements and social groups, genders and generations have little or no choice but to operate. The argument developed by John Stopford and me in *Rival States, Rival Firms* (1991) was based on this fundamental premise. Change in the production structure, brought about principally by the accelerating rate of technological change, was making it imperative for governments to negotiate with foreign firms, and vice versa, rather than exclude or punish them. Diplomacy had thus become triangular – between states and firms, and firms and other firms as well as between two or more states. But this was not as the result of any change in what the PIER writers refer to as the political structure.

IMITATING ECONOMISTS

For most of the last decade, a great deal of the literature in IPE written in the US has displayed a marked tendency to imitate the methods and concepts of liberal or neo-classical economics. Rosenau (1990), for example, applied to transnational relations the distinction borrowed from economics between theory at the micro and the macro level (i.e. at the level of individual behaviour and of systemic interactions). Keohane, led by his interest (and belief) in institutions, popularized if he did not pioneer the use of game theory to explain the failures of governments to co-operate in policies they professed to favour (Keohane, 1984; Axelrod, 1981). Others followed and the coincidental popularity of game theory applied to domestic politics allowed departments of political science to make joint appointments and develop courses for the study of both international and national politics.

I personally believe this trend to be mistaken, a journey down a blind alley that will inevitably and in the long run shut off IPE scholars – as too many economists are now shut off – from openness to the perceptions of historians, sociologists, demographers, geographers, psychologists and many others. But in the short term this imitation of economics has seemed to introduce a new rigour to the study of IPE, and to mark out around it narrower but much clearer boundaries. It has naturally appealed to the preference of academics for a defined area to work in and a defined group to work with. Within these confining walls, it is easier to ignore uncomfortable developments in the real world of business and government and disconcerting observations by scholars in other disciplines. As a teaching device, emphasizing logical thinking, game theory has obvious uses. As a research method, its foundation in the concept of bounded rationality has serious weaknesses. This concept originated in the work of an economist, Herbert Simon, in the 1950s. It was borrowed and much used by behaviouralist writers in international relations as well as by other economists. Essentially, Simon had suggested substituting *satisficing* for the classical concept in economics of *maximizing* or *optimizing* behaviour. This presumed that decision-makers could, and would, choose policies that would achieve, or satisfy, not one but a number of objectives, meeting certain (given) standards of acceptability in each one. But this assumption presumes that decisions are taken in a static world. The reality is that ministers of government departments, like managers of transnational corporations operate simultaneously, not just in one but in (at least) four power structures – which themselves are never static; that they are therefore obliged to play multiple games simultaneously; and most of all that their preferences, and those of their fellow players, are in a constant state of dynamic flux. Since consequently, in real life these decision-makers have to deploy a variety of means of limiting uncertainty and reducing transaction costs, the operational potential of game theory as a research tool to explain outcomes in the real world must be severely limited.

The magnetism of economics for political economists derives, of course, not only from its social prestige as the (supposedly) least unscientific of the social sciences, the one which lays strongest claims – never mind the record – to a potential for the discovery of regularity in behaviour and therefore of a capacity for prescience and prediction. It also derives from its claim to have developed a number of the general theories: general theories of economic development, of exchange rates, of inflation, unemployment, investment, and so on. The aspiration to emulate the supposed achievements of economics leads to the imitation of its methods. By this means, other academics seek to share both the economists' social and political prestige – and of course their access to resources.

My suspicion is that, as often happens with imitators, IPE scholars who imitate the economists will be left behind as their models move on to new ideas, new methods, new discourses. Already, the popularity of organization economics is leading some economists back to economic history – always in my view a much sounder basis for the study of IPE. The work of historians like Braudel, Cipolla or Polanyi exposes the complexity of structural and relational factors shaping outcomes. That complexity seems to be incompatible with any rooted attachment to the concept of rationality, bounded or unbounded.

WHAT NEXT, THEN?

The first thing that is needed for the further development of the study of international political economy is a redefinition of the study of politics. For too long, political scientists have imagined that politics consists of what governments do, how they function and how they behave to one another. The state, as someone said, came to 'colonize' the study of politics. Thus, we have courses in American (or British, French, Japanese, or whatever) politics, local government, comparative politics, world politics. The state is at the centre of them all. But as the French writer, Bertrand de Jouvenel (1954) pointed out some years ago, people engage in politics whenever one individual or group needs the support or assistance of others to achieve their ends.

That principle allows us to think quite differently about the nature of politics. It is no longer confined to the state, to the functioning of government by states. Thus, the chief executives of firms are engaged in politics when they seek the support and co-operation of their managers and their workers, or of their suppliers in meeting quality standards, or the continued confidence of their shareholders or creditors. Running a business – as anyone who has ever done it knows – is more than conducting a series of rational economic exchanges. Conflicting interests have to be reconciled, chains of command established. Areas of responsibility must be defined, and disagreements arbitrated. Above all, some leadership, some sense of purpose, some confidence have to be instilled in all the people involved.

Nor does politics outside government occur only on a grand scale. Charity organizers engage in politics. People who try to raise money for charities need 'the support and assistance of others to achieve their ends'. To some, the ends may be trivial – running a tennis club, for example, or negotiating a car-pool or a baby-sitting rota. But the process is still political, and calls for political skills more than economic rationality, as anyone who has done any of these things will agree. The heads of university departments, too, play a political role, in which they may excel or fail quite independently of their skills as teacher or scholar.

Once the point is conceded, it will be clear that the worlds of politics and economics are not, and cannot be, separate from each other. If those engaged in economic exchanges are also simultaneously engaged in politics, and those engaged in political negotiation – building a coalition, for example – are also engaged in raising finance and soliciting votes, both processes have to be studied, and analysed, together, and the structures analysed within which the processes take place.

The second thing is that the concept of power, too, has to be radically enlarged. The political theorists and sociologists have made a good beginning by extending the notion of power beyond the mere command of resources and beyond the use of direct coercion. Luhmann has emphasized the capability to apply negative sanctions, although it is not clear to me why he attaches less weight to positive sanctions since systems of patronage are as old as the study of politics itself. Lukes's (1974) idea of the three levels of power has been widely accepted. From direct coercive power, he extends the concept of power to what I would call structural power – not just power to set agendas but to shape institutions – and to power in the realm of ideas: what I call the knowledge structure in which definitions are made of legitimacy in authority, by which some kinds of logic and methods of argument and analysis are accepted and others rejected.

What is still unclear is whether the third level includes – as I believe it should – power that is exerted unconsciously, without intent or deliberate purpose. Involuntary power applies particularly to the power of markets – what many people think of as economic power – though I firmly insist that it is impossible to make any clear distinction between political power and economic power since there is always an element of each in the other. Those who think narrowly about politics find it hard to imagine that power can reside in anything as impersonal as a market. But in real life the power of the market operator may be difficult to separate from the way the market is organized. Think, for example, of the power exercised by De Beers over buyers and sellers of diamonds. The way the diamond market operates has been structured by De Beers – with the compliance and indeed co-operation of governments of South Africa – over nearly a century. It is therefore impossible to separate the power of De Beers as operator from the power of the market for diamonds in which the company operates: just as the structure of international society in which the mutual interest of all governments in their own survival sustains a whole set of conventions that could be summed up as 'dog does not eat dog'. Thus, the system itself confers power on the constituent states, just as the structures of the world market economy confer power on those who operate in the market, whether they seek such power or not.

This is not inconsistent with the analysis in Robert Cox's *Production, Power and World Order* (1987), although he gives special emphasis to the international political system as an intervening variable between social forces and outcomes, where I would separate the security structure sustained by the system of states from the financial, production and knowledge structures.

For these reasons, I would argue that both realism and neo-realism in the study of international relations, and liberalism and neo-classical notions of equilibrium in the study of economics, will prove to be blind alleys and should be abandoned. They are both culs-de-sac, *strade senza uscita*, no through roads – for IPE. Sooner or later, it will be necessary to go back and start again at the beginning if we are to achieve a genuine synthesis of political and economic activity.

The purpose should be to arrive at a clear analysis of the outcomes in the global household and how they were brought about. 'Outcomes' involve both distributive outcomes – who gets what – and those concerning the mix of values in the system as a whole. Does the way in which the international political economy functions continue to favour the production of wealth over the provision of justice? What room does it give for the exercise of autonomy or the freedom to choose? How much stability and security does it provide in the long run as well as in the short run? And for each of these values, there is the distributive question: for whom? For which social, economic, ethnic or religious groups does the system provide most wealth, most security, most justice or most freedom to choose?

Going back to the beginning, for me, means starting with what used to be called moral philosophy. As I understand it, moral philosophers were concerned with fundamental values – how they could be reflected in the ordering of human society and how conflicts between them might be resolved. They were – some still are – interested in analysing both the mix of values in any society and their distribution. The only difference now is that we have, in some sense at least, a global society and, sustaining it, a virtually worldwide political economy. The horizons of moral philosophy, as of the social sciences, no longer end at the frontiers of the state. To start, therefore, with moral philosophy is a powerful safeguard against nationalist, or any other partisan, bias when it comes to the analysis of IPE issues.

How far to go beyond analysis to prescription is a rather subjective question. Some individual scholars may be inspired by a normative motive – advocating the purposive promotion of a different mix of values and a different distributive outcome of particular values. Others may be concerned only to make an objective, accurate analysis of the arrangements, the structures of production, finance, security and knowledge – and of how they have come about. Like Ibn Khaldun, the North African contemporary of Machiavelli, their purpose is simply to discover 'how and why things are as they are' (Lacoste, 1984, p. 177). Where Thucydides regarded history as an art, Khaldun sought to make it into a science, looking for underlying causes of political change in his own North Africa in social and economic structures. The contrast with Machiavelli, the forerunner of realist thought in international relations, is striking. Machiavelli wanted to advise a ruler how to survive in control of the state and in its relations with others. For reasons which should now be plain, my feeling is that the study of international political economy today needs more Ibn Khalduns and fewer Machiavellis.

To sum up, translating these thoughts into practical terms of teaching and research, there are two imperatives. The first – whether applied to taught courses or to research projects – is to move the field away from too exclusively state-centred a focus. The focus of study and enquiry should be on the system, and on the mix of values in it. The questions should always begin by asking: 'By what political and economic processes, and thanks to what political and economic structures, did this outcome come about?' After causes, come consequences: Who benefited? Who paid? Who carried the risks? Who enjoyed new opportunities?

The second imperative is to apply in practice the two points made above: to extend the limits of politics; and to broaden the concept of power so that it includes structural as well as relational power, the power to influence the ideas of others, their access to credit, their prospects of security, their chances of a better material life as producers and as consumers. These two changes mean that when we look for causes, we shall look beyond states to markets and market operators, and to non-state authorities over them. And when we look at consequences, again, we shall look beyond states to associations of people other than 'nations': to classes, generations, genders, even species.

Notes

1 Kindleberger was, I believe, first in the field (Kindleberger, 1970) but he rather studiously avoided the problem of theoretical synthesis.
2 A notable example is Professor Rittberger and the team of scholars he has assembled at Tübingen University.
3 For example, by Andrew Shonfield in *Modern Capitalism* (1965) – his best book but the conclusions of which now seem hopelessly dated and over optimistic.
4 Diana Tussie's contribution, 'Trading in Fear? US Hegemony and the Open World Economy', to Murphy and Tooze (1991) is an example of the new generation of Latin American work in IPE. W. Ofuatey-Kodjoe's review of current African literature is another. A 1993 World Bank research project on the Asian miracle also casts serious doubt on some of the conventional economic wisdom.
5 Hence much ambiguity and misunderstanding in the use of the words 'structure' and 'structuralism'.

References

Axelrod, R. 1981: 'The emergence of cooperation among egoists'. *American Political Science Review*, 75, 306–18.
Baldwin, D. 1971: Money and power. *Journal of Politics*, 33, 578–614.
Blake, D. and Walters, R. 1976: *The Politics of Global Economic Relations*. Englewood Cliffs, N.J.: Prentice-Hall.
Brandt, W. 1980: *North–South: a Program for Survival*. London: Pan Books.
Colander, D. and Brenner, R. (eds) 1992: *Educating Economists*. Ann Arbor: Michigan University Press.
Cole, K., Cameron, J. and Edwards, C. 1983: *Why Economists Disagree: the Political Economy of Economics*. London: Longman.
Cooper, R. 1968: *The Economics of Interdependence*. New York: McGraw-Hill.
Corbridge, S. and Thrift, A. 1994 forthcoming: *Money, Space and Power*. Cambridge: Cambridge University Press.
Cox, R. 1987: *Production, Power and World Order*. New York: Columbia University Press.
De Jouvenel, B. 1954: *Sovereignty*. Paris: PUF.
Dicken, P. 1986 (2nd edn 1992): *Global Shift: the Internationalisation of Economic Activity*. London: Chapman.
Eichengreen B. 1992: *Golden Fetters: the Gold Standard and the Great Depression 1919–1939*. Oxford: Oxford University Press.
Giddens, A. 1990: *The Consequences of Modernity*. Cambridge: Polity Press.

Gilpin, R. 1987: *The Political Economy of International Relations*. Princeton, N.J.: Princeton University Press.

Higgott, R. 1991: Toward a non-hegemonic IPE. In Murphy and Tooze (1991), 97–128.

Hodgson, G. and Screpanti, E. 1991: *Rethinking Economics: Markets, Technology and Economic Evolution*. London: Elgar.

Holsti, K. 1985: *The Dividing Discipline: Hegemony and Diversity in International Theory*. London: Allen & Unwin.

Keohane, R. 1984: *After Hegemony: Cooperation and Discord in the World Political Economy*. Princeton, N.J.: Princeton University Press.

Keohane, R. and Nye, J. (eds) 1972: *Transnational Relations and World Politics*. Cambridge, Mass.: Harvard University Press.

Kindleberger, C. 1970: *Power and Money: the Economics of International Politics and the Politics of International Economics*. New York: Basic Books.

Krasner, S. 1983: *International Regimes*. Ithaca, N.Y.: Cornell University Press.

Lacoste, Y. 1984: *Ibn Khaldun: the Birth of History and the Past of the Third World* (tr. from French). London: Verso.

Lukes, S. 1974: *Power*. Oxford: Oxford University Press.

Mann, M. 1986: *The Sources of Social Power* vol. I: *A History of Power from the Beginning to A.D. 1760*. Cambridge: Cambridge University Press.

Morse, E. 1976: *Modernisation and the Transformation of International Relations*. New York: Free Press.

Murphy, C. and Tooze, R. (eds) 1991: *The New International Political Economy*. Boulder, Colorado: Rienner.

Rosenau, J. 1990: *Turbulence in World Politics*. Princeton, N.J.: Princeton University Press.

Shonfield, A. 1965: *Modern Capitalism: the Changing Balance of Public and Private Power*. Oxford: Oxford University Press for RIIA.

Sklair, I. 1991: *Sociology of the Global System: Social Change in Global Perspective*. London: Harvester Wheatsheaf.

Spero, J. 1977: *The Politics of International Economic Relations*. Hemel Hempstead: Allen & Unwin.

Stopford, J. and Strange, S. 1991: *Rival States, Rival Firms: Competition for World Market Shares*. Cambridge: Cambridge University Press.

Strange, S. 1970: International economics and international relations: a case of mutual neglect. *International Affairs*, April, 304–15.

Strange, S. 1972: International economic relations: the need for an interdisciplinary approach. In R. Morgan (ed.), *The Study of International Affairs*, Oxford, Oxford University Press for RIIA, 63–84.

Strange, S. 1983: Cave! hic dragones. In Krasner (1983), 337–54.

Strange, S. 1988: *States and Markets: an Introduction to International Political Economy*. London: Frances Pinter.

Whitman, M. 1984: Persistent unemployment: economic policy perspectives in US and Europe. In A. Pierre (ed.), *Unemployment and Growth in the Western Economies*. New York: Council on Foreign Relations.

8

Re-visioning Security

J. Ann Tickner

In the aftermath of the Second World War, E. H. Carr (1945, chapter 2) observed that the developments in military technology of the first half of the twentieth century were rendering the state an anachronism: it could no longer assure the military security or economic well-being of its citizens. As a solution to this dilemma, Carr suggested divorcing international security from its association with national frontiers and national sovereignty: the achievement of what he called 'pooled' or 'common' security would require some kind of world security organization with a standing international force at its command. Carr proposed a system of overlapping and interlocking units appropriate for different purposes, a world organized along functional rather than national lines. National units, however, should be retained to satisfy people's need for identity which, he believed, represented the constructive side of nationalism.

Nationalism and After (Carr, 1945) was written at the end of a major war, a time of heightened sensitivity to insecurity when the quest for new models for achieving international security is usually a major preoccupation. In many respects, Carr's vision was quite similar to contemporary 'common security' thinking, although Carr's world security organization involved more centralization of power than contemporary advocates of common security are willing to entertain. However, this vision was soon to be lost as the onset of a superpower cold war seemed to demand alliance-orientated, 'realist' prescriptions. Assessing the limitations of national security was postponed; collective security, a step on the road to Carr's world security organization, was dismissed as 'unrealistic' in a world of self-interested and power-seeking states.

With the ascendancy of the realist paradigm in the postwar period came realist claims that it was the failure of utopian schemes for collective security and Western policy-makers' unwillingness adequately to pursue their national security interests in the 1930s which were responsible for the Second World War (Morgenthau, 1973, chapter 24).

REALIST PERSPECTIVES ON NATIONAL SECURITY

For several decades, the predominance of the realist paradigm largely silenced the post-national security views expressed in *Nationalism and After*: ironically, Carr's earlier work, *Twenty Years' Crisis*, has been cited frequently to reinforce realism's world view. For realists, the meaning of security was subsumed under the rubric of power. Conceptually, it was synonomous with the security of the state against external dangers, which was to be achieved by increasing military capabilities. This focus on a state-centric definition of security grew out of realist assumptions of a sharp boundary between domestic 'order' and international 'anarchy', a 'state of nature' where war is an ever present possibility (Waltz, 1979, p. 102). Given the lack of an international authority with the power to curb others' aggressive ambitions, states must rely on their own capabilities for the achievement of security. As realists have acknowledged, this self-help system often results in what they describe as a 'security dilemma'; what are justified by one state as legitimate security-enhancing measures are likely to be perceived by others as a threatening military build-up (Smoke, 1975). Such behaviour can lead to destabilizing arms races which may decrease the overall security of the system and its member states. For realists, what stability does exist in such a world can be attributed to the balance of power.

These assumptions about the nature of the international system and the security-seeking behaviour of states fit with realist analysis of the behaviour of the great powers in the post-Second World War period. The escalation of the arms race between the US and the Soviet Union could be characterized as a classic case of the security dilemma, yet the tight bipolarity produced a balance which, for Kenneth Waltz and other realists, assured a considerable measure of security (Waltz, 1964). However, the stress of the Cold War epitomized by the 'emergence of a fabulous new technology of violence' (Beck and Berkowitz, 1966, p. 122) led to a new specialization in international relations, the field of national security which further cemented the meaning of security into a statist, military framework. Adopting a realist worldview and heavily dominated by US strategic thinking about nuclear weapons and the security problems of the US and its NATO allies, the field of national security was based on the assumption that, since nuclear wars were too dangerous to fight, security was synonomous with nuclear deterrence and nuclear power-balancing.

While the ideology of the Cold War corresponded with realism, the equating of international security with the strategic relationship between the great powers was not without its critics even during the Cold War period (Wolfers, 1952). Hedley Bull (1965) pointed to the ethnocentrism in security thinking as the focus in national security studies on the US–Soviet relationship meant that their security became equated with the security of the international system as a whole. With this emphasis on political/military issues, the work of scholars who raised issues about economic relations between states was consigned to the realm of 'low politics'.

Although bipolarity began to break down well before the end of the Cold War and economic issues moved onto the security agenda after the oil shocks of the 1970s, a fully fledged debate about the meaning of security did not begin until the early 1980s. The reintensification of the Cold War, which fuelled fears about the possibility of nuclear war, raised concerns as to whether the escalation of the arms race was compatible with the enhancement of security. Debates about extended deterrence centred on the credibility of the US promise to guarantee the security of Western Europe. By the 1980s nuclear weapons, deployed in the name of national security, were making certain people feel very insecure: paradoxically, national security thinking had reached its height at a time when, as the Reagan administration's Strategic Defense Initiative made clear, the state could no longer assure the security of citizens within its own boundaries. To those critical of realist strategic thinking, the military security of the state seemed synonomous with the insecurity of individuals held hostage to nuclear deterrence.

As the conflict between the great powers de-escalated rapidly at the end of the 1980s and the world seemed poised on the verge of another new international order, space opened up for broadening the security agenda to include issues that Carr so prophetically raised in 1945. Today, however, unlike half a century ago, the field of international relations is in disarray: a multiplicity of theoretical challenges to the realist paradigm assures that new definitions of security and prescriptions for its achievement will be more contested than the old. This emerging dialogue on security issues has already produced some fundamental rethinking, not only of the conceptual foundations upon which the traditional understanding of security was constructed but also of the epistemological foundations of the field more generally.

Contemporary re-analyses of security come from a variety of sources – policy-makers and academics in the West, 'new thinking' in the former Soviet Union, as well as scholars concerned with security issues in the South. Earlier realist thinking on security is being re-examined by realists themselves as well as by scholars critical of the realist tradition. Confronted with the sudden abdication of one of the superpowers from the nuclear arms race, even the strategic community has begun to debate the adequacy and morality of nuclear deterrence, the focus on great power relationships, and the utility of war itself (Booth, 1993). The focus on the military dimension of the security of the great powers, typical of the Cold War period, is being re-examined as the definition of security is being widened to include economic and ecological dimensions. Motivated both by the precarious economic position of the South and the extent to which Northern states now see their own security in terms of economic vulnerabilities, debates about a new international order have centred on a variety of issues ranging from the trade-offs between economic, military and ecological security to the likelihood of instability in the world economy associated with US hegemonic decline.

It is probably not coincidental that this re-analysis of security is taking place at the same time as a 'third debate' in international relations which is questioning the theoretical foundations of the field more generally (Lapid, 1989). These critical perspectives are claiming that an understanding of security more appropriate for the contemporary world requires a fundamental rethinking of the framing assumptions of realist analysis: in a highly interdependent world facing multiple security threats, critics of realism claim that state-centric analysis, which focuses exclusively on the political/military dimensions of security, is no longer adequate.

EXPANDING THE DEFINITIONAL BOUNDARIES OF NATIONAL SECURITY

The realist preoccupation with cross-border conflict and military power defined in terms of the interests and security of the great powers has come under a great deal of criticism from those who argue that its worldview is a poor fit with contemporary reality. Evan Luard (1988) notes the declining likelihood of war between the great powers as well as the erosion of the usefulness of military power as a factor in national security enhancement. Yet as Luard's study confirms, proponents of new security thinking who focus on the decline of military conflict run the risk of perpetuating the ethnocentrism that has long plagued the field of security studies (Nye and Lynn-Jones, 1988). To applaud the absence of war among the great powers at the core of the system is to ignore approximately 127 significant wars that have occurred since 1945, all but two of them in the South (Luard, 1988, p. 61).

Perspectives from the South

Where conventional national security thinking has analysed Southern security it has generally done so from the perspective of great power security interests: one irony of the removal of military conflict to the peripheries of the system during the Cold War may have been that the quest for systemic security actually increased Southern insecurity (Ayoob, 1991). From the perspective of the South, the Northern definition of security was seen as synonomous with the preservation of US hegemony, the security of the West, and the interests of international capitalism (Luckman, 1983, p. 204).

From a Southern perspective, military conflicts are rarely cross-border, but, rather, the result of domestic challenges to the legitimacy of political regimes frequently supported by outside intervention. Recent wars in the Middle East being the exception, security threats more often arise, not from outside aggression, but from the failure to integrate diverse social groups into the political process. Deterrence against external attack is not an adequate representation of security goals when it is internal insecurity that is the greatest threat: moreover, as Nicole Ball (1988, p. 40) points out, even the term 'internal security' is a misnomer since its purpose is rarely to make all citizens equally secure but, rather, to enable ruling elites to remain in power, often at the expense of the majority of the population.

While military conflict has and probably will continue to be a source of insecurity in the South, many scholars claim that security should not be defined solely in terms of military threats. Going beyond realist thinking, Edward Azar and Chung-in Moon (1988) define insecurity more broadly, as threats to values and identities, the nature of which will vary across time, space and issue area. Many regions of the South are more preoccupied with economic than military threats and, as Nicole Ball suggests, where both exist simultaneously, they are usually highly interdependent. Ball argues for an expanded definition of security on the basis of this interdependence: internal military conflicts often arise because elites are unwilling to alter exploitative social and economic relations and political systems which work to their advantage. Ball also points to the trade-off between military and economic security when resources are diverted from development to the military. She claims that military expenditures have a negative effect on economic growth (1988, pp. 163–7): the kind of technologies necessary for military development are of little use for providing the basic material needs of most people.

Caroline Thomas (1987) also stresses the economic dimensions of national security when she defines security, not only in terms of the internal security of the state, but also in terms of secure systems of food, health, money and trade. For Thomas, basic human needs provision is a dimension of national security; like Ball, she notes the interdependence between military and economic security when the failure to meet individuals' basic needs reinforces the problems of internal security as regimes, perceived as not working in the interests of people, arm themselves to protect against domestic unrest. Thomas also emphasizes the lack of control over the external environment where weak states operate in an international economic order that favours the powerful, who are both the rule-makers and the rule-enforcers.

As these redefinitions indicate, an examination of security in a Southern context exposes the limitations of contemporary great-power-orientated realist analysis. The arming of the South with advanced weapons, usually provided by the great powers and used primarily for internal security purposes, reinforces the claim of critics of nuclear deterrence that it is militarization itself which is becoming the greatest threat to security. Internal conflicts raise the issue of whose security is being assured and suggest that an adequate analysis of security demands consideration of security at the individual as well as the state level. Some scholars have even suggested that the term 'state', as it is used in the Western context, is not appropriate in certain areas of the South where 'quasi-states' derive their legitimacy from the international system rather than from the support of their own people (Jackson and Rosberg, 1982). In an international system which, in parts of the South, amounts to domestic disorder and stability of international borders, often upheld by the interventions and interests of the great powers, the realist assumption about boundaries between anarchy and order is turned on its head.

Perspectives from the North

Two sharply divergent trends in contemporary definitions of security in the North are emerging. One is associated with proponents of 'common' or 'comprehensive' security, who argue that military-centred notions of national security are fundamentally flawed in a highly interdependent world facing multiple security threats that are not amenable to traditional statist solutions. The other revives the more traditional notion of national security through a new and modified Pax Americana; after the demise of the Soviet threat, the US, with its continued strong military capabilities and the help of its Cold War alliance partners, is seen as having the potential to become the guarantor of global security, a role that is now less ambiguous and dangerous than it was during the bipolar rivalry of the Cold War.

Like those writing from a Southern perspective, proponents of 'common security' have adopted a multidimensional definition of security which emphasizes security interdependence rather than the zero-sum notion of security more typical of national security thinking. The contemporary definition of 'common security' was first given political prominence in the report of the Independent Commission on Disarmament and Security Issues (1982), which claimed that the nuclear paradox, the fact that the security of states depended on the insecurity of their citizens, had stretched the traditional concept of security to its limit. Common security assumes that there are global dangers which threaten the entire system and which cannot be solved by boundary protection; by emphasizing common dangers, it bases its appeal for co-operative behaviour, not on altruism, but on a larger sense of collective self-interest.

Elements of common security thinking entered into certain policy-making circles in the North in the 1980s. A 1980 Report on Comprehensive National Security to the Prime Minister of Japan defined security as protecting people's lives from various forms of threat both internal and external. According to this report, insecurity includes economic vulnerability as well as ecological threats and natural disasters (Barnett, 1984). In the mid-1980s, Mikhail Gorbachev proposed a comprehensive system of international security which would include disarmament as well as global economic and ecological security. Gorbachev urged an enhanced role for the United Nations as a global security provider: this enhanced role is compatible with expanded UN peacekeeping functions as well as UN involvement in humanitarian relief efforts in Somalia and the former Yugoslavia.

Some Northern scholars have also begun to define security in similar multidimensional terms. Richard Ullman (1983) defines national security as an attempt to protect against events that threaten to degrade the quality of life for the inhabitants of the state: among these threats he lists the inability to meet basic needs, environmental deterioration and natural disasters. Neo-realist Barry Buzan (1991) has broadened the traditional realist focus on military security to include economic and environmental dimensions. Jessica Mathews (1991) claims that the definition of security must be expanded to include environmental, resource and demographic issues; resource degradation and pollution together with population growth are causing damage that increasingly impacts on people's ability to meet their basic needs.

The multidimensionality of security defined in military, economic and ecological terms and the interdependence between them is at the heart of common security thinking. The World Commission on Environment and Development (1987) underscored the interdependence between economic and ecological dimensions of security when it called for 'sustainable development', a type of development compatible with preserving a healthy environment for future generations: it also emphasized universal basic needs satisfaction as an important aspect of sustainable development. This emphasis on individuals and the natural environment, stressed by all proponents of common security, calls into question the state as a security provider: the Independent Commission on Disarmament and Security Issues claimed in its report (1982) that, in the nuclear age, no state could find security by itself. Building on the tradition of Scandinavian peace research (Galtung, 1980), proponents of common security have proposed definitions of security which challenge the boundaries and institutions within which our traditional understanding of security is framed.

In sharp contrast to this global thinking, proponents of a new Pax Americana see security in terms similar to post-1945 realist thinking although they applaud the resolution of the uneasy tension between US hegemony and nuclear bipolarity which so preoccupied earlier national security thinking. Charles Krauthammer (1992) sees evidence of what he terms the 'unipolar moment' in which 'an ideologically pacified North seeks security and order by aligning its foreign policy behind that of the United States'. Claiming that 'the UN is a guarantor of nothing', Krauthammer maintains that we are entering an era of 'pseudomultilateralism' in which effective security can be guaranteed only by US military power. He asserts that most of the dangers are located in the South, where small and backward states are emerging as threats to both regional and global security. While they continue to focus on issues related to military security, certain proponents of this world view do acknowledge that there are trade-offs to be made between the US's military capabilities and its economic power.

Pax Americana, with its emphasis on the military policing role of the US, is an avowedly ethnocentric reformulation of earlier national security thinking, differing only in its shift from an East–West to a North–South perspective. While there are those who continue to see military dangers in a post-Cold War Europe, (Mearsheimer, 1990), much of the new thinking on security has made a similar shift towards a North–South framework, which has the potential for reinforcing a disturbing trend towards an increasing North–South polarization. In spite of the remaining problems of US–Russian de-nuclearization, the end of the Cold War has focused arms control discussions on issues of proliferation and arms sales to the South. From a Northern perspective, however, the continued development of high-technology weapons in the North for use against unacceptable Southern regimes appears, in certain areas, as at least as great a threat to security as internal conflict. Even voices sympathetic to the South may be reinforcing this new worldview which sees insecurity, whether it be in the form of war, economic deprivation, over-population, human rights abuses or environmental degradation, located only in the South. While not underestimating the severity of security threats in this region, an adequate re-analysis of security must resist new boundary distinctions which obscure global structures of inequality that contribute to making certain individuals and groups in both the North and the South more insecure. Re-analysing security, therefore, requires that we go beyond the polarities of traditional thinking. I shall now examine how realism and some of its contemporary critics are undertaking this re-analysis.

RE-VISIONING SECURITY

Reformulating Realism

Realist re-visions of security offer two contrasting perspectives which parallel the state-centric and common security definitions outlined above. First, there are realists who are analysing security in terms quite similar to the post-1945 era but adapted to the post-Cold War world. Assuming the state as a unitary actor, their definition of security prioritizes international order and stability to be achieved by a modified version of Pax Americana which includes co-operative collective security arrangements among the great powers. Acknowledging that US pre-eminence cannot last and that the US can no longer act alone, Henry Kissinger (1992) associates security with the re-creation of a concert of powers in the North: Northern states should also support attempts to create regional power balances in unstable areas of the South such as the Middle East. In similar terms, Charles and Clifford Kupchan (1992) propose a new version of collective security consisting of the major powers, similar to the nineteenth-century Concert of Europe. Defining security in terms of systemic stability, the Kupchans claim that universal collective security organizations are doomed to fail because they require an unacceptable loss of sovereignty and do not reflect power realities; one of the functions of the security group of the militarily powerful is to ensure that peripheral conflicts, examples of which are all taken from the South, are 'fenced off or resolved'. William Odom (1992) equates security with a new Pax Americana in which US military dominance in key strategic regions keeps the peace. He urges that US military forces increase their capabilities for rapid interventions in the South.

In the tradition of realism, all of these authors equate security with order and international boundary maintenance, to be achieved by the preservation of a hierarchical international system in which the great powers act as the world's policemen. This realist re-analysis does nothing to move us beyond the ethnocentrism of earlier national security studies. The emphasis on order, defined in terms of resolution of military conflict, does not begin to address issues of economic injustice and environmental degradation; those who argue for this broader definition of security claim that increasing military capabilities may actually contribute to increasing economic and ecological insecurities by draining resources away from civilian needs and from efforts to create a cleaner environment. They assert that modern military technology is not only expensive but carries huge environmental costs due to its high resource use and large-scale environmental pollution.

The most important and extensive re-examination of security from a neo-realist perspective which attempts to get beyond this military, state-centric focus is Barry Buzan's *People, States and Fear* (1991). Calling himself a 'liberal realist', Buzan includes issues raised by proponents of common security. Having broadened his definition of security to include freedom from military, political, societal, economic and environmental threats, Buzan makes a case for the need for a new field of international security studies which, in contrast to the traditional national security approach, would take as its starting point this multidimensional definition of security.

While Buzan examines security from the perspectives of the individual and the international system as well as of the state, he concludes that the most important and effective provider of security is likely to remain the sovereign state. Answering the claim raised by scholars analysing the South, that states can be a threat to rather than a source of security, Buzan argues that the evolution toward 'strong states', more typical of the West, will result in a greater degree of security for individuals. In terms of the international system, Buzan does not feel that the elimination of anarchy is the answer to the security dilemma. Accepting, in principle at least, the realist boundary distinction between domestic order and international anarchy, he predicts that, as the system moves towards what he terms 'mature anarchy', a more stable form of international anarchy which is co-evolving along with progress towards stronger states, international security will be enhanced. Buzan also claims that the integrative features of an increasingly interdependent global market economy contribute to the movement towards mature anarchy with its promise of greater international security.

By acknowledging the distinction between strong and weak states, Buzan has moved beyond traditional realist analyses which assume that the state is a unitary unproblematic actor in matters of national security. However, his assumption that strong states, which he equates with Western democracies, can be successful security providers for all their citizens has been questioned by certain critics (Smith, 1991). Buzan's claim that strong states can successfully provide security might be challenged by marginalized groups, such as women and minorities, whose economic security is often compromised when military security takes priority. The concept of the national interest, around which national security policies are framed, is usually defined by political and military elites; consequently, even strong states implement dubious policies that are not always formulated democratically.

While Buzan may be correct in basing his assumptions about mature anarchy on the fact that Western liberal democratic states seem disinclined to fight one another, there is no guarantee that they will not intervene militarily in weak states in other regions when their security interests are threatened. Peripheral states might also have trouble accepting Buzan's liberal assumption that their economic security can be improved by greater interdependence with the world economy. Moreover, environmental security, the least developed dimension of security in Buzan's work, may be at odds with the continued economic development of states and the world economy required for progress towards mature anarchy (Dalby, 1992).

Even though Buzan has broadened his analysis of security it remains rooted in a framework in which the North is the guarantor of global security. While Buzan sees a decline in military conflict as the system progresses towards mature anarchy and an increase in economic well-being as the world economy becomes more interdependent, the South sees security threats in a Northern build-up of high-technology weapons for wars of intervention, in Northern control of a highly unequal world economy, and in Northern overconsumption of natural resources with its negative consequences for the global environment. Buzan's critics would disagree with his liberal assumption that the benefits of progress can be available to all: political hierarchies and the uneven development of the capitalist world economy are structural constraints on the achievement of security for the poorest states and individuals. Reformed realism continues to privilege the security of the state: although less explicitly than traditional realism, it continues to equate security with an international system dominated by the great powers.

Critical Perspectives

Most approaches that are critical of realist and neo-realist perspectives are attempting to move security analysis towards a more comprehensive, less state-centric orientation. Critics of realism question what they see as the zero-sum, dichotomous thinking of traditional national security discourse. They also question whether the state can continue to be an adequate security provider when security is defined in terms that include economic and ecological as well as military dimensions.

Recent peace and conflict research has begun to define security from a multidimensional, multilevel perspective (Dunn, 1991). Using a definition of security similar to common security, which focuses on the elimination of all types of violence both direct and indirect, peace research first introduced the concept of structural violence in the late 1960s: structural violence extends the meaning of violence beyond its association with physical violence to the indirect violence done to individuals when unjust economic and political structures reduce their life expectancy through lack of access to basic material needs (Galtung, 1971; Wallensteen, 1988). While many peace researchers continue to address issues involving military conflict, they are also making links between military operations and environmental degradation, as well as drawing attention to trade-offs between military and social spending. Certain peace researchers are advocating non-offensive defence and de-nuclearization as ways of scaling down military spending and decreasing the likelihood of global war.

Like E. H. Carr, certain peace researchers are questioning whether the state system as presently constituted can continue to be an effective security provider; in an increasingly interdependent world, where weapons of mass destruction threaten both victors and vanquished alike, self-help is not considered a viable method of security provision. Many peace researchers have, therefore, postulated a new or dramatically reformed world order as a necessary step towards greater security; within this reconstructed global framework, the security of the individual takes precedence over the security of the state.

In the introduction to their volume on world security, Michael Klare and Daniel Thomas (1991) define security, not in statist terms, but as the attempt to enhance the long-term health and welfare of the human family and minimize human suffering. In the same volume, Richard Falk distinguishes his 'world order' approach to security from that of realism. He claims that new threats to security, which defy boundary protection and which cannot be solved by one state alone, complicate realist assumptions of self-help and demand new frameworks that analyse security from a more comprehensive perspective. Attention must be paid to democratic transnational social forces which are intensifying the interplay between domestic and international factors and which offer a strong challenge to the realist worldview. While this conceptual move from national security to global security is at the heart of the world order perspective, its proponents also claim that this human vision of security must start with the individual. Echoing Carr, proponents of the world order values of peace, economic well-being, human rights and environmental balance believe that they can best be achieved, not by state institutions, but by international or transnational functional institutions appropriate to the task.

Like proponents of this 'world order' approach, Ken Booth (1991) claims that individuals not states must be the fundamental referents of security. Arguing for an emancipatory vision of security, Booth criticizes 'unhelpful dichotomies' which have characterized the way we study international politics. According to Booth, the language in which security has been framed is one of division and exclusion; unless we cast off these old images and begin to think more interdependently, our images of the future will tend to replicate the past. Booth argues for a position that sees security from a holistic perspective rather than one that privileges the state and its military power. Labelling himself a 'utopian realist', he attempts to integrate what is best about the realist tradition with a politics of emancipation that looks to a democratic form of human security not achieved at others' expense.

Most critics of realism would agree with Booth that a politics of emancipation that can assure human security requires fundamental rethinking of the boundaries and identities within which our traditional understanding of security has been framed. Like Booth, R. B. J. Walker (1988) is critical of the language of division associated with realist thinking: he claims that assumptions that security can be provided only within states works in the interest of elites and reinforces boundary distinctions between self and other, friend and foe, citizen and foreigner, which set up barriers that inhibit the achievement of world security. These dichotomies, which reflect conventional understandings of political space, are necessary for the legitimation of the concept of national security but are incompatible with the search for world security and the security of individuals.

When national security is defined negatively, as protection against outside military threats, the sense of threat is reinforced by the doctrine of state sovereignty, which strengthens the boundary between a secure community and a dangerous external environment. For this reason, many critics of realism claim that, if security is to start with the individual, its ties to state sovereignty must be severed. While E. H. Carr argued for the retention of the nation-state to satisfy people's need for identity, those who are critical of state-centric analysis point to the dangers of a political identity constructed out of exclusionary practices. In the present international system, security is tied to a nationalist political identity which depends on the construction of those outside as 'other' and therefore dangerous (Walker, 1990). David Campbell (1992) suggests that securing the boundaries of this statist identity demands the construction of 'danger' on the outside: thus, threats to security in conventional thinking are all in the external realm. Campbell claims that the state requires this discourse of danger to secure its identity and legitimation which depend on the promise of security for its citizens. Citizenship becomes synonomous with loyalty and the elimination of all that is foreign. Underscoring this distinction between citizens and people reinforced by these boundary distinctions, Walker argues that not until people, rather than citizens, are the primary subjects of security can a truly comprehensive security be achieved.

Yet, as both Falk (1992b) and Walker (1990) claim, never before has the state system been so strong. Uneven development, fostered by a hierarchical international system of states and a global capitalist economy, is contributing to what Falk (1992a) and others are beginning to call 'global apartheid' – an analogy drawn from the interplay of racial domination and economic inequality in South Africa (Schelling, 1992). Falk claims that, whereas apartheid in South Africa was regarded as intolerable, the situation wherein the rich and powerful are located in states in the North with predominantly white populations and the poor and weak in Southern states comprised largely of people of colour is tolerated and accepted. Globalization of capital, along with policies that prevent the migration of people to the North, exacerbates this phenomenon, which appears to be increasing the security of the rich as it diminishes the security of the poor.

Yet Falk and others see forces at work that challenge these boundaries between the strong and the weak and the rich and the poor created by the state system and global capitalism. They claim that the creative energy for reformulating security in less exclusionary terms is coming from social movements which operate across national boundaries and which grow out of a concern for human security defined in economic and ecological as well as political/military terms (Walker, 1988; Reus-Smit, 1992). These authors suggest that social movements defy traditional concepts of political space which threaten to undermine the security of the least privileged; by rearticulating security in terms of those who are most vulnerable, security becomes a process which begins at the bottom. Social movements from below, which are concerned with peace, the environment, democracy, human rights and feminism, have the potential to disrupt the prevailing system and provide a vision of global security which assures the security of all individuals (Falk, 1992b). Falk claims that feminism is one such approach which is attempting to articulate this humanist vision of security: although they are rarely cited in the security literature, feminist perspectives are making an important contribution to these new visions of security.

Feminist Perspectives

Feminists from a variety of theoretical and disciplinary perspectives share a common concern for broadening knowledge to include the experiences of women and introducing gender as a category of analysis. Exposing relations of gender inequality and including women's experiences in security analysis can help to construct the more comprehensive definition of security that many contemporary critics of realism are searching for (Tickner, 1992). Since the military and national security functions of the state have always been considered 'masculine' issues, women have seldom been recognized by the security literature; yet women have been writing about security since at least the beginning of the century, when Jane Addams spoke out in favour of a new internationalism to replace the self-destructive nationalism which she believed contributed to the outbreak of the First World War (Addams, Balch and Hamilton, 1916). Women have generally favoured defining security in multidimensional terms, which include freedom from both physical and structural violence (Falk, Kim and Mendlovitz, 1991, pp. 392–402).

The National Organization for Women estimated, in its 1990 Resolution on Women in Combat, that 80–90 per cent of casualties due to conflict since the Second World War have been civilians, the majority of them women and children. The strategy of rape in the war in Bosnia has alerted the world to an atrocity that has always existed in wartime, although it is usually unreported. Women and children constitute 80 per cent of the global refugee population, a phenomenon usually attributable to military conflict: women are also the most frequent victims of domestic violence in all societies, a crime which is always under-reported, but one which ranges across regions, cultures and classes (United Nations, 1991). Violence against women is higher in militarized societies and in military families. Evidence such as this suggests that women are particularly vulnerable to militarism and war: it also suggests that the myth that women and children are protected by male soldiers, a myth that has persisted throughout history, must be re-examined (Stiehm, 1983).

Extending the definition of security to economic and environmental dimensions also highlights women's vulnerabilities. A 1981 report to the UN Committee on the Status of Women claims that while women represent half the global population and one-third of the paid labour force and are responsible for two-thirds of all working hours, they receive only a tenth of world income and own less than 1 per cent of world property (Jaggar, 1983, p. 138). Data such as these suggest that women are at greater economic risk in all societies. Women's work is undervalued because it is often performed outside the market, in the agricultural subsistence sector in the South or in households more generally. When women enter the labour market they earn less than men in all societies, either because they are disproportionately clustered in low-paying jobs or because they are paid less for performing similar work (United Nations, 1991, pp. 81–114). Women in the South provide low-paid wage labour for Northern multinational corporations and domestic servants for Northern households. In times of economic recession, when state welfare services contract, it is usually women who take up the burdens of caring for the elderly and the sick. In the South structural adjustment policies have impacted heavily on women, who must assume additional care-giving tasks when states are forced to cut back on social spending. Women are also particularly vulnerable to environmental degradation: in areas of Africa and Asia they are walking up to 10 kilometres a day to search for shrinking supplies of fuel-wood and water. Women's reproductive systems are particularly susceptible to the hazards of toxic wastes and industrial accidents.

This evidence of women's multiple insecurities worldwide can help to conceptualize a definition of security that is people-centred and transcends state and regional boundaries. Such evidence also reinforces the claim of theorists critical of realism that the state as presently constituted is not an adequate security provider for all its citizens. The unitary state actor model favoured by realists conceals the extent to which individuals' insecurities are dependent on race, class and gender, categories that also cross state and regional boundaries.

Feminist perspectives are also raising new questions about political identities and political boundaries that certain critics of realism claim are barriers to a comprehensive, non-exclusionary definition of security. As David Campbell notes, the discourse that is used to secure the identity of those on the inside, through the association of danger with those on the outside, is frequently framed in gendered terms. For example, representations by US nineteenth-century authors of Japanese people and people of Latin America as treacherous, child-like, emotionally disturbed and effeminate are gendered, and vestiges of them are still part of US foreign policy discourse today (Campbell, 1992, p. 238; Hunt, 1987). During the early Cold War, the labelling of communist or socialist thought as 'pink' stands in contrast to the imperatives of national security, which depended on the ability of strong men to stand up to the threats of communism (Campbell, 1992, pp. 176–7). In most states, citizenship has been associated with a militarized version of patriotism and the ultimate sacrifice of giving one's life for one's country. Excluded from military combat in almost all societies, women have, therefore, been perceived as second-class citizens or victims who lack agency in matters of their own protection. By questioning this protector/protected relationship and by seeing how these political identities are constructed in terms of gender inequalities, we can begin to understand how they, and other social relations of domination and subordination, can be obstacles to a comprehensive definition of security.

Feminist perspectives can also contribute to the reconsideration of boundaries that have locked traditional security analysis into its statist framework. By emphasizing the interrelationship of physical violence across all levels of society from military combat to family violence, which, like international conflicts, also takes place in a space that is under-protected by the law, feminist perspectives question the identification of security with state boundaries. The global feminization of poverty provides evidence which raises questions about economic boundary distinctions between North and South, increasingly prevalent in the new security literature. Just as poverty and homelessness inside Northern states demonstrate the existence of the South in the North, the North's negative presence is felt in the South when political and economic elites align with Northern states and global capital to the detriment of their own people. Since women have been disproportionately providing the free or under-remunerated labour upon which these inequalities are built, examining women's lives offers a new entry point into understanding how these phenomena are structurally linked (Mies, 1986).

Feminists believe, therefore, that evidence of women's insecurities demonstrates that the activities of the state and the global market are not neutral with regard to security provision for all individuals. However, looking at security from these feminist perspectives is not intended only to address women's insecurities; rather, its goal is to point out how unequal social relations can make all individuals more insecure. Understanding the shared experiences of women worldwide helps to overcome divisions between citizens and people and insiders and outsiders that some critics of realism have identified as detrimental to the achievement of comprehensive security. Many feminists claim that true security cannot be achieved until these hierarchical social relations and divisive boundary distinctions are recognized and substantially altered and until all individuals participate in providing for their own security.

CONCLUSION

Just as E. H. Carr wrote *Nationalism and After* (1945) at a turning point in the history of the international system, this review of some more recent thinking on security suggests that we are at a similar turning point today. The end of the Cold War, marked by the sudden collapse of one of the two superpowers and the continuing conflict in the peripheries of the international system, demands new frameworks for thinking about security. Multiple threats that defy military solutions have caused some neo-realists, as well as many of their critics, to search for a broader definition of security that encompasses not only freedom from physical violence but also the material well-being of individuals and the environmental health of the entire planet. While recognizing that the end of the Cold War does not necessarily signify a more peaceful world or a world where military issues will not continue to occupy the security agenda, those who argue for this broader definition do so on the grounds of heightened interdependence between these various security issues. The collapse of the Soviet Union and the growing militarization of certain regions of the South have highlighted the trade-off between the cost of sophisticated weapons of war, whose use is circumscribed by their potential for mass destruction, and the economic welfare of individuals. The Gulf War of 1991 demonstrated that modern warfare is also a serious threat to the ecosystem. For these reasons there is a growing sense among many contemporary scholars, and even some policy-makers, that preparing for war is becoming too costly and may actually detract from the achievement of national security: even those who continue to prioritize military issues often advocate collective rather than unilateral security arrangements.

If we believe that the various insecurities outlined in this chapter are interrelated, we must begin to take steps towards constructing a vision of security that can promote a viable ecosystem while at the same time working towards the elimination of both physical and structural violence. To do this we must begin to recognize that all these forms of violence are interrelated and that their diminution requires dismantling hierarchical boundaries between women and men, rich and poor, and insiders and outsiders which have contributed to an exclusionary divisive definition of security. Genuine security for all individuals requires a less militarized model of citizenship that valorizes different types of activities and allows women and men to participate equally in building the type of state institutions that are responsive to the security needs of their own people as well as to those on the outside. Such reformulated states could satisfy people's need for identity that

E. H. Carr felt was so important, while providing a type of security that is not achieved at the expense of the security of others. Although still in the distant future, the realization of this humanist vision of security that Carr alluded to fifty years ago requires a willingness to move beyond the exclusionary boundaries and identities within which our traditional understanding of security has been framed.

References

Addams, J., Balch, E. and Hamilton, A. 1916: *Women at The Hague: The International Congress of Women and Its Results*. New York: Macmillan.

Allison, G. and Treverton, G. (eds) 1992: *Rethinking America's Security: Beyond Cold War to New World Order*. New York: W. W. Norton.

Ayoob, M. 1991: The security problematic of the Third World. *World Politics*, 43, 257–83.

Azar, E. and Moon, C. (eds) 1988: *National Security in the Third World*. London: Edward Elgar.

Ball, N. 1988: *Security and Economy in the Third World*. Princeton, N.J.: Princeton University Press.

Barnett, R. 1984: *Beyond War: Japan's Concept of Comprehensive National Security*. Washington: Pergamon Brassey.

Beck, P.G. and Berkowitz, M. 1966: The emerging field of national security. *World Politics*, 19, 122–36.

Booth, K. 1991: Security and emancipation. *Review of International Studies*, 17, 313–26.

Booth, K. 1993: Strategy. In A. J. R. Groom and M. Light (eds), *A Handbook of International Relations Theory*, London: Frances Pinter.

Bull, H. 1965: *The Control of the Arms Race: Disarmament and Arms Control in the Missile Age*. New York: Praeger.

Buzan, B. 1991: *People, States and Fear: An Agenda for International Security Studies in the Post-Cold War Era*. London: Harvester Wheatsheaf.

Campbell, D. 1992: *Writing Security: United States Foreign Policy and the Politics of Identity*. Minneapolis: University of Minnesota Press.

Carr, E. H. 1945: *Nationalism and After*. New York: Macmillan.

Dalby, S. 1992: Security, modernity, ecology: the dilemmas of post-Cold War security discourse. *Alternatives*, 17, 95–134.

Dunn, D. 1991: Peace research versus strategic studies. In K. Booth (ed.), *New Thinking About Strategy and International Security*, London: Harper Collins, 56–72.

Falk, R. 1992a: *Economic Aspects of Global Civilization: The Unmet Challenges of World Poverty*, Princeton, N.J.: Princeton University Center of International Studies.

Falk, R. 1992b: *The Western State System*. Princeton, N.J.: Princeton University Center of International Studies.

Falk, R., Kim, S. and Mendlovitz, S. (eds) 1991: *The United Nations and a Just World Order*. Boulder, Colorado: Westview.

Galtung, J. 1971: A structural theory of imperialism. *Journal of Peace Research*, 8, 81–117.

Galtung, J. 1980: *The True Worlds*. New York: Free Press.

Hunt, M. 1987: *Ideology and US Foreign Policy*. New Haven: Yale University Press.

Independent Commission on Disarmament and Security Issues 1982: *Common Security: A Blueprint for Survival*. New York: Simon and Schuster.

Jackson, R. and Rosberg, C. 1982: Why Africa's weak states persist: the empirical and the juridical in statehood. *World Politics*, 35, 1–24.

Jaggar, A. 1983: *Feminist Politics and Human Nature*. Totowa, N. J.: Rowman and Allanheld.

Kissinger, H. 1992: Balance of power sustained. In Allison and Treverton (1992), 238–48.

Klare, M. and Thomas, D. (eds) 1991: *World Security: Trends and Challenges at Century's End*. New York: St Martin's Press.

Krauthammer, C. 1992: The unipolar moment. In Allison and Treverton (1992), 295–306.

Kupchan, Charles and Kupchan, Clifford 1992: A new concert for Europe. In Allison and Treverton (1992), 249–66.

Lapid, Y. 1989: The third debate: on the prospects of international theory in a post-positivist era. *International Studies Quarterly*, 33, 235–54.

Luard, E. 1988: *The Blunted Sword: The Erosion of Military Power in Modern World Politics*. London: I.B. Tauris.

Luckham, R. 1983: Security and disarmament in Africa. *Alternatives*, 9, 203–28.

Mathews, J. 1991: The environment and international security. In Klare and Thomas (1991), 362–80.

Mearsheimer, J. 1990: Back to the future: instability in Europe after the Cold War. *International Security*, 15, 5–56.

Mies, M. 1986: *Patriarchy and Accumulation on a World Scale: Women in the International Division of Labour*. London: Zed Books.

Morgenthau, H. 1973: *Politics Among Nations: The Struggle for Power and Peace*, 5th edn. New York: Knopf.

Nye, J. and Lynn-Jones, S. 1988: International security studies: a report of a conference on the state of the field. *International Security*, 12, 5–27.

Odom, W. 1992: Military lessons and US forces. In Allison and Treverton (1992), 337–48.

Reus-Smit, C. 1992: Realist and resistance utopias: community, security and political action in the new Europe. *Millennium: Journal of International Studies*, 21, 1–28.

Schelling, T. 1992: Rethinking the dimensions of national security: the global dimension. In Allison and Treverton (1992), 196–210.
Smith, S. 1991: Mature anarchy, strong states and security. *Arms Control*, 12, 325–39.
Smoke, R. 1975: National security affairs. In F. Greenstein and N. Polsby (eds), *Handbook of Political Science*, Reading, Mass.: Addison-Wesley, vol. 8, 247–362.
Stiehm, J. 1983: *Women and Men's Wars*. Oxford: Pergamon Press.
Thomas, C. 1987: *In Search of Security: The Third World in International Relations*. Boulder, Colorado: Lynne Rienner.
Tickner, J.A. 1992: *Gender in International Relations: Feminist Perspectives on Achieving Global Security*. New York: Columbia University Press.
Ullman, R. 1983: Redefining security. *International Security*, 8, 129–53.
United Nations 1991: *The World's Women: Trends and Statistics 1970–1990*. New York: United Nations.
Walker, R. B. J. 1988: *One World, Many Worlds: Struggles for a Just World Peace*. Boulder, Colorado: Lynne Rienner.
Walker, R. B. J. 1990: Security, sovereignty, and the challenge of world politics. *Alternatives*, 15, 3–27.
Wallensteen, P. 1988: The origins of peace research. In P. Wallensteen (ed.), *Peace Research: Achievements and Challenges*, Boulder, Colorado: Westview, 7–29.
Waltz, K. N. 1964: The stability of a bipolar world. *Daedalus*, 93, 881–909.
Waltz, K. N. 1979: *Theory of International Politics*. Reading, Mass.: Addison-Wesley.
Wolfers, A. 1952: National security as an ambiguous symbol. *Political Science Quarterly*, 67, 481–502.
World Commission on Environment and Development 1987: *Our Common Future*. Oxford: Oxford University Press.

9

The Level of Analysis Problem in International Relations Reconsidered

Barry Buzan

This chapter surveys the level of analysis problem in international relations. It looks at how the issue came into the field, how it developed, why it generated disagreement and conflict, where the debate is, and where, in my view, it should be going. The intellectual history approach is used because it seems to be the clearest and most compact way of covering this agenda briefly. The argument is that although the concept of levels of analysis has done much to improve the rigour of theoretical thinking in international relations, too little attention has been paid to the idea itself. A central confusion in understanding what 'levels' refers to arises from a widespread failure to distinguish between sources of explanation and objects of analysis.

THE 'LEVEL OF ANALYSIS PROBLEM' AND HOW IT CAME INTO INTERNATIONAL RELATIONS THEORY

In the social universe, events often have more than one cause, and causes can be found in more than one type of location. For example, it is easy to find statements like: 'The Second World War was caused by French insecurity, German revanchism, and a fatally weakened balance of power mechanism.' This multi-causality may reflect explanations that are all in the same type of location. In the example just given, the French and German causes are in the same type of location, both concerning the behaviour and motives of states. But a weak balance of power is a feature of the international system as a whole, a different type of location for explaining the war than those derived from the behaviour of individual states. Arguing that the war was caused by Hitler would be a third type of location, different from the state- and system-based ones, though of the same type as: 'The Second World War was caused by Chamberlain (or Stalin or Roosevelt).' The 'level of analysis problem' is about how to identify and treat different types of location in which sources of explanation for observed phenomena can be found.

The issue of levels of analysis came into international relations during the 1950s, as part of the broader impact of the behavioural movement, which was trying to introduce the methodology and rigour of the natural sciences into social science. The main concern was to encourage a more positivist, scientific approach in the discipline, stressing observed facts, quantitative measurements, hypothesis-testing, and the development of cumulative theory. This required that one specify and differentiate the sources of one's explanation. It also resulted in part from the impact of general systems theory as a way of thinking about a wide range of physical and social phenomena. Traditional approaches to international relations were informed more by history and law than by natural science, and at that time only a few analysts in the discipline had knowledge of scientific methods. Not everyone was convinced (then and now) that the use of natural science methods was appropriate in the social sciences. But for the behaviouralists, the problem was that explanation in international relations was methodologically confused and lacking in rigour. As in historical method, the typical analysis mixed different locations and sources of explanations, and this both weakened the attempt to create more general types of understanding (theory) and prevented the development of a cumulative science. The heated argument between behaviouralists and traditionalists eventually died down into an uneasy stalemate, but the behaviouralists did carry the point that whatever their approach scientists needed to be more conscious about the methodological, ontological and epistemological aspects of their work. In international relations, development of a general consciousness about levels of analysis was a principal effect of this debate.

The 'behavioural revolution' meshed with a long-standing epistemological debate in the social sciences about two primary approaches to understanding social events: *atomistic* and *holistic*.

In international relations these two approaches are more commonly known as *reductionist* and *systemic* after the usage of Kenneth Waltz (1979, chapters 2–4). Atomism/reductionism is the highly successful methodology of the natural sciences, and requires the fragmentation of a subject into its component parts. In the reductionist approach, understanding improves as one is able to subdivide and explain the component parts of the system ever more finely, as has been done with such astounding success in physics, chemistry, astronomy and biology during the twentieth century. A holistic/systemic approach rests on the premise that the whole is more than the sum of its parts, and that the behaviour and even construction of the parts are shaped and moulded by structures embedded in the system itself. Where the effect of structure is strong, a reductionist approach is inadequate, and on this basis holism established a claim to a distinctive social science approach to analysis.

The reductionist v. holist debate continues among philosophers of social science, with the holist claims rejected by 'methodological individualists', who insist that all structural explanations can and must be reduced to explanations couched in terms of individuals. Recently a 'structuralist' position has been developed that seeks to reconcile the two approaches with a complex argument that structures and units are mutually constitutive (Giddens, 1984). In the discipline of international relations, however, a pragmatic attitude towards levels of analysis by and large prevails, and except for a few enthusiasts, this philosophical debate (no matter how important it is) takes place at the margins of most people's thinking and understanding. The mainstream position in the discipline has been, and still is, that both reductionist and holistic approaches can and must be used if anything like a complete understanding of international relations is to be achieved. The use of levels of analysis therefore represents an eclectic, multi-causal position within reductionist and holist approaches.

Levels of analysis made a strong impact on international relations not least because the idea of levels seemed to fit easily and neatly into the organization of the discipline's subject matter in terms of individuals, states and systems. Three US writers were mainly responsible for bringing the level of analysis problem into the mainstream of thinking about international relations theory: Kenneth N. Waltz, Morton A. Kaplan and J. David Singer (Hollis and Smith, 1990, pp. 97–100). Waltz made the most durable impact by demonstrating the power of an explicitly 'levelled' approach in his still widely read 1959 classic (based on his 1954 Ph.D. thesis) *Man, the State and War*. In that book Waltz unpacked the classical literature on war, and showed how all of it could be organized around three distinct 'images', each reflecting a different location and type of explanation. Some writers explained war by human nature, others by the nature of states, and others by the nature of the international system. Waltz's scheme separated out the international system, and particularly its anarchic structure, as a location of explanation in its own right, and it was this development more than any other that shaped the development of levels of analysis thinking in the discipline.

Morton Kaplan picked it up in his 1957 book *System and Process in International Politics*, which started a vogue for system theory. Most of this took the form of attempts to construct typologies of international system types, usually on the basis of patterns in the distribution of power and/or the configuration of alliances, and then to infer hypotheses about behaviour from these patterns. Whereas Waltz favoured the system level as the dominant source of explanation, Kaplan argued more in favour of the dominance of the state level, and this began a debate which continues to the present day. One effect of this heightened interest in levels was to search for ways of theoretically comprehending what 'international system' meant. Its ontological meaning was clear enough (the sum of all its parts and their interactions), but only if something more than the sum of the parts – the structure or essence of the system – could be specified, could it be used as a basis for explaining international relations. The system level also had the attraction that it increased the distinctiveness of international relations as a field, and gave it some hope of establishing a claim to be a discipline in its own right. Singer's contribution was less substantive, but his 1960 review of Waltz's book, and his 1961 essay 'The Level of Analysis Problem in International Relations' were influential in moving awareness of the problem, and use of the term 'levels of analysis', into the centre of theoretical debate in the field.

These three writers opened the debate about levels of analysis, but they certainly did not close it. Once the importance of levels of analysis to any coherent understanding of international relations was accepted, two issues arose:

1 How many, and what, levels of analysis should there be for international relations?

2 By what criteria can these levels be defined and differentiated from one another?

On neither of these issues is the debate settled. A third issue, once a levels scheme is established, is how one puts the pieces back together again to achieve a holistic understanding. Debate on this has only just begun.

HOW MANY AND WHAT LEVELS?

The early stages of the level of analysis debate in international relations projected an unwarranted impression of simplicity about the whole idea. The neat fit between the idea of levels, and the natural division of the subject matter into individuals, states and system, seems largely to have forestalled any intense enquiry into the concept of levels itself. Indeed, within the discipline the literature on levels as an idea in its own right is remarkably thin considering the huge impact that the idea has had on the way international relations research is conducted. It is not clear, for example, whether levels of analysis is more an epistemological construct (and thus about different approaches to knowledge) or whether it is ontological (and therefore about the number and type of entities that are thought to actually exist in the international system). It is not at all clear what the rules are for designating something as a level, or for denying it that status. Consequently, there is no agreement on how many or what levels there are (or could be) for the study of international relations.

In practice, the discipline has proceeded along very pragmatic and simple lines, asking few fundamental questions, and not straying far beyond its starting point. Levels of analysis in international relations has been closely tied to the idea of system, defined as 'a set of units interacting within a structure'. Using this approach, two candidates for levels are immediately obvious: the units and the structure of the system. Waltz's original formulation used three levels: the individual, the unit or state, and the system itself in terms of its anarchic structure. Singer proffered two levels, system and state, but then hedged his bets by saying: 'it must be stressed that we have dealt here only with two of the more common orientations, and that many others are available and perhaps even more fruitful potentially than either of those selected here' (1961, p. 90). In his later work, Waltz ends up close to

Singer's original position, though for different reasons. Arguing from the general distinction between reductionist and holist theories, Waltz lumps together 'theories of international politics that concentrate causes at the individual or national level', classifying both as 'reductionist'. Theories that conceive causes operating at the international level he classifies as 'systemic' (1979, p. 18). In logic, this approach privileges the epistemological over the ontological, but in practice it simply blurred the distinction: system and unit could be (and were) seen as both objects of analysis and sources of explanation.

Following in the track set by Waltz and Singer, most international relations scholars accept at least three levels: individual (often focused on decision-makers), unit (usually state, but potentially any group of humans designated as an actor) and system. As Yurdusev argues, this basic classification is inclusive, even though it can be further subdivided, especially in the middle level (1993, pp. 80–2). Some writers insert a bureaucratic level between individual and unit (Jervis, 1976, p. 15; Hollis and Smith, 1990, pp. 7–9). Others insert a 'process' level between unit and system to capture the difference between explanations based on the nature of the units, and those based on the dynamics of interactions among units (Goldmann, 1979, pp. 1–2; Buzan, Jones and Little, 1993, chapter 5), others that the system level should be divided into two distinct levels, either structure and 'interaction capacity' (defined as the level of transportation, communication and organization capability in the system) (Buzan, Jones and Little, 1993, chapter 4) or 'international' and 'world' (Goldstein, cited in Yurdusev, 1993, p. 82). Some have their own schemes of levels that do not fit well with more conventional views: Rosenau suggests five – idiosyncratic, role, governmental, societal and systemic (1966, p. 43).

Much of this confusion can be removed by observing that what underlies these proposals is an unresolved dispute between two overlapping schemes for identifying what 'levels' are supposed to represent. One (ontological) sees levels as being about 'different units of analysis', and the other (epistemological) sees them as being about 'the types of variables that explain a particular unit's behaviour' (Moul, 1973, p. 495). Yurdusev proposes distinguishing between units of analysis and 'levels of abstraction' in methodology (philosophical, theoretical and empirical) (1993, pp. 78–9, 87), but in my view Moul's line is more fruitful in addressing the confusion in the levels debate.

The first, and simpler, scheme focuses on levels as units of analysis organized on the principle of spatial scale (small to large, individual to system). The term 'levels' does suggest a range of spatial scales or 'heights'. In this sense, levels are locations where both outcomes and sources of explanation can be located. They are ontological referents rather than sources of explanation in and of themselves. The introduction of levels of analysis into international relations by Waltz, Singer and Kaplan could be conceived in these terms, and much of the debate about levels of analysis has *de facto* taken place within this framework. In this perspective, levels range along a spectrum from individual, through bureaucratic and state, to region (subsystem) and system.

There are some advantages to thinking of levels in this way. In a recent book, Hollis and Smith (1990) offer an ingenious scheme which seems to allow them both to retain the simplicity of a basic dualism between system and unit, and at the same time to elaborate more levels. They argue (echoing the reductionist/holist debate) that 'the dispute between system and unit is a formal dispute which can be filled out according to what is claimed to be the relevant system and what the relevant unit'. They then offer four levels of explanation from international relations theory (international system, nation-state, bureaucracy and individual), grouping these into three possible pairs of system–unit dyads: system–state, state–bureaucracy, bureaucracy–individual (i.e. in each pair the left-hand level serves as the system within which the right-hand level is the unit – for individual units, bureaucracy is the system, for bureaucratic units, the state is the system, and so forth). Within each of these dyads, the debate is whether explanation proceeds top-down (system to unit, and therefore system-level theory) or bottom (unit to system, and therefore unit-level theory) (1990, pp. 7–9). Curiously, they do not consider a regional level, which would seem to be a logical component in any ontological system of levels.

In the second scheme, levels are understood as different types or sources of explanation for observed phenomena. In principle, anything that can be established as a distinct source of explanation can qualify. In practice, debate in international relations has largely developed around three ideas:

1 *Interaction capacity*, defined generally as the level of transportation, communication and organization capability in the system. Interaction capacity focuses on the types and intensi-

ties of interaction that are possible within any given unit/subsystem/system at the point of analysis: how much goods and information can be moved over what distances at what speeds and what costs.

2 *Structure*, defined generally as the principle by which units within a system are arranged. Structure focuses on how units are differentiated from one another, how they are arranged into a system, and how they stand in relation to one another in terms of relative capabilities.
3 *Process*, defined generally as interactions among units, particularly durable or recurrent patterns in those interactions. Process focuses on how units actually interact with one another within the constraints of interaction capacity and structure, and particularly on durable or recurrent patterns in the dynamics of interactions.

Each of these sources can itself be subdivided into more specific classifications along the lines of Waltz's three tiers of structure.

Levels in this sense are not in and of themselves units of analysis. The two schemes can be integrated as a matrix in which each unit of level of analysis contains, in principle, all of the sources or types of explanation. Thus structures, process and interaction capacity can be found as sources of explanation in individuals, states and the international system. Differentiating units of analysis and sources of explanation resolves much of the incoherence about how many and what levels.

Given the centrality of levels of analysis to most international relations theory, it is not clear to me why this fairly obvious and crucial distinction between units of analysis and sources of explanation has not surfaced earlier in the discipline's theoretical discourse. One possible explanation is the convenient overlap between them and Waltz's influential work, which blurred the distinction between system and structure (Buzan, Jones and Little, 1993, pp. 22–8). Another is the generally weak understanding of the philosophy of social science within international relations. As will be shown in the next section, the great bulk of debate about levels of analysis in the discipline has focused on the opening differentiation between system/structure and unit/state levels. This debate confused both system and structure, and the location of explanation with its source at the unit level.

WALTZ AND THE STRUCTURE VERSUS UNIT DEBATE

To understand why basic questions about levels of analysis in international relations remain either unanswered or unexplored, it helps to return to the intellectual history. Much of the explanation for what has not been done can be found in the story of what has preoccupied debate within the discipline since the late 1970s. At the centre of this debate has been Kenneth N. Waltz, his 1979 book *Theory of International Politics*, and the responses to it, both positive and negative. What might be called the Waltz–Singer dyadic approach to levels of analysis, focusing mainly on system/structure and unit/state is unquestionably still the dominant one in the field, despite much unhappiness with its severe simplification. Surprisingly, there has been little attempt to follow up Singer's escape clause 'that many other [levels] are available and perhaps even more fruitful potentially than either of those selected here'.

Most of the action has been concentrated on how to distinguish between the (collective) unit and the system level. Neither Waltz nor Singer attempted much precision in his early works. The individual and state levels were seen as largely self-evident, and Singer defined the system level rather hazily as 'encompassing the totality of interactions which take place within the system and its environment'. In his later work, Waltz made it his principal aim to specify the two levels clearly, and thus to define the boundary between them:

> Structure has to be studied in its own right, as do units. To claim to be following a systems approach or to be constructing a systems theory requires one to show how system and unit levels can be distinctly defined. Failure to mark and preserve the distinction between structure, on the one hand, and units and processes, on the other, makes it impossible to disentangle causes of different sorts and to distinguish between causes and effects. Blurring the distinction between the different levels of a system has, I believe, been the major impediment to the development of theories about international politics. (1970, p. 78).

Waltz defined a system simply as 'composed of a structure and of interacting units.' Following his earlier division of the universe of international political theory into reductionist and systematic categories, he defined the unit level of the system as 'the attributes and interactions of its parts', and the system level 'by the arrangement of the system's parts and by the principle of that arrangement' (1979, pp. 18, 79, 80). His purpose in focusing on system level theory was to 'explain why different units behave similarly . . . Political structure produces a similarity in process and performance so long as a structure endures' (pp. 72, 87). He then went on to elaborate in considerable detail a three-tiered conception of structure (chapter 5). The deepest tier was the principle of arrangement of the units, and in the political universe the options were anarchy or hierarchy (respectively absence or presence of central government). The next tier concerned the differentiation of units by function, but Waltz closed this off, arguing that under anarchy states were always 'like units'. This view is contested, but the debate is beyond the scope of this chapter (Ruggie, 1986, p. 148; Buzan, Jones and Little, 1993, pp. 37–47). The third tier was the distribution of capabilities across units. This is essentially about polarity: how many great powers does the system contain? This conception of structure has dominated the discipline. Though it has many critics, it has no serious rivals. Interestingly, nobody has questioned the status of Waltz's innovation of subdividing a level into three tiers, or asked why each tier does not have the status of a level in its own right.

Waltz's principal concern was to define system structure. His project was thus about a single unit (system) plus a single source of explanation (structure), though the general perception throughout the debate was that these two things constituted a single level. His reasons for concentrating on this single level were perfectly sound: he thought (1) that it was the most important for explaining the general characteristics of international relations, and (2) that within the discipline system and structure were much less well understood than units, and therefore more in need of development. But because the book became so influential, this lopsided attention to system structure distorted the debate about levels of analysis in a number of unhelpful ways. One way of understanding what happened is to see it in terms of a conflation between the deeper philosophical debate about reductionist and holist approaches on the one hand, and the more pragmatic issues of levels of analysis on the other. In effect, Waltz presented his argument in such a way as to make the two indistinguishable. This not only confined debate to two different types of level (structure and unit), but also saw them as constituting the whole universe of levels. This formulation choked off the possibility that other levels might be explored and, indeed, made it difficult to find a place for them in the scheme of things.

Part of the problem was generated by Waltz's choice of terms. Because of the very close linkage in his argument between the issue of reductionist versus systemic approaches, and the specific choice of structural and unit levels of analysis, Waltz used the terms 'system level' and 'structure' interchangeably. This conflation went largely unnoticed, and had the effect of shutting off thinking about other systemic qualities (such as interaction capacity) that might count as levels of analysis. It meant that Waltz's notably parsimonious definition of structure effectively occupied both the entirety of the holist position, and the meaning of the term 'system level'. Following the reductionist/holist logic, Waltz then defined everything that is not structure as belonging to the unit (i.e. reductionist) level: 'structure includes only what is required to show how the units of the system are positioned or arranged. Everything else is omitted' (1979, p. 82). Since he had defined structure in highly restrictive terms (as well as inadvertently restricting its use to the system level) he could not avoid pushing a vast array of causes and effects down to the unit level, which had then to contain all other units of analysis and all other sources of explanation.

Waltz's restriction of the levels of analysis debate to the confines of the reductionist/holist one thus had three distorting effects. First, it rammed the whole debate about levels into an inappropriate dyad, confining it to only two levels, and importing into the relationship between those two levels the oppositional qualities associated with reductionism versus holism. Second, it created a very narrow conception of holism/system, confining it to Waltz's sparse definition of political structure. Third, it created a bloated and incoherent 'unit' level, to which Waltz paid relatively little attention.

While many people in the discipline acknowledge the important contribution that Waltz's ideas on structure have made to the development of international relations theory, few are comfortable with his conclusion that all else is thereby relegated to the unit level. As Keohane and Nye argue it, 'making the unit level the dumping ground for all unexplained variance is an impediment to the development of theory' (1987, p. 746). But because Waltz's two-level scheme has not been adequately challenged, there has been continuous pressure to push what Waltz counts as unit-level factors back into the structural level. Waltz acknowledged 'how difficult it is to keep the levels of a system consistently distinct and separate' (1986, p. 328), but uncompromisingly defended his strict boundary. This struggle over the boundary has too easily ignored the possibility that Waltz's mistake lay not in the placement of the line between structure and unit levels, but in confining the debate to only two levels, in blurring the distinction between units of analysis and sources of explanation, and in assuming that structure is the only source of explanation at the system level.

The argument about the nature and placement of the boundary between the system and unit levels (and therefore about their content) sets much of the tone of response to *Theory of International Politics*, as indicated by the title of the 1986 volume *Neorealism and Its Critics*. One main line of criticism is that Waltz's theory is too narrow, in part because of its restriction to the international political sector, and within that confine, to his sparse definition of structure. In combination, these two restrictions exclude, or marginalize, a range of factors that others see as being: (1) 'structural', (2) important to outcomes, and/or (3) lying both beyond a strictly political domain, and above a strictly unit level of analysis. The debate over defining the levels here spills over into that about what counts as a level. Ruggie focuses on 'dynamic density', defined as 'the quantity, velocity and diversity of transactions that go on within society' (1986, p. 148). Keohane looks at richness of information, rules and institutions in a similar light (1986, pp. 190–7). Keohane and Nye highlight processes and patterns of interaction among states, referring to 'non-structural incentives for state behaviour' and 'the ability of states to communicate and cooperate' (1987, p. 746). Both Ruggie and Cox also want to bring socio-economic factors into the analysis: Ruggie drawing attention to the linkage of property rights and capitalism to political sovereignty, and Cox wanting to include the social forces engendered by the organization of production (Ruggie, 1986, pp. 141–8; Cox, 1986, p. 220).

In their various ways, Waltz's critics all think that a holist/systemic approach needs to contain more than Waltz's structure. Their concerns with factors such as 'dynamic density', information richness, communication facilities and suchlike do not obviously fit into Waltz's structural level or into the unit one. They cannot be made to do so because, as argued above, that dyad is itself incoherent. The problem goes right back to the basic definition of system as units, interactions and structures. Because his thinking is dominated by the epistemological opposition of reductionism versus holism, Waltz sees interactions as part of the unit (reductionist) level, varying according to the dispositions and capabilities of the units as mediated by structural pressures. Many of his critics think that the interaction component of system needs a higher profile in the theory, but are blocked by Waltz's pre-emption of structure as the sole system level component of neorealist theory, by the blending of units of analysis and levels of explanation, and by the confinement of the debate of two levels of analysis.

Many of these problems can be solved by separating units of analysis from sources of explanation, and seeing them as a matrix as described above. In this matrix, all of the units of analysis between individual and system are quite familiar and straightforward. Because of Waltz's work, structure is by now also familiar as a source of explanation. Though only spelled out at the system level, its applicability to other levels (where any unit can be defined as a system à la Hollis and Smith), is clear enough. But interaction capacity and process are not yet clearly articulated in a widely understood formulation.

Interaction capacity is about the technological capabilities, and the shared norms and organizations, on which the type and intensity of interaction between units in the system, or within a unit, depend. These things clearly fall outside the meaning of structure, and represent a different source of explanation from it. As new technologies of transportation and communication spread, they change the quality and character of the interactions among and within units in the system as a whole. The sharing of norms and values is a precondition for establishing organizations, but once established, such organizations greatly facilitate, and even promote, interactions that shared norms and values make possible and desired. Political communication in a system or a unit with no such shared norms or institutions will be quite different in scale and character from one that is richly endowed with them. Interaction capacity captures both the technical and the social aspects of capabilities that are system or unit wide. These capabilities are both a defining characteristic of all units of analysis, and a distinct source of shoving and shaping forces playing alongside those from the structural level.

The standing of interaction capacity as a distinct source of explanation is demonstrated by its profound impact on the operation of neo-realism's whole structural logic. As the basic definition of system indicates, the absolute quality of interaction capacity is fundamental to the existence of a system. How much interaction, and of what type, is necessary before one can say that an international system exists? This question has not been addressed in neo-realism. Yet so basic is the effect of interaction capacity that unless its level and type are specified first, one cannot say whether structural logic will operate or not. In historical perspective, the impact of low density on the logic of anarchy becomes very clear: the variable of interaction crucially affects the meaning and construction of the system. When interaction capacity is low, even the existence of a meaningful international system is in question. Structural logic is suppressed or weakened by thinness of interaction. Waltz simply presupposes that an adequate level of the right type of interaction (strategic) exists to make structural logic work, but in fact this has not been the case for most of history. Interaction capacity is a distinct variable, not a constant (Buzan, Jones and Little, 1993, chapter 4).

Process is also a distinct source of explanation applicable to all units of analysis. Looked at from the bottom up, explanations in terms of interactions among or within units seek to understand behaviour and outcomes in terms of the ways in which units at any level respond to one another's attributes and behaviours. Looked at from the top down, process is about the dynamics of a system or a unit. These are essentially action–reaction theories, in which the key element is a dynamic of stimulus and response. In international relations, many recurrent patterns have been found at the system and subsystem levels in these often very complex dynamics, including war, alliance, the balance of power, arms racing and the security dilemma, and the whole range of international political economy patterns arising from protectionist and liberal policies on trade and money. The concepts of international society and the related idea of regimes are also process phenomena. Process dynamics can also be found within all types of collective organizations, and within individual human beings.

Taking all of this discussion into account, one version of definitions and differentiations for levels of analysis in international relations theory might begin to be arranged as in figure 9.1.

Units of analysis	Sources of explanation		
	Interaction capacity	Structure	Process
System			
Subsystem			
Unit			
Bureaucracy			
Individual			

Figure 9.1 *Levels of analysis in international relations theory*

THE FALSE CONFLICT BETWEEN STRUCTURALISM AND UNIT LEVEL ANALYSTS

One unfortunate consequence of the confusion between the epistemological argument about holism/reductionism, and the debate about levels of analysis is that it generated an unnecessary confrontation between structuralists and foreign policy analysts. The central issue was whether or not structural explanations were thought of as deterministic. If they were, foreign policy analysis as a mainstream approach to the study of international relations was drastically devalued. Many took Waltz to be a structural determinist, and interpreted *Theory of International Politics* as a dismissal of reductionist approaches to analysis. Waltz was fully aware that structural causes could never offer more than a partial explanation of international outcomes, and that it was important 'to keep open the theoretically interesting and practically important question of what, in different systems, the proportionate causal weights of unit-level and of systems-level factors may be'. He says this in many places throughout his works, and these are not the statements of a structural determinist (1979, pp. 48–9, 78, 87, 123; 1986, pp. 328–9, 343; 1990, p. 34).

Again, the confusion between levels of analysis and the epistemological debate about holism/reductionism is apparent. The necessity to choose between systemic and reductionist approaches is one position within the wider, and still unresolved, epistemological argument. It is not necessary to transfer this opposition to the level of analysis debate. The important issue in international relations theory is which units of analysis and which sources of explanation tell us most about any given event or phenomenon. No one level of unit or source of explanation is always dominant in explaining international events.

Taking this perspective sweeps away a host of irrelevant questions about who is winning, whether the unit level is about to have a resurgence, and whether it is time to 'bring the state back in'. Because it was a fresh development, and powerfully argued, structural logic dominated international relations theory during the 1980s. It also gained a boost from the Cold War, because its concern with polarity (the structural effects of the number of great powers in the system) in general, and Waltz's argument in particular that bipolarity was a desirable structure, resonated with the world events going on around the theory. Now the pendulum is swinging back. With the Cold War over, it is easier to assert arguments from other levels. Fukuyama's fashionable writings about the triumph of the liberal state, and 'the end of history', stem from the unit level, and build on an argument made much earlier by Gourevitch that powerful states project their domestic characteristics out into the international system (Gourevitch, 1978); Fukuyama, 1992). Arguments about regimes and international society stem from the process at the system and subsystem levels, and much of the argument about interdependence reflects the systemic effects of changes in interaction capacity.

In this perspective, the question of which level is winning (or losing) is not a very interesting one except in relation to some specific phenomenon to be explained. In international relations generally, all the levels are powerfully in play. The important theoretical question is: if two or more units and sources of explanation are operating together, how are their different analyses to be assembled into a whole understanding? To this there is yet no clear answer. Waltz's position, probably widely shared, suggests that explanations on different levels can be added together and assigned relative weights in relation to any given analysis. But it is not clear how this weighting might be done, or even whether it is methodologically sound (Moul, 1973, p. 499; Hollis and Smith, 1990, pp. 6–7). There is also a rather complex debate going on in the background about the relationship between 'agents' (units) and structures (Giddens, 1984; Wendt, 1987; Buzan, Jones and Little, 1993, chapters 6–7). The ideas of structure developed by Waltz are, unlike some conceptions of structure, dependent on units. Structure of this sort cannot precede units but only grow up with them. Because of this, it is possible to argue that units and structures are mutually constitutive: states make the structure, and the structure makes states. Once this line of reasoning is entered into, the whole differentiation of units of analysis is brought into question. This form of reassembling the whole is much more complex than that envisaged by Waltz, and its implications for the standing of levels of analysis as an approach to the study of international relations is not yet clear. Can levels be reassembled without undoing the initial validity of their separation?

CONCLUSIONS

There can be no doubt that the idea of levels of analysis has had a profound impact on the way international relations is studied. It has forced analysts to be more systematic about how they present explanations. It has structured much of the mainstream debate about theory, and it has provided a potent way of dividing up the vast and complex subject matter of international relations. It has stimulated thinking about what the concept 'international system' actually means. It has begun to raise awareness in the discipline of the need to consider a range of epistemological and ontological questions. What counts as knowledge in discipline, and what are the legitimate methods of explanation? What is the relationship between analytical constructs and 'real' entities that exist in the world? It has therefore done much to increase the rigour of analysis in the field, and it has opened lines of theory that would otherwise have been difficult to find. In some areas quite major advances have been made, most notably Waltz's conception of structure.

But much remains to be done, many core issues and concepts are still poorly understood, and many serious questions are unanswered or unaddressed. International relations theory is still in its infancy, and there is no disguising the fact that the discipline is still theoretically primitive. Few have bothered to enquire as to how levels relate to the practice of dividing the international system up into political, economic, military and societal sectors. The debate about levels of analysis remains confined largely within the political and military sectors, and this inhibits linkage to increasingly important bodies of international relations work (international political economy, historical sociology) that deal with the economic and societal sectors.

Nevertheless, thinking in terms of levels of analysis is now firmly established as part of international relations theory. It has been a potent and useful stimulus to theory in the discipline even though the concept of levels is still not properly understood in its own right. Levels of analysis has defined a way of thinking about the international system that has dominated theory for several decades. The work of several generations of academics has been shaped by it to such an extent that it is now crucial to an understanding of a good deal of the discipline's theoretical discourse. But like much else in international relations theory it is as yet only a very partial construction on which much work still needs to be done.

Note

I would like to thank Hayward Alker, Nils Petter Gleditsch, Richard Little, Jaap de Wilde, Ole Wæver and the editors for comments on earlier drafts of this chapter.

References

Buzan, B., Jones, C. and Little, R. 1993: *The Logic of Anarchy: Neorealism to Structural Realism*. New York: Columbia University Press.

Cox, R. 1986: Social forces, states and world orders: beyond international relations theory. In Keohane 1986b, 204–54.

Fukuyama, F. 1992: *The End of History and the Last Man*. London: Penguin.

Giddens, A. 1984: *The Constitution of Society: An Outline of the Theory of Structuration*. Cambridge: Polity Press.

Goldman, K. 1979: Is my enemy's enemy my friend's friend? Lund, Sweden: *Cultural Indicators, The Swedish Symbol System, 1945–75*, Report No. 1.

Gourevitch, P. 1978: The second image reversed: the international sources of domestic politics. *International Organization*, 32 (4) 881–912.

Hollis, M. and Smith, S. 1990: *Explaining and Understanding International Relations*. Oxford: Clarendon.

Jervis, R. 1976: *Perception and Misperception in International Politics*. Princeton, N.J.: Princeton University Press.

Kaplan, M. 1957: *System and Process in International Politics*. New York: Wiley.

Keohane, R. O. 1986a: Theory of world politics: structural realism and beyond. In Keohane (1986b), 158–203.

Keohane, R. O. (ed.) 1986b: *Neorealism and Its Critics*. New York: Columbia University Press.

Keohane, R. O. and Nye J. S. 1987: Power and interdependence revisited. *International Organization*, 41(4), 725–53.

Moul, W. B. 1973: The level of analysis problem revisited. *Canadian Journal of Political Science*, 61(1), 494–513.

Rosenau, J. N. 1966: Pre-theories and theories of foreign policy. In R. B. Farrell (ed.), *Approaches to Comparative and International Politics*, Evanston: Northwestern University Press, 27–92.

Ruggie, J. G. 1986: Continuity and transformation in the world polity: toward a neorealist synthesis. In Keohane 1986b, 131–57.

Ruggie, J. G. 1993: Territoriality and beyond: problematizing modernity in international relations. *International Organization*, 47(1), 139–74.

Singer, J. D. 1960: International conflict: three levels of analysis. *World Politics*, 12(3), 453–61.

Singer, J. D. 1961: The level of analysis problem in international relations. In K. Knorr and S. Verba (eds), *The International System: Theoretical Essays*, Princeton, N. J.: Princeton University Press.

Waltz, K. N. 1954/1959: *Man, the State and War*. New York: Columbia University Press.

Waltz, K. N. 1979: *Theory of International Politics*. Reading, Mass.: Addison-Wesley.

Waltz, K. N. 1986: Reflections on *Theory of International Politics*: a response to my critics. In 1986b, 322–45.

Waltz, K. N. 1990: Realist thought and neorealist theory. *Journal of International Affairs*, 44(1), 21–37.

Wendt, A. E. 1987: The agent-structure problem in international relations theory. *International Organization*, 41(3), 335–70.

Yurdusev, A. N. 1993: Level of analysis and unit of analysis: a case for distinction. *Millennium Journal of International Studies*, 22(1), 77–88.

10

The Post-Positivist Debate: Reconstructing Scientific Enquiry and International Relations Theory After Enlightenment's Fall

John A. Vasquez

For over two decades, various criticisms of positivism – some justified and some fatal wounds on men of straw – have swept through the social sciences. International relations has been no exception to these debates, but, as is usual for it, they have come to the discipline late. The criticisms are of two sorts. The newest and most profound criticism stems from the postmodernist critique. The more familiar, which I will call the post-empiricist critique, looks at a number of criticisms made by philosophers of science such as the impossibility of a value-free, neutral and objective science; the lack of an Archimedean point to build knowledge; the absence of an independent data base, etc. Together post-empiricists and postmodernists have pushed social science into a post-positivist era. In this chapter I seek to assess the contribution of postmodernism and post-empiricism to the field by examining their implications for scientific enquiry, specifically, and international relations theory, generally. I hope to reconstruct a philosophical foundation of the essential aspects of both the latter two projects, at least in outline form. The chapter closes with a brief discussion of the implications of these meta-theoretical concerns for the ongoing inter-paradigm debate.

The post-positivist debate is occasionally called 'the Third

Debate' (see Lapid, 1989), which sometimes leads to it being confused with the inter-paradigm debate (see Banks, 1985). The two are distinct in that one deals with the question of science and its applicability to the study of world politics; whereas the other deals with whether the realist paradigm is adequate or superior to alternative paradigms. It is important to keep the two debates separate because it is very unclear how, if at all, the post-positivist debate will favour or advantage one international relations paradigm over the other – although it will definitely shape how and whether such assessments can even be made.

THE PROMISE AND PITFALLS OF POSTMODERNISM

More of an attitude than a position, postmodernism means different things in different fields. Within international relations, it has not completely arrived and may be abandoned in favour of a more critically reasoned post-structuralism even before it has much of a foothold. Although there are many technical differences between post-structuralism and postmodernism, for the purpose of this chapter, the main difference that will be the focus of analysis concerns the question of relativism. Whereas post-structuralists, particularly those who are inspired by Foucault, flirt with relativism, postmodernists, like Lyotard and Baudrillard, embrace it. This is particularly the case in international relations where many of those who write in the post-structuralist vein are heavily influenced by critical theory and resist the charge of relativism. Despite these nuances, the use of postmodernism and post-structuralism promises to make important contributions to the field and to international relations theory specifically.

I see five major insights which constitute the promise of postmodernism. All of these in one way or another involve freeing us from our conceptual gaols. And for this there is much reason to celebrate. The so-called third debate (Lapid, 1989) is not a dead end. Rather than jumping to conclusions and dismissing claims, this is an important time for listening. If that is done, not only will we learn a great deal but there may actually be some fresh air to breathe.

Nevertheless, these insights are not without potential pitfalls, so while I present them here as working assumptions which when applied to existing international relations theory are apt to lead to some important contributions, this does not mean that I do not have reservations about each of the claims – and in some cases, as will be clear in the next section, rather severe reservations. For now, let me say that one of the major pitfalls is that some of these insights, if taken as universal claims, easily become over-generalizations that simply are not true. The claim that reality is a social construction is perhaps the most glaring example. Having made this caveat, I try to present in what follows the case postmodernism is making that is most relevant for international relations theory and the scientific study of world politics.

The arbitrary nature of modernity

The first contribution of postmodernism and the one that is on the verge of assassinating the Enlightenment deals with the arbitrary nature of modernity. To the children of the Enlightenment, modernity is the path of progress, perhaps even culminating in the perfection of humanity. To be modern is to be free from superstition and ignorance and a set of institutions and ideas that shape destiny at birth. Even today modernization with its concomitant ideas of economic and political development connotes these sentiments. Beneath them is the firm belief that there exists an optimal way, and perhaps only one way, to progress and that reason, science, and technology will uncover that way.

Postmodernism denies the Enlightenment on two grounds. First, it denies the idea of progress and, in its stead, it places the idea of discontinuities. This is one of Foucault's (1972) major insights. History is not moving forward or backward. It lacks teleology, as well as evolution. Second, postmodernism not only denies the idea of progress, but rejects the notion that the purported end of the Enlightenment, the modern, is the end of history, the perfection of humanity, or even a worthwhile goal. For the postmodernist, there is no optimal way of doing things. There are many ways and one is not necessarily better than another. Likewise, there is no one truth (with either a capital T or small t) but many truths. Postmodernism rips aside capitalism's mask of science and denies modern economics' claim that there is solely one way to solve the problem of food and shelter and that other forms of organizing economies will be less efficient or beneficial, if they 'work' at all. At the same time, it denies Marxist claims that certain modes of production are appropriate to certain conditions of history. For the postmodernist, 'nothing is written'.

What this means is that modernity and its claims need not have been the products of history, although they were the products of Western European history. Modernity is not a model, it is simply an instance. Modernity was not inevitable, nor was it necessary. It is a project. Something else could equally well have occurred. Modernity is arbitrary, and may or may not have served as well as other projects.

More important than these insights themselves are the implications derived from them. Postmodernism not only insists that modernity is an ongoing project, but denies its benevolence. It stands in opposition to the homogenizing role modernization has played both within and between states. What it fears most is the bureaucratic/all-seeing/scientific investigating/liberal social engineering/technology-wielding world reformer that will make everyone the same and drown all cultures in one global culture. It stands for the different, the dissenter, the non-conforming. To postmodernism, the ideas of economic and political *development* are just so many modernist conceits in a litany of conceits that have been imposed on the weak and the defeated. Modernity is not progress. It is not optimal. It is not superior. It is culturally and ethically arbitrary.

Once the illusions of the Enlightenment are stripped away, the modern era comes to an end and the postmodern era begins. Postmodernism, then, refers not only to a philosophical position but to a historical era which we have entered. Because of the ambiguity of the term, it is possible for post-structuralists to write about the postmodern without always embracing all of postmodernism (see Der Derian and Shapiro's (1989) Preface for an example).

Choice posing as truth

The second contribution of postmodernism is the realization that what exists in the world is choice posing as truth. This insight flows naturally from the first; for if it is the case that nothing is necessary (because historicist conditions or positivist causes do not determine things as they are), it follows that the arrangements that do exist were created by human beings either consciously or unconsciously. Such constructions were in fact choices that were made. How much freedom went into the choices is a matter for historical research, but they were choices in the sense that other arrangements could have been selected by struggles within history.

Human beings, however, have not been satisfied to call these outcomes choices that were contingent on preference, cultural biases or political fights. Instead they have sought to cloak them as the outcome of metaphysical categories – God, Reason or History. Rather than seeing things as arbitrary choices coming out of power and interests, the victors have justified their choices in terms of divine law, natural law or scientific analysis. Even when choice is recognized, these warrants make any other choices sinful, unnatural and unreasonable, or unscientific. Such claims when seen in the context of Enlightenment beliefs about the inevitability of progress take on an added weight. The postmodernist denies all of this.

Reality is a social construction

The third contribution, which is naturally derived from the second, is that reality is a social construction. If what exists is at one and the same time arbitrary and the product of human choice (at some level), it follows that what exists must have been socially constructed by people. Reality is created and constructed by beliefs and behaviour. Structures do in fact shape beliefs and behaviour the way some positivists thought, but these structures are the product of human action. Reality is not God- or Nature-given, but human-imposed. And, some would add, *this* is an imposition.

Foucault (1972) is responsible for much of this contribution, but his thinking on this point fitted in nicely with other intellectual currents in hermeneutics, anthropology and sociology (especially the work of Berger and Luckmann, 1966). As a result, something of a wide consensus exists on this point, although thinkers arrive at it from very different starting positions. What can remain of positivist social science, however, if this point is accepted in its entirety?

Exploring how beliefs and social science in particular help construct reality leads to the fourth contribution.

Language and conceptual frameworks are prone to self-fulfilling prophecies

Whenever ideas spread and people believe and act on them, part of the world the ideas portray actually comes into being. In this way realities are constructed. As certain rules and norms are obeyed, institutionalized and enforced through a variety of social control mechanisms, a reality comes into existence. Since people often conform to such cultures, it is possible to have a science, like economics, that appears accurately to predict and explain patterns.

Because of this effect, social science cannot be entirely value-free or neutral. Of course, it must be pointed out that when positivists argue in favour of a value-free, neutral and objective science, they do not necessarily mean that values play no role in motivating research, and they certainly do not mean that science should have no impact on the lives of people. What they mean is something much narrower, and that is simply that a scientist should act as an impartial judge in terms of which specific theories and explanations are accepted, rather than as an advocate.

Nevertheless, scientific enquiry is not wholly value-free because it helps build structures that support and nourish some lifestyles or forms of life and starves and kills other forms of life. Science is not simply a useful tool, but a practice that creates a mode of life that consciously destroys other ways of thinking and living. This is even more evident in the social sciences. Modern economics, for example, is very supportive of capitalism both in terms of providing an ideological veneer and in solving and researching real problems. The contemporary emphasis on rational choice can be read in this light. Rational choice is seen as a modernist conceit that makes choice pose as truth. To the extent rational-choice analysis can become a rigorous science will depend very much on the extent to which people or leaders accept its rules to guide their behaviour. In doing so, they will not only create a reality but people who are 'rationally calculating individuals'. Such a science succeeds in explaining more and more of the variance not because it is able to uncover the 'causes' of behaviour, but because it produces them.

Postmodernism directs us toward researching how language, conceptual frameworks and paradigms shape the world. In international relations one would clearly want to know how power politics and the realist paradigm constructed reality (see Vasquez,

1993). In democratic polities one would want to explain how liberal social thought constructed reality. Objectively, for example, which is generally seen as the absence of a point of view, is seen from the postmodernist perspective very much as a point of view and a pernicious one at that. To insist that everything must be seen from two or more sides makes all kinds of assumptions about truth, the way knowledge should be sought, lifestyles, and so forth.

From the ideas of social construction and self-fulfilling prophecy, the fifth contribution of postmodernism follows.

The process of identification and the construction of identity is a form of power and an act of violation

Identity is probably one of the more intimate forms of social construction that is imposed on individuals. There can be no doubt from a postmodernist point of view that identity is a social construction. Why one identity rather than another? Who decides and with what consequences? Since identity is often associated with wars and/or persecution, not to mention privilege/victimization, what one's identity is can have profound influences. Whoever controls identity obviously has profound influence over the destiny and life of an individual, group or society. Because of this, it is an act of power. Because identity is typically not chosen (at best it can be rejected with pain and agony), it is a violation of human freedom.

These five contributions of postmodernism cut across all enquiry, and their implications have had dramatic and sometimes long-lasting effects in certain disciplines, particularly literary criticism. In international relations and comparative politics their implications have not been fully explored. Their potential impact on social thought is profound, particularly on the question of modernization and the creation of a new homogenizing world order. Already within international relations theory, the impact of the small band of scholars writing under the post-structuralist label has been significant. Scholars like Ashley, Michael Shapiro, Der Derian, R. B. J. Walker, David Campbell, Jim George and Bradley Klein, as well as feminist theorists like V. Spike Peterson and Christine Sylvester, have influenced how we think about international relations theory and have changed the terms we use to describe and conceptualize its project, as well as our understanding of international relations theory's past and its future (see Der Derian and Shapiro, 1989).

In addition to these contributions, however, there is a looming pitfall which Lapid (1989) and Pauline Rosenau (1992), among others, have pointed out, and this is the question of relativism. Within the philosophical writings of Jean-François Lyotard and Jean Baudrillard it is clearly evinced. For Lyotard (1984), the grand narratives shaped by the Enlightenment, including universalistic claims about freedom, rationality, and human rights, are just so many attempts to master and suppress differences. For Lyotard, specific communities supply their own meaning and truth for themselves, and any evaluation across communities is an act of power seeking to destroy differences. With Baudrillard (1990), the idea of representing the world is entirely overturned and replaced with the notion that only simulation is possible, because there is no reality or truth to be represented; indeed the distinction between truth and falsity is blurred.[1]

The spectre of relativism stemming from the postmodernist critique and from constructivism, in general, questions the legitimacy of the modernist conception of knowledge. Theory and science are not embodiments of truth from this view, but constructions of reality which are imposed arbitrarily by acts of power. For postmodernists, the role of the theorist should not be to invent and impose further meaning, but to deconstruct and expose such impositions. In many ways, this kind of postmodernism is a logical outcome of the hermeneutic approach, which maintains that only the analysis of meaning is possible. The scientific project, which includes Marxism and critical theory as well as positivism, says more than this is possible, because while meaning may be imposed arbitrarily, there is more to be analysed than the meanings humans attribute to their experience.

It is not an accident that postmodernism has had its most profound impact on literary theory. Literary theorists, after all, deal with fiction, so for them empirical truth is never really a concern; for them there is only metaphysical truth or constructions of meaning (i.e. texts). There are no pre-given texts. There is no nature; there is no animal inheritance; there is no biology; there is no chemistry, no genetics. There are no human brains, but only creations of human minds and imagination. For them, humanity and its world are plastic – authorless – where every reader can make his or her own meaning.

This fundamental assumption, which underlies all constructivism, is postmodernism's one essentialist sin; it provides a universalistic understanding of human nature and facts as a grand narrative of history. This produces a fundamental self-contradiction that is postmodernism's logical refutation. For if everything is a social construction and nothing is permanently true, how can postmodernism's view of the world and history as a set of constructions be anything but a social construction? And if it is a social construction, in what sense can it be true? Indeed, if the postmodernist conception of humanity is accurate, how could postmodernism's analysis conceivably be correct? And why would a postmodernist try to give an explanation of history and human cognition and behaviour that was invariant across time? Let me suggest that the very foundation upon which postmodernism makes its appeal is in fact parasitic upon an alternative epistemology and view of the world. The very charge of essentialism, which is postmodernism's warrant philosophically to dismiss any statement, is in fact an empirical question that is best answered through empirical research and not philosophical analysis. This opening provides a way of reconstructing scientific enquiry and addressing some of the post-empiricist criticisms that make positivist science so vulnerable.

RECONSTRUCTING SCIENTIFIC ENQUIRY: DEALING WITH THE POST-EMPIRICIST CRITIQUE

The most basic question that needs to be addressed in any attempt to reconstruct the scientific project is whether one conception or framework is as good as any other, or, put another way, whether there is any non-arbitrary way of distinguishing among concepts on the basis of (what science calls) their truth or falsity.

Empirically, we know enough about the world to conclude that not every imaginative narrative can be imposed on the world. People make mistakes and recognize them as such and not simply as a change in beliefs. Utopian efforts are unable to be put into practice even when the utopians have immense power. Schizophrenics live in a very real and meaningful world of their own making, but they are dysfunctional. Many theories fail to work in natural science and in the social world. *The word 'reality' refers to this resistance of the world to conform to every imaginable conception humans create.* We can imagine unicorns, even develop very coherent and meaningful texts about them. In a sense they are real in our lives, but they do not exist in the world, only in our imaginations. Likewise, we can develop worlds of witches, devils, angels, ghosts and goblins, and these can be real and dangerous, but as far as we know they do not exist in the world either. Humans are constantly creating social worlds, but only some can survive careful and rigorous scrutiny.

The *differences* between accuracy and error, reality and fiction, truth and falsity are in fact constructed by concepts. Concepts and words do construct a world around us; yet we need not be prisoners of this world. We are free to reject concepts on some basis other than whim or personal taste. Not all concepts or theories are equal; there are good reasons for accepting some concepts and theories over others.

Of the various criticisms made by post-empiricists (see Hollis and Smith, 1990, for an overview, and Nicholson, 1983, for a defence of empiricism), there are two that question the possibility of rejecting concepts or theories on any scientific basis. The first looks at the empirical foundation for testing theories and argues that there are no independent facts, data bases or 'reality' to test theories. The second looks at the process of making inferences about the inadequacy of theories and argues that science is not based on logic, but on an act of power that imposes its criteria for determining truth on the culture.

The first area where some post-empiricists believe science has not been reconstructed is in still holding on to the 'naive' belief in 'an independent data base'. Post-empiricists rightly argue that facts do not simply exist in the world, but are the products of concepts, which in turn are a function of theories, or at least theoretical assumptions. It is argued that facts are not independent of theories, and therefore cannot be used to test theories. Since theories create facts, facts can always be found to support theories. These post-positivist philosophical claims in and of themselves are not definitive, but they are often treated that way to dismiss empirical findings. At first blush, this analysis, because it can be quite sophisticated, appears persuasive, but on further inspection it is at best paradoxical. While it is true that the way we see the world and what constitutes its facts are a function of the concepts we employ, this does not mean that no observations or puzzles existed before the theory. Theories and concepts often follow observations and are meant to explain or account for a pattern. Theorists are not so much interested in 'facts' *per se* as they are in the relationships between 'facts' (variables, etc.).

Post-positivists argue, however, that because concepts create facts, any operational definition derived from concepts does not create an independent data base. All data are theory-laden. Any good social scientist would agree with this, but the word 'independent' means different things to each side. For the post-empiricist critic, it seems to mean that any data set will always be biased in favour of the theory that informed its collection. The implication here is that data sets will always produce confirmation rather than falsification of an explanation or theory. As Hawkesworth puts it:

> if what is taken to be the 'world', what is understood in terms of 'brute data' is itself theoretically constituted (indeed, constituted by the same theory that is undergoing the test), then no conclusive disproof of a theory is likely. For the independent evidence upon which falsification depends does not exist; the available evidence is preconstituted by the same theoretical presuppositions as the scientific theory under scrutiny. (1992, pp. 16–17)

This view is widely accepted by political philosophers, and I venture to say that one reason it is, is that they have never really tried to test a hypothesis that was incorrect. If in fact this presumption were true, we should have thousands of strong findings in international relations. Instead we have hardly any! Data are not independent in the sense that they have no connection with concepts, but they are independent in the sense that they do not assure confirmation of theories. Data bases can be considered independent if two competing explanations of the same behaviour (i.e. set of observations) have the same chance of being rejected. We know this is often the case, because, in international relations the most frequent finding is the null finding.

The second area where some post-empiricists think scientific enquiry still needs further reconstructing and where their criticisms are much more telling has to do with science's epistemological foundation. The early logical positivists had hoped science and its method could be established on logic, so that its conclusions would be *compelling*. No such epistemology and logical solution has been established. The most recent effort to do so and the focus of much post-empiricist criticism has been that of Popper (1959). He attempted to rest scientific criteria for acceptance of beliefs on the principle of falsification.

However, as most are prepared to concede, Popper's efforts fall down because the principle of falsification, as well as the other standard criteria for rejecting theories, must be seen as decision rules, norms if you will, and not as logical conclusions compelling belief. From this view, science becomes a project for making decisions about belief according to fairly rigorous rules, norms and definitions. Establishing a consensus on rules becomes the basis for reconstructing science in the postmodern era.

These rules and norms need not be seen as philosophically arbitrary because they are justified on the basis of good reasons. They also are not arbitrary at the practical level in that the rules they embody are applied to make appraisals in a rigorous manner that limits the intrusion of personal preferences. In this way, science can act as a self-correcting mechanism and is one of the few ways people have to save themselves from self-delusion. Although science is a language game, like all other language games in a culture, it can claim adherence over competing games because of its self-correcting mechanism and its ability to settle differences on empirical questions once its procedures are accepted. Ultimately, while science draws upon aspects of the correspondence and coherence theory of truth, it rests as a final check on the pragmatic theory of truth. Putting ideas to test and examining evidence are important strategies that should not be cavalierly discarded by those interested in political enquiry.

This conception of science concedes much to post-empiricist criticisms, but it reconstructs the scientific project on firmer philosophical ground. In addition, it makes it clearer exactly what role science can play in society. Science, however, is more than just a tool, although it could be reduced to that. It must be conceded that at the very centre of the scientific spirit are values and practices that make it a way of thinking; indeed it can be argued that they constitute a way of life. The commitment to truth and the search for truth as the highest values are more than just preferences – they are fundamental value commitments. Truth is not simply a semantic concept, but a value that guides enquiry. To say that truth is the primal value means that theories and beliefs should be accepted or rejected solely on the basis of their ability to be consistent with the evidence and not because their acceptance will have beneficial consequences, promote a particular economic or political interest, be consistent with preconceived revealed doctrine, or provide an enabling function that allows a society to shape the world by controlling people and resources. These other considerations, one or more of which are often important criteria in ethics, religion or public policy for the acceptance of statements, are in competition with the scientific spirit. Even those who take an instrumental philosophy of science position (and prefer to speak of adequacy or utility rather than truth) still see what I am calling 'truth' as the central value commitment of the scientific project. Science insists that for empirical questions its value commitment to the search for truth must be taken as guiding, and its practices privileged as the best way of attaining knowledge. In non-empirical matters, it is willing to give way; i.e. it recognizes the legitimacy of using additional and sometimes other criteria for accepting or rejecting non-empirical statements.

Science, then, is an act of power in that it imposes its criteria for determining truth on the entire society. At a particular point in Western history, science emerged as a discourse that competed with other discourses and institutions for the control of language and belief in certain domains, and after a long struggle, which still continues in certain quarters, it won the battle. Although this was a political battle, this does not mean that there are not good reasons (both epistemological and practical) for choosing scientific criteria of truth over others in the questions science has demarcated within its domain.

All of this does not mean that postmodernism's insights about the Enlightenment are ill-founded or incorrect. They stand and should make scientific enquiry more humble, more cautious about human learning and 'progress', and more mindful of the corrupting nature of power. Nevertheless, building on the post-empiricist criticisms of logical positivism to establish a new rational foundation for science on the basis of decision rules makes it possible to avoid the abyss of relativism. To do so concedes to the critics that science is a system of conventions for decision-making and not an Archimedean fulcrum lifting us to irrefutable knowledge.

OVERCOMING RELATIVISM IN SCIENTIFIC AND PRACTICAL THEORY

Efforts to overcome relativism centre on the question of establishing criteria for theory appraisal. Within international relations, this has been seen as a crucial area of concern both because of post-positivism and because of the inter-paradigm debate (see Lapid, 1989). While some have celebrated the idea of theoretical pluralism, the idea of building knowledge requires some appraisal of existing beliefs, explanations, theories and paradigms. Elsewhere (Vasquez, 1992, pp. 840–4), I have presented a set of criteria for appraising international relations theories – both empirical and normative.

The criteria of adequacy for scientific theory I present are based on the assumption that good theory must be true. The criteria are justified on the basis of the argument that following and using them increases the probability that a theory, research programme or paradigm that satisfies the criteria is less likely to be false than one that does not. If one prefers not to accept a philosophically realist view of theories (see Nagel, 1961, pp. 117–18, 141–52, 196), then in more instrumental terms, a theory that satisfies these criteria can be said to be more promising for achieving and making progress toward the ultimate goal of science, which is the acquisition of knowledge.

There are six criteria (all of them standard in philosophy of science) that are relevant for international relations enquiry. 'Good' theories should be:

1 accurate;
2 falsifiable;
3 capable of evincing great explanatory power;
4 progressive as opposed to degenerating in terms of their research programme(s);
5 consistent with what is known in other areas;
6 appropriately parsimonious and elegant.

I label these, respectively, the criteria of accuracy, falsifiability, explanatory power, progressivity, consistency and parsimony.

Some of these criteria are more important than others. The first two are essential; if a theory is not accurate or falsifiable (in at least the broad sense of specifying at some point what evidence would lead the theorist to say the theory was inaccurate), it cannot be accepted regardless of how well it satisfies the other criteria. Having great explanatory power, which is defined here as being able to resolve puzzles and anomalies (theoretically) that could not be explained before, is of little use if the explanation turns out to be inaccurate or is non-falsifiable. Likewise, the case for parsimony is often given too much weight in international relations. Theories, as Craig Murphy (personal communication, 1993) argues, should have an appropriate degree of complexity. They should not include all possible variables without regard for their relative potency; nor should they leave out important factors to keep the explanation simple. What is crucial is that theories be able to pass tests – first in principle and then in fact.

A criterion that is of great relevance to the inter-paradigm debate is that research programmes must be progressive rather than degenerative. This is the key criterion used by Lakatos (1970) to overcome some of the problems Kuhn (1970) identified about paradigms and their alleged incommensurability (on the latter see Scheffler, 1967). Lakatos shows that while it is logically compelling for one valid test to falsify a theory, there is no logical reason to prohibit a reformulation of a theory on the basis of an almost infinite number of auxiliary hypotheses. Thus, while specific theories or explanations may be falsified, it is very difficult to falsify a research programme with a single underlying theoretical perspective; i.e. what Kuhn would call a paradigm. Suffice it to say here that paradigms that are always developing *ad hoc* propositions and/or having their theories reformulated or emended because they are not passing empirical tests should be considered as degenerating and not as progressive. Finally, good theories should not contradict what is known in other fields of knowledge. Assumptions about motivation or cognition in international relations should be consistent with what is known (as opposed to theorized) in psychology, for example.

While such criteria will make theory appraisal rigorous, it is important that they not be applied too early in a theory's development so as to close off an avenue of enquiry prematurely. All in all these criteria must be seen as goals toward which we should strive, with concerns being raised if theorists no longer seem able to move toward the goals with the explanations being developed.

In addition to empirical work, most of the history of international relations theory has had a strong normative component, and one would expect significant work along these lines as the intellectual climate moves further away from positivist biases. While postmodernism and post-empiricism have made space within international relations enquiry for normative analysis, such work has not been very rigorous, and if it is to gain more respect it too must have criteria for appraisal.

Since the purpose of practical theory is to guide practice, it can be assessed in terms of the extent to which it provides an enabling function; that is, how well it guides practitioners. This can be done directly in terms of whether the theory actually provides information practitioners need to know and can use. A philosophy and theory of practice can also be tested by the policies and actions to which they give rise. Practical theory, therefore, can be appraised both by looking at some of its intrinsic characteristics (e.g. the kinds of information it provides) and by the quality of policy prescriptions it produces. I have delineated seven criteria of adequacy; a 'good' guide to practice must:

1 have a good purpose and consequences;
2 be able to be implemented in practice;
3 provide comparatively complete and precise advice as to what should be done;
4 be relevant to the most difficult policy problems of the day;
5 have anticipated costs (including moral costs) that are worth anticipated benefits;
6 achieve success and avoid failure.

I label these, respectively, the criteria of goodness, practicability, completeness, relevance, anticipated utility and success–failure (see Vasquez, 1992, pp. 842–4). To this we can add a seventh:

7 the latent empirical theory of a practical theory must be scientifically sound.

I call this the criterion of empirical soundness. To the extent to which practical theory has an empirical domain, and almost all do, it can be evaluated by some of the scientific criteria of adequacy, especially accuracy. However, practical theory needs its own criteria to ensure that it is satisfactorily meeting its own purpose, which is different from that of scientific theory despite the narrowing of the philosophical differences between empirical and normative analyses.

The criterion of goodness is the most fundamental in that it is a prerequisite for the rest. The key is in defining 'good', which can be determined (or contested) only by the larger ethical, religious, professional or organizational goals guiding the group or, in foreign policy, the state. One of the contributions of post-empiricism and critical theory is to invite more discourse on this topic. What are and should be the purposes of foreign policy; what are the consequences of policy; and do the consequences live up to certain ethical or other social standards? The criterion of practicability acknowledges that there are many fine theories, but that they lose much when they are implemented; i.e. their most interesting aspects cannot be implemented. Likewise, the criterion of completeness recognizes that some theories, like the realist notion of national interest, provide general rules, but no advice as to how to apply the rule in a specific situation. Realism, for example, provides little guidance as to how to determine which option in a crisis is really in the national interest or what a rational choice might be before the fact. Although no general advice can be entirely complete, analysts must have some clear way of deriving guidance in a specific situation, if the theory is to be of any use. Ultimately, practical theories tend to be judged by their success or failures. Dramatic failures, like Munich in 1938, destroy a policy and the theory associated with it, even when that might not be legitimate. Likewise, once a practical theory is in place, only a dramatic failure leads to its displacement, even if all the other criteria have been flouted.

From the lists above, it is clear that one of the main differences between normative and empirical analysis remains the criteria used to accept or reject statements. In addition, since normative analysis involves a variety of values in defining 'good' and scientific analysis assumes the truth is the highest value, the criteria for practical theory are going to accept a variety of positions, approaches and lifestyles as fairly adequate. There is nothing necessarily wrong with this. In the areas of meaning, interpretation and lifestyle, variety may be seen as an intrinsic good – a diversity many postmodernists celebrate. Nevertheless, the criteria provide some basis for a reasonable discussion among alternatives. In empirical matters, the commitment to truth applies more stringent criteria, especially that of accuracy, which makes rejection of theories more possible. Although the criteria make truth more of a process than an end product, the very idea of truth implies ultimately a single accurate explanation rather than a plethora of equally true theories.

These empirical criteria can be used to place scientific enquiry on a new foundation, answering some of the major criticisms of post-empiricism and avoiding the potential relativism of post-modernism. In the concluding section I discuss the implications of the post-positivist debate for the future of the inter-paradigm debate.

POST-POSITIVISM AND THE FUTURE OF INTERNATIONAL RELATIONS THEORY

Post-positivism has placed the scientific study of world politics in a serious crisis. Many in the field take glee in this, for they believe it sounds the death knell for a form of analysis they never liked and which they found boring and difficult. They underestimate the extent to which a threat to scientific enquiry may also be a threat to much of what they do. Surely, a critique of all empiricism, let alone the entire Enlightenment, is not without severe implications for a variety of approaches within the field.

For me the real crisis in international relations enquiry is the absence in both empirical and normative analysis of serious, sustained and rigorous theory appraisal. Postmodernism brings this crisis to a head. In both the scientific and practical realms, the inability to evaluate stultifies cumulation and learning and hampers research progress. The reasons for this lack of appraisal are twofold: first, the dearth of criteria and, second, the lack of discipline in applying what criteria there have been. Let us turn first to how this has affected the inter-paradigm debate.

Contrary to Lapid (1989), I do not see the field as one where there are many contending theories competing with one another. Many of the so-called different theories are really not theories at all, but conceptual frameworks with a few explanations attached to them. Most of these are not competitive since they are seeking to explain different phenomena. The problem here is not choosing among them, but synthesizing and integrating them into a coherent whole; i.e. the problem is theory construction rather than theory appraisal.

A similar but more extensive problem of theory construction exists for those taking a data-based approach. Along with the charges of post-empiricism has been the charge that the scientific study of world politics has been a waste of resources and energy and has not found anything of importance (Ferguson and Mansbach, 1988, p. 220, but also see their qualification in Ferguson and Mansbach, 1991; Puchala, 1991). Part of the problem here lies with data-based scholars who have not really paid sufficient attention to integrating findings (see Dessler, 1991). Given differences in measurement as well as specification of propositions, a variety of findings should not have been unexpected. Some of the findings, however, are much less contradictory than is widely believed and can be integrated (see Vasquez, 1993).

Puchala's (1991) claim that data-based research is not as productive as theorizing sets up a false dichotomy. Theory construction based on findings and/or committed to testing its claims on the basis of evidence is part of the scientific process. To say that the main *theoretical* (his emphasis) contribution of behaviouralists like Kaplan or Deutsch is when they were performing as metaphysicians rather than positivists (p. 40) is to deny (by definition) that theory construction is not an essential part of the scientific process. Theory, because it synthesizes all knowledge, will always appear more valuable, but theory not based on research is doctrine, and anyone who lived through the one-dimensional realist thinking of the 1950s should know the dangers of that. To separate theory from science, and to call the latter positivism and scientism, sets up false issues. What we need is not further traditionalist theorizing but more scientific theory construction – with traditionalists paying more attention to operationalizability and what evidence will falsify their claims and behaviouralists paying more attention to evaluating and synthesizing findings into a coherent explanation.

In my view, the main reason for the lack of cumulation has been that the set of theoretical approaches the scientific-orientated have been testing – realism – is probably wrong. In fact, one of the messages scientific research has been persistently giving us is that the dominant realist paradigm is not providing a very fruitful and progressive guide to enquiry (see Vasquez, 1983). Part of the lack of rigour in the field is to dismiss all too quickly the method rather than the theory. What makes this a rather serious issue is that the main opponents of data-based work are often those most tied to realism and neo-realism. While some traditionalists questioned early on the ability of scientific enquiry in international relations to find anything that was not trivial, they have not been able to show why a supposedly flawed method has had more success when it has tested hypotheses that have deviated from the realist research programme than when it has tested hypotheses central to realism (see Vasquez, 1983, pp. 183–94, 201). If realists and neo-realists are to be taken seriously, they must specify at some point precisely what evidence they will accept for rejecting their theory. The time for that specification is long overdue.

Realists have always had a problem with evidence. Typically the early realists, like Morgenthau (1960), would support their case by going through history to collect examples that supported their point. This procedure, of course, was highly unsystematic in that it did not provide an equal chance for cases that did not support the proposition to emerge. Such an approach was derided as 'ransacking history'.

Nevertheless, there still are today scholars who might be called neo-traditionalists, who eschew all data-based work and findings and see international relations primarily as making good arguments. The danger of relying on argument as primary or in many cases as the only method is that there is now emerging a large number of scholars who actively publish on questions of security, including peace and war, who feel they can write on alliances, crises, bargaining, the onset of war and the conditions of peace without dealing with any of the quantitative work on these topics. They probably feel they can do this on two grounds. First is the notion that this research is contradictory and not very informative. Second is the belief that quantitative work is not really evidence and can be picked apart by questioning measures, research designs and theoretical misspecification, and therefore can be safely ignored.

The end result is a failure to come to grips with data-based evidence. To use anecdotal evidence and ignore entire research programmes is hardly excusable. The consequences of this failure for just normal discourse, let alone the inter-paradigm debate, are best seen by examining a concrete example. One of the most discouraging aspects of Mearsheimer's (1990) otherwise interesting article on bipolarity and post-Cold War stability was the absence (and apparently even an unawareness) of very relevant empirical research on the question. That research shows that a bipolarity of power is associated with frequent but not severe wars, while a multipolarity of power is associated with infrequent but severe wars, like the two world wars (see Bueno de Mesquita, 1978; Wayman, 1984). These findings make it clear that polarity is not related to the onset of war or conditions of peace, but to different types of war(!) (Vasquez, 1993, pp. 248–58). An examination of this research would have shown how much of the debate was misplaced. At one point, Mearsheimer (Hoffmann, Keohane and Mearsheimer, 1990) replied to Stanley Hoffmann's use of anecdotal evidence by saying that it is an empirical question whether bipolarity is more stable than multipolarity and that no historical survey had been done on the question. Of course, a literature review of the *Journal of Conflict Resolution* or the *Journal of Peace*

Research would have shown that there was systematic empirical research on the question covering the 1815–1965 period. If this were only a matter of the oversight of one person, this would not be such a problem. It is equally significant that Hoffmann, the early critic of American social science, also resorted to anecdotal evidence (citing the single case of the Peloponnesian war) rather than systematic evidence. Science and its empiricism always insist on arguments being based on evidence and the rules of evidence, and not simply logic.

The criteria I have offered would replace this kind of dismal procedure, which has dominated so much of international relations policy analysis, with a much more rigorous procedure. If neo-traditionalists prefer historical case-studies to data-based work, there is no problem with that, but there has to be some effort to compare theoretical claims with a systematic review of evidence and within the larger context of the other criteria of adequacy. In addition, they will have to come to terms with what quantitative evidence exists, if for no other reason than the criterion of consistency. But the latter criterion cuts both ways; quantitative scholars need to take account of comparative historical case-studies. If both sides proceed in this manner, some actual progress and cumulation can be made by settling certain issues.

While even a modicum of rigour will help general discourse, a much more systematic application of the criteria will be needed to make any headway with the inter-paradigm debate. Lakatos and Kuhn point out that paradigms cannot be falsified by an application of what I have called the criterion of accuracy. This is because any decent theory, which a dominant paradigm would have to have had to become dominant in the first place, will be articulated along a number of lines. Part of the reason realism has been extensively articulated, however, is that it is constantly being reformulated in the face of anomalies and discrepant findings. Realism's penchant for predicting contradictory things (and embodying contradictory propositions – often added to save the paradigm in light of discrepant evidence) violates Popper's (1959) criterion of falsifiability, as well as Lakatos's (1970) concern about innumerable auxiliary propositions. The violation of this principle explains why realism lives on in the face of devastating conceptual criticism, historical anomalies, a large number of null findings and a general dearth of strong empirical findings. I agree with Hollis and Smith (1990, p. 66) that the realist paradigm's ability to reformulate itself accounts for its persistence in the field, but unlike them I do not see this as an indicator that it is a progressive research programme. To the contrary, the proliferation of emendations exposes the degenerating character of the realist paradigm's research programme. If that were not the case, at some point the research programme would have progressed not by playing on its ambiguity by saying this or that specification is the real realism, or by coming up with new propositions couched in a new conceptual language, but by actually passing empirical tests.

Only by applying all the criteria of adequacy in a systematic fashion and by shaping research in the light of the theory appraisal's agenda can the inter-paradigm debate be resolved. In addition, a focus on the inter-paradigm debate can help bring both neo-traditionalists and data-based scholars together to work on a common agenda without compromising divergent methodological emphases. Whether this will be the case depends very much on whether we collectively are willing to exercise more discipline and rigour in our discussion of international relations theories. An application of the criteria of adequacy of practical theory can also place normative theory on a new foundation of rigour. The post-positivist debate, then, need not lead to a dividing discipline or to silencing the dominant approaches of the immediate past, but to a more conscious selection and evaluation of scientific theories, as well as restoring normative practical theory to its rightful place within international relations discourse.

In conclusion, while the third debate has placed the scientific study of world politics in a position where it must reconstruct its philosophical foundation, this need not necessarily jeopardize its research approaches. Instead, treating science as a self-contained system with its own rules and norms based on scholarly conventions and reason rather than irrefutable principles of logic places the scientific approach on a more adequate epistemology. Eventually, of course, the postmodernist critique will affect most approaches to international relations and not just quantitative approaches. Nevertheless, the critique has ended much of the myopia associated with logical positivism and created a more congenial space for normative and legal approaches, as well as theory construction in general. Post-positivism and postmodernism can have beneficial effects so long as they do not become the new orthodoxy. The danger is that some traditionalists will use post-positivism as a weapon to replay the second debate (on traditionalism v. science) and to dismiss and ignore quantitative research rather than to engage it on its theoretical and substantive merits. Such an outcome will further divide the discipline and reduce rigour at a time when more comparison of research findings using different methodologies and more rigorous appraisal of theories and paradigms is needed.

Notes

My thanks to Ken Booth, David Campbell, David Dessler, Yale Ferguson, Maire Heneham, Yosef Lapid, Jack Levy, Craig Murphy, Michael Nicholson, V. Spike Peterson, Steve Smith, Harvey Starr and for thoughtful comments and criticisms. Although I have not always taken their advice, I have benefited from their suggestions. Nevertheless, the views and content herein are strictly my responsibility.

1 It should not be assumed, however, that the position of Lyotard and Baudrillard is necessarily embraced by international relations scholars working with postmodernism. While several have dealt with the question of relativism explicitly, it is fair to say that their position on the underlying epistemological issues is still in the process of being elaborated.

References

Banks, M. 1985: The inter-paradigm debate. In M. Light and A. J. R. Groom (eds), *International Relations: A Handbook of Current Theory*, London: Frances Pinter, 7–26.

Baudrillard, J. 1990: *Seduction*. New York: St Martin's Press.

Berger, P. L. and Luckmann, T. 1966: *The Social Construction of Reality*. New York: Doubleday.

Bueno de Mesquita, B. 1978: Systemic polarization and the occurrence and duration of war. *Journal of Conflict Resolution*, 22 (June), 241–67.

Der Derian, J. and Shapiro, M. J. (eds) 1989: *International/Intertextual Relations: Postmodern Readings of World Politics*. Lexington: Lexington Books.

Dessler, D. 1991: Beyond correlations: toward a causal theory of war. *International Studies Quarterly*, 35, 337–55.

Ferguson, Y. H. and Mansbach, R. W. 1988: *The Elusive Quest: Theory and International Politics*. Columbia, S.C.: University of South Carolina Press.

Ferguson, Y. H. and Mansbach, R. W. 1991: Between celebration and despair: constructive suggestions for future international theory. *International Relations Quarterly*, 35, 363–86.

Foucault, M. 1972: *The Archaeology of Knowledge*. New York: Pantheon.

Hawkesworth, M. 1992: The science of politics and the politics of science.

In M. Hawkesworth and M. Kogan (eds), *Encyclopedia of Government and Politics*, London: Routledge, 5–39.

Hoffmann, S., Keohane, R. O. and Mearsheimer, J. J. 1990: Correspondence: back to the future, part II. *International Security*, 15, 191–9.

Hollis, M. and Smith, S. 1990: *Explaining and Understanding International Relations*. Oxford: Oxford University Press.

Kuhn, T. S. 1970: *The Structure of Scientific Revolutions*, 2nd edn, enlarged. Chicago: University of Chicago Press.

Lakatos, I. 1970: Falsification and the methodology of scientific research programmes. In I. Lakatos and A. Musgrave (eds), *Criticism and the Growth of Knowledge*, Cambridge: Cambridge University Press, 91–196.

Lapid, Y. 1989: The third debate: on the prospects of international theory in a post-positivist era. *International Studies Quarterly*, 33, 235–54.

Lyotard, J. F. 1984: *The Postmodern Condition*. Minneapolis: University of Minnesota Press.

Mearsheimer, J. 1990: Back to the future: instability in Europe after the Cold War. *International Security* 15, 5–56.

Morgenthau, H. J. 1960: *Politics Among Nations*, 3rd edn. New York: Knopf.

Nagel, E. 1961: *The Structure of Science*. New York: Harcourt, Brace & World.

Nicholson, M. 1983: *The Scientific Analysis of Social Behaviour: A Defense of Empiricism in Social Science*. New York: St Martin's.

Popper, K. 1959: *The Logic of Scientific Discovery*. London: Hutchinson.

Puchala, D. J. 1991: Woe to the orphans of the scientific revolution. In R. Rothstein (ed.), *The Evolution of Theory in International Relations*, Columbia, S.C.: University of South Carolina Press, 39–60.

Rosenau, P. M. 1992: *Postmodernism and the Social Sciences*. Princeton, N.J.: Princeton University Press.

Scheffler, I. 1967: *Science and Subjectivity*. Indianapolis: Bobbs-Merrill.

Vasquez, J. A. 1983: *The Power of Power Politics: A Critique*. London: Frances Pinter.

Vasquez, J. A. 1992: World politics theory. In M. Hawkesworth and M. Kogan (eds), *Encyclopedia of Government and Politics*, London: Routledge, 839–61.

Vasquez, J. A. 1993: *The War Puzzle*. Cambridge: Cambridge University Press.

Wayman, F. W. 1984: Bipolarity and war: the role of capability concentration and alliance patterns among major powers, 1816–1965. *Journal of Peace Research*, 21(1), 61–78.

11

Neo-realism in Theory and Practice

Andrew Linklater

The argument that neo-realism is flawed in theory and stultifying in practice has been explored at length in critical circles in recent years. The advocates of critical perspectives have argued that global political structures are mutable, and the future need not be like the past. Two claims which are robustly defended by Kenneth Waltz have been challenged as a result. The first is that the international system, which has been remarkably similar across whole millennia, will endure indefinitely. The second is that the anarchic system will thwart projects of reform as in the past. The neo-realist riposte has been that advancing the moral case for a different world order will not prevent the recurrence of old patterns of inter-state rivalry and war.

With the demise of the Cold War era, the differences between neo-realist and critical theories of international politics should acquire even greater importance. The neo-realist argument advanced by John Mearsheimer (1990) develops Waltz's (1964) point that the advent of nuclear bipolarity was the main reason for the high level of international stability since the Second World War. In Mearsheimer's view, the passing of bipolarity creates new dangers and instabilities. Critical accounts of long-term trends in international relations remain underdeveloped, but one of the more detailed approaches, which is found in the writings of Robert Cox, refers to the rising fortunes of multilateralism and middle-powermanship in the emerging post-Westphalian world order (Cox, 1989). Although competing visions of future possibilities divide critical theory and neo-realism, there has been very little debate between their proponents about the likely shape of the post-Cold War world or about the significance of their differences for the future of international theory.

This chapter links debates about whether long-term processes of change have gathered momentum following the demise of bipolarity to the ongoing controversies between neo-realism and critical theory, specifically between the former's emphasis on the cyclical quality of international history and the latter's emphasis on the prospects for development and change. The chapter is in four parts. Part 1 considers Waltz's argument that neo-realism is not only different from realism but an advance upon it. Parts 2 and 3 compare neo-realist arguments about the stability of the bipolar world with some recent analyses of the changing nature of state structures and emerging patterns of closer co-operation. The argument of these sections is that neo-realism underestimates the extent to which state structures are changing in the industrialized parts of the world. Part 4 highlights three respects in which neo-realism is being superseded by critical theories of international relations which, it is argued, contain a superior account of the relationship between the units and the international system, a deeper grasp of the significance of the cultural dimensions of world politics and a clearer recognition that the main challenge of the post-bipolar world is to create new forms of political community.

REALISM AND NEO-REALISM: PRIMARY DIFFERENCES

Waltz has long been critical of the idea that war will be eradicated by tapping the best in human nature or by creating legitimate domestic political systems. In *Man, the State and War* (1959), he argued that the international system had dashed liberal and socialist hopes that the rise of legitimate regimes would bring an end to war. In *Theory of International Politics* (1979), Waltz restates the argument that non-conformist regimes have been socialized into the dominant ways of the anarchical system when criticizing the reductionist belief that the system can be explained by understanding the sovereign parts.

What reductionism cannot explain, in Waltz's view, is why states behave in very similar ways despite their diverse political systems and contrasting ideologies. The problem is solved, according to neo-realism, by assuming that systemic constraints are interposed between states and their foreign policy behaviour. Neo-realism endeavours to demonstrate that these systemic forces are responsible for the remarkable similarities of foreign policy behaviour.

Reductionism underpins classical liberal and socialist writings about international relations, but realists often commit the same error, according to Waltz. Classical realism understood the constraints inherent in anarchy but failed to develop a serious account of its structure. Realists often focused on national foreign policies in the belief that they held the key to the dominant forces in world politics. Exemplifying this position, Raymond Aron maintained that the realm of international politics was impossible to theorize because it was shaped by diverse economic, political and ideological forces (Waltz, 1990, p. 25). The realist error was to suppose that no clear distinction between the system of states and the nature of the sovereign units could be drawn. As we shall see, the relationship between the units and the system remains a deeply contested theme in Waltz's thought.

Waltz acknowledges that economics, politics and culture are intertwined, but adds that a theory of international relations can be developed by abstracting the international system from other domains. Failing to disentangle the international system in this way, realists such as Aron were confined to developing crude generalizations about foreign policy (Waltz, 1990, p. 33). Neo-realism begins with the premise that a theory of international relations and a theory of foreign policy are not the same.

Waltz maintains that neo-realism advances beyond realism just as the physiocrats progressed beyond earlier analyses of different national levels of economic prosperity and uneven rates of growth. What gave the physiocrats the advantage over earlier economic thinkers was the boldness of their decision to abstract the economy from society and politics when, in reality, no firm boundaries separated these realms. Recognizing the need for abstraction, the physiocrats proceeded to develop a superior understanding of the primary determinants of economic growth. The neo-realist abstraction of the international system from the wider socio-political domain equally distorts reality, but it has similar utility. It ensures that the propelling forces in international politics are properly identified while future probabilities are more clearly ascertained (1990, pp. 22–31).

To achieve its aim of explaining the uniform behaviour of different nation-states and the constancy of international political life across whole centuries, neo-realism omits many of the factors which were important in realism (Waltz, 1979, p. 66). It resists the temptation, to which realists invariably succumbed, of being waylaid by the contingent, the transitory and the unforeseen (pp. 5 and 8). Neo-realism assumes that the 'regularities and repetitions' in international politics are clues to the operation of deep structural constraints. Its greatest advance beyond realism, it is argued, is the decision to conceptualize international politics 'as a system with a precisely defined structure' (Waltz, 1990, pp. 29–30).

Several analysts observe that the continuities between realism and neo-realism are more striking than the ruptures and breaks (Gilpin, 1984; Little, 1985). They are right to stress differences of emphasis. Neo-realism highlights the uniformities of foreign policy and the long-term reproduction of the anarchical system, but realism also emphasized these themes, and it is unhelpful to make too much of the differences between Waltz and Morgenthau. However, differences exist. Waltz's neo-realism seeks to emulate developments in the philosophy of science and structuralist modes of social-scientific explanation which are absent from classical realism. This quest for methodological rigour is central to the principal neo-realist endeavour, which is to delineate the main structural features of the system of states.

For Waltz, the structure of the international system is distinguished from the structure of domestic political systems according to three criteria: the ordering principle of the system, the character of the units and the distribution of their capabilities. In domestic political systems the organizing principle is hierarchy; in the international system the operative principle is anarchy. In hierarchic domestic systems, relations of command and obedience exist, and individuals are free to specialize within a complex social division of labour; in anarchic systems, where there are no relations of super- and subordination, the basic units tend towards functional similarity. Individuals within hierarchic orders are functionally alike and endowed with unequal capabilities whereas states in the anarchic realm have an unequal ability to perform exactly the same functions (Waltz, 1979, p. 104).

The ordering principle of international relations has remained unchanged over several centuries, and states have relied on the principle of self-help when faced with the security dilemma which is inherent in anarchy (Waltz, 1979, pp. 187–8). States such as the former Soviet Union, which believed that the structure of international relations was malleable, failed to break the mould. Economic interdependence exists, but it is low compared with the level of economic and social integration found within states. In the context of anarchy, each state tries to avoid dependence on others, and each is afraid of receiving a lesser share of the economic gains of interdependence (pp. 105–6; Grieco, 1988). The organizing principle of international relations has forced states to become like units (Waltz, 1979, p. 93).

Neo-realism stresses continuities but it does not deny the existence of change. Change *within* the international system has occurred because there have been alterations in the configuration of military power, but no change *of* its organizing principle has occurred, nor has it ever seemed probable or imminent (Waltz, 1979, p. 100). Anarchy may give way to hierarchy at some future date but, Waltz argues, no logic of economic and political change powerful enough to transform the condition and consequences of anarchy currently exists. Alterations in the balance of power will continue to occur, but no rearrangement of the configuration of military forces will alter the basic structure of international relations or radically modify the behaviour of its sovereign parts. For neo-realism, however, the current reconfiguration of the global balance of power is no minor matter.

BIPOLARITY, NUCLEAR WEAPONS AND INTERNATIONAL STABILITY

Waltz wrote that in the nuclear age it became necessary to reject the conventional wisdom that bipolarity is less stable than multipolarity: the bipolar world was a world of unusual stability (1988, p. 620). Because the barriers to acquiring superpower status had never been so insurmountable, and the continued survival of the Soviet Union seemed assured, Waltz argued that the bipolar system was not only stable but likely to persist (1979, pp. 95 and 183).

The bipolar world turned out to be more precarious than most analysts had realized. But, as previously noted, Waltz does not think that a breakdown of the balance of power transforms the international system. The prediction is 'not that a balance, once achieved, will be maintained, but that a balance, once disrupted, will be restored' in some other way (1979, p. 128). Following the demise of the Soviet Union, neo-realists such as John Mearsheimer have argued that the end of bipolarity is a reason for concern rather than celebration.

Four reasons have been offered by neo-realists in support of the claim that the bipolar world was more stable than the multipolar world which it replaced. First, the bipolar world was free of war between the great powers because the main threat to their security and survival stood out in bold relief. Caution in foreign policy and a keen sense of the dangers of over-reaction underpinned the long peace. By contrast, dangers were much less specific, responsibilities were confused and definitions of vital interests were unclear in the multipolar age (Waltz, 1964, pp. 881–90). The attendant danger was that states would miscalculate the power of their rivals or underestimate the exact strength of their resolve, so unleashing a sequence of events which culminated in major war (Mearsheimer, 1990, p. 14). Ambiguities prevail in multipolar systems because shared understandings of national rights and obligations are notoriously difficult to achieve (p. 17).

Second, the dangers of miscalculation are compounded in multipolar systems by the existence of military alliances comprising approximately equal powers. In the multipolar context, the defection of any one state immediately jeopardizes the security of the rest. In the modern bipolar world, the unequal military capabilities of partners meant the superpowers were largely unaffected by acts of defection. The superpowers could concentrate on preserving the central strategic balance untroubled by 'free floaters' (Mearsheimer, 1990, p. 14).

Third, because crisis might have embroiled the superpowers in war, the long peace could not have rested on bipolarity alone. Had both superpowers been armed with conventional weapons, they might have been tempted to attack their principal adversary whenever military success looked probable. Nuclear weapons were a crucial source of stability in the bipolar world because neither superpower could suppose that victory was possible or derive any comfort from thinking that the consequences of military defeat would be bearable (Waltz, 1988, pp. 624–7; Mearsheimer, 1990, pp. 19–20).

Waltz has argued that the controlled spread of nuclear weapons to other societies could have equally stabilizing effects, in which case nuclear proliferation is to be welcomed rather than feared (1981, p. 30). Mearsheimer has argued that the 'limited, managed proliferation' of nuclear weapons in the post-Cold War world, and the admission of Germany into the ranks of the nuclear powers, could preserve stability in Europe, although the future will be more dangerous than the past (1990, p. 8). But problems arise for neo-realism at this stage. If an orderly transition to stable nuclear multipolarity occurs, the number of powers must be less significant than the nature of their destructive military power and their willingness to collaborate. And if the ability to act in concert is an important variable, Stanley Hoffmann is right to deny that the anarchic character of the international system is more important than the nature of sovereign states in determining the level of war or peace (Mearsheimer, 1990, p. 12; Hoffmann, 1990, p. 192). This is a crucial issue to return to later.

Fourth, mutuality of dependence, which is a feature of multipolar systems, compels each state to observe others with suspicion (Waltz, 1979, p. 209). If interdependence is high, there are many occasions in which states can come into conflict (Mearsheimer, 1990, p. 45). Unusual levels of economic self-sufficiency in the years since the Second World War reduced the prospects for war between the superpowers (Waltz, 1979, pp. 138 and 144).

Neo-realism will remain central to analyses of long-term trends in international relations if Mearsheimer (1990, p. 56) is correct that the stability of the last forty-five years is unlikely to be repeated in the next few decades. However, the relationship between the units and the system remains unclear. It has been argued that realism is less useful for understanding international politics between the core industrial powers than for explaining relations between peripheral states where military competition remains paramount (Goldgeier and McFaul, 1992). If this is correct, states in the industrial core are capable of overriding the systemic logic which neo-realism regards as an unavoidable consequence of anarchy. Richard Rosecrance (1986) has argued that instability may result unless a new concert of great powers emerges quickly, but a strong domestic commitment to liberal-democratic and free-market thinking on their part could smooth the path ahead. Even Waltz nods in the direction of liberalism. Unbalanced US power is a matter for concern in the post-Cold War era, but there is some truth in the liberal claim that peace usually exists between liberal-democratic societies, and the spread of liberal democracy should be welcomed for external and internal reasons as a result (Waltz, 1991, p. 670).

Waltz argues that the relative importance of the units and the system changes over time. The 'international system is more likely to dominate' the units in a bipolar world whereas, with multipolarity, states possess greater flexibility regarding military alignments (1964, p. 901). Yet there is no meaningful discussion of how states can display flexibility or virtuosity in other respects – by institutionalizing norms which pacify relations between the great powers for example. The whole tenor of neo-realism discourages the analysis of unit-driven change. It stresses how non-conformist powers such as the Soviet Union were forced to comply with the dominant patterns of international behaviour, and suggests that civilian powers and reformist states will succumb to a similar fate or face irrelevance in the future (Waltz, 1979, pp. 128 and 152). In Waltz's view, Morgenthau's claim that superpower detente would be more secure if it rested on a common moral framework committed the reductionist fallacy of assuming that the main contours of international relations are moulded by the domestic characteristics of states. Morgenthau's attendant error was to believe it was important to 'do something to change the internal dispositions of the internationally important ones' (Waltz, 1979, p. 62). Waltz's own remarks about the positive, if qualified, achievements of liberal democracies point towards a different and less bizarre conclusion which raises further difficulties for neo-realism. If nothing prevents liberal democracies from behaving peacefully in their relations with one another, the neo-realist distinction between the unit and the system, and its denial that fundamental international reform is possible, are immediately suspect. International stability may come to depend less on the number of great powers, or on the nature of their destructive capabilities, than on the principles of international relations they espouse and the moral constraints which they recognize.

THE DECLINING RELEVANCE OF NEO-REALISM?

The belief that the spread of liberal democracy could help refashion the international system (Doyle, 1986) is a minor theme in Waltz's writings but a major point for some of his critics. Francis Fukuyama (1991) refers to deep currents of global change in which relations between the liberal-democratic, industrial powers have come to rest on consensus rather than force. Fukuyama argues that Michael Doyle's thesis that liberal-democratic societies form a unique zone of peace was bolstered by the zeal for democratization which transformed the Soviet Union and Eastern Europe. John Mueller (1989) maintains that modern warfare has become increasingly repulsive in the industrialized world, just as the duel fell into disrepute in nineteenth-century Europe. Ray (1989) has observed that just as moral development led to the abolition of slavery in the nineteenth century, contemporary moral progress proclaims the obsolescence of force. Are these writers correct that cultural change within nation-states has already checked the neo-realist logic of anarchy? Are they right that 'anarchy is what states make it' (Wendt, 1992)?

Although the neo-Kantian thesis remains controversial, there is a significant consensus that the spread of liberal democracy is an encouraging development which supplements other patterns of change in the industrialized world. Unquestionably, the major powers are less inclined than their predecessors to rely on force to resolve their political differences. The nuclear revolution not only helped to maintain the peace but ended the reliance on 'mass armies' which has been a crucial linchpin of modern nationalism (Mearsheimer, 1990, p. 21). In industrialized societies more pacific cultures are the result. Although the struggle for territory continues in world politics, none of the great powers is gripped by past assumptions that the conquest of territory is necessary for economic growth (Gilpin, 1981, p. 138; Rosecrance, 1986). What Rosecrance calls the rise of the trading state represents a watershed in the evolution of international society in this regard. Not only have the great powers replaced military conflict with peaceful economic competition but, *contra* neo-realism, they may be more willing as a result to perform specialized roles within an international division of economic and political responsibilities (Rosecrance, 1986, pp. 24 and 101). Developing a similar theme, Robert Cox (1989, pp. 827–8) has argued that the prospects for multilateralism and middlepowermanship have improved with the decline of US hegemony: the same is true of the world after bipolarity.

A related argument concerns the impact of international interdependence upon the sovereign state and its willingness to co-operate with others and comply with the rules established within international organizations. Robert Keohane (1989) accepts the neo-realist postulate that states are rational egoists but employs game-theoretical resources to explain how states can widen their conception of self-interest through their involvement in international institutions. There are parallels between this approach and English rationalism in that both think the concept of anarchy is of limited explanatory value (Keohane, 1990). The international system is anarchic but it is normatively regulated too. From the vantage point of these perspectives, neo-realism has underestimated the role of normative constraints upon states in the past and the potential for further development in the future.

Greater opportunities for moving towards multilateral forms of global governance exist in the post-bipolar world, but it is clear that the transfer of power and authority from states to global institutions is not the only challenge to lie ahead. The nation-state is under pressure on two fronts – because globalization has seriously reduced its scope for independent action and because subnational groups demand greater representation and autonomy. As Aron (1968) noted many years ago, nationalism and globalization travel in tandem: inequalities of progress fragment the human race. The rapid demise of bipolarity is the most dramatic shift in world politics in forty years but the collapse of state socialist societies must be understood in conjunction with these dual patterns of change – the subnational revolt and the process of globalization – which are eroding the foundations of the Westphalian system.

The above-mentioned perspectives differ from neo-realism in four fundamental respects. First, neo-realism argues that strategic factors are still the primary determinants of the shape of great power relations. Strategic relations are susceptible to change, and pacification may prove to be temporary. The opposing perspectives deny that the redistribution of power is the only significant change in world politics; each claims that the pacification of great power relations is a dominant logic in contemporary world politics (Richardson, 1992, 1993). Second, neo-realism and its critics disagree about the relative importance of cultural forces in world politics. Waltz argues that a systemic theory of recurrent patterns should ignore beliefs and traditions (1979, pp. 81–2). The critics point to a revolution in statecraft which systemic explanation neither registers nor explains – this is the transformation of values in world politics (Morse, 1976). Third, the critics argue that neo-realism is an inadequate guide to the dominant forces in world politics precisely because it analyses the states-system in isolation from the sovereign units and the complex processes of economic and cultural change to which states are now subject. Not only is the international system far more dependent on the character of the units than Waltz suggests, but states have the ability to initiate radical change in world politics. Fourth, neo-realism argues that its concern with the question of power and security should remain paramount since idealist visions will fail to leave any impression on the system of states. The critics argue that neo-realism is too quick to endorse prevailing realities, and its legitimation of the status quo should come to an end. The approaches outlined above often share a normative commitment to understanding the alternative paths of historical development which are immanent within contemporary global structures.

THE SUPERSESSION OF NEO-REALISM

Three criticisms of neo-realism remain for discussion as we turn to the issue of what the debates above imply for future directions in international theory. First, neo-realism lacks an adequate account of the relationship between the units and the system, and underestimates the capacity of states to promote international political change. Second, by lifting the system of states out of the cultural practices in which it is embedded, neo-realism fails to grasp the immense significance of contemporary moral and cultural change. Third, neo-realism has set its normative sights too low and devalues the contribution which critical approaches are making to the study of international relations.

Competing perspectives on unit and system

Waltz argues that realists failed to take account of the effects of structure. Neo-realism differs from realism by explaining how structural constraints force states to become functionally alike, but neo-realism does not deny that some of the 'causes of international outcomes are located at the level of individual units' (Waltz, 1990, pp. 34–36). Three reasons are proferred for taking unit-level phenomena seriously.

First, the analysis of unit-level characteristics is essential to explain 'why different units behave differently despite their similar placement in a system' (Waltz, 1979, p. 72). Second, states are not powerless to influence the system; the causal flow runs two ways, from the structural level to the units and from the units back again to the system (Waltz, 1990, p. 34). Third, unit-level analysis is necessary because 'the proportionate causal weight of unit-level and of systems-level factors' varies over time (Waltz, 1979, p. 49). (The neo-realist observation that the units had more influence in a multipolar system than in the bipolar world exemplifies the basic point.) Extending this theme, Waltz argues that a theory which explains the relative importance of unit and system in different epochs is unattainable at present, although one might be developed in future. Current limitations are no reason for abandoning the quest for theory, however. The most sophisticated approach available should therefore consider the international system in isolation from the units, set out its unique structure and explain how its constraining influence produces similar behaviour among states.

Waltz argues that systemic theory can ignore the domestic nature of the units because while they are able to influence the system they are powerless to change it. This portrayal of the relationship between the units and the system is precisely what is at stake in the debates between neo-realism and its critics, although some of the latter deny that Waltz has a coherent and unchanging position on the way they are related. Martin Hollis and Steve Smith (1990) argue that Waltz softens his systems-determinism in his major riposte to his critics. In his response, Waltz argues that 'the shaping and shoving of structures may be successfully resisted', adding that structural constraints can occasionally be overcome by using the requisite amount of 'skill and determination'. In particular, 'virtuosos transcend the limits of their instruments and break the constraints of systems which constrain lesser performers' (1986, pp. 343–4).

To what extent does this grant more influence to the units than Waltz allowed in *Theory of International Politics*? In part, the answer depends on the meaning of virtuosity. Waltz's definition is not immediately clear, but his comment that unit-level processes should be analysed when there is 'a deviation from the expected' may offer a clue (1979, p. 71). The neo-realist could choose to define virtuosity as the imaginative exercise of security and foreign policy to achieve national goals which strategic conditions seemingly place out of reach. If this is Waltz's intended meaning, his position is unchanged since the publication of *Theory of International Politics*.

However, Waltz's argument that unit-level phenomena do not generate significant systemic change forecloses the discussion at a crucial point. As already noted, Waltz (1979, p. 62) criticized Morgenthau's conception of the prerequisites of detente for converting domestic political developments 'into matters of direct international concern'. A systemic account of international relations has no interest in 'whether states are revolutionary or legitimate, authoritarian or democratic, ideological or pragmatic'

(p. 99). Yet the decision to place unit-level phenomena on one side clashes with other remarks about keeping 'open the theoretically interesting and practically important question' of how the influence of unit-level and systems-level factors varies historically (pp. 48–9). Clearly, Waltz's more recent comments on the positive international effects of the spread of liberal democracy should upgrade the importance of unit-level analysis. But so should his earlier observation that the international 'standards of performance' are currently higher than they were when social Darwinism encouraged the belief that military prowess provided unambiguous evidence of national virtue (1979, p. 137). Understanding changes in the standard of performance inevitably leads to the social and cultural forces operating inside and across nation-states.

Waltz's argument that he is concerned with developing a theory of international politics as opposed to a theory of foreign policy should therefore be treated with suspicion. He maintains that systemic theory explains the impact of structural constraints upon state behaviour, but it does not explain the whole of foreign policy. However, Waltz simultaneously argues that the units can transcend structural constraints and castigates Morgenthau for taking unit-level phenomena too seriously and for attaching too much importance to foreign policy. Waltz cannot have it both ways. Either the system determines the principal moves which states make, in which case foreign policy analysis is a residual enterprise, or states can profoundly influence the system, in which case reductionist and systemic theories deserve equal standing.

Different policy implications are inherent in these contrasting points of view, and the import of the gulf between them is immense especially in the post-Cold War age when traditional assumptions about what is possible and impossible in international relations have come under question. Neo-realists such as Mearsheimer argue that the age-old struggle to create international stability will continue under the more exacting conditions of an emerging multipolar world. The critics, such as Rosecrance, Fukuyama, Mueller and Cox, argue that neo-realism fails to appreciate the importance of 'far-reaching changes . . . in national goals and values' (Jervis, 1988, pp. 343–4). Neo-realism misjudges the initiative that trading states and middle powers can take to raise the standard of performance in international relations, although Waltz observes that the spread of liberal democracy may prove helpful in this regard. It is important to go much further by arguing that raising the standard of performance under contemporary conditions requires efforts to rework political community to give subnational and transnational identities greater importance. Promoting this pattern of change requires virtuosity with regard to political ideas and culture rather than virtuosity with regard to strategic circumstances. This deeper form of virtuosity requires efforts to make national political communities less exclusionary.

Structure, culture and change

The way in which neo-realism conceptualizes the relationship between the units and the system obscures one form of political change which is different from an alteration in the balance of power or a change in the organizing principle of the whole system. The missing dimension is cultural change, which John Ruggie (1983) stressed in the first major critical essay on neo-realism. Neo-realism failed, in Ruggie's view, to consider the shift from medieval international society to the modern system of states. This was a transition between different types of international anarchy in which membership of a wider Christian society was replaced by the divisive principles of sovereignty and territoriality. What changed were the legal and moral rights and duties which constituted independent political actors and regulated their interaction. Ruggie describes this development within international anarchy as the metamorphosis of the principles of separability.

Contemporary critiques of neo-realism which argue that Waltz does not consider how the state is constituted, but simply takes its egotism for granted, take this point further. Richard Ashley and Alexander Wendt argue that neo-realism fails to note that the meaning and importance of sovereignty are socially constructed and change over time (Ashley, 1984, pp. 240–1; Wendt, 1992). The main point is that state egotism is acquired rather than given in anarchy itself; new conceptions of the state and political community are possible; anarchy might endure but, given the capacity of states to co-operate, it need not exist as a realm of structural constraint (Linklater, 1990b, pp. 28–32).

Earlier references to the fact that states no longer regard territorial conquest as central to economic development shed further light on this notion of the constitution and reconstitution of states. In early modern Europe, it is often argued, violence was endemic partly because the absolutist state assumed that economic growth required conquest and war. False expectations of the economic benefits of territorial expansion compounded the tensions which led to the First World War (van Evera, 1985). The twentieth century has witnessed the rise of the trading state which eschews the use of force for strategies of global commerce and investment. The absolutist state and the trading state both belong to an anarchic system but their code of conduct is clearly not the same and the nature of anarchy is different because of it. Neo-realism fails to consider the changing nature of state structures and therefore cannot account for the possibility of an anarchical system which is not only peaceful but responsive to subnational identities and cosmopolitan moral sentiments. It rules out the possibility that the modern system of states might be the first system to change peacefully rather than revolve around the axis of the balance of power until it is finally destroyed by empire.

Surprisingly little exists in the way of a sociology of state structures which explains how states construct their legal or moral rights and duties and how these cultural inventions change over time. The sociological project envisaged here runs counter to neo-realism and has been delayed by structuralism and ahistoricism. The problem can be traced back to Waltz's important and enduring work, *Man, The State and War*, which distinguished three images of war, which locate its cause in human nature, type of domestic regime and international anarchy respectively. At no point did the analysis focus on the ways in which states construct the legal and moral rights and duties which separate them from, and relate them to, the outside world (Linklater, 1990a, 1992). Neo-realism neglects a possible fourth image which focuses on the construction of community and its potential and desirable reformation to respond to the interests of the systematically excluded (Linklater, 1990a).

Community and critique

Since the 1980s the critique of neo-realism has been centred on epistemological issues. Richard Ashley (1981) employed Jurgen Habermas's trichotomy of knowledge-constitutive interests to defend a critical-theoretical alternative to the technical realism of Waltz with its orientation towards manipulation and control, and the practical realism of Morgenthau with its orientation towards diplomatic understanding and consensus. Subsequently, he described neo-realism as 'an apologia for the status quo' (1984,

p. 257). Assuming that prevailing realities are 'natural', Ashley argued, neo-realism focuses on ways of 'expanding the reach of control' and 'parades the possibility of a rational power that need never acknowledge power's limits' (p. 228). In the same period Cox (1981) distinguished between neo-realism, or problem-solving theory, with its interest in the management of great power relations, and critical theory with its very different orientation towards understanding and promoting global change. According to Cox, neo-realism took the existing system for granted and asked how it could be made to function more smoothly, while critical theory asked how the system had developed and whether it might be changing. Whereas neo-realism helped to legitimate an order which the powerful found congenial, critical theory looked for immanent possibilities that it might be transformed to satisfy the interests of the marginal and excluded.

Three different points need to be made about these criticisms. First, the claim that neo-realism is simply about expanding the reach of control is either imprecise or false. Waltz recognizes that a state can act against its own interests by amassing so much military power that others have little choice but to respond aggressively towards it. Second, neo-realism takes issue with foreign policy which substitutes the pursuit of vague ideological goals for the sober assessment of vital security interests and attainable national goals. When it performs this role, neo-realism counterbalances excessively ideological or xenophobic foreign policies which obstruct the development of co-operation and community.

Third, however, neo-realism fails to make any significant positive contribution to strengthening international community between states and peoples. In Ashley's (1981) terms, neo-realism is constituted by a technical interest in manipulation and control as opposed to the practical interest in promoting diplomatic agreement and understanding, exemplified by the writings of classical realists such as Hans Morgenthau. In short, neo-realism cannot envisage a form of statecraft which transcends the calculus of power and control. No importance is attached to the practical efforts of states to create new global norms or to theoretical attempts to articulate new conceptions of political community and foreign policy. The emphasis is placed on the doomed utopianism of reformist projects. Significantly, then, neo-realists such as Mearsheimer alert the exponents of the Whig interpretation of history to dangers lying ahead, argue that in the end the balance of power is all that is possible and provide, however unwittingly, legitimacy for the status quo (Cox, 1981, p. 132). Recent developments in theory and practice suggest different modes of analysis. The neo-realist belief that the theory of international relations should explain recurrence and repetition is rejected by critical theorists who argue for the analysis (and defence) of immanent trends which run counter to the dominant logic of the system. This critique is reinforced by recent discussions of changing state structures in the industrialized world and the long-term pacification of great power relations. These developments in theory and practice suggest that neo-realism has to do more than issue warnings about the dangers which may eventuate now that the bipolar age is over.

The most important post-realist positions in the current debates share the assumption that one of the central purposes of studying international relations is to promote the well-being of the marginal and the excluded. In their different ways, Frankfurt school critical theory, postmodernism and feminism take issue with the classical principle of state sovereignty and make the case for new forms of political community. All three perspectives deny that while domestic politics may be governed by discourse and dialogue, international politics are condemned to revolve around power and force. All three are far more inclined than neo-realism to identify and give direction to promising trends in world politics.

Critical-theoretical approaches deny that the interests of insiders naturally take precedence over the interests of outsiders; they reject the supposition that in the event of a conflict between duties to fellow citizens and duties to humanity, the former inevitably come first. The emphasis is on extending political community to include outsiders, on universalizing norms, on realizing a cosmopolitan ethic (Linklater, 1990b). This cosmopolitan rejoinder to neo-realism is challenged by postmodern writers, who are equally keen to criticize the principle of state sovereignty and the rituals of power politics, but who fear that cosmopolitan perspectives are insensitive to cultural difference (Walker, 1988, 1993). Similar themes have emerged in feminist thought. Many feminists argue that neo-realism provides a gendered interpretation of world politics because it fails to understand how the political world might be changed by harnessing aptitudes for conflict reduction which are often more pronounced in the lives of women. But some feminists are suspicious of cosmopolitan ethics which disregard the personal traits of individuals in order to arrive at moral principles which are true for all. Their argument is that cosmopolitan thinking frequently downplays the ethic of care and responsibility for specific persons which has governed the traditional role of women within the family (O'Neill, 1989, p. 443; Grant and Newland, 1991).

Despite their differences, all of these perspectives argue for new forms of political community which are less exclusionary towards outsiders and more sensitive to their interests and needs. Critical theory argues for new political structures which take greater account of the interests of outsiders; postmodernism stresses the interests of those who are different, including minorities and indigenous groups; feminists argue that the exclusion of women from the public domain has meant that important ethical skills and orientations have been confined to the private sphere. Despite their differences these perspectives are complementary. A cosmopolitan ethic which denies value to diversity is unattractive, as the postmodernists observe, but so are claims for special cultural rights which constrain subordinate groups and willingly sacrifice the interests of outsiders (O'Neill, 1989). The real challenge is to strike the right balance between universality and difference in new forms of political community which transcend both moral parochialism in their dealings with outside groups and the exclusionary treatment of minorities within. What has been described elsewhere as the problem of community in international relations (Linklater, 1990c) is the longer-term problem posed by the post-bipolar age yet barely noticed by neo-realism.

CONCLUSION

Finally, what contribution has neo-realism made to the theory of international relations and, in the light of recent theoretical and political developments, what influence does it seem likely to exercise over future disciplinary debates? The first point is that neo-realism has helped to introduce greater sophistication to a field which has been shy of theory and insulated from the controversies which are central to other social sciences. In particular, there can be no doubt that neo-realism surpasses realism in rigour and sophistication. Neo-realism developed a magisterial account of the persistence of the international system, the remarkable similarities of state behaviour and the virtues of bipolarity. But it pays a heavy penalty for its abstractions and omissions. The contention that the international system should be analysed in isolation from the nature of the constituent states is not an advance beyond realism. In contrast with realism, neo-realism overstates the importance of structure. More importantly, it fails to recognize that the propensity for conflict is not the inevitable consequence of anarchy, but partly a product of the way in which states have been constituted historically. Although neo-realism recognizes that states can influence the nature of the international system, it underestimates their capacity to transform it. More importantly still, neo-realism does not consider the possibility that nation-states could (and should) be transcended by new forms of political community which are responsive to traditionally excluded identities and loyalties.

Various recent theoretical developments within the field may derive encouragement from the collapse of the bipolar world, for here is evidence that the future need not be like the past. The differences between neo-realist pessimism and progressivist interpretations of long-term patterns of change will no doubt persist, but there is a need to ensure that they are more systematically debated. What the more recent theoretical developments bring to this debate is a series of propositions which challenge neo-realism at its foundations. These propositions urge a more careful analysis of the powers of initiative which reside within the units, a greater emphasis upon the cultural dimensions of world politics and a normative engagement which seeks to recover the idealist project in international relations. Although it may be unwise to argue that neo-realism was no more than the bipolar age comprehended in thought, it did reflect that world and it did provide legitimacy for it. During the last decade, the task facing those who are committed to analysing and defending international political change has been to challenge the hegemony of neo-realism. The theoretical challenge has succeeded; the next stage is to understand more about the prospects for restructuring political community at the end of the cold war age.

References

Aron, R. 1968: *Progress and Disillusion: The Dialectics of Modern Society*. London: Harmondsworth.

Ashley, R. K. 1981: Political realism and human interests. *International Studies Quarterly*, 25, 204–36.

Ashley, R. K. 1984: The poverty of neorealism. *International Organization*, 38, 225–86.

Cox, R. W. 1981: Social forces, states and world orders: beyond international relations theory. *Millennium: Journal of International Studies*, 10, 126–55.

Cox, R. W. 1989: Middlepowermanship, Japan and the new world order. *International Journal*, 44, 823–62.

Doyle, M. 1986: Liberalism and world politics. *American Political Science Review*, 80(4), 1151–69.

Fukuyama, F. 1992: *The End of History and the Last Man*. London: Hamish Hamilton.

Gilpin, R. 1981: *War and Change in World Politics*. Cambridge: Cambridge University Press.

Gilpin, R. 1984: The richness of the tradition of political realism. *International Organization*, 38, 287–304.

Goldgeier, J. and McFaul, M. 1992: A tale of two worlds: core and periphery in the post-Cold War era. *International Organization*, 46, 467–91.

Grant, R. and Newland, K. (eds), 1991: *Gender and International Relations*. Buckingham: Open University Press.

Grieco, J. M. 1988: Anarchy and the limits of cooperation: a realist critique of the newest liberal institutionalism. *International Organization*, 42, 485–507.

Hoffman, S. 1990: Back to the future, part II, international relations theory and post-Cold War Europe. *International Security*, 15, 191–1.

Hollis, M. and Smith, S. 1990: *Explaining and Understanding International Relations*. Oxford: Clarendon Press.

Jervis, R. 1988: Realism, game theory and cooperation. *World Politics*, 40, 317–49.

Keohane, R. O. 1989: *International Institutions and State Power*. Boulder, Colorado: Westview Press.

Keohane, R. O. 1990: Back to the future, part II: international relations theory and post-Cold War Europe. *International Security*, 15, 192–4.

Linklater, A. 1990a: *Beyond Realism and Marxism: Critical Theory and International Relations*. London: MacMillan.

Linklater, A. 1990b: *Men and Citizens in the Theory of International Relations*. London: MacMillan.

Linklater, A. 1990c: The problem of community in international relations. *Alternatives*, 15, 135–53.

Linklater, A. 1992: What is a good international citizen? In P. Keal (ed.), *Ethics and Foreign Policy*, Canberra: Department of International Relations/Allen & Unwin, 21–43.

Little, R. 1985: Structuralism and neo-realism. In M. Light and A. J. R. Groom (eds), *International Relations: A Handbook of Current Theory*. London: Frances Pinter.

Mearsheimer, J. 1990: Back to the future: instability in Europe after the Cold War. *International Security*, 15, 5–56.

Morse, E. L. 1976: *Modernisation and the Transformation of International Relations*. New York: Free Press.

Mueller, J. 1989: *Retreat from Doomsday: The Obsolescence of Major War*. New York: Basic Books.

O'Neill, O. 1989: Justice, gender and international boundaries. *British Journal of Political Science*, 20, 439–59.

Ray, J. L. 1989: The abolition of slavery and the end of war. *International Organization*, 43, 405–39.

Richardson, J. L. 1992: Questions about a post-Cold War international order. Working paper, Department of International Relations, Research School of Pacific Studies, Australian National University, Canberra.

Richardson, J. L. 1993: The end of geopolitics? In J. L. Richardson and R. Leaver (eds), *Charting the Post-Cold War Order*, Boulder, Colorado: Westview Press, 39–50.

Rosecrance, R. 1986: *The Rise of the Trading State: Commerce and Conquest in the Modern World*. New York: Basic Books.

Ruggie, J. 1983: Continuity and transformation in the world polity: toward a neorealist synthesis. *World Politics*, 35, 261–85.

Van Evera, S. 1985: Why did cooperation fail in 1914? *World Politics*, 38, 80–117.

Walker, E. B. J. 1988: *One World, Many Worlds: Struggles for a Just World Peace*. Boulder, Colorado: Lynne Rienner.

Walker, R. B. J. 1993: *Inside/Outside: International Relations as Political Theory*. Cambridge: Cambridge University Press.

Waltz, K. 1959: *Man, the State and War*. London: Columbia University Press.

Waltz, K. 1964: The stability of a bipolar world. *Daedalus*, 93, 881–909.

Waltz, K. 1979: *Theory of International Politics*. Reading, Mass.: Addison-Wesley.

Waltz, K. 1981: The spread of nuclear weapons: more may be better. *Adelphi Papers*, no. 171.

Waltz, K. 1986: Reflections on *Theory of International Politics*: a response to my critics. In R. O. Keohane (ed.), *Neorealism and Its Critics*, New York: Columbia University Press, 322–45.

Waltz, K. 1988: The origin of war in neorealist theory. *Journal of Interdisciplinary History*, 18, 615–28.

Waltz, K. 1990: Realist thought and neorealist theory. *Journal of International Affairs*, 44, 21–37.

Waltz, K. 1991: America as a model for the world? A foreign policy perspective. *PS: Political Science and Politics*, 24, 667–70.

Wendt, A. 1992: Anarchy is what states make it: the social construction of power politics. *International Organization*, 462, 391–425

Further reading

Bull, H. 1984: *Justice and International Relations*. The Hagey Lectures, Waterloo, Canada: University of Waterloo.

Carr, E. H. 1962: *The Twenty Years' Crisis: 1919–1939*. London: MacMillan.

Gaddis, J. 1991: Great illusions, the long peace, and the future of the international system. In C. W. Kegley (ed.), *The Long Post War Peace: Contending Explanations and Projections*, New York: Harper Collins, chapter 1.

Rosecrance, R. 1992: A new concert of powers. *Foreign Affairs*, 71(2), 64–82.

Ruggie, J. 1989: International structure and international transformation: space, time, and method. In E.-O. Czempiel and J. Rosenau (eds), *Global Change and Theoretical Challenges: Approaches to World Politics for the 1990s*, Lexington, Mass.: Lexington Books.

Waltz, K. 1990: Nuclear myths and political realities. *American Political Science Review*, 84, 731–45.

12

International Politics and Political Theory

Jean Bethke Elshtain

My task in this chapter is to make a case for what students of international politics might learn from the study of political theory, including those classical writings constitutive of this rich tradition of discourse. To say I can only scratch the surface is to understate. I begin with a brief account of how it came to be that the two enterprises became severed, one from the other, and the damage this split has done to the political acumen and explanatory possibilities of each. Second, I display but a few of the ways international theory today should draw upon and help to extend and deepen our appreciation of political theory texts. I go on to argue that the primary political passion of our time is, and will be, nationalism and that both international relations scholars and political theorists must 'go back to school' and learn (or re-learn) history, geography, cultural studies, most especially the power of religious and national belief and identity, if they are to have anything interesting or intelligible to say about the politics of the next century. Drawing upon Raymond Aron, I conclude by suggesting what has gone wrong with international relations theory and how things might be put right, at least from the perspective of the sort of political theory I endorse.

IN THE BEGINNING

In the beginning (of the political sort, that is) the Greeks created the *polis and the world-beyond-the-polis*, a world composed of foreigners or aliens (*barbaroi*, or barbarians), or other Greeks poised in potential contest with one's own political body. This emergent historical reality represented no fall from an Eden-like paradise. The pre-*polis* Homeric warrioring world was scarcely bucolic. From what we know of other ancient ways of life, none seems an exemplary instance of harmony from which the human race, at one point, took a rather severe tumble. Some might evoke original sin here; others patriarchy's triumph over some mythical golden age of matriarchy; yet others a state of nature, whether more or less pacific or more or less violent. Whatever. My point is that there is *no such original* point of departure. We are always 'in the empire', so to speak, always in a world in which power figures and reconfigures; in which human artifice must struggle with human necessities; in which notions such as justice, freedom, compassion, and autonomy, authority, legitimacy, security and force animate, constrain and enable human beings in each and every arena within which they engage one another. The Greeks sorted this out by evolving rules that pertained *within* the *polis*, on the one hand, and, on the other, those standard practices that came into play externally, that governed dealings with 'foreigners', all those who were not members of one's city.

As I have suggested elsewhere, these rules were at once straightforward and complex. Within the *polis*, according to Athenian thinking (and it is this thinking that 'founds' several discursive traditions), different spheres of rule-governance, implicit and explicit, specified rights and wrongs, the just and the unjust. A sharp internal/external split prevailed. Justice governed relations among citizens within the *polis*; force came into play between Athenians and 'others'. What would be counted a wrong against a citizen is not so adjudged if it comes into play between citizens collectively and some external group. Diplomacy and arbitration might mediate relations with external others but the presumptive divide – them/us, what is wrong in one case may be right in another – holds (Elshtain, 1988, p. 443). To be sure, only incomplete justice pertained within the *polis*, or, perhaps better put, limiting instances of the rule of *polis* justice prevailed where women and slaves were concerned. Similarly, something of the justice of the *polis* might be called upon to blunt the sharp edges of the rule of force externally.

Several beginnings are here signalled: them/us, citizen/foreigner and limits to the discourse of justice and equality internally with precious few limits to the reign of force externally. At least that is the way the story is usually told and there is great force in its telling. It ricochets through the *locus classicus* of American academic 'realist' discourse: idealists (those who are not realists) v. realists (those who are . . .). The idealists are those who would extend the reign of *polis*-type justice throughout the world. The realists are those who know no such thing can be done, and were one to attempt it a terrible war for hegemony followed by the 'peace' of empire would be the likely result. This would seem to make secure 'the realist regime' and, as a bonus, to underscore the so-called 'levels of analysis' assumed by systemic realists, namely, that any 'explanation' of things international 'beneath' the level of the 'state system' itself is perforce inadequate, not robust enough for the task at hand. (As all students of international politics know, the levels of analysis doctrine derives in large part from Kenneth N. Waltz's classic, *Man, the State, and War*, in which Waltz discerns three 'levels' of explanation for 'why war?' – the nature of humans themselves, the nature of the 'internal' or domestic system, and the international arena within which state interactions occur.) It also, by default, secures the domain of domestic politics (the reign of justice) as the world of, and for, political theorists, saving international politics for specialists in what 'states' do given the 'system' within which they must operate.

Note that the levels of analysis formula posits a number of rather stark antinomies – not only between first-second-and-third-image approaches, but between humans and society, society and state, state and international anarchy. These various splits have defined the task for contemporary international politics on the one hand, and political theory on the other. On closer critical examination, however, the secure fortress surrounding these and related categorical presumptions is rather easily and, to my mind, persuasively breached. I will bring forward just one example – drawn from where it all is said to have begun, with the Greeks – and tie in a number of other themes that radiate out from or are entangled with my case in point. In other words, the example will lead me into my second main concern: how international relations may draw upon political theory in order to deepen our appreciation of those texts that help to constitute the tradition of theorizing in the West.

MAKING THE TASKS OF THEORY MORE COMPLEX

One problem with the splits, levels and spheres of theoretical influence we have inherited is that they make things too simple and all our tasks less complex, less daunting, they ought to be. For, as Rousseau reminds us, when we treat the worlds of men, women, nations and states we must not avert our eyes from certain terrible realities:

> I open books on law and ethics and listen to the scholars and legal experts. Permeated with their persuasive talk, I lament the miseries of nature, admire the peace and justice established by the civil order, bless the wisdom of public institutions, and console myself for being a man by looking upon myself as a citizen. Well versed in my duties and happiness, I shut my book, leave the classroom, and look around me. I see unfortunate nations groaning under yokes of iron, the human race crushed by a handful of oppressors, a starving crowd overwhelmed with pain and hunger, whose blood and tears the rich drink in peace, and everywhere the strong armed against the weak with the formidable power of the law . . . I raise my eyes and look into the distance. I see fires and flames, the countryside deserted, towns pillaged. Savages, where are you dragging those unfortunate people? I hear a terrible noise; what an uproar! I draw near; I see a scene of murder, ten thousand butchered men, the dead piled in heaps, the dying trampled under horses' hooves, everywhere the face of death and agony. So this is the fruit of these peaceful institutions! Pity and indignation rise from the bottom of my heart. Barbarous philosopher! Come and read us your book on the field of battle! (1991, pp. 42–3)

This is Rousseau at his indignant best. Were these passages simply part of a Rousseauian screed against the perfidy of philosophers when confronted with the realities and fruits of civilization, we could read it, appreciate the rhetorical power, and go back to business as usual. But Rousseau here hits upon a conundrum he articulates although he sees no way out, save, perhaps, the *deus ex machina* of a new and altogether more virtuous rebirth of civic freedom tied to respect for the civic freedom of other similarly ordered republics. That conundrum is precisely the one deeded to us by the Greeks, one that simultaneously marks the divide between 'domestic peace' and external alienation and war; between political theory which takes as its object civil society and international relations which takes as its object what goes on at the boundaries between, the space created by all 'states' in their relations.

But perhaps we should take a closer look by examining, briefly, one of the founding texts of international politics, Thucydides'

The Peloponnesian War. Is it really an account of 'the behaviour of states' given a distribution of power of a certain sort? Or, rather, of the way in which speech and action constitute *particular* civic identities – and these, in turn, are further revealed, and either reaffirmed or undone, through the terrible and tragic events Thucydides unfolds? For if it is the latter, the presumptive divide between what goes on 'inside' and what happens 'outside' comes under heavy pressure to succumb to the press of 'real life', if I dare use such a phrase in this day and age. What is 'inside' spills over and determines, or helps importantly to constitute, the context within which political bodies vie. The tasks of political theorists and practitioners of international politics flow freely back and forth, or should, if Thucydides' contextual and historical representation of the unfolding of a terrible tragedy remains potent and apt – and I believe it does. (Rousseau clearly believed this, too!)

Here classical scholars help us to get inside the world Thucydides lays bare, de-simplifying our reading and theorizing and cautioning us against moving, oversimply, to derive laws of behaviour by performing radical surgery on his dense account. For example, Nichole Loraux, in her wonderful work, *The Invention of Athens*, explores the importance of the eulogy or funeral oration in constituting the city, for 'the citizen-soldier finds in himself . . . the civic norm', and it is this renunciation of his own life for the city that somehow 'decided through him', reaffirming the city and creating 'the model of a civic choice that is both free and determined' (1986, pp. 102, 104). The ideal of *pro patria mori* is here given one of its most powerful expressions and this ideal is central to any compelling account of how it is that human beings not only incur obligations but embrace loyalties of a civic sort.

There is no easy way out for a powerful reason: the peace of civic bodies internally is *sufficient* to pit them against others externally. For once human beings have 'cohered', some are inside and others are outside – unless the 'peace' of one body is extended to encompass that of outside others. Then we have something called empire, a Pax Romana, say. The relationship between 'domestic' and 'international' relations is not only complex but mutually defining.

Contra Hobbes, Rousseau insists that the natural condition of humankind is not war. But the civil condition of humankind is, for the very simple reason that 'the existence and behaviour of civil societies produces war and the state of war. War, therefore, is a relationship not between individuals in the state of nature but between states formed by the movement of men into civil societies' (1991, from the editor's introduction, p. xvii). Thus 'war and the state of war emerge out of the very effort to establish order and justice between men in civil society' (p.xviii). We here find intimations of the Hegelian construction of war as the expression of the universalism of the state – its demand for recognition. In this scheme of things, war flows not from the unleashing of aggressive human urges but from the demands of political struggles in a world that is by no means anarchic but, rather, exquisitely relational. For were we not engaged with one another the occasions for competition, comparison, enmity and alliance would not be, as they clearly are, so exigent.

THE IMPORTANCE OF ETHICS AND NATIONALISM

This brings me to a third consideration. I argued at the outset that international relations theorists (I daresay labourers in the vineyard of political science more generally), fared rather poorly when the time came to ante up and say something compelling about the break-up of the Soviet Empire. But this was just the latest in a long line of relative failures, in part because the notorious severing of ethics from politics, often embraced by international relations theorists who fancy that they traffic in remorseless realities – what's ethics got to do with it? – yielded impoverished models, concepts, paradigms and predictions. Moral concerns are central to politics – all politics, domestic and international. The two worlds flow back and forth into each other; hence, no tidy separation of the 'justice' of the *polis* from the necessities of statecraft is either possible or desirable. The citizen, as Rousseau understood so well – and, before him, St Augustine and many others – is a torn creature, at once commited to his or her polity and to some other idea or ideal. For Rousseau this 'other' consisted of a set of more universalist yearnings for peace between peoples; for Augustine a more universalist yearning for comity, yes, but also for a full understanding and peace achievable only in end-time. The misery derives from the fact that these yearnings clash. More precisely, the loyalty and love for the polity may well pit one in antagonistic, even ferocious, competition or battle with others who are similarly loyal and torn in much the same way.

But the picture is yet more complex, in ways Augustine understood and Rousseau understood and lamented. For our torn creature may be split not once but several times over. Why? Because his or her loyalty is often divided along the model of mitosis rather than straightforward inner/outer dualism. It is not simply a matter of loyalty v. universalist aspiration but of loyalty itself at odds. Religious identity may trump civic loyalty, for example: this Augustine understood and Rousseau wanted to stamp out. Religious conviction is by definition universalist in scope – I am united not just as a citizen to other citizens within my polity but as a believer to other believers outside my polity, perhaps outside the boundaries of my own culture itself.

Political and international relations theorists consistently understate the power of religious conviction and its role as a defining, shaping, and constitutive force in world affairs. Force of belief is a form of power; it is, or may be, fungible. The events in Central Europe are quite literally unthinkable without consideration of the role of the Catholic Church. To be sure, the power of Catholicism varies from place to place. In Hungary the Church was less significant than in Poland and it was the Protestant Church in the German Democratic Republic that played the central political role. But my point here is lodged not only on the level of belief as a motivation for individual action and group solidarity against a repressive regime, but, more importantly, on the overall influence of Pope John Paul II's *Ostpolitik* in reshaping the entire balance of power in the region. The Church is the oldest continuing player in diplomatic life in the West but you would never know this from contemporary accounts of the sort taught to students of international politics. Perhaps it is because religion itself presents something akin to an embarrassment for Western intellectuals and this embarrassment leads to conceptual inadequacy and theoretical ham-handedness. Perhaps Freud's quip is here apt: 'Theory is good but it doesn't prevent things from existing.' Islam shapes the lives of some 800 million human beings. Orthodoxy is alive and well in Russia. Evangelical, fundamentalist and charismatic Protestantism is growing in Latin America. Should these potent phenomena continue to fall through the grid of our explanatory frameworks? Religious belief refuses to abide by a domestic/international cleavage and our analyses should follow by example.

But it is nationalism I want to concentrate on for a moment. If political and international relations theorists ignore religion at their peril and in the interest of promoting orthodoxies of their own, we do pay some attention to nationalism; but often in a tone best described as hand-wringing (Nairn, 1993). This is not the best place from which to offer a cogent analysis of what is going on, whether for good or ill, in one's world. There are some things we ought by now to have learned. One is that the imperial suppression of particular national identities is bound to be temporary and, moreover, that these identities, once they are unchained, may be expressed in militant forms. Why should this surprise us? As Sir Isaiah Berlin points out: 'People tire of being spat upon, ordered about by a superior nation, a superior class, or a superior anyone. Sooner or later they ask the nationalist questions: "Why do we have to obey them?" "What right have they?" "What about us?" "Why can't we?"' (1991, p. 20).

Liah Greenfield points out, in her important work on nationalism, that: 'National identity is, fundamentally, a matter of dignity. It gives people reasons to be proud.' Peoples historically – including our own foremothers and forefathers – fought 'over respect due to them, rather than anything else' (1992, pp. 487–8). The nation-state model may have emerged historically as a Western invention with the Treaty of Westphalia in 1648 but this form has been embraced worldwide. Aggrieved peoples want, not an end to the nation-state, or to sovereignty, or national autonomy, but an end to Western colonial or Soviet or other external dominance of their particular histories, languages, cultures and wounded sense of collective identity. Once *inside* the world of nation-state civic identity, they are pitched into that *outside* world of state competition.

THE IMPORTANCE OF HISTORY AND THE NEED FOR INTERPRETATION

Hand-wringing aside, how do we get a grip on these events? Through being meticulously historical, sophisticatedly interpretative and determinedly anti-specialist in the stultifying way so many now are – to the detriment of their, and our, understanding of domestic and international politics alike. As Sanjay Seth commented recently, 'international theory has not suffered because domestic theory has prospered, but rather . . . both are marked by the signal failure to grasp the implications of, and to theorize adequately about, nationalism' (1993, p. 76). Seth goes on to argue that neither modern political nor international relations theory has adequately grasped the importance of the nation in the category 'nation-state', despite the fact that nation or nation-state is a traditional building block of standard international relations texts. Nationalism is political particularism of the sort that creates loyalty to one's people. But modern nationalism also bears within itself distinctly modern and universalistic yearnings and concepts – human rights and self-determination, first and foremost. We are in desperate need of theories of the nation-state that put together its particularistic and universalistic imperatives. Such a theory would disdain any requirement that one construct one's account in a way that abides by the domestic/foreign divide.

Nationalism is neither good nor evil *per se*; it is and can be both. But it is pervasive and it is bursting out everywhere. And we seem singularly ill-equipped to come to grips theoretically with this most powerful of all political phenomena in our time, perhaps because the hold of national identity on people's minds and hearts is difficult to conceptualize; easier, by far, to have recourse to the notion of irrationalism or atavism. Stanley Hoffman observed recently that 'the problem of order has become even more complex than before. One reason for this is the unexpected increase in the number of independent states; even five years ago no one predicted the end of the Soviet Empire in Eastern Europe and the break-up of the Soviet Union itself' (1992, p. 37). Timothy Garton Ash unpacks the difficulties the West (especially the Western left) experienced in coming to grips with Solidarity in Poland, for example, because of its religious and national aspirations, its ability to forge 'a quite original mixture of ideas drawn from diverse traditions' – liberal democracy, local self-government, cultural conservatism, free-market entrepreneurialism plus aspects of social democracy, national identity without aggressive nationalism (1993, p. 338).

A DEFENCE OF THEORETICAL MODESTY

Perhaps it is best to throw down the gauntlet at this point. Given what I have thus far argued, my claim is that there can be no *grand, formalizable, universal theory* of international politics. Indeed, I will push that claim a little further: the quest for a comprehensive and overriding theory is itself suspect. The will to theorize, *if* undertaken with relentless solemnity as a quest for an overarching schema or Archimedian point from which the theorist can survey all he (and historically such characters have tended to be 'he') beholds and pronounce predictions, is not only, in principle, unachievable; it yields, at best, elegant formulations that tell us precious little about the inelegant, messy, dense, historically suffused world of international politics. This is a lesson I bring from political theory of an interpretative and modest sort and it is a lesson all we practitioners of the *Geisteswissenschaften* should by now have learned. If 1989 taught us nothing else it should have taught us humility. An empire collapsed and many, if not most, practitioners of international relations were entirely unprepared. It seems that precisely when theories of international politics should have best served us, they failed rather strikingly, overtaken, as they were, by politics itself. This recognition is borne not of a positivist chimera that prediction is the only authentic yield of theory but, rather, that a 'will to theorize', to create abstracted accounts that pay precious little attention to history, including those forces that many academics believed should have been overcome by now, the most important being religion and nationalism. My argument, then, is not against the hope for multiple *theories* of international politics but is an exercise in deep scepticism where the 'will to theorise' is concerned. This will be clearer as I proceed.

In his book *Plausible Worlds*, Geoffrey Hawthorn argues that

> generalisable answers of what we conventionally think of as a causal kind have ceased to be persuasive. The casual connections or runnings-on that we have been able to detect in human states of affairs have turned out either to have to be phrased at a level that is so general as to be insufficiently informative and not address our interests in explanation; or to be so conditional as not to be general; or, when they have generated testable predictions, to be false. Because the answers to questions about social change, we now see, have to be hedged with so many conditions, any account of any particular change, if it is to respect the conditionality of the instance, has itself to be relatively particular and accordingly complex. And the more complex it becomes . . . the more it suggests alternatives which reduce even such certainty as we can have about the particular itself. (1991, pp. 160–1)

Hawthorn follows up with a list of 'indicative false predictions' proffered quite confidently by social scientists, including practitioners of international relations theory, over the years. Those of particular relevance to the concerns of the present volume include the conviction that the world was so much in the grip of a generalizable secularization and a move away from parochial allegiances to more universal attachments that one's theories could simply assume this, or ignore it altogether, and get on with what was *really* important. And what was really important lofted heavenward into the ether of the systematically generalizable, forces operating on the level of a 'macro-order', theorizable formally in tune with macro-economics. This, at least, has been a quest for many students of international relations. Belief in a system or structure untethered to, or untainted by, considerations of cultural and historical specificity turns out to have been a big part of the problem for labourers in the vineyard of international politics. Far too little attention was paid to conditions 'on the ground', so to speak. International relations theorists, fuelled by positivist optimism, ignored *verstehen* particularities and limits.

Let me make one thing clear at the outset. By challenging the conviction that there is, should, or can be a unified theoretical or systemic account of international politics, I by no means include within my sights as a target Hedley Bull's notion of an 'international society'. The context for the conduct of international relations is not a world of thoroughgoing anarchy but, rather, a world laced through and through with historically constituted and reconstituted understandings, rules and notions about what is or is not a clear-cut (as opposed to a murky) occasion for reaction and response ranging from diplomacy to boycotts to war. But that recognition reinforces rather than undermines my initial claim, for these understandings, rules and notions are open to affirmation or negation, to renegotiation or reinforcement.

This, too, is a lesson practitioners of international politics can (and should) draw from political theory. Sometimes it is a lesson to be drawn negatively – why Plato's *Republic* could never be implemented in practice, for example – and sometimes positively: how the Machiavellian world of diplomatic manoeuvring, fractious discontents, and limits as well as inducements to action can never be altogether overcome in some future-perfect order. The international community is too diverse, composed of wondrously various communities, and the reality generated by these multiple communities in their dealings with one another too dense, for any sustainable and compelling theoretical overcoming. Far better to consign that aspiration to the dustbin of history than the aspirations that continue to animate the world's peoples, among the most vital and important being religious belief and identity and national or nationalist aspirations and quests for recognition. These latter are what we most need supple and coherent accounts of and what, strikingly, we most lack if we confine ourselves solely to the world of international relations theory.

THE AMBIGUITY OF, AND NECESSITY FOR, THEORY

In his 1967 essay 'What Is a Theory of International Relations?', Raymond Aron points out that few words are more ambiguous and more promiscuously overused than 'theory'. In international studies, he continues, observations as commonplace as 'the virtues of nonalignment' or 'the influence that the priority of economic considerations in modern societies allegedly exerts in favour of peace', are presented in full regalia as 'theory' (1984, p. 166). Aron goes on to note that the first meaning of theory, emerging with the Greeks, was theory as contemplative knowledge. That, clearly, is not what practitioners of international politics seek; rather, they prefer theory as a hypothetical, deductive system consisting of testable hypotheses. Such 'theorists' – not all international relations theorists are of this type, of course, but the aspirations and claims of those who are haunt all other projects – want to be able to predict: that takes priority over deep understanding, over the interpretative '*verstehen*' turn in the human sciences associated (in the Anglo-American world at least) with Ludwig Wittgenstein's later works. Physical science seemed to offer the 'perfect model' for predictive science, Aron comments (p. 167). But something went awry: all sorts of important insights were derived from models of econometrics and related enterprises, but the complexities characteristic of politics failed to 'fit', hence fell through the grid of econometrism, whether in its roughest barefoot empiricist form where generalizations are sought once 'large numbers' are collected, or in its more impressive ('purer') economic theory form modelled on macro-economics. Aron notes a few of the troubles – a veritable swarming host of troubles.

Here is a by no means exhaustive shopping list of a few of the seemingly intractable problems students of international politics – indeed of *all* politics – must contend with, according to Aron. Politics is characterized by doctrinal conflict. Politics is unusually susceptible to the influence of a single ruler. Politics is swayed by the passions as well as the interests and 'calculations of utility' of masses of people, whether subjects or citizens. Politics takes place in a particular spatio-temporal figuration of states, nations and regions, thick with life, dense with history – history not as icing on the cake of identity but as constitutive of identity itself. Here I refer to the fact that being 'English' (as but one example), as George Orwell pointed out, is not, for the vast majority of Englishmen and women, an incidental and not terribly interesting fact about their lives, but an integral feature of who they are, what they think, what they hope for and what they fear. Politics undertaken by such encumbered beings is always complex and always in need of interpretation. Political action is never wholly transparent. Undertaken in the heat of action, there is no single law to cover how persons act politically, for, depending upon the situation, one factor may trump others equally important but, at that moment, less exigent.

Aron thinks that American political scientists, those most determined to make the 'scientific turn' in the post-Second World War era, took the wrong way, or, at best, a not terribly fruitful one. For them (Hans Morgenthau is his particular point of reference but Aron casts his net more widely), the way to theorize was to begin with general concepts – power and conflict – and then to map international politics as a species of an abstract genus, 'as illustrations of special cases of universally human phenomena . . . setting up power, thus defined, as the unique and highest goal of individuals, parties, or nations does not constitute a theory in the scientific sense but rather amounts to a philosophy or an ideology' (1984, p. 170). The ideological commitments undergird and give energy to the theory but go unrecognized – repressed and denied as having foundational force and thus serving as a rationale for 'the theory' itself.

This is rather similar to the case I made in a 1985 essay, 'Reflections on War and Political Discourse: Realism, Just War, and Feminism in a Nuclear Age'. Unpacking the dominant 'scientized realism' of the American academy, I argued that this perspective presumes what actually needs explaining. That is, the 'theory' posits: 'a world of sovereign states as preposited ontological entities, each seeking either to enhance or to secure its own power. State sovereignty is the motor that moves the realist system as well as its (nearly) immutable object . . . Wars will and must occur because there is nothing to prevent them.' Note that states, *not* nations or nation-states, are the actors and each state is conceptually 'alike' (Elshtain, 1985, p. 40). No state within this general framework, I continued, can from itself entertain any hope that through the actions it takes, or refrains from taking, it may succeed in transforming the wider context.

Missing from this schema – domimated as it is by the 'big booming categories' (power, first and foremost; security as an overriding interest, indeed perhaps the only legitimate interest) – is precisely what Aron indicates as needed in order that we begin to 'grasp what distinguishes this field from other social fields, what differentitates relationships among politically organized communities from all other social relationship' (1984, p. 170). In his masterwork, *Peace and War: A theory of International Relations*, Aron notes, he begins by trying to assess 'what constitutes the distinctive nature of international or interstate relations' and he concludes that it rests, finally, in the legitimacy and legality of the use of military force, 'for only in the international arena is violence considered more or less "normal."'(p. 171). This is no doubt somewhat austere but it forces us to look at what we often prefer to avert our eyes from. This needs some explanation.

Whatever one thinks of where Aron winds up (which is also the place at which he begins), it at least has the virtue of recognizing that political systems and political and social events can never be defined exhaustively and (so to speak) *from the outside*, from a position removed from any concern for historically specific and contingent features, for politics is both experienced and enacted by human actors and agents themselves. International society is a world the reality of which is that its members can, and all too often do, resort to force. Further, this resort to force, which may be negotiated and limited diplomatically, challenged militarily, deplored ethically or celebrated ideologically, cannot be ruled out of court definitively in the way 'domestic' violence can – and is. *Pace* Kant, perpetual peace is nowhere in sight. History offers up many bitter lessons and this, surely, is one. But this latter recognition should not lead the theorist to pursue the chimera of a precise, unclouded divide between 'inner' and 'outer' forces and factors – each counts in every engagement of states and peoples, one with the other.

Any persuasive study of international relations must be 'concrete' – it must be both 'sociological' and 'historical' (Aron, 1984, p. 178). In the absence of a nuanced attunement to different countries and their stories, hence the strategic cultures they represent to the world, all attempts at theorizing must needs be shallow.

The 'old world', Aron rather delicately suggests, perhaps understands this better than the buoyant, even adolescent go-getting enthusiasts of 'solutions' and 'predictions' and 'control', of the new. By wanting every proposition to be 'operational', those dedicated to an over-inflated view of what a 'science of politics' might accomplish are pursuing phantoms, for 'political science or the science of international relations is not operational and will perhaps never be so, at least not until the time when politics per se, that is, the rivalry between individuals and the community to determine what is good in itself, will have disappeared' (1984, p. 181).

But this by no means precludes 'doctrines of action' and rules of thumb. The best diplomats and presidents and prime ministers do work through a loosely structured conceptual grid but, hopefully for all our sakes, they are not bound up in the rigidity of lawlike 'behaviours'. Theorists must appreciate what practitioners have always known: they must 'bear in mind the multiplicity of aims pursued by actions in the international system', and to the extent that they bear this in mind, 'the less he [the diplomat] will be a prisoner of an oversimplified representation of *Homo diplomaticus* and the more chance he will have of understanding his allies and his enemies by understanding the diversity of perceptions that govern their conduct' (Aron, 1984, p. 184).

Surely the time has come for us to cease being perplexed, frustrated and disappointed that the world does not fall into line with our theorizing. Perhaps that says something about our theorizing. Perhaps we should try to catch up with the world. Perhaps we should enter, in and through our work, the endless *agon* called 'politics', that grand and sometimes terrible human activity that regularly mocks our carefully delimited categories and systems and predictions yet cries out for our understanding. By understanding I mean much more than impressions or reactions to specific events, although these are no doubt important; rather, I have in mind a way of undertaking theory that can take coherent account of ways of life and histories far different from our own without abstaining, as we do so, from offering up perspicuous contrasts and even judgements. Stepping back from the 'will to theorize' places a heavier burden on the theorist. For he or she must take to heart 'what exists' and what might be possible given what exists. This is not to move away from abstract concepts – we cannot manage theory of any kind without them – but it is a cautionary note about what I am tempted to call 'abstracted' categories, those couched at such a remove from what they purport to explain that we are bound to miss the vital truths that lie in the details of things, in their many sided complexity and inherent thickness.

References

Aron, R. 1984: 'What is a theory of international relations?' In M. B. Conant, (trans. and ed.), *Politics and History*, New Brunswick, N.J.: Transaction Books, 166–85. Originally published in *Journal of International Affairs*, XXI, (2) (1967), 185–206.

Ash, T. G. 1983: *The Polish Revolution: Solidarity*. New York: Scribner's.

Berlin, I. 1991: Two concepts of nationalism. Interview by N. Gardels, *New York Review of Books*, 21 November, 19–23.

Elshtain, J. B. 1988: The problem with peace. *Millennium: Journal of International Studies*, 17(3), 441–49. (For a genealogical account of this story see R. B. J. Walker 1993: *Inside/Outside: International Relations as Political Theory*. Cambridge: Cambridge University Press.)

Elshtain, J. B. 1985: Reflections on war and political discourse: realism, just war, and feminism in a nuclear age. *Political Theory*, 13(1), 39–57.

Greenfield, L. 1992: *Nationalism. Five Roads to Modernity*. Cambridge, Mass.: Harvard University Press.

Hawthorn, G. 1991: *Plausible Worlds*. Cambridge: Cambridge University Press.

Hoffmann, S. 1992: Delusions of world order. *New York Review of Books*, 9 April, 37–44.

Loraux, N. 1986: *The Invention of Athens*. Cambridge, Mass: Harvard University Press.

Nairn, T. 1993: Demonising nationalism. *London Review of Books*, 15(4), 25 February, 3–6.

Rousseau, J.-J. 1991: The state of war. In S. Hoffmann and D. P. Fidler (eds), *Rousseau on International Relations*, Oxford: Clarendon Press, 33–47.

Seth, S. 1993: Political theory in the age of nationalism. *Ethics and International Affairs*, 7, 75–96.

13

Questions about Identity in International Relations

Marysia Zalewski and Cynthia Enloe

Who are 'we' in international relations? Who becomes identified as important in international political events? Which identities are perceived as relevant and which are not? Which groups are allowed to self-identify? What role does the politics of identity play in contemporary international relations theory and practice? These are just some of the questions about identity being asked by students and scholars trying to make sense of international political events.

IDENTITY QUESTIONS

The break-up of the Soviet Empire, together with the demise of Cold War polarization, has resulted in the revival or eruption of a large number of nationalist conflicts. The war in the former Yugoslavia is only the most obvious example. There were, of course, nationalist conflicts during the Cold War but the 'New World (Dis)Order', about which so much has been said recently, seems to have opened up spaces for people to reassess their identities and for groups to claim the right to their identity often in response to a perceived threat (Milić, 1993). These identity claims take many forms: seats at the bargaining table, control of land, new languages taught in schools, but also wars, ethnic cleansing, racist graffiti, increasing tensions. The process of integration in Western Europe similarly has created room for many new considerations of identity to emerge (Wæver et al., 1993, p. 3). Some European peoples who belonged to previously submerged minority nationalities (Basques, Catalans, Welsh, Scots,

Romani ('gypsies'), German Turks and black Britons) have fought and continue to fight to claim their public voices. Outside Western Europe, political life is being remade too as Aborigines in Australia, Sikhs in India, Tamils in Sri Lanka and black people in South Africa each speak up collectively, refusing to keep on acting publicly as though their own identities were trivial or obsolete.

It is ethnic or racial identity that makes the headlines. But identity has many more faces. When an Arab man travelled in the 1980s to Afghanistan to fight in a guerrilla army against the Soviet army he may have been motivated by his own sense that he was a Muslim, that he was defending a people sharing his religious identity. Likewise, a Mexican woman travelling to Canada in the 1990s to form a group calling for an end to sexist international trade agreements was acting out of not only her sense that she was Mexican, but also out of her newly politicized sense that she was a woman.

Students and researchers have not been immune to these events. Since the 1980s these developments 'out there' have pushed some international relations observers to rethink their methodologies and to reassess their theories for explaining what has been happening in the world. And one topic that seems to be flashing in neon is 'identity'. Who do people think they are and how does this shape not just their local but their international actions? Who did Yitzak Rabin think he was when he (hesitantly) shook hands with Yasser Arafat in the White House rose garden in September 1993? Who did the British soldier think he was when he heard he was being sent to join UN forces in Bosnia that same month? How is a Vietnamese woman defining herself when she weighs whether this week to apply for a job in the new Australian-owned garment factory opening in her town? How does a Croatian anti-rape activist respond when the local press calls her a traitor? Until recently most international relations theorists imagined that they did not have to be curious about these questions. Today some of us are realizing that when we avoided these questions we were being intellectually naive.

Scholars critical of mainstream international relations theory have therefore insisted that questions about identity should not be left just to sociologists and psychologists. Feminist scholars in particular have called on all international relations researchers to become curious about identity politics (Moghadam, 1993; Peterson, 1993). Why? Why should it be feminist international relations students and scholars who have been most insistent that their colleagues take on identity? First, a feminist awareness makes anyone wary of seeing 'France' or 'Japan' as naturally cohesive actors on the world stage because feminism has revealed how few women in any country actually make those policies so glibly labelled 'national' policies. A feminist consciousness thus nudges any international relations observer to look deep into the 'nation-state' and ask who actually is getting to speak for the nation or for the state and who is being marginalized and silenced. Second, even feminists who are not personally involved in political movements have learned from activists that identities informing international relations are fluid and complex. They have learned, for instance, that John Major's actions in Northern Ireland or Hong Kong cannot be fully explained unless one wonders when (and how and why) his sense of his manliness, his whiteness, his upwardly mobile Englishness *each* shape his decisions and when any one of these facets of his identity lies dormant politically. Feminist theorists, joined now by critical theorists and postmodernists, thus have raised questions about the construction and ascription of identity and the effects that these everyday processes have on the ways alliances are sustained, the ways wars are waged, the ways foreign investment is attracted. The rise of empirical and philosophical identity questions means that as students of world politics we have to be much more systematic and rigorous in considering questions about identity.

QUESTIONS ABOUT IDENTITY

Who we are, what our identity is, and who defines us each have far-reaching consequences. We now know that each of the following examples has shaped local but also international politics profoundly. Being identified by others as Jewish in Nazi Germany in the 1930s and 1940s meant your life was in severe danger, even if perhaps you defined yourself as a German. These identity politics have to be explained to understand some of what happened in the Second World War. Being identified by others as a communist in McCarthyite America in the 1950s likewise increased your chances of being hunted out and branded as anti-American, even if you defined yourself as thoroughly American.

In the 1990s, too, identity politics have to be understood by anyone wanting to explain the post-Cold War world. Here are three examples. Being identified as a female foetus in present-day

China severely diminishes its chances of being born, while simultaneously making it an object of international human rights monitors as female foeticide, assisted by the rapid international spread of pre-natal diagnostic technology, takes the place of female infanticide. Being identified as middle-class in Britain today improves your chances of being given the opportunity of a university education, which in turn increases your chances of being able to find well-remunerated employment, and may also encourage you to support the integration of the European Community. Being seen as first and foremost a woman in Saudi Arabia means you will not be able to vote or drive a car without a chaperone, even if you see yourself as politically sophisticated or technically adept. But, beyond these local consequences, being identified as a Saudi woman has made the United States government nervous about your activism because it could destabilize the United State's ally, King Fahd. Each of these three processes of identity politics is helping to shape the landscape of post-Cold War international events and processes and in each of these instances, one will notice, the identity that will often determine one's fate is not dictated by the person whose life is being channelled. Instead, identity is being fashioned – and constructed – by others, others who have a stake in making up certain social categories and in trying to make people conform to them. But it is a mistake to imagine that people are mere puppets, passive marionettes whose identity strings are being pulled by omnipotent others. Rather, we need to think of identity politics as a process in which both the person seeking to answer 'Who am I?' and others who want to influence the answer are pushing and pulling each other, though often with unequal resources. Thus, how many middle-class British secondary school students prefer to think of themselves as 'natural' entrants into university and thus do not need much outside pushing to embrace this comfortable identity? And how many Saudi women think that they would not be 'respectable' if they climbed behind the wheel of their husband's Toyota, and so were scandalized, not encouraged, when a small brave group of Saudi women held a 'driving protest' on the eve of the Gulf War.

The consequences of who we are, how we identify ourselves, how we are identified by others (parents, police, journalists) are enormous. Identity determines how you are treated, what is expected of you, what you expect of yourself, what jobs will be available to you, what jobs you will even apply for, what your health will be, whether you will be allocated as a primary carer for children, whether you will be seen as an enemy or a friend. In the conventional perception of international relations we can start thinking about the effects of identity politics by seeing which identifiable groups become the privileged referents. That is, who or what do mainstream international relations observers bother to pay attention to or expect anything of? Why do we consider states to be a major referent? Why not men? Or women? And even when we do look below the state, why is it we pay most attention to economic class or national or ethnic identity? For example, we privilege business managers' and trade union members' relations to the North American Free Trade Agreement (NAFTA) and Scottish or French relations to the EC. But as international relations analysts, we spend far less energy making sense of how and why women see themselves as women when they react to NAFTA or the EC (Griffin Cohen, 1987; Duchen, 1993).

One might think that the answer to the question, why do we consider states to be a major referent, is obvious. We pay attention to the state of China when we are watching nuclear proliferation because it is the Chinese government, not all Chinese men, not Chinese workers, who are making nuclear decisions. Perhaps. But what if we were more curious; what if we dug deeper and investigated whether the current Chinese officials making nuclear policy were all men and whether they made at least some of their nuclear decisions in order to prove to the Russians and the Americans that they too were 'real men' in international politics? But we will never know how much this has affected international nuclear politics if we persist in talking simplistically about 'China decided' or 'the US decided'.

Or take another example. The largest media companies would have us believe that Bosnian Muslims in the 1990s would automatically regard the Serbs and the Croats as enemies taking ethnicity as their own primary identity. Yet if we pause and consider other forms of identity, we might discern that a large number of Bosnian Muslim women feel they have more in common with Croat and Serbian women victims of mass rape, that is, other women, than they do with some Bosnian Muslim men. When we as theorists, explainers, privilege ethnicity over gender in our investigations, we act as though women's identities as women (and men's identities as men) explain nothing about how the Yugoslav war is being waged. Are we so sure? If we do not pause, if we do not carefully assess how ethnic and gender identities congeal and fragment in the former Yugoslavia, we are likely to provide inadequate help to such international bodies as the UN War Crimes Tribunal (Stiglmayer, 1994).

Thus, while for generations international relations researchers have made the state, the government, their privileged referent, that analytic choice is questionable (Tickner, 1992; Peterson, 1992a; Peterson and Runyan, 1993). The ending of the Cold War and the consolidation of the European Community, the emergence of private multinational giants, the dependence on UN peacekeeping forces for international stability, all have compelled even some mainstream international relations theorists to have second thoughts about relying on states as the principal actors. Whereas the old, and still widely used, security agenda was about states and their sovereignty, expressed chiefly through the accumulation of military power, the new security agenda, as identified by some Western scholars, is about societies and their complex and fluid webs of identity. 'Societies are fundamentally about identity', according to Barry Buzan, identity for him being 'what enables a group of people to refer to themselves as "we"' (Wæver et al., 1993, pp. 5–6). The desire and ability of a society to sustain its traditional patterns of language, culture, association, religious and national identity and custom are perceived as central to the new security agenda. Changing the referent therefore changes what we think of as 'us' and thereby changes what we perceive as threats to 'us'. Ann Tickner underscores this point by challenging her colleagues in international relations to give up their comfortable notion that states are sovereign entities. For this assumption of sovereignty is suspiciously akin to the assumption that men as fathers and husbands are the 'heads of households', an assumption that for years has lured policy-makers into their naive view that the 'family' acts as a single cohesive unit and that the adult male can always speak for the desires of all members of the family. Thus, becoming curious about identity formation below the state and surrendering the simplistic assumption that the state is sovereign will, Tickner (1992) suggests, make us much more realistic describers and explainers of the current international system.

Referring unquestioningly to state governments as actors also has far-reaching philosophical consequences. It makes any government's officials *seem* as though they actually are speaking for all the people living within their state's territory. That, in turn, unwisely implies that there is validity to most officials' wishful claims that they do represent the 'nation', that their state is not merely a state, but a 'nation-state', a political system in which virtually all people identify with the central state and feel represented by its officialdom. Think about the language used by officials and many observers to justify certain actions carried out 'on behalf of the nation': in 1986 the United Kingdom felt obliged to allow the United States to use British bases to send aircraft to bomb Libya. The fact that Britain had 105 United States military installations is linked to its membership of NATO, which was created in 1949 by officials of Canada, the United States and a handful of postwar European governments. There is something very troubling, analytically, about these two seemingly bland sentences. Did in fact 'the United Kingdom' feel obliged to accommodate 'the United States'? Is that really what went on? No. It seems far more accurate and thus realistic to say that 'the all-male elite security officialdom of the British government, under both Conservative and Labour Party rule, came to believe that they had to oblige their United States male counterparts, under both Republican and Democratic administrations, when the topic on the table was military'. Now admittedly, this alternative sentence is longer and less elegant but it exposes dynamics rather than camouflages them. It prompts us as readers of the sentence to launch our own research into some necessary questions.

1 Did this handful of British men develop some sort of masculinized bond when they met in secret with the United States national security men to discuss such deeply masculinized issues as military strategy?
2 Did all British women for whom the United Kingdom officials spoke know that they were being identified as willing supporters of such a foreign basing policy?
3 What would women as women, or as mothers, or as black Britons, or as feminists, each do once they did find out?

The original two sentences for all their brevity imply a lot, but say little. They imply some sort of reciprocal protective relationship; they also imply a democratic process. Indeed the principle of reciprocity is enshrined in NATO doctrine. If, during the Cold War, British people had been actively threatened with mass extinction, the identity of 'British' would imply that the United States government would have been more likely to come to their assistance than if they had had another identity, such as East German. In the 1990s NATO is the only major inter-state military alliance still standing but the European identity it formerly relied on has been shaken. Thanks to the grassroots peace movements in countries such as Britain, Germany, Greece and Spain, NATO no longer looks as though it rests on a secure foundation of European individuals' identity as state citizens in the democratic system (Kaldor and Anderson, 1987; Liddington, 1989).

WHAT IS IDENTITY?

So far we have treated identity as a self-evident concept, but the issue is not as simple as that. Do you know how to identify yourself, who you are, where you belong? To be able to claim your identity without fear of persecution or discrimination seems to be a deeply held value, even though it is sometimes impossible to express without paying a high price. Clearly, one's felt need to claim identity or to restore lost identity will depend on whether there is or has been a threat to that identity. This applies at many levels. Think of African-American Sojourner Truth's impassioned challenge to white-American men and women at a suffrage congress in 1851. She had to demand that her male and female co-suffragists recognize her as a woman despite her 'blackness' and her muscled body caused by years of hard work. She simply asked: 'Ain't I a woman?' (quote in Adams, 1989, p. 23). Think also of British novelist Radclyffe Hall's plea in 1928 for recognition of female homosexuals: 'Acknowledge us, of God, before the whole world. Give us the right to our existence' (1956, p. 437). Since the 1970s lesbians and gay men in many cultures have 'come out of the closet'. That is, they have demanded that parents, co-workers and government officials recognize *all* of their identities, not just those identities that confirm the current social and international order. When gay men and lesbians have asserted their identities, they have challenged the workings of the World Health Organization, scores of state militaries, international human rights lawyers, and, of course, states' immigration bureaucracies (Tatchell, 1992). 'Give us the right to our existence' is surely the rallying cry of other claims to identity. Some international relations work to keep closet doors firmly shut; others work to pry those same doors open. 'Closets' can be internationalized spaces.

And making claims to identities involves asserting the legitimacy of collective beliefs and customs without discrimination or persecution. Still, what is it that defines the identities of, for example, the Welsh or the Australians? Does a common language define the

Welsh when only 20 per cent (approximately) of those living in Wales speak the language? Or is it the commitment to revive Welsh culture which might imply that non-Welsh speakers could define themselves as Welsh. Who are 'we' in Wales? What about Australian identity? Some Australians want to distance themselves from the British to claim distinctive Australian identity. Others wish to claim that they are the true Australians (Pettman, 1992). We might assume that identity is about the 'we', the 'us' and the 'them' (Hall, 1993. Curthoys, 1993; Brah, 1993; Bhavani, 1993). But Spike Peterson (1993) argues that a new and urgent question revolves around 'who we are'.

For Peterson it is no longer adequate to rely on the conventional boundaries that we have traditionally used to define who 'we' are. She argues that conventional categories are no longer self-evident, and goes on to claim that the conventional definition of group identification assumes an exclusionary form, 'us versus them, insiders versus outsiders, citizens versus foreigners, differences among people are in tension with contemporary requirements to compatible identities and global cooperation' (1993, p. 2). This adversarial perception of identity arguably locks us into a vision of an anarchical international system tormented by an inevitable and unending conflict between the demands of national identity and the need for the global community in terms of solidarity and political co-existence. Do we have to be content with the continuation of the success of particular national identities at the expense of other subnational and transnational identities (p. 11)?

Peterson also urges us to ask other, more searching, questions about identity and what really constitutes the international. It is not enough to confine ourselves to the seemingly insurmountable tension between national or state identity and today's widely felt need for global community. Or to assume that identity is a given and fixed phenomenon (1993, p. 3). Or that we have only unitary and not multiple identities. We perhaps intuitively believe that the claiming of identity is a natural, universal phenomenon. To have the right to retain one's own land or language or culture seems, almost instinctively, to be what we would all want for ourselves. Feelings of national identity are felt extremely strongly by large numbers of people. Think of football matches and other major sporting events. Press reports following the 1993 peace accord between the Israeli government and the leadership of the PLO featured a soccer match between a Palestinian team and a visiting

French team. When journalists saw the Palestinian fans (mostly men?) waving their flags enthusiastically for their team, they took it as evidence of newly legitimized national identity. Even where to hold future Olympic games has the potential to spark off huge surges of nationalistic pride and feelings of identity and belonging. But we should be wary of anything that seems to be either natural or inevitable. Many things have seemed natural or inevitable which have turned out to be products of deliberate calculation. Think of Western government policies designed to sustain the barriers keeping people of colour out of the senior ranks of the military or out of universities, elite clubs and decision-making posts in secretive intelligence agencies. Official statements regarding the allegedly 'normal' roles for women or putative racial personalities are usually backed up by an appeal to naturalness and inevitability precisely because that protects the speakers against critical inspection (Harding, 1993).

Some of the most subtle analyses of the constructing processes surounding identity come today from women scholars who are feminists in ex-colonial societies or women of colour in post-industralized societies (Mohanty, 1988; Yuval-Davis and Anthias, 1989; Anthias and Yuval-Davis, 1993). This is not just a coincidence. It is these scholars who seem most aware of how contradictory identity construction can be, how hard those contradictions can be to live with, to cope with, to reconstruct. Think for a moment about how some of the international events of the 1990s appear to women. For example, the woman who has thought of herself since childhood as 'female' and 'Muslim' and 'Kuwaiti', but in the time since the Gulf War has come also to see herself as a 'citizen' and as a 'potential voter'. But if she wants to be a 'voter' some Kuwaitis may force her to give up her identity as a 'good woman' or as a 'loyal Kuwaiti' (Tetreault, 1992). Think too of a woman living in Britain who has seen herself as Afro-Caribbean and British and Protestant but who now is rebuked by the very community leaders she used to respect because she wants to redefine black British notions of 'community' so that it will be wide enough to include female autonomy (Sahgal and Yuval-Davis, 1992). These writings should make international relations observers pause before they settle for exploring only national, state and societal identity. That triad may be in fact only the tip of the identity iceberg.

International relations may always have been shaped significantly by the other identities suggested in all the examples above.

Race, ethnicity, class, gender, religion, age, income, each of these may, not necessarily, not automatically, serve as a launching-pad for people to join together in a way that affects international politics. Thus in the 1980s and the 1990s international relations analysts could be seen scurrying to make sense of the newly mobilized international Islamic fundamentalist movement. Many of these same observers were caught off guard too when a new international Women's Coalition successfully lobbied the UN human rights agency to rewrite the definition of a 'human right' to include the right of a woman to be free from police rape and domestic violence (Defeis, 1991; Kerr, 1993; Tomasevski, 1993).

THE INTERNATIONAL POLITICS OF IDENTITY CONSTRUCTION

The construction and ascription of identities play significant roles in international politics. Some extremely innovative work has been carried out in this area since the 1980s. An early example of such work is Carol Cohn's much quoted (in feminist circles) article 'Sex and Death in the Rational World of Defense Intellectuals' (1987). Cohn spent a year among United States defence intellectuals, working with them and becoming (almost) a member of their closely knit community. These defence intellectuals are civilians, mostly men, but with government contracts and top security clearances only a state can bestow. They sometimes work in government, sometimes in universities or think tanks. Cohn discovered that these men created identities for themselves, and a sense of community derived from those identities, in large part by denying the lethalness of the project they worked on every day. Cohn concluded that 'they formulate what they call rational systems for dealing with the problems created by nuclear weapons: how to manage the arms race; how to deter the use of nuclear weapons; how to fight a nuclear war if deterrence fails' (p. 688). Her aim was to understand more about what they thought and how they thought it. Her goal was to discuss the nature of nuclear strategic thinking and in particular the specialized language, which she called technostrategic.

Although Cohn does not talk about identity formation as such, her discussion about how the language used by these defence intellectuals helps to create a particular understanding of nuclear weapons and nuclear war is useful for our purposes in this chapter. Language, after all, is often taken to be a key indicator of identity. But language is not simply a naming device, it is also a creative device. This means that language has the power to create meaning. Cohn claimed that the language used to discuss nuclear war was extraordinary, with elaborate use of euphemisms and abstractions. Clean bombs, surgical strikes, collateral damage, all phrases which gloss over the realities of death and destruction and all phrases which many of us in the West will be more familiar with since the Gulf War. She also discusses the 'fun' and 'sexy' way in which technostrategic language was used. Snappy, jargon-filled talk was common, with frequent reference to 'slick'ems' (SLCMs – submarine-launched cruise missiles), 'glick'ems' (GLCMs – ground-launched cruise missiles) and SRAMS (short-range attack missiles). As Cohn claims, 'the words are fun to say; they are racy, sexy, snappy. You can throw them around in rapid-fire succession. They are quick, clean, light; they trip off the tongue. You can reel off dozens of them in seconds' (1987, p. 704).

The language used by these defence intellectuals arguably plays a central role in constructing part of strategic identity. As strategists, they have the grave responsibility of constructing US nuclear defence policy. The implications of the construction of strategic identity which inhibits discussion of such things as death, pain and destruction is surely profound. 'Clean bombs' and 'collateral damage' leave little room to imagine a seven-year-old boy with his flesh melting away from his bones or a toddler with her skin hanging down in strips (Cohn, 1993, p. 232).

In a more recent essay Carol Cohn recalls a story told to her by a white, male physicist:

> Several colleagues and I were working on modeling counterforce attacks, trying to get realistic estimates of the number of immediate fatalities that would result from different deployments. At one point, we remodeled a particular attack, using slightly different assumptions, and found that instead of there being thirty-six million immediate fatalities, there would only be thirty million. And everybody was sitting around nodding, saying, 'Oh yeah, that's great, only thirty million', when all of a sudden, I *heard* what we were saying. And I blurted out, 'Wait, I've just heard how we're talking – *Only* thirty million! *Only* thirty million human beings killed instantly?' Silence fell upon the room. Nobody said a word. They didn't even look at me. It was awful. I felt like a woman. (1993, p. 227)

Cohn goes on to say that the physicist declared that he was careful never to blurt out anything like that again. She argues that the discourse in which strategic language is positioned is fundamentally *gendered*. All that is associated with femininity, in this case emotions, blurting out, becomes devalued. As such, ways of behaving, speaking and thinking associated with femininity (and the substantive content changes) are rarely included. To include them results in, in the words of the white, male physicist, feeling like a woman; awful. In this sense, gender and specifically that which is identified as belonging to femininity acts as a pre-emptive deterrent to certain modes of thought, action and speech. If the constructions of strategic identity has the power to inhibit what can be said and thought in this way it is indeed a powerful tool with potentially very damaging consequences.

Similar claims can be made about the constructions of military identity. A number of scholars (e.g. Holden and Ardener, 1987; Isaakson, 1989; Cock, 1992) claim that the construction of gender identity plays a large part in scores of different societies' military thinking and ideology. The values of traditional Western masculinity are systematically invoked in basic training in the military. Recruits learn that to be a man is to be a soldier not a woman (Hartsock, 1989, p. 134). The virility and manhood of and in war are constantly invoked by those involved, and in particular a specific configuration of manhood which is not weak or wimpish but strong and powerful. There is little space for anything associated with femaleness or femininity. Commander of US Marines until 1983, General Robert H. Barrow, had this to say:

> War is a man's work. Biological convergence on the battlefield [by which he means women serving in combat] would not only be dissatisfying in terms of what women could do, but it would be an enormous psychological distraction for the male, who wants to think that he's fighting for that woman somewhere behind, not up there in the same foxhole with him. It tramples the male ego. When you get right down to it, you have to protect the manhood of war. (quoted in Hartsock, 1989, p. 134)

The consequences of this particular construction of masculine identity are even more evident when it comes to war. John McNaughton, Assistant US Secretary of Defense in 1965, summed up United States aims in the Vietnam War as 10 per cent to permit the people of Vietnam a better way of life, 20 per cent to keep the territory away from the Chinese and 70 per cent to avoid a humiliating defeat (Hartsock, 1989, p. 147). The image of United States failure and emasculation in Vietnam is constantly invoked when similar circumstances occur (Jeffords, 1989; Weber, forthcoming). The American way of life is not meant to include being 'humiliated by a bunch of skinny little Orientals in black pyjamas' (Hutchinson, 1990, p. 58).

It is not only this particular construction of masculinity which plays a role in identity formation and war. Abouali Farmanfarmaian argues that the construction of sexual and racial identities were a determining factor in the Gulf War. Farmanfarmaian takes us back to the time just before the Gulf War, claiming that when George Bush and the United Nations issued the 15 January deadline, many in the United States were not at all convinced that a war would take place. People inside and outside Congress expressed a measured level of disapproval (1992, p. 113). However, by the end of December 1990 the United States showed overwhelming support for war. Farmanfarmaian argues that the appeal to the people in the United States to accept the choice of war was made primarily on the level of morality rather than reason. He goes on: 'by positioning the United States as the righteous protector of the world and Iraq as an evil destructive force, George Bush managed to rally and unite public opinion in favour of a military strike' (p. 113).

Farmanfarmaian claims that the campaign to identify Iraq as intrinsically immoral began to centre on Iraqi atrocities and in particular sexual atrocities. A month before the deadline there were increasing media reports of the continuation of the 'violation of Kuwait's sovereignty' which became increasingly tied to sexual atrocities committed by the Iraqis. Infanticide, rape and torture had become the main focuses of attention. A report on the story that Iraqi soldiers took babies out of incubators in a Kuwait hospital and watched them die was waved in outrage by George Bush on national television to point to the intrinsic, sadistic evil residing in Iraqi soldiers (p. 114). The story ultimately turned out to be untrue.

The 'rape' of Kuwait became an increasingly used concept. The *New York Times* ran a report on its front page with the lead 'more than four months after Iraq's invasion, Kuwaitis are being subjected to looting, rape, torture'. The newspaper also quoted an 'unidentified senior US official' who identified Middle Eastern culture as 'the culture of rape'. Farmanfarmaian's claim is not that rapes and torture did not occur but he seeks instead to show 'how easily and naturally certain constructs get lined up and emphasised over the national consciousness' (p. 114). He argues that the panic about mass rapes, torture and infanticide committed by the Iraqis moved the issue of war outside the realm of real casual threats and appealed to notions and anxieties that are an intricate and integral part of American consciousness. 'The image of an Other and the boundaries set against that Other in favour of the Self. The war took place against that image, against the representation of Iraq, not Iraq itself' (p. 115; see also Parker et al., 1992).

The ascription of Iraqi identity in this case is intricately tied up to concepts of racial otherness. As Farmanfarmaian points out, clearly rapes were committed, largely on migrant female workers in Kuwait. But to imagine that rape 'is not one of the facets of military life everywhere in the world is an illusion. The difference lies in people's perceptions and their willingness to react' (p. 115). He claims that whereas rapes committed by Iraqi soldiers elicit a massive retaliation, rapes committed by United States soldiers are dismissed. He argues that the 'international division of attributes' implies that the label of rape sticks to the racial other (p. 116). This also applies within the United States army itself. Black GI's based in British bases in the Second World War were far more likely than white GI's to be convicted of sexual offences (Enloe, 1989, p. 70).

Our discussion of the construction and ascription of identity and the implications for international events is not meant to be understood as simply symbolic or metaphorical but as real and concrete. But, as Farmanfarmaian points out, any such project linking the construction of sexual identities, or masculine identities, or racial identities, to concrete international events suffers from lack of information (1992, p. 133). Sexuality, masculinity, concepts of racial otherness are hidden not just in an empirical sense but in an epistemological sense. It is usually very difficult for students and scholars of international relations to understand that there may be concrete and important links between such things and the enactment of 'real-life' international events such as war. This has important implications for international relations theorizing, a point which we will discuss in the final section.

IMPLICATIONS FOR INTERNATIONAL RELATIONS THEORY

This section will attempt to link the earlier discussion of identity to current debates within international relations theorizing, specifically the inter-paradigm debate (Banks, 1985; Whitworth, 1989) and the post-positivist debate (International Studies Quarterly, 1989).

The phrase 'inter-paradigm debate' was coined by Michael Banks (1985), who claimed that the study of international relations had become focused on three main paradigms: realism, pluralism and structuralism (alternatively known as globalism). This is now a widespread approach in the study and teaching of international relations (Holsti, 1985; Little and Smith, 1991; Viotti and Kauppi, 1993). What we want to do now is to think about the questions that discussions of identity pose for these three paradigms.

Since the 1940s realism has been the dominant paradigm in the discipline of international relations. (We use the term realism somewhat reluctantly especially as realism has been, in practice, rather naive and *un*realistic, particularly on the issue of power. See Enloe, 1989.) Within this paradigm the key actors in the international system are deemed to be states, which are seen largely as unitary and rational actors. States are thus assumed to make planned, considered decisions and policy, the main concern being national military security. Realist scholars focus on the relationships between states and particularly on the potential or actual conflict between states. Such conflict is deemed to be an intrinsic part of state behaviour, particularly as states exist in an anarchical international system. The type of questions that are important to realists revolve around stability, sovereignty, force and power. Such questions include: how to maintain stability; how and why it breaks down; how to retain sovereignty; when and how to use force to maintain stability and sovereignty. Power is a central feature of realist analysis. It is seen largely as one of the guiding principles of the international system of states, founded on a largely Hobbesian view of the world and human nature. Power is also deemed to be an important commodity as, in such a Hobbesian world, power is necessary to prevent others taking from you. What space is there within the realist paradigm to theorize or think about identity?

Given the realist's commitment to states and inter-state conflict one would rightly assume that there is no space at all to think about identity. Realists would not consider specific groups such as women or ethnic groups or children as relevant to the understanding of the workings of the international system. Realists would urge contemporary international relations theorists to 'return to the fundamental purpose of the discipline: the investigation into the causes of war, and the condition for peace, order and security' (Kal Holsti quoted in Whitworth, 1989, p. 267). The call to move away from an assumed further fragmentation of the subject of international relations was reinforced by Kenneth Waltz (1993), when he claimed that 'international relations cannot be a theory of everything. It's a theory about some things regarded as important in the world.' For Waltz the only important actors are states, which he claims are the dominant unit of international politics (1986, p. 338).

This seems a very plausible counter to those critics of realism who claim that the paradigm ignores the lives of women or ethnic groups or children or any number of similarly marginalized identities in the international arena. The experiences of such groups are not dismissed as *unimportant* by realists; rather, as ultimately *irrelevant* to the workings of the international system. In part they are irrelevant to realists because they wield so little political influence. That this is true seems to become particularly clear when issues of 'high politics' come to the fore, the classic example being that of war. Realists do not deny that women suffer in wartime and that they suffer in particular ways. Off the record (not in print, not at the podium) a realist may acknowledge the common use of rape as a weapon of war. But the realist will not go further. He or she will not accept that the construction and articulation of gender identity, or sexual identity or racial identity, might play an important part in the causation, enactment and continuation of war. The actors who matter to the realist, the people the realist thinks it is worth watching and listening to, are only that handful of people – usually male, usually members of the dominant ethnic group – with enough power to steer a state. *They* are the causal factors. Everyone else is a mere consequence, or coincidence.

Sandra Whitworth argues that, although realism's ontological commitments to states and statesmen probably precludes the possibility of analysing gender, there still may be epistemological spaces within realism which, in principle, allow theorizing about gender (1989, pp. 267–8). She is specifically thinking of more classical realism, which allows for the possibility that such things as the national interest, power and the states system are not just pre-given in the sense that they are not 'natural' categories but, rather, are historically contingent. Thus, there is some space to allow for thinking about the construction of the meanings of such things. This might allow us to imagine, for example, that realist thought has the space to theorize about the construction of military identity and the enactment of war.

Does this mean that we can integrate or even ask our questions about identity within a realist framework? Following Sandra Whitworth we would agree that the realist commitment to structural forces and states as the key units in the system makes it difficult to think how realism could seriously deal with the questions and issues of identity that we have raised. As to the possibility of epistemological space for theorizing about identity, we would argue that the positivist underpinnings of realism foreclose any space that might feasibly be there. We will return to this point in our discussion of the post-positivist debate.

What about the possibilities for theorizing about identity within the pluralist paradigm? Pluralism differs from realism in that non-state actors, such as multinational corporations, and bodies such as the United Nations and the European Community, are regarded as relevant to the study of international politics. The state itself is not seen as a unitary actor but as something which has competing demands and interests both within the state itself and from non-state actors. The hierarchy of world issues is also subject to change and not dominated by matters of military security. Key concepts within the pluralist paradigm are interdependence and transnationalism. A classic example of the pluralist approach is the world society or 'cobweb' model of the world put forward by John Burton (1972).

Within the pluralist paradigm international relations theorists are able to widen the agenda of what is considered relevant. Does this mean we can adequately think about identity within this paradigm? Essentially the widening of the agenda is largely at an empirical level and, as Whitworth suggests, this might imply that the study of women and international relations is allowed for within the pluralist paradigm (1989, p. 269). Similarly, we might include other identifiable groups such as ethnic or religious groups. This clearly represents an advance for those scholars who regard the realist depiction of international relations as too narrow. But again the positivistic underpinnings of pluralism make it doubtful that there would be any space for theorizing about the construction of gender identity or sexual identity or racial identity and the enactment of international events and processes.

Within the structuralist/globalist paradigm, the main actors in the international system include a mixture of states, societies and non-state actors which are seen to operate largely within the parameters of a capitalist world system. In this sense all actors are viewed within an overarching capitalist global structure. International relations are viewed from a historical perspective, especially the continuous development of world capitalism. The focus is on patterns of dominance within and among societies, with economic factors assuming prime importance.

As with the pluralist perspective, structuralism/globalism allows for a widening of the empirical agenda which might permit the consideration of some identities not included on the realist agenda. But essentially all three paradigms are ontologically, and ideologically, committed in relatively stringent ways, which restricts the view of what can be considered as relevant to the study of international relations. Clearly, the three perspectives are not mutually exclusive. As Viotti and Kauppi (1993, p. 11) note, realists such as Robert Gilpin do not deny the importance of economic factors in international relations; he would merely differ with pluralists and structuralists/globalists as to the relative importance of political-military factors compared to economic factors.

Essentially, realists are far too committed to states and military-political affairs; pluralists are far too committed to the empirical nature of transnational processes; structuralists/globalists are far too committed to economics and classes to allow much room for the consideration of questions of identity in international relations as we have raised them. All three paradigms are too restricted ontologically, methodologically and epistemologically, and in ways which ultimately render them unable to theorize or think adequately about identity. This suppression of the investigation of issues like identity undermines their claims to have an accurate picture of 'what does the work' in world politics. Earlier in this chapter we stated that methodological and theoretical developments within the subject since the 1980s have brought new questions on to the agenda. It is to those developments that we now turn in a concluding discussion of identity and international relations theory.

POST-POSITIVISM

Alternatively called the third debate, the post-positivist debate involves several streams of thought and a number of different groups of scholars, most notably some feminist theorists, critical theorists, postmodernists and post-structuralists. Each group has a different agenda but they all agree that it is necessary to challenge the positivist underpinnings of most of international relations theory, including realism, pluralism and structuralism/globalism. Post-positivists claim that mainstream international relations theorists are locked into a problematic way of understanding theory and reality which inhibits their ability or even desire to widen or change their existing agendas for international relations theory. In short, paradigms such as realism, pluralism and structuralism/globalism are ontologically and ideologically committed to seeing a particular picture of the international, as a result of which they are also theoretically and epistemologically constrained. In fact it is their theoretical and epistemological limitations which fundamentally structure what they see and think of as important in international relations. Briefly put, the simple structures they describe in international relations are no more than reflections of the simple theoretical structures in their heads. Questions about identity are not therefore only of practical consequence, but they have implications which go to the heart of the study of international relations.

This is all quite complex but it is important to have some understanding of these issues in terms of our questions about identity. In particular, it is important to begin to understand the problems inherent in saying that international relations cannot be a theory about everything and assuming that this then lets one off the hook in terms of thinking about the lives and experiences of marginalized identities or the ascription of identities in the world, leaving the state as the central referent. The problem with the older paradigms is that they rely on an understanding of the world which involves seeing the world as being divided into distinct bits of reality, already there, which are in need of illumination. Theory is then something used by international relations theorists either to explain or to understand these pieces of reality, with the added possibility of predicting future international events. It is not insignificant that the failure of the academic community of international relations theorists to predict the demise of communism or indeed the mutual recognition by Israel and the Palestine Liberation Organization has been the source of some embarrassment.

The positivist conception of the world and reality typifies much of mainstream international relations theory in the 1990s despite the emergence of the 'third debate' or the so-called post-positivist revolution. This understanding of the world allows the possibility of thinking that defining specific referents or identities as the central issues in international relations theory is not a particularly political or epistemologically significant act; it is merely one of choice. In other words, the choice of referent is seen as a neutral activity by positivists. Waltz can choose to study states, wars and the activity of leaders, others can look at the situation of women or whatever group they wish. Each then collects data and facts about the chosen group and ultimately develops theories about them. Jim George calls this the 'spectator theory of knowledge, in which knowledge of the real world is gleaned via a realm of external facts' (1993, p. 204). Mark Neufeld similarly talks about 'truth as correspondence' (1993, p. 55). This involves believing that there is a distinct separation between 'theory' and the 'real' world, 'the former, the realm of "internally" generated "invention" – the latter, the "external" repository of laws which theories (retrospectively) explain, order and systematise . . . theory . . . always remains distinct from that world' (George, 1993, p. 209). The key point to be taken from this is that theory is represented as a 'cognitive reaction to reality rather than integral to its construction. Theory, in this context, takes place after the fact' (p. 213).

But theory does *not* take place after the fact. Theories, instead, play a large part in constructing and defining what the facts are. This is a central claim made by those scholars working on post-positivist perspectives in international relations theory but it is not a new claim. Albert Einstein once pointed out that 'on principle it is quite wrong to try founding a theory on observable magnitudes alone. In reality, the very opposite happens' (quoted in MacKinnon, 1989, p. 106). However, it is a claim resisted strongly by mainstream international relations theory, which remains, despite recent claims to the contrary, entrenched in a realist-positivist paradigm (Runyan and Peterson, 1991; Peterson, 1992b; George, 1993). When vilified for serving the interests of the powerful and preserving the status quo, classical and neo-realists simply reply that they are 'telling things the way they are' (Runyan and Peterson, 1991, p. 70).

'The way things are' for the realist/positivist core implies an image of the world in which some things become regarded as *central* and *important*, in relation to international events, whereas others are seen as *specific* and *local* and as such essentially *irrelevant* to the practice of international relations theory and the workings of the international system. Central and important includes states, leaders, wars; local and ultimately irrelevant includes conceptions and constructions of masculinity, femininity, sexuality, religiousness, ethnicity and racial otherness. To be sure, religion or ethnicity might be accepted as exacerbating conflictual situations, or used to whip up support. But for the vast majority of neo-realists, who still dominate within international relations theory, systemic theories emphasizing the balance of power between states do not seriously consider such 'variables' as being relevant to the workings of the international system and international events.

However much we might want to simplify the international system, whether in the form of states, nations, societies or regions, the politics of identity plays a crucial but complex part. The construction, ascription, internalization, refusal or reclaiming of identities continually works behind, below and on the stage of world politics. The very boundaries created to separate one part of this international system from another functions to form an identifiable self ('us') within the boundary and an identifiable other ('them') outside the boundary. Indeed, the very concept of a nation is not thinkable without the notion of 'others' or 'foreigners'. Migrants pre-date the formation of the nation-state. It is the formation of those boundaries that constructs those migrants as 'foreigners'.

It is worthwhile spending some time thinking about boundaries, especially the insight that boundaries often become visible, at least clearly, only when they are overstepped. This does not have to be only in a physical sense, although the crossing of 'enemy lines' is a dangerous thing to do. Several British men have learnt this to their cost when crossing over the border from Kuwait to Iraq in recent years. The Protestant man killed in a Catholic bar by other Protestants in October 1993 in Northern Ireland paid a high price for crossing another boundary line. Presumably he did not want to accept that line but was ultimately forced to pay dearly for that refusal. Boundaries often change even though people do not physically move but suddenly they find themselves behind 'enemy lines', suddenly identitifed as 'other', a 'foreigner': for example, Serbs in Croatia, Bosnian Muslims in Serbia, non-Europeans in a newly defined Western Europe which is starting to define its citizens on ethnic and racial gounds (Kofman and Sales, 1992; MacDonald, 1993; Anthias and Yuval-Davis, 1993). It is as if with the aid of smoke and mirrors, as in an illusion or magic trick, new boundaries appear, new or newly defined identities emerge, whether those identified want them or not, and people, quite frequently, suffer or even die as a result.

SO WHO ARE WE AND WHAT ARE WE?

It may be becoming somewhat of post-positivist cliché to claim that we are living in a complex world and thus simplistic theories will be of little explanatory or descriptive use. But if we are trying to understand more about the world and in particular those events which cause pain and destruction, why would anyone not want to include insights which might help us do that? If realist scholars want genuinely to investigate the causes of war in a sophisticated and systematic manner, why not investigate the construction and internalization of certain images of masculinity in military ideology? If they want to argue that students be better equipped, intellectually and conceptually, to understand international politics, why not extend their analyses to include concepts of identity?

There may, of course, be ideological resistance to thinking about these issues. The assumption is made that sexual identity or gender identity can have nothing to do with the causation and enactment of war. But although these are just assumptions they do a great deal of work in defining what is and is not relevant to consider. When this ideological commitment is linked with a limited epistemological understanding of the construction of reality, it becomes easy for scholars within international relations to think that such things as the politics of identity can have no real importance to our understanding of the international system. Additionally, it implies a lot more work in the sense that more books have to be read (ones that many realist scholars might think irrelevant), new methodological tools have to be learned and old positions have to be rethought.

Kal Holsti (1993) is one who laments the increasing theoretical expansion of the discipline of international relations. This expansion, he argues, is not necessarily evidence of progress. Unless we can agree on, at least, the purposes of the theoretical enterprise and on what some of the fundamental problems in the real world are, the 'menu [of international relations theory] threatens to become tasteless for all but the few that inhabit the rarefied sanctuaries of the Universities' (p. 408). Why should this be the case? If, as Holsti suggests, our 'consumers' are students and policy-makers and what they want most of all is to know 'what is going on in the real world' (p. 407), it seems to make eminent sense to find out more about how that 'real world' works by asking more, deeper and searching questions. What apparently seems to be 'staring us in the face' (p. 407) in the world may well be an example of what psychologists call a perceptual illusion. In these illusions what stares one person in the face cannot be seen at all by another person. The same can be true when we move from a psychologist's drawing to the 'reality' of politics on a global scale. The simple questions 'Who am I?' and 'Who defines who I am?' might be as revolutionary for the discipline of international relations as that of the little boy who questioned not the magnificence of the Emperor's clothes, but whether he had any at all!

In a global age, one characterized by a global menu, global music and global time, the resurgence of claims to identity might be seen as a response to a fear of disappearing into bland sameness. We can drink Coke, eat sushi and watch *Neighbours* and be in practically any country in the world. The fight for identity may, at one level, be an example of resistance to such an image of global uni-identity. Alternatively, the struggle for identity may be a reaffirmation of belonging, in a postmodern, post-local age. This desire may be fuelled by nostalgia, a nostalgia for 'tradition', which might be construed as a nostalgia for the nation-state, the icon of modernity. Identities in this view may be increasingly fluid and multiply at ever more rapid rates as we approach the twenty-first century. But those properties do not make them analytically irrelevant to the international relations analyst. Who we are, how we are, who defines us, how international processes and events are moulded and manipulated by identities: these are all questions relevant to international politics. Anyone trying to make sense of international political trends in the near future who treats these maddeningly complex and infuriatingly dynamic identities as a mere mosquito to be swatted away risks being surprised.

Note

Marysia Zalewski would like to thank Richard Wyn Jones and Ralf Goldak for their insights about identity and Ken Booth and Steve Smith for their editing skills.

References

Adams, M. L. 1989: There's no place like home: on the place of identity in feminist politics. *Feminist Review* 31, 22–33.

Anthias, F. and Yuval-Davis, N., with Cain, H. (eds) 1993: *Racialized Boundaries, Race, Nation, Gender, Colour and the Anti-Racist Struggle*. London: Routledge.

Banks, M. 1985: The inter-paradigm debate. In M. Light and A. J. R. Groom (eds), *International Relations: A Handbook of Current Theory*, London: Frances Pinter, 7–26.

Bhavani, K. K. 1993: Towards a multicultural Europe? 'Race' nation and identity in 1992 and beyond. *Feminist Review*, 45, 30–46.

Brah, A. 1993: Re-framing Europe: en-gendered racisms, ethnicities and nationalisms in contemporary Western Europe. *Feminist Review*, 45, 9–29.

Burton, J. 1972: *World Society*. Cambridge: Cambridge University Press.

Cock, J. 1992: *Women and War in South Africa*. London: Open Letters Press.

Cohn, C. 1993: Wars, wimps, and women: talking gender and thinking war. In M. Cooke and A. Wollacott (eds), *Gendering War Talk*, Princeton, N.J.: Princeton University Press, 227–46.

Cohn, C. 1987: Sex and death in the rational world of defense intellectuals. *Signs*, 12(4), 687–718.

Curthoys, A. 1993: Feminism, citizenship and national identity. *Feminist Review*, 44, 19–38.

Defeis, E. F. 1991: An international human right: gender equality. *Journal of Women's History*, 3(1), 90–107.

Duchen, C. (ed.) 1993: A continent in transition: issues for women in Europe in the 1990s. *Women's Studies International Forum*, 15(1) (special issue).

Enloe, C. 1989: *Bananas, Beaches and Bases: Making Feminist Sense of International Politics*. London: Pandora.

Farmanfarmaian, A. 1992: Did you measure up? The role of race and sexuality in the Gulf War. In C. Peters (ed.), *Collateral Damage*, Boston: South End Press, 111–38.

George, J. 1993: Of incarceration and closure: neo-realism and the new/old world orders. *Millennium: Journal of International Studies*, 22(2), 197–234.

Griffin Cohen, M. 1987: *Free Trade and the Future of Women's Work*. Toronto: Garamond Press.

Hall, C. 1993: Gender, nationalism and national identities: Bellagio Symposium report. *Feminist Review*, 44, 97–103.

Hall, R. 1956: *The Well of Loneliness*. London: Barrie and Jenkins.

Harding, S. (ed.) 1993: *The 'Racial' Economy of Science*. Bloomington: Indiana University Press.

Hartsock, N. 1989: Masculinity, heroism and the making of war. In A. Harris and Y. King (eds), *Rocking the Ship of State*, Boulder, Colorado: Westview Press, 133–52.

Holden, P. and Ardener, A. (eds) 1987: *Images of Women in Peace and War*. London: Macmillan.

Holsti, K. J. 1965: *The Dividing Discipline. Hegemony and Diversity in International Theory*. Boston Mass.: Allen & Unwin.

Holsti, K. J. 1993: International relations at the end of the millennium. *Review of International Studies*, 19(4), 401–8.

Hutchinson, M. 1990: *The Anatomy of Sex and Power*. New York: William Morrow and Co.

International Studies Quarterly 1989: 33(3), September (special issue).

Isaakson, E. (ed.) 1989: *Women and the Military System*. Brighton: Wheatsheaf.

Jeffords, S. 1989: *The Remasculinization of America: Gender and the Vietnam War*. Bloomington: Indiana University Press.

Kaldor, M. and Anderson, P. (eds) 1987: *Mad Dogs: The US Raids on Libya*. London: Pluto Press.

Kerr. J. (ed.) 1993: *Ours by Right: Women's Rights as Human Rights*. London: Zed.

Kofman, E. and Sales, R. 1992: Towards fortress Europe? *Women's Studies International Forum*, 15(1), 29–39.

Liddington, J. 1989: *The Long Road to Greenham*. London: Virago.

Little, R. and Smith, M. (eds) 1991: *Perspectives on World Politics*, 2nd edn. London: Routledge.

MacDonald, S. (ed.) 1993: *Inside European Identities*. Oxford: Berg Publishers.

MacKinnon, C. 1989: *Towards a Feminist Theory of the State*. Cambridge, Mass.: Harvard University Press.

Milić, A. 1993: Women and nationalism in the former Yugoslavia. In N. Funk and M. Mueller (eds), *Gender Politics and Post-Communism*, London: Routledge, 109–22.

Moghadam, V. 1993: *Identity Politics: Cultural Reassertion and Feminisms in International Perspectives*. Boulder, Colorado: Westview Press.

Mohanty, C. T. 1988: Under Western eyes: feminist scholarship and colonial discourses. *Feminist Review*, 30, 60–88.

Neufeld, M. 1993: Reflexivity and international relations theory. *Millennium: Journal of International Studies*, 22(1), 53–76.

Parker, A., Russo, M., Sommer, D. and Yaeger, P. (eds) 1992: *Nationalisms and Sexualities*. New York and London: Routledge.

Peterson, V. S. (ed.) 1992a: *Gendered States: Feminist (Re)Visions of International Relations Theory*. Boulder, Colorado: Lynne Rienner.

Peterson, V. S. 1992b: Transgressing boundaries: theories of knowledge, gender and international relations. *Millennium: Journal of International Studies*, 21(2), 183–206.

Peterson, V. S. 1993: The politics of identity in international relations. *The Fletcher Forum of World Affairs*, 17(2), 1–12.

Peterson, V. S. and Runyan, A. S. 1993: *Global Gender Issues*. Boulder, Colorado: Westview Press.

Pettman, J. 1992: *Living in the Margins: Racism, Sexism and Feminism in Australia*. Sydney: Allen & Unwin.

Runyan, A. S. and Peterson, V. S., 1991: The radical future of realism: feminist subversions of IR theory. *Alternatives*, 16(1), 67–106.

Sahgal, G. and Yuval-Davis, N. (eds) 1992: *Refusing Holy Orders: Women and Fundamentalism in Britain*. London: Virago.

Stiglmayer, A. (ed.) 1994: *Mass Rape: The War Against Women in Bosnia Herzegovina*. Lincoln, Nebraska: University of Nebraska Press.

Tatchell, P. 1992: *Europe in the Pink: Lesbian and Gay Equality in the New Europe*. London: GMP Publishers.

Tetreault, M. A. 1992: Democratization and women in Kuwait. Paper presented at the annual meeting of the International Studies Association – Midwest, Michigan State University, East Lansing, MI, 20–21 November.

Tickner, J. A. 1992: *Gender in International Relations: Feminist Perspectives on Achieving Global Security*. New York: Columbia University Press.

Tomasevski, K. 1993: *Women and Human Rights*. London: Zed.

Viotti, P. and Kauppi, M. 1993: *International Relations Theory: Realism, Pluralism, Globalism*, 2nd edn. New York: Macmillan.

Waltz, K. 1986: Reflections on *Theory of International Politics*: a response to my critics. In R. O. Keohane (ed.), *NeoRealism and Its Critics*, New York: Columbia University Press, 322–45.

Waltz, K. 1993: The new world order. Lecture given at University of Wales, Aberystwyth.

Wæver, O., Buzan, B., Kelstrup, M. and Lemaitre, P. 1993: *Identity, Migration and the New Security Agenda in Europe*. London: Frances Pinter.

Weber, C. forthcoming: Something's missing: male hysteria and the US invasion of Panama. *Genders*.

Whitworth, S. 1989: Gender in the inter-paradigm debate. *Millennium: Journal of International Studies*, 18(2), 265–72.

Yuval-Davis, N. and Anthias, F. (eds) 1989: *Women-Nation-State*. London: Macmillan.

14

International Relations and the Concept of the Political

R. B. J. Walker

A POLITICS OF SPACE

Theories of international relations express a historically specific account of what political life is all about. They do so by affirming a familiar understanding of where it can occur. Politics, they insist, is something that is proper to the life of people living within the borders of modern territorial states. More accurately, theories of international relations affirm a claim that only within the secure borders of territorial states is it possible to engage in a serious politics, a politics that aspires to some kind of moral status on the basis of some kind of community. This is the politics deemed suitable for the refined aspirations of a proper political theory. Outside these borders, relations between states are supposedly more primordial, struggles for power and survival that waver between anarchy and utilitarian co-operation but are always fated to betray the standards of civilized conduct at home.

Despite the insistence of many analysts who link capitalist modernity with a self-conscious historicity, modern politics is a spatial politics. Its crucial condition of possibility is the distinction between an inside and an outside, between the citizens, nations and communities within and the enemies, others and absences without (Wight, 1966; Linklater, 1982). Modern accounts of the political occur as twin, though mutually contemptuous, discourses: as a properly political theory, or a sociology, of life within, and a more wretched theory of relations between territorial states. Political theorists are supposed to pursue their ambitions for justice, freedom and law absorbed by the potentials of life within particular communities. Even at their most pluralistic, or their most radical, they usually assume the unitary identity of the singular state, or at least of the integral law governing the broad structure of, say, capitalism, or some world system, of which states are assumed to be just subordinate parts. It is left to the theorists of international relations, and to some extent the anthropologists and critics of 'development theory', to express the bad conscience of a civilization that prefers to forget that the great ideals of the political and social theorists, and not least their hopes for history, development and other temporal destinations, have been articulated in relation to particular communities among other communities. The characteristic universalisms of so much modern political and social theory, they remind us, demand a concerted amnesia towards the geopolitical fragmentations within which specifically modern accounts of universality have been articulated.

Theories of international relations can thus be read as a primary expression of the limits of modern politics (Walker, 1993a). They, especially, frame these limits spatially. Politics, real politics, they suggest, can occur only as long as we are prepared – or able – to live in boxes. Not everyone is persuaded that such an understanding of the political is either convincing under contemporary conditions or desirable as a guide to ways in which we might now live. But limits are limits. To try to conceive forms of politics other than those framed as a spatial distinction of here and there, self and other, is to recognize that even the imagination of an alternative politics is constrained by accounts of escape that keep us firmly where and what we are (Walker, 1990).

These brief observations inform three assumptions I want to rely on in order to address the relationship between some recent critical understandings of the limits of theories of international relations as a discourse about limits in space, and various claims about the changing spatio-temporal character of contemporary politics.

One involves a simple reminder of the historicity, of the historically constructed and continually reconstructed character, of human existence. Though many theorists of international relations have been prone to rash claims about the connection between the modern spatial account of what political life can be and the eternal necessities of the human condition, the historical specificity, indeed the rarity of the understanding of the political that is affirmed by theories of international relations and its constitutive divorce from the political theory of particular communities is fairly obvious. In the grand schemes of macro-historians, systems of states must jostle for attention among tribes and empires as only one of the organizing principles of human conduct. It is of course true that one particular states system, the one constructed in early modern Europe, has dominated both our recent experiences and our collective memories, although it has not erased other experiences or other memories quite as much as modern political theorists or theorists of international relations often assume. Nor have the ahistorical structuralisms that have been so influential in recent theories of international relations entirely erased a concern with the historicity of the modern states system (Wight, 1977; Mann, 1986; Vincent, 1987; Hall and Ikenberry, 1989). It is also true that the spatial understanding of political possibility that developed in early modern Europe drew in turn upon the fateful and even paradigmatic achievements of the Greeks and their *polis*, and especially on their account of the good life possible within the bounded community. There are undoubtedly good reasons both in our experiences and in our selective memories to be impressed by the resilience of the spatial politics of both *polis* and state, but it requires a fair degree of historical myopia to give much credit to the claim that these experiences and memories tell us what and where the political *must* be, or even what and where it now is.

The second assumption involves an equally simple but in some quarters more provocative claim about the normative character of all theories of international relations. As connoisseurs of the limits of modern politics, theorists of international relations have become specialists in cynicism and violence. They deflate the pretensions of the political theorists if not with wit and charm then with tragic lamentations about the way things are. But their claims about the way things are invariably depend on a prior – normative – understanding of what and where political life is supposed to be. For all their cynicism, theorists of international relations cling tightly to the normative ambitions of political theory, although these ambitions are usually expressed as a deferred moralism, as a hope for a properly moral community to be constructed at some future time, though only in a future that can never come closer. Theories of international relations have been constructed largely as a negation of assumptions about political life within the authentic statist community, as a discourse of absence made possible by a prior discourse of presence. As a negation, they are also an affirmation of specific normative ideals that remain visible behind even the most cynical apologies of power politics and the most positivist claims to objective knowledge.

The third assumption involves the highly problematic status of change and temporality in so many theories of international relations. As spatial framings of political life, theories of international relations experience tremendous difficulty accounting for temporal transformation of any kind (Gaddis, 1992/3; Kratochwil, 1993; Walker, 1993a). They are especially troubled, I will suggest in this chapter, by claims about beginnings and endings. Claims about novel political practices, about new world orders, interdependencies, integrations, globalizations, and so on, quickly run up against the counterclaim that international relations is simply a realm of structural continuity and repetition. To the extent that claims about novelty are considered plausible, the concepts used to grasp their contours express a spatial imagery of extension in space far more readily than of possibilities in time. Thus as discourses of limits in space, theories of international relations can also be read as discourses of limits in time. Challenges to these limits, and to the spatial framing of inclusions and exclusions that have made them possible, constitute the crucial condition under which we might be able to renegotiate our understanding of the political under contemporary conditions, not least because they render quite untenable so many familiar accounts of who this 'we' is/are.

BEGINNINGS AND ENDINGS

Contemporary commentary on political life has become obsessed with endings. Eras have supposedly stopped. Cold War has finally expired in a collapse of walls and empires. Capitalism has leapt to yet another developmental stage. Modernity and colonialism have spawned their own ambivalent obituaries and their characteristic crises of posthumous identity. Even history, some excitable Hegelian souls have come to think, has finally run its course. Or, at least, this multidimensional obsession with endings has been an event that once gripped the imagination in a few crucial sites of political discourse in what now seems rather a long time – even years – ago (Fukuyama, 1992; Anderson, 1992; Held, 1993a).

This discourse of endings has often been enthusiastic, even triumphant, but also often negative: nostalgic, apocalyptic or simply baffled. At least the Cold War, with its rank orderings of saved and damned, centre and periphery, and First, Second and Third Worlds, offered some semblance of order, even if an order of considerable violence and injustice. At least it provided some sense of what it means to engage with a politics as usual, whether as the everyday policy of established authorities or as attempts to capture and redeploy authority. At least it was relatively easy to think one knew what was involved in struggles for 'emancipation' or 'liberation' or 'revolution'. But in an era of endings, even the certainties of 'progressive' politics have become artefacts of nostalgia, measures of what it once meant to be serious about aspirations for other ways of being human.

Eras of apparent endings also attract readings of new beginnings. For a short while at least, new optimisms for initiatives long stifled by a geopolitics of nuclear fixation flourished amid a sense of millennial transformations. These readings, of a new world order or of cosmopolitan democratizations, retained their resonance for only a few moments before being sapped by the spectre of killing fields and the shrug of political cynicism. Even so, the rapid switch from euphoria to pessimism has not erased the pervasive sense that we are not simply witnesses to business as usual. Claims about *some* kind of new world (dis)order or *some* kind of (highly selective) cosmopolitan democratization are not entirely far-fetched (Held, 1993b). The difficulty posed by claims to new beginnings is not the absence of evidence that things are not what they used to be. On the contrary, only those befuddled by metaphysical claims about the permanent tragedies of the human condition – claims that have found a special ideological niche in modern theories of international relations under the dubious name of political realism – could ignore the sense of pervasive historical and structural transformation that has been charted by legions of social and political analysts over many generations. Rather, the difficulty arises from the extent to which accounts of such transformations, of new beginnings and new possibilities, have come to be framed within historically specific accounts of what it means to begin, or to end, or to become other than we are now.

Claims about beginnings or endings may well be impossible to affirm or refute, but they do function as more or less transparent legitimations of authority and authorities. And there are different ways of framing beginnings and endings, of fixing the constitutive orders of temporality into the expectations of common sense and the legitimation practices of struggling powers. Authority and authorities depend on myths of origin and projections of the edge of time. Despite all claims to brute reality and concrete necessity, political life is unthinkable without deployments of metaphysics. The difficulty posed by claims about brute realities and eternal necessities of the kind affirmed by so many theories of international relations is not simply that they depend on metaphysics as such, but that they depend on, and work to affirm, a very restricted repertoire of metaphysical possibilities, while pleading innocence of all metaphysical responsibilities and thus of all responsibility. Affirmations of brute reality are never convincing except as evidence of the authoritarian stance of those who hide behind the affirmation.

MOVEMENTS

Illustrations of the kind of difficulties these considerations pose for modern theories of international relations can be found in diverse literatures, but two that may be especially telling involve claims about the present significance of certain kinds of social movements, on the one hand, and claims about the significance of speed or temporal acceleration in the organization of later-capitalist/postmodern life, on the other.

The literature on social movements, especially those that are somehow 'new', is now quite voluminous. It has attracted all the methodological sophistication one might expect of those sociologists who are comfortable with the statist conceptions of community and society that have made sociology as a disciplined enquiry possible in the first place. For a crucial limitation is already built into most attempts to ask questions about the novelty of specific social movements. The horizon of enquiry is already given by historically specific understandings of what it means to speak of a community, a class, an interest, an identity, or a movement of action orchestrated in space/time. Working within these horizons, these constitutive boundaries of social possibility, it is reasonable to enquire whether social movements are a break from or a continuation of class politics, an abandonment of the state or an affirmation of civil society, a continuation of liberal pluralism or a struggle to take pluralism beyond the homogenizations of liberal accounts of diversity. Even where social movements are understood in terms of – celebrated or castigated for – their anti-statism, analysis inevitably seems to work within statist assumptions about what it means to be statist or anti-statist. The image of the singular spatially circumscribed community seems as difficult to avoid as the image of the all-powerful god has proved to be for the modern secular imagination. And, indeed, it is useful to remember that time, and movement, once came to a stop at the edges of eternity, somewhere among the angels crowded on the almost but never quite infinite point of transition from here to there, from life to death, from the City of Man to the City of God. To speak of a movement now, even a movement firmly rooted in the secular necessities of capitalist modernity, is to do so in languages and concepts that have not quite lost their theological resonance.

The problems posed by very general considerations like these have been reinforced by the preoccupation of so much social movement analysis with the specific tendencies of European and North American welfare states, and to a lesser extent with those societies – primarily Latin American and Eastern/Central European – in which struggles to construct more effective arrangements within civil society to counteract the centralized power of state have been so important. There is no doubt that the reconstruction of civil society, the collapse of the unitary labour movement as *the* paradigm of what a serious social movement is supposed to be, the exploration of multiple social identities, connections between personal life and the structural power of state and capital, and so on, have all been crucial aspects of contemporary political life, and have received especially extensive examination in the literature on social movements in such societies. But even here, the image of *the* society, of the singular spatial container in which some kind of society can cohere, can permit or even require class conflict or pluralist identities, is rarely put into question. For all the sophistications of the literature on social movements in this context, it still seems bound by conceptions of political possibility that preclude debates about what it would mean to put established conceptions of political community or identity into question. In this respect, the term *social* movements seems tellingly appropriate. It signifies an affirmation that whatever social movements are and do, they are artefacts of the social processes that are already constructed within the borders of established political unities. They come to be understood as political only within terms set by a specific rendition of what it means to be political, and of where the political is to be found. The possibility of novelty is circumscribed by what appears to be a very effective substitute for eternity

(Walker, 1988; Magnusson and Walker, 1988; Magnusson, 1990, Magnusson, 1993).

Claims about the significance of social movements rest on observations of a great many struggles around many different issues in many different places. Difficulties of interpretation arise from their diversity, their specificity and their almost invariably contradictory character. Claims about the increasing significance of temporality, and especially about the acceleration of historical change, are also difficult to interpret, primarily because their formulation is fairly abstract and is concerned with the characteristics of very large-scale social processes. Marx, for example, once made some acute observations about the inherent tendencies of capitalism in this respect, drawing attention to its dynamics of destruction and reconstruction of the condition of human existence. Weber, too, characterized capitalist modernity in terms of a specific temporal trajectory, with a project of disenchantment that generates a fundamental political crisis, a crisis especially in relation to the twin moments of spatial autonomy – the individual subject and the territorial state – that Weber wanted to save from the ravages of modern rationality (Walker, 1993b).

While one may be sceptical of either or both of these paradigmatic accounts of the problem, and especially of the solutions that have been legitimized in their name, few would deny that their preoccupation with the problematic character of modern temporality has been crucial for attempts to rethink the character of political life. On the face of it, they seem to pose a crucial challenge to the account of politics reified in the spatial categories of theories of international relations. For the most part, however, this challenge has been successfully contained. Marx has been read partly as an economist with little to say about politics, and partly as a utopian with little to say about enduring political forms; either way, his progressive historicism is judged to have blinded him to the supposed eternal truths of geopolitics. (In other contexts, of course, Marx has been subjected to even more stunning interpretative abuse, but his portrayal by theorists of international relations is almost entirely a product of Cold War literary devices.) Weber's own ambivalence towards modernity has encouraged him to be read as two quite different people: as a kind of utilitarian theorist of convergence on a global scale or as the rather dubious theorist of the power state and the existential subject as the only solutions to the dilemmas of politics in a disenchanted world. Either way, his reading of modern temporality is rendered irrelevant. For some it merely affirms the spatial claims of states and for others it merely affirms the imminent disappearance of states in some unprecedented global system.

It seems increasingly difficult, however, to restrain intimations of the crucial importance of temporality within the rhetorical strategies that have tamed the insights of Marx, Weber and other theorists of modernity as an epoch of temporal acceleration as well as of spatial fragmentation. Claims about speed and simultaneity have entered into the clichés of modern life (in the context of international relations, recent discussions include Gill, 1991; Luke, 1991; Der Derian, 1992; Luke, 1993). The front pages of the newspapers may still affirm a world of spatial fragmentations, but the business and financial sections speak more clearly in a language of temporal simultaneities. Yet to invoke temporalities in this way is immediately to court irrelevance in the discourses of modern politics. Modern accounts of the political are still framed spatially: here and there, inside and outside, First World and Third World. It is within that framing that modern conceptions of temporality, or progressive history and development, have found their political purchase. Without that framing, it is difficult to make sense of politics at all. Modern accounts of the political have assumed that the puzzles of temporality can, and indeed must be solved in territorial space. Although theories of international relations are certainly concerned with the transformative character of contemporary events, the terms used to capture these transformations – interdependence, integration, regime, world order, globalization, and so on – betray the enormous authority of spatial imagery in this context. As with the images drawn from the experiences of *polis* and state, of boxes that can be called home, of a secular substitute for eternity in the unchanging sovereignty of states, it is far from clear that they capture the dynamics and fluidities of contemporary political life with much conviction. As Machiavelli might have predicted, the terrors of temporality cannot be tamed by fixed fortresses in territorial space as easily as the modern political imagination has come to suppose.

TAMING TEMPORALITY

The modern theory of international relations is perhaps the most significant discourse of eternity to be found in modern political life. As such, it is of crucial importance, despite the extent to which it is effectively ignored by those social and political theorists who believe that claims about eternity have long been left behind by secular claims to history, progress and development. And certainly, by the standards of many other disciplines, the theoretical practices that characterize the analysis of international relations can appear to be fairly crude and unsophisticated. But crude unsophistication can itself be a form of sophistication and refinement – a form, moreover, that is already made possible by the practices that encourage the distinction between the refined and the crude, the civilized and the barbarian. The disciplinary division of labour in the contemporary social sciences builds on rich, and rather suspicious, historical and cultural foundations.

As a discourse of eternity, international relations is prone to various manifestations of the claim that the basic realities and necessities of relations between states conform to a few unchanging rules. Most of these concern the supposed inevitability of power struggles among competing interests, struggles that may or may not be mitigated by quasi-institutional structures (a balance of power), the responsible acts of statesmanship, of the constitution of a complex (legal, cultural, functional) 'society' of states. To the extent that this story of eternal tragedy is effected by claims about temporality, the options seem to involve either a gradual progress from potential hell on earth (war) to the pursuit of self-interest by rational, and thus co-operative states (Kantian or utilitarian visions of international order) or the radical transcendence of relations between states within some as yet unforeseeable global community in which humanity finally comes to realize its own authentic identity – the option that has largely come to define the meaning and irrelevance of contemporary utopianism.

Part of the legitimacy of international relations theory as a discourse of eternity can be traced to the constant invocation of a long list of canonical names of those who have somehow grasped the perennial wisdom required to understand the way things are, indeed the way things must be. But it does not require too much reading to realize that the texts of at least two of the best known of those writers are often obsessed with the tremendous difficulty of all claims to eternity in a secular universe. The construction of a canonical tradition of international relations theory may be understood not only as an attempt to legitimize a specifically twentieth-century account of what political realism must be, but also to affirm a specifically modern understanding of the place of time and movement in political life generally. It is perhaps useful, therefore, to reflect on the significance of claims about movement and temporality in an era of increasingly global trajectories in relation to the different responses to the puzzles of secular politics articulated by Machiavelli and Hobbes. It is especially useful to do so because of the tremendous inhibitions placed on thinking about new forms of political practice in a global context exercised by those who have persuaded themselves of a secular theology of eternal damnation, a theology in which hard-headedness and 'realism' work as a perverse ritual of faith in the arbitrary limits of modern political order.

Machiavelli, especially, was hypersensitive to the difficulty of beginnings. *The Prince* may have been taken as an account of the character and necessities of political life in general, but it is quite explicitly framed as a study of a very specific problem, the problem of founding. It was the new beginnings, the creation and sustaining of completely new principalities, for which Machiavelli saved all his good examples. The prince is conceived, in good classical fashion, as the agent of *virtù*, as the site of pure creativity, the artist of innovation in a world of shifting energies but no fixed forms. Machiavelli also worried about endings, about the failure of flawed virtuosities to sustain community or memory. He worried especially about all those who would not learn that things change. Reliance on what has worked before, or on a fixed place, a fortress in which one might lie to wrestle with the wiles of *fortuna*, was, for Machiavelli, a sure sign of impending failure. So much, it should be said, for Machiavelli as the source of the eternal wisdom of international relations theory, unless eternal wisdom is framed, paradoxically, as an affirmation of earthly contingency.

Hobbes was also highly sensitive to the importance of beginnings; so sensitive, in fact, that he was satisfied with nothing less than completely new beginnings as the condition for any serious politics. Erase the Aristotelian essentialisms, out with the greatest good. A proper politics requires the constitution of a new – modern, scientific, nominalist – language, one that does not confuse words with things; a language, moreover, that permits an account of the past (the state of nature) in the language of the present – of the natural (that is, historical) condition of *modern* humankind – and which also permits an account of sovereignty as the eternal necessity of a life of freedom and equality under the eternal law of reason.

Hobbes, of course, knew very well that his account of sovereign power is pure fiction. He may have wanted to affirm the reality of sovereign power, and considerable numbers of commentators have certainly indulged his ambition in this respect, but Hobbes is quite aware that his nominalism must lead to awkward questions about how people are to be persuaded that sovereignty is indeed in their own best interests. Hobbes's familiar story about reason and fear is precisely a familiar story, one of those strategies of legitimation that require us to read Hobbes as a theorist of ideology, of how historical creatures are to be persuaded of the necessity of eternal necessities. The central move of Hobbes's story is precisely to deprive people of their history, to construct a myth of origins in which individuals arise out of an imaginary moment of utilitarian calculation: a fabulous story that continues to mesmerize those economistic utilitarians seated obediently on the patriarch's knee. It is certainly a very different story from the tales of temporal seduction told by Machiavelli.

Both Machiavelli and Hobbes recognize the problematic character of endings and beginnings. And both figures, it might be said, have informed some of the very different theoretical strategies that have come to share the name of realism in international relations. But it is Hobbes who has come to dominate the claims of this discipline. He does so not because of the accuracy of his account of the world (in any case, he goes to some trouble to deny the applicability of his account of atomistic individuals in a state of nature to the condition of mere war among those states that are in principle so much more than individuals writ large). He does so largely because Hobbes's treatment of beginnings and endings resonates so closely with the specifically modern principle, institution and practices of state sovereignty. The consequences of state sovereignty, it is usually assumed, are exactly what theories of international relations are supposed to examine: geopolitical fragmentation, potentially limitless conflict and possible accommodations in a world bereft of a common power. It is perhaps more useful, however, to look at how the principle, institution and practices of state sovereignty work to constitute the theory of international relations as a discourse of eternity, one that has few qualms about reading any marginally pessimistic text from the past as a confirmation of its own catechism of reifications.

In this context, Machiavelli's political artistry in time might be read as somehow congruent with the necessities of *realpolitik* in a fragmented world; but it can also be read as a radical subversion of the atemporal reifications of human existence that the principle, institution and practices of state sovereignty struggle to sustain.

Hobbes is perhaps easier to read as a corroboration of the eternal necessities of *realpolitik*, but only if his explicitly normative aspirations are read naively as the way things are, and his explicit comments on relations between states are resolutely ignored. There is clearly something very important going on in the manner in which the theory of international relations has been able to sustain itself as a discourse of eternity, and how theorists who have understood the highly problematic character of all claims to eternity have been so easily co-opted as canonical sources of everlasting wisdom. This something is not merely of abstract theoretical interest, for the simple reason that state sovereignty, while usually treated only as a formal principle, is also both an institution and a practice. It has a very tangible reach into the immediate struggles of peoples and movements as well as into the apparatuses of states that speak so comfortably in its illustrious – but still nominal – name. To pose questions about movements, acceleration or speed and their capacity to challenge the way we have become is necessarily to confront state sovereignty as the discourse of limits in time and space that the theory of international relations reproduces in such a domesticated manner.

STATE SOVEREIGNTY

Claims about state sovereignty led a rather charmed life among theorists of international relations in the Cold War era. Always supposedly present as the primary constitutive principle of modern political and international order, it remained notable for the silence that surrounded it as an object of critical analysis, especially among those who sought to ground theories of international relations in the image of a more or less positivistic social science. State sovereignty remained firmly on the agenda of literatures of international law, in relation both to specific disputes about specific claims to sovereignty and to more general debates about intervention, domestic jurisdiction, and so on. Somewhere in the more obscure margins of the literature, also, it is possible to trace evidence of important enquiries into the historical emergence of sovereignty (Hinsley, 1986; Onuf, 1991) or even of more theoretically self-conscious debates about what sovereignty is supposed to be (Ashley, 1989; Ashley and Walker, 1990; Shapiro, 1991; Dillon, 1992; Weber, 1994). The marginal significance of such concerns within the discipline of international relations, however, is perhaps confirmed most tellingly by the lack of interest shown in the challenges posed to liberal constitutionalist accounts of sovereignty by Carl Schmitt, widely recognized to be one of the most important writers on sovereignty in this century and a key voice behind Hans J. Morgenthau's dominating vision of what the analysis of international relations must involve (Schmitt, 1985; Sollner, 1987).

More recently, state sovereignty has again begun to receive serious attention, not only because its status seems to have become even more uncertain in the wake of post-Cold War turmoils and claims about accelerating globalization, but also because the broader philosophical principles of modernity, which have so clearly shaped the most influential accounts of what sovereignty is supposed to be, have also come under widespread challenge. Whether explicitly, as it has been in major works by people like Michel Foucault, or implicitly, as with a wide range of people pursuing diverse strategies under the more or less incoherent labels of postmodernism, post-structuralism, feminism, genealogy, and so on, claims about the possibility and consequences of sovereign identities have become one of the crucial obsessions of political and scholarly dispute.

This revival of interest in state sovereignty, and the broader cultural resources that sustain its legitimacy, offers considerable scope for diverse strategies of enquiry. The connection between the claims of state sovereignty and the constitutive principles of modernity have seemed to me to be especially important, and also relatively straightforward.

As a formal principle, state sovereignty seems to have emerged over a considerable period and obviously must be understood in the context of very complex developments usually subsumed into stories about the rise of the modern state and of capitalism in early modern Europe. Moreover, it came to be articulated as a solution to a wide range of problems generated by these developments. Political theorists, for example, rightly focus on the significance of state sovereignty as a solution to the increasingly unstable authority of personal rule, on the one hand, and the uncertain status of 'the people', on the other. States became specifically modern states, abstracted from both ruler and ruled. In a broader frame, however, state sovereignty can be understood as part of a solution to a wide range of problems arising primarily from the collapse of hierarchical modes of knowing and being, of which the puzzles of political authority and identity were only a part. Where the Great

Chain of Being permitted acounts of a world of continuities, a culture of resemblances, an ethics of greater and lesser, and thus of a politics rooted ultimately in monotheistic theology, modern European life increasingly developed as a culture of chasms, of Cartesian dualisms, Protestant and bourgeois individualisms, epistemologies of objectivity and subjectivity, of horizontal spaces and enclosed, spatialized times. State sovereignty came to work in a new universe of expanding horizons and spatial demarcations. It marked a world concerned less with the move from time to eternity or the subservience of lesser to greater than with the move from here to there and the absence of natural order among agents of sovereign identity. (Ruggie (1993) is an important exception to the general silence of international relations theorists on this crucial shift, but his analysis remains severely constrained by a curiously uncritical affirmation of the modern epistemologies that are part of the spatialization of subjects and objects that his analysis helps to explain.)

It is in this context that state sovereignty can be read as a very elegant and specifically modern resolution of three philosophical problems that had once received a more theological treatment, most notably through the categories of faith and redemption and the ministrations of the Church on earth. Puzzles about the relationship of time to eternity came to be framed instead as puzzles about relationships in terrestrial space (Walker, 1993a, especially chapter 8).

The relationship between the claims of the one and the many, for example, came to receive a double resolution. For all that state sovereignty is described as a source of fragmentation, it also expresses a unitary account of the system within which sovereign states can exist in the first place. To begin with, this system also had a precise cultural identity, whether specified in relation to Christian or European sources. Increasingly, the key unity has been understood in relation to a universalizing culture of capitalist modernity, a culture that has been shared even where particular states have been reluctant to participate in, much less endorse, it (this is a key but underrated theme in the writings of Hedley Bull, as in Bull and Watson, 1984; on the contemporary context of cultural production on a global scale, see Tomlinson, 1991). This resolution of one system, many states permits another resolution, one articulated primarily by theorists of political life within states anxious to show how the problems of modern fragmentation, especially individualism, might be made compatible with claims to universal reason. Not surprisingly, the state itself came to be understood precisely as the institution that would permit both particularity and universality, usually through the invocation of universal necessity as the ultimate ground for a properly human freedom; the formulations of Hobbes, Kant and Hegel have been especially influential in showing how this resolution might be articulated with some plausibility.

This double resolution of the relationship between universality and particularity depends on a clear demarcation between an inside and an outside, a self and an other. Inside the particular, aspirations for the universal can be pursued within a secure and authoritative order, although it is best not to think about the behaviours required at the margins of society where violence may be necessary to sustain the claims of righteousness within. Outside, there are only other particulars, an absence of a cohesive community, a pure anarchy according to some, a decentralized society of states according to others, but a realm, certainly, of difference, competition, insecurity, domination and conflict: a realm in which others can be turned into Other, and the Other may be subjected to the familiar practices of projection, negation, orientalism and obliteration.

As a demarcation of an inside and an outside, state sovereignty specifies a politics of spatial containment; one, moreover, that specifies a new range of possibilities for a human existence in time. Machiavelli's art of politics in the face of approaching *fortuna* gives way to the fixing of temporality within the ordered jurisdiction of the territorial state. After reason: history, the gradual realization of universality in time. Outside the state: the anarchy of contingency, an absence of progress and the seductions of utopian visions turned away from the irredeemable realities of earthly struggles.

These three resolutions – of universality/particularity, self/other and space/time – did not appear overnight, but in retrospect their elegance has seemed overwhelming, rational, reasonable, intrinsically right. They perhaps rest upon other resolutions, notably of the finite and the infinite within the claims of a self-identical individuality, the modern autonomous subject torn between alienation and self-realization. They permit other resolutions in turn, notably of the appropriate relation between the sovereign identities of the (macro) state and the (micro) individual. But to frame the principle of state sovereignty as a principle that draws upon, and in turn offers a guarantee of, the claims of modernity as a specific historical way of life, is perhaps to gain some insight into how it works as a practice of legitimation that serves to render other ways of being human, other ways of being both one and many, of relating self to other, or articulating space/time – almost unimaginable. State sovereignty works because it has come to seem to be simply there, out in the world, demarcating the natural orders of here and there. But the lesson that theorists of international relations have consistently refused to learn from Hobbes is that sovereignty is never simply there. And what was never simply there can never simply disappear.

AFTER ETERNITY

Claims that state sovereignty is either about to disappear or is fated to be with us for the foreseeable future are an expression of one of the most powerful discourses of modern politics. It informs scholarly categories and popular imaginaries. And it is possibly the most misleading guide there is to whatever futures we may succeed in fashioning out of the ruins of the present.

This discourse of eternal presence and imminent absence is itself produced by the philosophical resolutions that state sovereignty both expresses and guarantees. State sovereignty, that is to say, produces its own account of the only alternatives to itself that we can readily imagine. Like heaven, these alternatives are impossible to reach except as mysterious possibilities beyond life as we know it. This discourse cannot offer a guide to what it might mean to say that state sovereignty is somehow obsolete. Rather than working within philosophical resolutions that state sovereignty has served to naturalize as common sense and legal principle, therefore, it seems to be more productive to examine ways in which, say, people struggling to survive, or the dynamics of capitalist restructuring challenge the resolutions that make this discourse of eternity possible: to ask what it means to be caught up in practices of both universality and diversity; to negotiate alternative conceptions of self and other; to explore spatio-temporal possibilities not envisaged by the cartographers of containment or the children of Hegel's ghost.

It is in the context of challenges to these resolutions that one might usefully ask questions about what it now means to be critical or even novel. It is in this context, also, that one might begin to read *some* social movements as practices in search of the political rather than simply a sociological phenomena working within a particular account of what and where the political must be. It is in this context, furthermore, that one might read highly specific local struggles in relation to broader, even global, processes without assuming that one must bow down to the sovereign state as the only intermediary between local and global or here and there.

Many phenomena in the contemporary world seem to me to be susceptible to this kind of reading, not all of them of a kind that fills me with hope and warm feelings. But to the extent that one can glimpse opportunities for something better than we have now, it seems to me to lie in great part with those who are able to explore the relationships of unity/diversity, self/other and space/time without deifying the undoubted charms of a discourse of eternity that never has been able to bring history to an end, but shows every sign that it can now sustain its charms only at the cost of ever increasing misery and violence.

The trouble with what we have come to regard as the serious politics that aspires to some kind of moral status on the basis of some kind of community – the politics that is affirmed by theories of international relations and their characteristic negations of the solipsistic universals of modern political theory – is that it is widely admitted to be in serious trouble. As a normative aspiration, it remains very attractive for a great many people. Some can even envisage its continuing capacity to inform better ways of acting together. But for many others, the character and location of community are highly problematic; aspirations for moral status rooted in an uncertain community are obviously tricky, and many attempts to respond to the most pressing problems of our time on the basis of what we have come to regard as a serious politics would be quite amusing if they were not so massively tragic.

The contemporary political agenda is full of exceptionally difficult questions. We may ask what democracy could be if not rooted in a territorial community (Connolly, 1991a, 1991b); or what obligation might mean if not delineated only in relation to one's fellow citizens; or what the relation of global to local might be if not simply mediated by statist monopolies of all relations of universality and particularity; or what political identity might be if not subsumed into the totalizing claims of citizen, nation and subject, if not disciplined by a Schmittean politics of the exception (Campbell, 1992), or theologized by the fundamentalist forms of self-righteousness that states have so often deployed to turn themselves into gods on earth; or what it means to act in relation to biospheric necessities or the needs of the world's most desperate people; or what it means, in a world of leaking boundaries, to act on the basis of claims about gender, race, culture or class.

To try to work through any of these questions, or even to try to ask them in a plausible fashion, even though the literatures attempting to do so are now vast (McGrane, 1989; Butler and Scott, 1992; Lash and Friedman, 1992; Campbell and Dillon, 1993; Agamben, 1993; Said, 1993, among many others), is to realize just how fragile modern accounts of the location and character of the political have become. They are certainly much too fragile to permit much confidence in the capacity of modern theories of international relations to tell us where or what the political can now be. Some sense of this fragility is currently expressed by contemporary debates about the dangers of dissolving subjectivities and the consequent need for some kind of 'standpoint', whether this is framed in strategic, tactical or even logistical terms. The ease with which various forms of 'identity politics' lapse into elitisms of one kind or another (often in ways reminiscent of earlier positions associated with Georgy Lukacs, Karl Mannheim or Leo Strauss) or even in more virulent forms of self-righteousness, is especially troubling in the context of theories of international relations, which can be read precisely as discourses that seek to place limits on the politics of self-righteousness that is intrinsic to modern states. It may be the case that the emancipatory practices of specific groups require some kind of 'standpoint' in order to act in the world with some semblance of effectiveness, but it is also the case that a politics of self-righteous identity is all too likely to reproduce the codes of inclusion and exclusion that have made theories of international relations what they have become. Surely we have had enough of a politics of little boxes.

Note

I would like to express my thanks to the organizers and participants in the Conference on Social Movements, Civil Democracy and the New Global System held by the Center on Human Rights Development and the Graduate School of International Studies, University of Denver, March 1992, at which the first draft of this chapter was given as a keynote address.

References

Agamben, G. 1993: *The Coming Community* (trans. M. Hardt). Minneapolis: University of Minnesota Press.

Anderson, P. 1992: The ends of history. In P. Anderson, *A Zone of Engagement*, London: Verso, 279–375.

Ashley, R. K. 1989: Living on border lines: man, post-structuralism, and war. In J. Der Derian and M. J. Shapiro (eds), *International/Intertextual Relations: Postmodern Readings of World Politics*. Lexington: Lexington Books, 259–321.

Ashley, R. K. and Walker, R. B. J. 1990: Reading dissidence/writing the discipline: crisis and the question of sovereignty in international studies. *International Studies Quarterly*, 34(3), 367–416.

Bull, H. and Watson, A. 1984: *The Expansion of International Society*. Oxford: Clarendon Press.

Butler, J. and Scott J. (eds) 1992: *Feminists Theorize the Political*. New York: Routledge.

Campbell D. 1992: *Writing Security: United States Foreign Policy and the Politics of Identity*. Manchester: Manchester University Press.

Campbell, D. and Dillon, M. (eds) 1993: *The Political Subject of violence*. Manchester: Manchester University Press.

Connolly, W. E. 1991a: *Identity/Difference: Democratic Negotiations of Political Paradox*. Ithaca, N.Y.: Cornell University Press.

Connolly, W. E. 1991b: Democracy and territoriality. *Millennium Journal of International Studies*, 20(3), 463–84.

Der Derian. J. 1992: *Antidiplomacy: Spies, Terror, Speed, and War*. Oxford: Blackwell.

Dillon. G. M. 1992: Stat(e)ing Australia: squid, jigging and the masque of state. *Alternatives*, 17(3), 281–312.

Fergusson, K. 1993: *The Man Question: Visions of Subjectivity in Feminist Theory*. Berkeley: University of California Press.

Fukuyama, F. 1992: *The End of History and the Last Man*. London: Hamish Hamilton.

Gaddis, J. L. 1992/3: International relations theory and the end of the Cold War. *International Security*, 17(3), 5–58.

Gill, S. 1991: Reflections on global order and sociohistorical time. *Alternatives*, 16(3), 275–314.

Hall, J. A. and Ikenberry, G. J. 1989: *The State*. Minneapolis: University of Minnesota Press.

Held, D. 1993a: Liberalism, Marxism, and democracy. *Theory and Society*, 22, 249–81.

Held, D. (ed.) 1993b: *Prospects for Democracy: North, South, East, West*. Cambridge: Polity Press.

Hinsley, F. H. 1986: *Power and the Pursuit of Peace*, 2nd ed. Cambridge: Cambridge University Press.

Kratochwil, F. 1993: The embarrassment of changes: neo-realism as the science of *realpolitik* without politics. *Review of International Studies*, 19(1), 63–80.

Lash, S. and Friedman, J. (eds) 1992: *Modernity and Identity*. Oxford: Blackwell.

Linklater, A. 1982: *Men and Citizens in the Theory of International Relations*. London: Macmillan.

Luke, T. W. 1991: The discipline of security studies and the codes of containment: learning from Kuwait. *Alternatives*, 16(3), 315–44.

Luke, T. W. 1993: Discourses of disintegration, texts of transformation: re-reading realism in the new world order. *Alternatives*, 18(2), 229–58.

Magnusson, W. 1990: The reification of political community. In R. B. J. Walker and S. H. Mendlovitz (eds), *Contending Sovereignties: Redefining Political Community*, Boulder, Colorado: Lynne Reinner Publishers, 45–60.

Magnusson, W. 1993: Social movements and the state: presentation and representation. In G. Albo, D. Langille and L. Panitch (eds), *A Different Kind of State? Popular Power and Democratic Administration*, Toronto: Oxford University Press, 122–30.

Magnusson, W. and Walker, R. 1988: Decentring the state: political theory and Canadian political economy. *Studies in Political Economy: A Socialist Review*, 26, 37–71.

McGrane, B. 1989: *Beyond Anthropology: Society and the Other*. New York: Columbia University Press.

Mann, M. 1986: *The Sources of Social Power*, vol. 1: *A History of Power from the Beginning to A.D. 1760*. Cambridge: Cambridge University Press.

Onuf, N. G. 1991: Sovereignty: outline of a conceptual history. *Alternatives*, 16(4), 425–46.

Ruggie, J. G. 1993: 'Territoriality and beyond: problematizing modernity in international relations. *International Organization* 47(1), 139–74.

Said, E. 1993: *Culture and Imperialism*. New York: Knopf.

Schmitt, C. 1985: *Political Theology: Four Chapters on the concept of Sovereignty* (trans. G. Schwab). Cambridge, Mass.: MIT Press.

Shapiro, M. 1991: Sovereignty and exchange in the orders of modernity. *Alternatives*, 16(4), 447–77.

Sollner, A. 1987: German conservatism in America: Morgenthau's political realism. *Telos*, 72, 161–72.

Tomlinson, J. 1991: *Cultural Imperialism*. London: Frances Pinter.

Vincent, A. 1987: *Theories of the State*. Oxford: Blackwell.

Walker, R. B. J. 1988: *One World, Many Worlds: Struggles for a Just World Peace*. Boulder, Colorado: Lynne Reinner.

Walker, R. B. J. 1990: Sovereignty, identity, community: reflections on the horizons of contemporary political practice. In R. B. J. Walker and S. H. Mendlovitz (eds), *Contending Sovereignties: Redefining Political Community*, Boulder, Colorado: Lynne Reinner, 159–85.

Walker, R. B. J. 1993a: *Inside/Outside: International Relations as Political Theory*. Cambridge: Cambridge University Press.

Walker, R. B. J. 1993b: Violence, modernity, silence: from Max Weber to international relations. In Campbell and Dillon (1993), 137–60.

Weber, C. 1994: *Writing the State: Political Intervention and the Historical Constitution of State Sovereignty*. Cambridge: Cambridge University Press.

Wight, M. 1966: Why is there no international theory? In H. Butterfield and M. Wight (eds), *Diplomatic Investigations: Essays in the Theory of International Politics*. London: Allen & Unwin, 17–34.

Wight. M. 1977: *Systems of States* (ed. H. Bull). Leicester: Leicester University Press.

15

Dare not to Know: International Relations Theory versus the Future

Ken Booth

Political theories, whether domestic or international, have invariably been ideas of their times. It is not surprising, then, that today's confused and fractured world should produce a troubled discipline of international relations. We wonder whether history is at an end or only at a beginning. We wonder whether we can possibly know the future, when we are so divided about the past. We begin to fear that there may not be a future, or at least much of one, for those who will be alive in the middle of the twenty-first century. We ponder who 'we' are. What should we think? How should we think? Why should we think? Many Western intellectuals have become deeply uncertain in recent years as methodological disquiets have interacted with worrying global trends and end-of-century atmospherics; it has led to a perceived need to reinvent the future. These disquiets have been evident in the study of international relations, as in other disciplines, and the individual chapters in this book have shown how they manifest themselves in debates about theory, method, curricula and political agendas. This final chapter will try to focus these disquiets in relation to international political theory and the future, and suggest a way forward. Ours is a troubled discipline, but it is increasingly one which has a claim to be the subject of all subjects in the social sciences.

REGARDING THE FUTURE

If you wanted to repair your car you would go to a mechanic, and to restructure your house you would go to a builder, but if you wanted to reinvent the future would you naturally go to a professor of international relations? You could not be blamed if you did not, because we have not dealt with the future very well. This was obvious for all to see in the radical surprise of the revolutions of 1989 in Eastern Europe, and the soon-to-follow abdication of a superpower.

That year, 1989, rounded off a difficult decade for professors of the subject, in which the Humpty Dumpty discipline of international relations increasingly split into a number of competing paradigms. It seemed the final indignity when the Berlin Wall had a big fall. If academic international relations theory could not adequately describe, explain or predict such a turning point of history, should it not be discarded as another of the failed projects buried by the rubble of the Wall? Following this experience, one would understandably hesitate before hiring a professor of international relations to reinvent the future. But where else might you go? Other disciplines possess some insight and visions about the future, but can they actually offer a great deal in the way of practical wisdom? Theology and science, for example, both make claims on our attention regarding the future, but how far can they take us? Faith and Hope they can offer: but what about Polity?

Despite all the inadequacies of international political theory, it is not evident that other subjects have any better disciplinary claim to be reinventers of the future. It is therefore time for all the academic men and all the academic women to try to put the 'divided discipline' (Holsti, 1985) back together again. I believe that such reconstruction is necessary, though not along traditional lines if we want to think usefully about the future of 'who gets what, when, [and] how' (Lasswell, 1950) across the globe, which is what I take 'world politics' to mean.

The injunction 'Dare not to know' turns on its head Kant's motto for the Enlightenment (Reiss, 1989, p. 54). It has been chosen as the title of this chapter because 'established knowledge' in international relations has tended to become an oxymoron. Knowledge in the subject is no longer established: it is contested. For many years, and still today in part, international relations teaching has been more like Sunday school than university education. Set questions elicited set answers. Choice quotations were learned from the sacred books. The quality of thinking was judged by the extent to which it replicated the canons of the past. Students were quickly socialized into professional norms which channelled rather than challenged thought. Students did not know things as they were, but as they were taught they were, and what they were taught often distanced them from rather than engaged them with the lives of human beings across the world. If what is known and taught is impoverished, academic international relations needs reinventing before we can think usefully about reinventing the future of global society.

The implications of saying 'Dare not to know' in international relations are profound. They entail a revolution in the ontology, epistemology and agenda of the discipline. Dare not to know means: re-examining basic concepts; opening up to what has been closed out; rehumanizing what has been dehumanized; de-gendering what has been gendered; celebrating confusion rather than certainty; dethroning the logic of anarchy with the logics of anarchy; denaturalizing established common sense; populating the frontier zones between international relations and other academic disciplines; ideologizing the supposedly 'objective'; re-imagining the humanly constituted; contextualizing the tradition; making normativity a norm; and listening carefully to the subject's 'screaming silences'.

To accept such a programme obviously entails the risk of academic international relations being sucked into the black hole of philosophy. Thinking about thinking always threatens to undermine any confidence we may have in what we know and how we act. This is particularly disturbing for a subject such as international relations, which has always been thought about as a policy science, intimately concerned with decisions and their consequences. Implicitly, international relations has operated on the old principle that 'there is nothing so practical as a good theory'. A reinvented future for the subject requires consideration of the interplay of practice and theory. Dreams that are not operationalized leave the world as it is. Putting all this together, politically speaking, means that we cannot wait for philosophy to deliver final judgements about beauty and truth. The world is confronted by numerous immediate and long-term problems, so we have to demonstrate the 'courage of our confusions' if we hope to get from here to the future in good shape. For several reasons, the year 2045 can be taken as the symbolic marker of the future.

That year will be the centenary of the dropping of the first atomic bomb, on the city of Hiroshima. It is a convenient future to think about – a middle-aged mind can conceive half a century – and we are already half way there. The atomic bomb dropped in 1945 represents the culminating point of traditional rationality about the games nations play. The destruction of Hiroshima was not a tragedy: that was its tragedy. It represented, in its way, the triumph of rationality and the vindication of good. It was the culmination of several centuries of international relations dominated by the Westphalian states system, Machiavellian ethics and the Clausewitzian philosophy of war – all kitted out with the technology of 'science rampant'.

The single-bomb destruction of a city did at least leave a unique crystal ball among the radioactive ruins. It showed where traditional rationality (the 'common sense' of the powerful) might lead. Despite this warning, the rationality that had led to the destruction of Hiroshima continued to dominate how practitioners and academics conceived international politics during the Cold War. As a result we have lost a great deal of time. When we contemplate the foreseeable problems the world will face in the next half-century, it quickly becomes apparent that human society will be in deep trouble if we cannot transcend the common sense of 1945. That is why the phrase 'international relations theory versus the future' is the subtitle of this chapter. One test of human society having transcended the logic of 1945 would be if those reading this today who will be alive at the centenary of Hiroshima will then be able to look back at that event with all the horror and incomprehension with which we now look back on other social inventions we have transcended, such as slavery, or burning people for their religious views – or lack of them. Social inventions like international relations cannot be uninvented overnight, but they can be reinvented, over time.

VERSUS THE FUTURE

The common sense of 1945 seamlessly became the basis of the strategies of the Cold War. The circumstances were also right for international relations to take off academically. During these years it was a subject running on steroids, and in its simplest realist/strategic mode it became the Ben Johnson of the social sciences. Like that infamous and tragic athlete, it was pumped up and into toughness; it powered straight ahead, not willing to look at what was happening down other academic lanes; it was well sponsored and discounted ethics; it was reluctant to ask awkward questions; and it was focused on the here and now, leaving the future to take care of itself. During the Cold War there were five major reasons that international relations specialists left the future to take care of itself.

International relations specialists did not believe in the future International political theory has been dominated by two versions of realism, both of which see international relations as a 'timeless present'. The classical realists (strongly influenced by Christian pessimism) see conflict between states as a manifestation of a flawed and unchanging human nature. The neo-realists see an endless interplay of states wanting to survive, within different distributions of powers, in a condition of anarchy. Exponents of both viewpoints – Niebuhr and Waltz, for example – look back over twenty-five centuries of unbroken struggle and shake hands with Thucydides (Niebuhr, 1938; Waltz, 1979). For his part, Thucydides would feel at home today in seminars about the international politics of the Middle East, with all the talk of crises, aggressions and self-interest, with the powerful doing what they can, and the weak what they must. For realists the Melian dialogue is the timeless script of states (Thucydides, 1972, pp. 400–8).

From the dominating realist theoretical perspective, reinventing the future has never been the issue, since the game of states does not change. Asking realists to reinvent the future would be like asking Brian Johnston to reinvent cricket. For realists, like revered cricket commentators, reinvention is unthinkable: the task is to tell the story of reincarnation. The game (whether cricket or international relations) is endlessly replicated, in different circumstances and forms, but its soul remains the same. So does the script. This timeless present is seen as both natural and the best of all possible worlds.

The 'archive' of international relations theory has been impoverished Over the last half-century the mainstream texts taught to students have been inbred and distorted. Running on steroids is not healthy for an academic discipline, but the Cold War tempted international relations down that path. During this period the subject developed largely in ignorance of developments in sociology, philosophy and other currents of intellectual life.

The study of international history, for example, was little more than self-fulfilling hindsight, based on realist assumptions.

The 'archive' (Said, 1985, pp. 41–2) comprised an authoritative 'tradition' of thought which emphasized an unbroken list of realists. Peace theorists and others who did think about the future were dismissed as 'utopians', and were not admitted into the canon; they were often ridiculed, and were marginalized or ignored in the construction of courses. But even those classical thinkers who were admitted into the archive – Hobbes, Machiavelli, Augustine, and others – were somewhat decontextualized so that they became, in Michael Donelan's apt phrase, merely 'ventriloquists' dummies' to speak the words of their manipulators (1990, p. 142). The archive was a means of controlling the present, not a resource for thinking about the future.

International political theory has largely been Western ideology It was hardly a coincidence that the dominating realist/strategic mode of thinking flourished in the Anglo-American world. Power-political theory was congenial to those with the big battalions, politically and militarily, and the academically prestigious. The West did not want a different theoretical future because it was dominating the practical present. No space was allowed for ideas about transcendence or emancipation. Ideas such as dependency theory or world-systems theory were shunned as un-American academic activities.

If E. H. Carr (1961) was right, when he argued that all history is contemporary history, it presumably follows that all political theory is contemporary political theory. So the image of the ventriloquist's dummy is perhaps too cosy. It would be more pertinent to say that Hobbes, Machiavelli and the rest became conscripts in the Cold War – the intellectual front-line for the Ayatollahs of nuclearism and global military confrontation. Philosophers looking forward to perpetual peace (like Kant), world society thinkers (like Falk) and other 'radicals' in Cold War terms were seen as fools or fellow travellers – usually both. In different ways, the iron curtain imprisoned everybody.

The explanation of who got what in world politics, as told in these years by white male Anglo-American professors of international relations, looked very different from that which would have been told (had we had a chance to hear it) by, say, a genitally mutilated, child-worn, hungry young woman from a war-torn part of Africa. This is not to say that the story we heard from the professors did not contain elements of reality, only that the story we did *not* hear also contained elements of reality. But for those seeking truth, the silence of the powerless has more to say than have the selfish words of the powerful. 'We don't see things as they are, we see them as *we* are', said Anaïs Nin. As the theorists of the powerful, Cold War Anglo-American professors of international relations did not easily or professionally embrace theories of future change, or empirical studies which might have given rise to cognitive uncertainties or ontological revolutions.

The desire of international relations specialists for policy-relevance Power generates knowledge; it also attracts academics, as participants, servants and voyeurs. The desire for policy-relevance has meant that international relations specialists have attended to the agendas of politicians, who, infamously, think about the next election, not the next generation. And many international specialists, especially in the US, have been interested not only in studying power but in having some (however little, however vicariously). If the search for policy-relevance and policy-involvement on the part of academics becomes all-embracing, then they become little more than the scribes of whatever is the prevailing idea or power or policy of the moment. The more academics 'go native' with the policy-making community, the more they will understand and the more, naturally, they will forgive. International relations as the cult of the statesman and strategist has always had glamour, but like all cults it demands that its followers accept specific and unquestioning interpretations of the world. If academics simply attend to the agendas of politicians and bureaucrats, they will not be in a position to have any say in the reinvention of the agenda of the world.

The subject's words do not work A sound theoretical structure for thinking about the future cannot be built with porous materials. Some key words in international relations have been and are politicized or sloppy; some have changed their meaning; and others less accurately describe what they purport to describe. A few common examples will make this clear.

1 We talk about 'peace' (as in 'We've had peace since 1945') in such a way that peace can mean only the 'absence of world war'. This is a bizarre conception, and also a distorted picture of reality, when it cloaks well over 20 million violent deaths.

2 We have been discussing the 'coming obsolescence of the nation-state' for many years, ignoring the fact that very few nation-states have ever actually existed. (What for the most part have existed have been multi-national states, dominated by a hegemonial nation.) Yet again this simple term reflects the discipline's top-down view of reality.

3 We emphasize the 'state' as the basic unit of analysis, but say little about its multiple characteristics. State forms vary considerably, yet we theorize instead according to some textbook notion of *the* state. Many states exist only juridically, not as 'social facts' (Jackson and Rosberg, 1982).

4 We rest a great deal of our thinking on the theory of sovereignty, while all the time actual state autonomy is declining. The gap between studying sovereign states and studying world politics widens annually, as space opens up between the traditional legalist conception of sovereignty and the increasing incapacity of all governments to shape political and economic life in the manner they would choose.

5 We in the West coined a term 'Third World', and believe the label still explains several continents. But there are differences within the so-called Third World which are as great as between parts of the First and Third Worlds. Singapore and Sudan have less in common than Mostar and Mogadishu, while the underclass of the American 'City on the Hill' share lives of 'Hobbesian fear' with the downtrodden of the Third World. Both 'Worlds' are dominated by elites who enjoy the goods and privileges of the global market-place and local power.

6 We have employed the euphemistic jargon of nuclear strategy, and have utterly distanced ourselves from the subject matter – the possible extinction of civilization. Nuclear weapons themselves created a historic disjuncture between destructive power and political purpose, but the euphemistic language of strategy tried to bring them back into a rational Clausewitzian relationship.

7 And at the heart of the matter we crudely equated power with military power. They are not synonymous. Chairman Mao famously said that power rolls out of the barrel of a gun; and Stalin infamously asked: 'How many divisions has the Pope?' But the over-identification of power with military might have led us to overlook other causal factors during the Cold War, and miss important questions. This was one of the reasons the collapse of communist power in Eastern Europe came as such

a surprise. Realism focused our attention on the wrong indicators of 'power'. Looking proudly at the way his photographs, manpower, ideology and organization are now scattered through Eastern Europe, the Pope today might well ask: 'How many statues has Stalin?'

If these and other key words in academic international relations have not been naming things properly, how could the future be usefully conceptualized? If concepts do not correspond to phenomena, never mind noumena, how can the theories they create help us discern the future? It is not only philosophical problems that arise – as Wittgenstein put it – when 'language *goes on holiday*' (1992, p. 19, §38).

For the five reasons just discussed, international relations specialists during the Cold War did not develop a habit of thinking usefully about the future. Even if their methodologies were sound, they failed to ask crucial questions (Hopf, 1993). These problems did not improve in the short term in the difficult decade of the 1980s, when history accelerated and the subject divided.

DECONSTRUCTING THE FUTURE

If the realist/strategic mode of international relations theorizing during the Cold War could be described as the Ben Johnson of the social sciences, in the 1980s the subject as a whole resembled a Monty Python relay race:

1 The realists continued to power straight ahead, but although they remained dominant there were rather fewer of them than before, and they were subjected to constant criticism.
2 A breakaway mainstream team decided it might be a good idea to let everything settle down for a while. Somewhat nostalgic about the Cold War and the doubt-free subject of their student days, they turned their backs on the finishing post for the moment, and escaped into the study of history.
3 There was a new team of postmodernists. They very much enjoyed the idea of being able to run about between the lines, but since they could not accept that the finishing post should be privileged over the starting post, they stayed where they were, and left everybody else to get on with their own business.

4 A normative team slipped quietly in, after a 'forty-year detour' (Smith, 1992), looking for the action. They provoked their critics in the crowd by shouting threatening 'f-words', like Frankfurt, foundationalism and Foucault. This was a team of big ideas and big names, with no merely four-letter words in its vocabulary.
5 A growing number of individuals decided that since they were not sure they could now reach the finishing line, they would simply amble along, and move into different lanes to talk to sociologists, economists, philosophers and others. They did not quite know where they were going, but they were sure who should travel with them.
6 One school willing to cross the lanes was that of the historical sociologists. They tried to bring in the state, at first sight a curious idea for a discipline which was criticized for being state-centric. It remained to be seen whether there was room for their analyses of state and society to be fitted in.
7 There was a reinvented critical theory team. They had an occasional spurt forwards, but they knew that they would never finally arrive. That did not matter: the aim was to travel hopefully. They were more confident of where they were coming from than where they were going to. This did not matter: they regarded the race as open-ended, and were cheered for it by a discriminating group in the crowd.
8 Only one team faced disqualification. This was because they were the wrong sex. International relations had never been friendly to women either in theory or in practice. Nevertheless, a small group of feminist theorists claimed some space and questioned the way the powers that be had constituted both the subject and the race – the human race, that is.

A major difficulty for those watching all this activity (students) was that each participant in this academic cockpit (their teachers) seemed to have to define the subject himself or herself as the price of entry. From being Sunday school, academic international relations overnight became a multifaceted disputation. There was a major crisis of representation in the subject. It was labelled the 'Third Debate' (Lapid, 1989).

It might be thought that by describing the discipline as a Monty Python relay race there is a hint of criticism, since indiscipline is the essence of Python. Far from it. With hindsight these developments can be seen as representing a decisive and beneficial stage in the evolution of the subject. The confusions of the post-positivist phase actually helped rescue the discipline from historical complacency and intellectual irrelevance (Smith, Booth and Zalewski, forthcoming). In contemplating the next stage of the subject, I hope that false hopes are not being raised by the repetition of a poetic line from Nietzsche: 'one must have chaos in one, to give birth to a dancing star' (1969, p. 46).

What did the 'post-positivists' add in the 1980s? What progress might emerge out of the chaos?

Postmodernists began asking questions about language, contextuality, the foundations of knowledge, the structure of authority and the relationship between power and the agenda (professional and political). What can we know? Critical theorists started to ask questions about the ideological basis of knowledge, the self-interested nature of theory, the importance of ethics, the open-endedness of politics and the role of intellectuals. Do we philosophize to pass the time, or to change the world? Historical sociologists began asking questions about the historical context of state growth, the historical variability of state forms, the interrelationships between state, culture and economy, and the 'fit' between society, state and international system. What is this thing we call the state?

And feminist writers started to ask questions about identity, the nature of the 'political' and gender bias in theory and practice. They asked a virtually all-male discipline to open its doors and minds to profoundly unsettling arguments about gender. They faced (indeed still face) enormous obstacles. Examples are everywhere, but one illustration is the last paragraph of Fukuyama's famous article 'The End of History?'. It represents a typical but nevertheless breathtaking expression of a gendered view of what the world is all about. Fukuyama talks about the ending of the 'struggle for recognition . . . of the worldwide ideological struggle that called forth daring, courage, imagination and idealism' (1989, p. 18). These words are pure Rambo-speak, showing no recognition in themselves or their author of the daring, courage, imagination and idealism in the daily lives of women who dare to cope in violent domestic and other situations, who courageously give up their lives to care for the old and handicapped, whose imagination makes birthdays and holidays special, and whose idealism runs charities and peace movements (as well as, often, families and jobs). If women's lives are completely invisible in these ways, it is no wonder they are not recognized as playing a part in making the world go round. If the study of international politics is blind to gender, what else does it fail to see?

Together, these forms of post-positivism – postmodernism, critical theory, historical sociology and feminist theory – added yet more fissures to a discipline already divided by the inter-paradigm debate of the early 1980s. This 'debate' – for the most part a set of isolated monologues – consisted of three dominant approaches: realism, pluralism and structuralism/globalism (Banks, 1985). Realism remained by far the dominant paradigm, the more so as it became apparent that pluralists shared many of the same assumptions. No sooner, therefore, had students of international relations grown used to thinking in terms of three paradigms than they were thrown into the confusions of the third debate. These new approaches (new for students of international relations at least) provoked or inspired, depending upon one's taste, but they were collectively beneficial. The post-positivists shared one central concern with traditional theorists, and that was power. For some reason the subtleties of the profoundest founders of realism – Carr and Niebuhr, for example – became lost in the 1950s, so that for the most part the post-positivists engaged with their less subtle and less profound disciples and interpreters. Unlike the school of realism which had developed by the 1980s, the post-positivist approaches did not concentrate on describing the surface forms of power politics, but instead attempted to uncover the deep structures of power knowledge.

Students of international politics had understood since Carr's *The Twenty Years' Crisis* (1946) that all politics of significance is power politics; now some of them were learning that all knowledge of significance is power knowledge. Where, then, is truth? In such uncertainty is fertilized the seed of ontological revolution. The post-positivists began asking good simple questions, though not always in good simple ways. They are questions which some of us – increasing numbers of us – will spend the rest of our professional lives trying to answer. Sunday school is over. This is the creative chaos one has to have in one. What chance is there that it will create a 'dancing star'?

By a 'dancing star' I mean a reinvented discipline, a subject put back together again, an international relations theory *for* the future. There are three main reasons why this is an important project.

First, world politics is the appropriate academic site for the discussion of the crucial human questions for the future. Political science and sociology make sense only in the context of the global. Most of us were taught to think of international relations as a branch of political science, but it has become increasingly evident that political science can be seriously studied only as a branch of the study of politics on a global scale. In disciplinary terms, the traditional answer to the question 'Who surrounds whom?' must be reversed. World politics is the home of political science, not vice versa. Kant was right: political theory has to be international theory (Reiss, 1989, especially pp. 47–9). World politics is the new metaphysics, a global moral science.

Second, whatever its faults, no one could criticize traditional international relations for not being hard-nosed. When political or academic heads have drifted into the clouds, its specialists have always asked down-to-earth questions. They remind those who propose perfectly logical plans for a future saner world that they must deal with Rousseau's warning that 'to be sane in a world of madmen is in itself a form of madness' (quoted by Waltz, 1959, p. 181). And they remind those who look towards progress through good people setting an example that they must deal with Niebuhr's dismissal of those 'who want to live in history without sinning' (quoted by Donelan, 1990, p. 43). Academics in general have the duty of speaking truth to power. Students of international relations have always embraced the responsibility of speaking power to truth.

Third, another special quality of academic international relations is that since its birth it has been a policy science. Many of its students find the interplay of theory and practice its most fascinating aspect. In reinventing the future the devil is in the doing even more than in the reconceiving. International relations specialists are used to getting their intellectual hands dirty.

Because of its global scope, its concern with power and truth, and its practical wisdom world politics justifies the claim made in the chpater opening that it should be regarded as the subject of all subjects in the social sciences.

CONCEIVING THE FUTURE

What is the transcendent human science that has to be put back together? How are we to define it? What are its parameters? For many years, like other teachers of the subject, I was sure what it was, and was satisfied to repeat Charles Manning's formula that international relations is a subject with a focus but not a periphery. That focus was relations between states. Such a formulation (concentrating on what diplomats and soldiers do) has become increasingly inadequate in explaining who gets what, when and how in global perspective. A better formulation is Nicholas Rengger's paraphrasing of Pascal, to the effect that international relations is a 'fearful sphere whose centre is everywhere and whose circumference is nowhere' (1990, p. 61). This is an apt image, but to tell students, especially new ones, that the subject they are studying has no focus or frontiers might be thought to be pushing the celebration of confusion too far.

One strategy for putting the subject back together does not require that students subscribe to one paradigm or methodology. Instead, it argues for a return to the subject's origins. When it all began, in Aberystwyth in 1919, the academic enquiry into international relations was explicitly constituted to grapple with the great issues of the day. These were obviously the great issues of peace and war. We might well move forward to the 'next stage' not by theoretical arm-wrestling, though this has a place, but by focusing our diverse perspectives on the great issues of our day. To a greater or lesser degree, scholars of all ontological persuasions might agree that the agenda of the subject, and thus of the world, over the next fifty years can be expressed in three ideas: community, security and emancipation. These concepts embrace the key questions for what could be a qualitatively different world order – depending on how well or how badly we reinvent our collective futures.

We have lived in a global political system ever since the European states system expanded, but we now have a possible world order of a new type. The phrase 'world order' is here being used in Hedley Bull's technical sense (1977, pp. 20–2) not in George Bush's vague, propagandistic and quickly discredited sense. By 'world order' Bull did not mean international order among states but patterns of activity among humankind as a whole that sustain the primary goals of social life (which he identified, not uncontentiously, as survival, truth and property). It is both possible and desirable to think about order among humans as a whole (beyond merely order among states). It is possible because we now live locally in only the most trivial sense (in that our feet are in one place at a time). It is desirable because world order is more fundamental and primordial than order among states, and is morally prior to it (p. 22).

The first great issue of future world (human) order is: what are the limits of political community, and how should community be organized (Linklater, 1990b)? The common sense of 1945 is not calculated to create a healthy world order by 2045. If it was not evident at the time, the intervening half-century has given us little reason to suppose that the society of states can deliver a humane world order. In face of cosmopolitan hopes about human community, communitarian traditions and identities are obviously very powerful, and most would argue much more powerful than any conceivable cosmopolitan values. But to express the choices in this way presents the problem and the opportunities too starkly.

Despite the praise given earlier, the third debate had some negative side-effects, and one was the encouraging of a new generation of unhelpful binaries, especially the juxtaposition of communitarian *versus* cosmopolitanist philosophies and identities. The next stage should seek to avoid treating communitarian and cosmopolitan outlooks as mutually exclusive. Instead of simple nineteenth-century identity classifications, we need in the twenty-first century to think of complex and overlapping identities, with a constant conversation taking place between cosmopolitan and communitarian values. They can cohabit.

What does this mean in practice? Bhikhu Parekh (1993) has recently written in the spirit just proposed in respect of democracy and human rights. He has argued that these concepts give us a language for global politics, and that they embody values which resonate widely. They have universal meaning, and are not simply specific to Western culture. But space can and must be found for local definition and variation. In this sense communitarian values are operationalized within a cosmopolitan framework. Local interpretations can evolve within a safety net of global norms. Difference within limits is the operating principle to follow in global politics more widely. The search for community should not be used as an excuse for the obliteration of difference, but culture should not be used as an excuse for torture (on the latter see Robson, 1993).

Cosmopolitan frameworks do exist. While showing cultural sensitivity, we should also be aware of cross-cultural affinities. It is as misleading to black-box 'cultures' as it is to black box 'states'. The framework for a qualitatively different world order is made up of such factors as globalized physical communications; several world languages; increasing 'world' images and symbols; the power of capitalism which has created a universal contemporary history (Linklater, 1990a); a scientific culture which respects empirical evidence (Rosenau, 1990, pp. 425–9); the declining territorial principle: an embryonic global civil society; and a society of states sharing the eighteen norms Mervyn Frost identified, including metanarratives like democracy and human rights (1986, pp. 120–60).

In many aspects of life the growing influence of the global over the local is evident. This is the case despite the signs of resurgent nationalism. James Rosenau is right when he argues that virulent/heroic nationalism is in decline (1990, pp. 431–6). When extreme nationalism is manifest – at the time of writing notably in the former Yugoslavia – it is mesmeric precisely because it is a throwback to the past and bears little relevance to the complexity of today's problems. This is not to say that there is any shortage of nineteenth-century minds at the end of the twentieth century; consequently, war between nations is not about to disappear. It is, however, losing its utility. Something profound in world affairs is surely under way when one superpower can abdicate without a shot being fired against it, and the other can elect a draft-dodger as its president and commander-in-chief. It is difficult to imagine any similar conjunction of events in any other period of international history.

The communitarian/cosmopolitanist cohabitation which has been projected will not necessarily produce a perfectly harmonious world order, but there is reason for hoping that the domestic analogy for global politics on these lines will bear more resemblance to the ramshackle polity of India rather than to the tribal wars of the former Yugoslavia. The interplay between globalization and fragmentation points to a new century which may be more like the patchwork Middle Ages than the statist twentieth century, but with lessons learned from both.

The second great issue ahead is: what is security, and who will be secure? Inter-state (as opposed to civil) war is in historical decline as governments are running out of justifications for sending troops across their borders in large numbers. Expressed simply, the costs are going up and the benefits are going down (Knorr, 1966). Inter-state war will be less of a problem for the twenty-first century than it was for the twentieth. But there will be plenty of intra-state violence and other threats; today most people on earth actually have more to fear from their own government (through tyranny or incompetence or both) than from a neighbour's army. In addition to traditional threats there is a range of new challenges arising from economic pressure, disease and environmental stress.

Some analysts argue that one of our problems in dealing with the future is that we presently lack an easily identifiable enemy (in contrast with the days of Hitler and Napoleon). This is misconceived. We do have an enemy, and an enemy of global proportions at that. The enemy is us. Western consumerist democracy, living in what J. K. Galbraith (1992) calls a 'Culture of Contentment', is the problem. Take environmental issues, for example. It is extremely doubtful whether the planet can endlessly sustain the expanding wants of Western appetites and the expanding needs of the rest. Of the two, the former is the greater threat to the planet. But in a capitalist-constituted world the consumer is sovereign: the individual subject is constituted by its capacity to consume: 'I shop therefore I am.' Ideally, each shopping trip should be negotiated with the global conscience, but it rarely is in societies where we are what we buy. When the enemy is us, victory entails the enormously difficult task of reinventing our own (contented) societies. The global environment will have to suffer much more before the global economy will really take seriously the need to treat it better.

This leads to the third great issue: what is emancipation? And who will be emancipated? An inevitable consequence of living in a wired world is that people will ask questions about the way they live in comparison with others. Emancipation has been an issue throughout the twentieth century and there is no reason for it not to be so in the twenty-first. Some will welcome the choices on offer, others will react against them (but even living in 'traditional' ways these days is a lifestyle choice). Emancipation means freeing people, as individuals and groups, from the social, physical, economic, political and other constraints which stop them carrying out what they would freely choose to do. It is the other side of the coin to security (Booth, 1991b).

Security and emancipation are broader concepts than peace and war as traditionally conceived. An obvious implication of giving them priority is that the usual intellectual tools of international relations are not suitable to deal with them. Students of world politics have therefore to learn much more about the theories and methods of other disciplines.

The logical polity for a world order which would foster community, security and emancipation can be described as a global 'community of communities' within a much looser state framework. Decision-making power, which now tends to focus on the state, would be devolved downwards to meet the social and other needs of regional or more local groups and upwards to continental or global functional organizations to deal with those environmental and other issues for which the individual state is helpless (Falk, 1980, 1987). When it comes to decision-making on a global scale, neither 'small is beautiful' nor 'big is best'. The test is what is appropriate, and statism does not pass it.

The organization of diversity just suggested offers some hope of achieving both rational and humane governance. In contrast to the prescriptions of the advocates of world government, this polity is based on decentralizing rather than centralizing power. There is something to be said, for example, in favour of a more democratic rather than a stronger UN – two positions which tend to be mutually exclusive. In world-historical terms a representative and norm-creating UN will be of more benefit than an organization through which the great powers impose their order on the world. It is only through such norm development and legitimization that the UN will become an expression of a genuine international community rather than merely an arm of the most powerful in the international system.

We obviously cannot achieve such a global polity easily or quickly. Nor should we try to over-manage the long-term future, since we cannot control or predict distant events or developments. This being so, the most rational posture to adopt, academically and politically, is one which can be described as 'utopian realism' (Booth, 1991a). It is too much to expect that we can create a 'hard' science of the human future, but it is certainly not too soon to expect a more future-sensitive subject of international relations to guide our thinking in the present.

Traditional thinking about international relations was criticized at the start of this chapter for being taken by complete surprise by the historic events of 1989: the end of the Cold War and the eventual disappearance of the Soviet Union. This is fair criticism, for as John Lewis Gaddis has argued, many mainstream theorists in international relations during the Cold War repeatedly set themselves the task of forecasting, while the 'case' – the eventual collapse of an international system – was hardly an insignificant one (1992/93, p. 53). This criticism immediately raises questions: will whatever passes as the new thinking which has developed in the subject since the early 1980s serve us any better? Will it be more future-sensitive? Will it be a more helpful guide to our thinking in the present? Will it assist practice? Encouragingly, there are several reasons for believing that once we have made the proponents in the inter-paradigm debate listen to one another, assimilated the post-positivist contributions, and learned some lessons from recent developments about the subject and the world, we should be in better shape to think about the future.

We can look into the crystal ball at once and predict with utmost confidence that accurate prediction will always be an impossibly demanding standard for any subject dealing with the total sum of human beings. The problems of prediction are familiar (see, *inter alia*, Gaddis, 1992/93, pp. 17–18; Hopf, 1993, pp. 205–7). Without hindsight, how can we know which theorists to believe? How should we assess a prediction which is broadly correct in terms of developments, but radically inaccurate in terms of timing? How are lucky guesses and hunches to be accounted? Is there any merit to predictions which are right, but for the wrong reasons? And what about the self-denying possibility of all political predictions, because they might encourage counter-trends? As long as forecasts and predictions *about* human behaviour are also factors *in* human behaviour, the social sciences will never fully live up to their name. Nevertheless, as international relations struggles to reinvent itself as a subject, it can be said with some confidence that it is becoming a potentially more future-sensitive subject than hitherto. It is developing more sophisticated skills to provide more accurate pictures of the world; it is open to a wider set of ideas and conceptualizations; it has a more subtle understanding of the interrelationships between agency and structure; it is more self-aware about the problems of knowledge; and it has begun to conceive the future as something other than an extension of a timeless present, because it is pulling down its traditional reified structures and is bringing humans (with more complex identities) back in. In contrast to the ontologically challenged subject dominated by realism, it now offers the scope through disciplinary cross-fertilization to ask more challenging questions, to produce a closer correspondence between concepts, phenomena and explanations, and to develop academic and political agendas resting on more sophisticated normative and empirical enquiries.

All the above represents an improvement on the situation described at the start of the chapter, even if it necessarily falls short of the holy grail of accurate prediction. The realistic function of international political theory is not to try to describe the future in detail, but to prevent its dangers from materializing. At the minimum we should be seeking to develop and utilize theory to minimize the worst actualities (such as hunger and war) and worst possibilities (such as nuclearism and the destruction of nature). More than this is a bonus. The aim of international political theory can therefore be seen in terms of bringing about a convergence of the 'science' of Marx and the 'science' of Morgenthau into the art of utopian realism: the problem of international political theory is to try to change the world through understanding it, and to try to explain the world through changing it.

ANCHORING THE FUTURE

The subject matter of international relations is political action as well as theory, yet there is a congenital tendency on the part of intellectuals to hesitate before doing anything right, for fear of doing something philosophically wrong. In the aftermath of the post-positivist debate, international relations specialists have become somewhat more sensitive to this than previously. The anti-foundationalists have shaken the confidence of many students of the subject in the bases of their beliefs. But the 'foundationalism v. anti-foundationalism' debate is yet another unhelpful binary generated by the third debate.

Architectural language (like 'grounding' and 'foundations' and 'Archimedean points') is inappropriate – too absolutist – for life in society across historical time. Human society is always changing, self-reconstituting, and demanding different rationalizations in different historical eras. Rationality may be timeless but in some historical eras it may have to be explained through myths rather than logic. 'We' and 'society' are mutually constitutive. The Cartesian 'I' cannot be regarded as ahistorical, but as the product of time and place. Identities evolve and words change their meaning. States are not steady. 'We' are an invention and reinvention. Consequently, rather than thinking of immovable 'foundations' as the bases for political thought and action, it is more appropriate to think of 'anchorages'. These do not represent absolutist philosophical, religious or ideological positions, only the securest points in a stormy and changing environment from which to discuss how best to meet the needs of humanity. Anchorages are needed so that we can argue that 'this way is better than that' in the endless global debate about the manner in which we live – or fight – together.

But who should choose our anchorages? In the next stage of the discipline's development I hope that empirical and normative theory will give more attention to the powerless rather than to the powerful, to the victims of world politics, and not just to the victors. Traditionally, the global perspective offered by the subject has been very much top-down rather than bottom-up – philosophically in power terms and literally in geographical terms. So, as a start, let us ask the victims of world politics to reinvent the future (a living experiment of Rawls's 'veil of ignorance'). The world they would conceive would surely point to 'justice as fairness' more closely than the world traditionally described and explained by the academics of the powerful. The victims of world politics would indicate different anchorages from which to start reinventing the future.

Victims suffer the failures of traditional theories about world politics and the structures that sustain those theories. In thinking about reinventing the future, it would be interesting to rewrite the UN Charter, starting not with the famous words 'We the peoples . . .' (1945 propaganda for 'We the Great Powers') but 'We the victims . . .'. Short of a revolutionary Universal Victims Charter, it would be an interesting start if a delegation of victims of world politics (represented by non-governmental organizations) be given a seat on the Security Council. Victims always bring special experiences to decision-making bodies.

Kenneth Boulding, who died recently, liked to say that 'we are as we are because we got that way'. Running through this chapter is the belief that we can reinvent the subject of world politics, and our collective future, in such a way that we could become what we dream to become. But this is by no means guaranteed. The dangers are manifold and we cannot be confident about the prospects of overcoming them. Indeed, what hope have we of reinventing the world when academic international politics remains such a divided discipline?

For the moment, therefore, the doubts about international relations theory and the future expressed at the beginning of the chapter must remain. We still have chaos in the subject rather than a dancing star. But it has been argued that there is good reason for hope, as agendas broaden, explanations deepen and new skills develop. Consequently, if the issues discussed here were to be raised again in ten years' time I am sure that I would be much more confident than now that I could recommend a professor of international relations to reinvent the future of politics on a global scale. In comparison with the analyses and prescriptions that have been given by those who have dominated the subject so far, I have no doubt that she would do better.

Note

This chapter was originally a lecture in the 1993 Global Security Lectures at the University of Cambridge. The overall theme was 'Reinventing the Future: Dangers, Dreams and Prospects', and the series was organized by the University's Global Security Programme. The lecture has been edited and slightly expanded, and references have been added, but as far as possible the style of the original has been maintained. Thanks are due to those on the Programme for providing a congenial intellectual home during 1992–3, and to the Joseph Rowntree Charitable Trust and the University of Wales Research Fund for making the sabbatical leave possible.

References

Banks, M. 1985: The inter-paradigm debate. In M. Light and A. J. R. Groom (eds), *International Relations: A Handbook of Current Theory*. London: Frances Pinter, 7–26.

Booth, K. 1991a: Security in anarchy. Utopian realism in theory and practice. *International Affairs*, 67(3), 527–45.

Booth, K. 1991b: Security and emancipation. *Review of International Studies*, 17, 313–26.

Bull, H. 1977: *The Anarchical Society: A Study of Order in World Politics*. London: Macmillan.

Carr, E. H. 1946: *The Twenty Years' Crisis: 1919–1939*. London: Macmillan.

Carr, E. H. 1961: *What is History?* Harmondsworth: Penguin.

Donelan, M. 1990: *Elements of International Political Theory*. Oxford: Clarendon Press.

Falk, R. A. 1980: Anarchism and world order. In R. A Falk and S. S. Kim (eds), *The War System: An Interdisciplinary Approach*, Boulder, Colorado: Westview, 37–57.

Falk. R. A. 1987: *The Promise of World Order*. Philadelphia, PA: Temple University Press.

Frost, M. 1986: *Toward a Normative Theory of International Relations*. Cambridge: Cambridge University Press.

Fukuyama, F. 1989: The end of history? *The National Interest*, 16 (Summer), 3–18.

Gaddis, J. L. 1992/93: International relations theory and the end of the Cold War. *International Security*, 17(3), 5–58.

Galbraith, J. K. 1992: *The Culture of Contentment*. London: Sinclair-Stevenson.

Holsti, K. J. 1985: *The Dividing Discipline: Hegemony and Diversity in International Theory*. Boston, Mass.: Allen & Unwin.

Hopf, T. 1993: Getting the end of the Cold War wrong. *International Security*, 18(2), 202–8.

Jackson, R. H. and Rosberg, C. G. 1982: Why Africa's weak states persist: the empirical and the juridical in statehood. *World Politics*, 35, 1–24.

Knorr, K. 1966: *On the Uses of Military Power in the Nuclear Age*. Princeton, N.J.: Princeton University Press.

Lapid, Y. 1989: The third debate: on the prospects of international theory in a post-positivist era. *International Studies Quarterly*, 33(3), 235–54.

Lasswell, H. D. 1950: *Politics. Who Gets What, When, How*. New York: Peter Smith.

Linklater, A. 1990a: *Beyond Realism and Marxism: Critical Theory and International Relations*. London: Macmillan.

Linklater, A. 1990b: The problem of community in international relations. *Alternatives*, 15(2), 135–53.

Niebuhr, R. 1938: *Beyond Tragedy: Essays on the Christian Interpretation of History*. London: Nisbet and Co.

Nietzsche, F. 1969: *Thus Spake Zarathustra* (trans. and with an introduction by R. J. Hollingdale). Harmondsworth: Penguin Books.

Parekh, B. 1993: The cultural particularity of liberal democracy. In D. Held (ed.), *Prospects for Democracy*, Cambridge: Polity Press, 156–75.

Reiss, H. (ed.) 1989: *Kant's Political Writings*. Cambridge: Cambridge University Press.

Rengger, N. J. 1990: The fearful sphere of international relations. *Review of International Studies*, 16, 361–8.

Robson, A. 1993: Torture not culture. *AIBS Journal* (Sept/Oct), 8–9.

Rosenau, J. N. 1990: *Turbulence in World Politics*. Brighton: Harvester Wheatsheaf.

Said, E. W. 1985: *Orientalism: Western Concepts of the Orient*. Harmondsworth: Penguin.

Smith, S. 1992: The forty years' detour: the resurgence of normative theory in international relations. *Millennium: Journal of International Studies*, 21(3), 489–506.

Smith, S., Booth, K. and Zalewski, M. (eds) forthcoming: *Theorising International Relations: Positivism and After*. Cambridge: Cambridge University Press.

Thucydides 1972: *History of the Peloponnesian War* (introduction and notes by R. Warner). Harmondsworth: Penguin Books.

Waltz, K. N. 1959: *Man, the State and War*. New York: Columbia University Press.

Waltz, K. N. 1979: *Theory of International Politics*. Reading, Mass.: Addison-Wesley.

Wittgenstein, L. 1992: *Philosophical Investigations*. Oxford: Basil Blackwell.

Index

Compiled by Meg Davies